VAULTS
MIRRORS
AND
MASKS

VAULTS MIRRORS AND MASKS

Rediscovering U.S. Counterintelligence

Jennifer E. Sims and
Burton Gerber, Editors

In cooperation with the
Center for Peace and Security Studies
and the George T. Kalaris Memorial Fund
Edmund A. Walsh School of Foreign Service
Georgetown University

Georgetown University Press
Washington, D. C.

Georgetown University Press, Washington, D.C. www.press.georgetown.edu

Library of Congress Cataloging-in-Publication Data

Vaults, mirrors, and masks : rediscovering US counterintelligence / Jennifer E. Sims and Burton Gerber, editors.
    p. cm.
"Published in cooperation with the Center for Peace and Security Studies and the George T. Kalaris Memorial Fund, Edmund A. Walsh School of Foreign Service, Georgetown University."
    Includes bibliographical references and index.
    ISBN 978-1-58901-267-7 (pbk : alk paper)
    1. Intelligence service—United States. I. Sims, Jennifer E. II Gerber, Burton L. III. Georgetown University. Center for Peace and Security Studies.
JK468.I6V38 2008
327.1273—dc22

2008030356

⊗ This book is printed on acid-free paper meeting the requirements of the American National Standard for Permanence in Paper for Printed Library Materials.

15 14 13 12 11 10 09 08   9 8 7 6 5 4 3 2
First printing

Printed in the United States of America

CONTENTS

PART III: STRATEGIES

FIGURES

PREFACE

THIS VOLUME has been long in gestation. First conceived after the publication of *Transforming U.S. Intelligence* in October 2005, the volume has been delayed by what our students sometimes call "life stuff": health, family, finances, and the press of the academic calendar at Georgetown University. That the volume is going to press at all is testimony to the incredibly hard work of excellent research assistants whose diligence, knowledge, attention to detail, and unfailing good humor made the journey as pleasant and productive as any edited volume can be, as well as substantively better than it would have been without them: Andrew J. Sawka, Chuck Prahl, and especially Anand Prakash and Megan Jackson. Megan brought this book to closure with true professionalism, providing valuable editorial and substantive suggestions, many of which we adopted. We also wish to thank those experts who offered comments and constructive criticisms along the way, including Richard Betts, David Kahn, Robert Jervis (also an author), Matthew Walker, James J. Clapper, Daniel Byman, John MacGaffin, Mark Lowenthal, Paul Redmond, and Roy Godson. Their advice, though varying in degree, was valuable to us and to the authors, some of whom acknowledge others as well in their separate chapters. We would also like to acknowledge the contributions of David Charney, MD, who presented his ideas and insights on insider spies at the authors' conference in November 2007. We thank him for deepening our knowledge of the psychological motivations underpinning insider espionage. Of course, we take full responsibility for any errors of fact and omission that may remain in these pages.

We owe much, of course, to the leadership and staff of Georgetown University Press and the Center for Peace and Security Studies (CPASS) at Georgetown University, who helped make this volume possible and provided substantial material and logistical support. There are too many people to list here, but among those deserving our particular thanks are Don Jacobs, acquisitions editor at Georgetown University Press; CPASS's Jennifer Park and Kirsten Lundgren, who organized the authors' conference; Brandon Cox for his administrative help; the CPASS executive director, Ellen McHugh, for her guidance and patience; and of course our program chair and CPASS director, Daniel Byman. Our decision to collaborate on this volume and venture down this road had much to do with the professionalism and encouragement we have found in this remarkable group of associates.

This volume probably could have been finished without the support and patience of family and friends, but our lives would have been miserable and the effort not worth it. Instead, their patience and encouragement kept us going.

Bob Gallucci deserves special thanks for putting up with piles of books and papers on the breakfast (lunch and dinner) table. And in return, Jennifer has acknowledged his request for no more edited volumes as houseguests. Now it is in writing. And Burton thanks his dear friends Clinton Finch and Anthony and Kari Van Vuren for their steadfastness whenever he faltered.

INTRODUCTION

Jennifer E. Sims

Democracies and Counterintelligence
The Enduring Challenge

DECISION MAKERS matching wits with an adversary want intelligence—good, relevant information to help them win. Intelligence can gain these advantages through directed research and analysis, agile collection, and the timely use of guile and theft. *Counterintelligence* is the art and practice of defeating these endeavors. Its purpose is the same as that of positive intelligence—to gain advantage—but it does so by exploiting, disrupting, denying, or manipulating the intelligence activities of others. The tools of counterintelligence include security systems, deception, and disguise: vaults, mirrors, and masks.

But counterintelligence involves much more. Indeed, insiders correctly tout *positive* intelligence as one of counterintelligence's best assets. Intelligence collectors can uncover penetrations of their own side by penetrating another, or by running agents with good access.[1] For this reason and their common objective, intelligence and counterintelligence should be considered two sides of the same cloth—a fabric cooperatively woven on behalf of decision makers. Ideally, this fabric reveals the adversary in fine detail on one side and displays illusions for opponents on the other, while shrouding the user for the purpose of surprise. The collaborative weaving of such tapestries and their use for strategic advantage constitute perfection in the intelligence enterprise. It is a standard rarely met, particularly in democracies, where, after all, the citizenry holds shrouds and illusions suspect—especially when they are employed by their governors.

The U.S. Counterintelligence Problem

The United States in particular has struggled with its counterintelligence instrument. The images from the Cold War were less those of jointly woven fabric than of "walls" between the operations of the Federal Bureau of Investigation (FBI) and the rest of the intelligence community. Routine as bureaucratic connections may have been before 9/11, few in the Central Intelligence Agency (CIA) seemed to have believed that counterintelligence, including helping the FBI, was as important as collecting and analyzing new information for policymakers for the president's daily intelligence briefing.[2] TIPOFF, a central government database for tracking terrorists and operatives located in the State Department's Bureau of Intelligence and Research (INR), was regularly starved for attention and funding during the 1990s as larger State Department appropriations took a nosedive. Few in the FBI viewed their role as empowering national security decision making; instead, their mission, as they understood it, was to stop spies, prosecute them, and thus uphold the law. In important ways, of course, these beliefs were right. When establishing stronger oversight of intelligence in the 1970s, Congress had chastised both the CIA and the FBI for their too cozy relations and too creative stratagems in support of presidential designs.[3]

By the 1990s, however, the old constraints had become handicaps to effective counterintelligence. Rapid changes in technology permitted transnational groups, including terrorists and criminals, to organize more effectively against U.S. interests. And those same technological changes, combined with the U.S. position as sole remaining "superpower," prompted a diverse set of foreign governments to increase their collection against the United States. At the century's turn, U.S. counterintelligence officials were at a particular disadvantage in their developing contest with newly aggressive state intelligence services and transnational groups such as al-Qaeda. In an indictment of pre-9/11 counterterrorist intelligence, one observer noted that the U.S. government "had no way of knowing what it knew about the terrorist threat. Even the FBI, hampered by inability to get funding for up-to-date information technology, did not really know what it knew. When it did learn something from foreign intelligence, the FBI was hamstrung by its understanding of constitutional limitations on the use of such intelligence in criminal investigations."[4] At the strategic level, the U.S. government's capacity to combine what it knew about how the enemy was behaving against us with what it knew it could do to beat him, was missing. This flaw in the national security process was not a problem of foreign intelligence alone; it was not a problem of counterintelligence alone. It was a flaw within the loom of security policymaking as a whole, which was unable constructively and creatively to weave the two together in the service of action and strategy.[5]

Since 9/11 the foreign intelligence threat has not abated; it is also not just a terrorist one. At the time of this writing, China apparently tops the list of those trawling for intelligence on the United States. Defense-related technologies have been a particularly attractive target. The Defense Security Service reported in 2006 that 106 countries had engaged in this activity in 2005, compared with 37 in 1997.[6] It added that the majority of collection against defense industries was focused on information systems (21.8%), followed by lasers and optics (10.7%). The threat from China seemed perhaps the fastest growing: In early 2008 the

Immigration and Customs Enforcement officials rated Beijing's activities as "the leading threat to the security of U.S. technology."[7] The chairman of the United States–China Economic and Security Review Commission echoed this view, testifying that China's espionage activities were "the single greatest threat to U.S. technology and strain [to] the U.S. counterintelligence establishment."[8] Chinese tradecraft is well honed: "There is a long record in China going back over two centuries of sending government directed missions overseas to buy or shamelessly steal the best civil and military technology available, reverse engineer it, and build an industrial complex that supports the growth of China as a commercial and military power."[9]

Such testimony suggests that espionage activity against the United States has both increased since the early post–Cold War years and changed in its primary sponsorship. One way to measure foreign intelligence activity, though not necessarily the best way, is to calculate the number of arrested spies. Foreign intelligence officers operating under diplomatic cover are usually sent home when they are caught. Agents of foreign powers who are not foreign government officials with diplomatic immunity can be prosecuted under U.S. espionage statutes.[10] According to David G. Major, president of the Centre for Counterintelligence and Security Studies, of the 247 foreign agents arrested between 1945 and early 2008, 49 percent were spying for the Soviet Union or Russia.[11] Of the 37 arrested since 2000, however, most have been either Chinese (11 cases) or Middle Eastern (13 cases). Moscow has been connected to three espionage cases and al-Qaeda to two during this later time period.[12] Given this level of diversity in the foreign espionage threat, and particularly the rapid rise of China, the United States is facing a structurally different kind of challenge than it did during the Cold War.

The Counterintelligence Challenge for the Next Century

With these issues as a backdrop, it should not be surprising that since 9/11, some of the hottest issues in the intelligence domain have continued to be matters of counterintelligence policy: the role of the federal government in protecting cities; the ownership and security of ports and shipping lanes; the appropriateness of creating a U.S. version of Britain's MI-5 to provide counterintelligence for homeland defense; the legality of the National Security Agency's (NSA) programs for domestic communications surveillance; renditions, interrogations, and secret detentions of alleged terrorists; and the risks involved in partnering with foreign liaison services, such as those of Pakistan and Syria, for intelligence on terrorists. Even the question of how a German source called Curveball misled policymakers about Saddam's weapons of mass destruction, an issue that pundits mined for its clues to analytic incompetence or politicization, was equally plausibly related to failures in strategic counterintelligence. To wrestle with such issues, the 9/11 Commission recommended the elevated position of director of national intelligence and called for a new era of cooperation among all sixteen intelligence and counterintelligence agencies. In the intelligence reform legislation of 2004, which implemented these recommendations, the counterintelligence apparatus itself, including the FBI and its relationship with the newly created Department of Homeland Security (DHS), was—rather remarkably—left untouched.

Seven years after 9/11, problems with U.S. counterintelligence persist. Sometimes the evidence is clear, as when the media report security breaches, faulty background checks on employees, and computer vulnerabilities at the FBI and CIA.[13] At other times, however, the indications are more subtle. Shortly after the U.S. Senate confirmed Admiral Michael McConnell as the new director of national intelligence (DNI) in the spring of 2007, he introduced his 100-Day and then 500-Day plans. Building on the National Intelligence Strategy (NIS) issued by his predecessor the previous year, the new DNI emphasized six pressing "focus areas." Counterintelligence was not among these central priorities, though it was mentioned elsewhere.[14]

The reasons for this omission were, at least at one level, maddeningly bureaucratic. Despite the lessons of 9/11 and the subsequent bureaucratic reforms, the DNI, as head of the intelligence community still lacks full authority for developing a counterintelligence strategy that balances effectiveness with civil liberties. By law the National Counterintelligence Strategy is the responsibility of the National Counterintelligence Executive.[15] The strategy is a document that must be derived annually from the National Threat Identification and Prioritization Assessment, which is approved in turn by an interagency board chaired by the FBI and composed of representatives from the Department of Justice, the CIA, and the Department of Defense.[16] Shaped by a largely defensive and law enforcement orientation, the National Counterintelligence Strategy may therefore be only loosely aligned with the DNI's National Intelligence Strategy and, by extension, policymakers' diplomatic and defense strategies more generally. Such a bureaucratic tangle suggests that the United States may be, at least as far as counterintelligence is concerned, a kind of modern-day Gulliver—bound by old policies or practices that, minor in isolation, become potentially devastating in their cumulative effects.

Whatever the historical reasons for such disconnects, this is a particularly bad time for poor intelligence coordination and the loss of agility it causes. Although sometimes reactions may be overblown, the threats posed by new technologies and their applications, including individuals' heightened capacities to organize fanaticism, vigilantism, and terror, are real. Information and counterinformation technologies are changing the nature of the combatants and how they fight. If communications security has always been important to warfare, a history well recounted in David Kahn's epic work *The Codebreakers*, it is now playing a starring role.[17] Smart sensors and communication networks are allowing the militarily weak to hunt the strong on the Internet.[18] Using store-bought computers, software, encryption, and communications—or borrowing all the above from Internet cafés—modern adversaries can conduct attacks orchestrated from afar. Intelligence and counterintelligence are becoming the foundation for success in asymmetric warfare. The advantages of an illuminated battle space will flow to those who can still minimize their presence, or "footprint," there and, at the same time, manipulate their opponents' perceptions. It therefore makes sense to provide a scene setter for this volume by reviewing the technologies that will likely compose the counterintelligence landscape for the twenty-first century, and the political culture that will shape the American response.

New Technologies

Technology affects counterintelligence both by influencing collection methods and by changing the relationship between analysts and policymakers. The modern era has brought particularly rapid changes in both these areas. Perhaps most obvious, advances in digital information and communications technologies have revolutionized the processing, exploitation, and sharing of data. The power of computers, their miniaturization, and their connectivity through broadband services have provided substantially increased flexibility in the routing of intelligence to people who need it. Developments in nanotechnology are allowing sensors and their power sources to get smaller and easier to disguise.[19] Robotics and microengineering are producing land-based machines that can carry sensors onto denied terrain that used to be accessible only from remote collectors. Over five thousand robots are in use in Afghanistan and Iraq and, between FY 2006 and 2012, the U.S. government will invest about $1.7 billion on ground-based military robots.[20] Robotics offer more than just an innovative new platform, however. Advances in "sociable robots" are creating humanlike machines because they are both "situated" (able to sense their environment and respond to it) and "embodied" (having a physical system that can to interact with others).[21] In other words, sociable robots already learn. From an intelligence standpoint, robots' purposeful mimicry and their ability to learn present interesting collection opportunities as well as counterintelligence challenges; roboticists (those who make robots) seem inevitably to reveal much about themselves in their creations.[22]

In any case, with such advances in engineering, energy, information, and communications, particularly since the Cold War, the nature of the intelligence competition has been rapidly changing. This change implicates the private sector in both evolving threats and the capacities for counter them. For example, the miniaturization of sensors, combined with rapid expansion of bandwidth through fiberoptic cables, means that the era of "static robotics"—smart systems that stay in place—is upon us. This is no small matter: It is one thing to have a companionable, trainable machine to help with grocery shopping; it is quite another to live inside of one. Recently, National Public Radio did a program on "Counter Intelligence" that discussed smart kitchens: refrigerators that know when butter runs low, spoons that detect the absence of salt in the soup, and ovens that warn when the roast is getting too crisp.[23] Similar technologies on a grander scale are making buildings clever. New technologies can open and close vents to adjust to outside air and pollutants; identify employees as they enter, enveloping them in air bubbles designed to preclude allergens; and adjust room temperatures, lighting, and audio systems to automatically accommodate individual preferences.

Technology is thus rendering fixed architectural spaces into tightly integrated intelligence collectors that, if brought into the service of the state, could help detect terrorists, biological pathogens, and other threats in urban centers and then act on the information. Unfortunately, these same collectors would be, as all collectors are, vulnerable to misuse by authorities or hijacking by a hostile service or transnational group, turning benign intelligence assets into tools of crime or technological double agents. Countering such hostile takeovers requires the cooperation of the private sector, including landlords, insurance companies, and telecommunications entities that have a vested interest in the security and privacy of their capital investments. A similar kind of cooperation between the private and public sectors would seem to be necessary to monitor, control, and counter hostile access to dual-use technologies such as bioengineered germs and nuclear material.[24] These private entities do not, of course, always see their governments as benign players.

Another technological advance that is likely to influence collection and deception strategies are those related to holograms and artificial reality. Advancing fast in the gaming industry, these technologies are becoming increasingly convincing and, at least in theory, easily adoptable by adversaries. One can think of holograms in simple terms as a stand-alone tool for tamperproof seals or, alternatively, as a sophisticated means for deception. In the latter case, they offer a three-dimensional counterpart to the "Photoshop route" to imagery alteration: modifying what a collector sees by just enough to convince him that reality is not what it is or, alternatively, creating three-dimensional images that reveal tampering.[25] Unlike YouTube displays in which altered video purports to show UFOs drifting over palm trees, holograms would not alter the video but rather the space the video records. In either case, the collector is potentially deceived; but in the second case nothing can be found wrong with the camera, its recording apparatus, or its processors. The diagnostics for counterintelligence are changing or, perhaps more accurately, will change should this and similar technologies take off.[26]

The rapid growth in worldwide data processing, open-source information, and commercial encryption has fundamentally changed the twenty-first-century counterintelligence challenge in ways that are particularly problematic for democracies. In open societies terrorists can survey their targets, take pictures of them, and research them on the Internet. Microsoft is even championing a new capability called Photosynth, which merges digital photos of sites taken by anyone—private citizens, pilots, businesspeople, or mapmakers—to create publicly accessible three-dimensional images of them—complete with interior tours of, for example, the Capitol, New York City's Grand Central Station, or the Sears Tower in Chicago.[27] The implication is clear: Terrorists will soon be able to conduct surveillance and plan attacks on significant sites using remote image collection and processing tools and Internet applications freely available and constantly being enriched on the Web. Of course, the flood of unclassified information available on almost any topic also makes counterintelligence potentially easier as digital footprints allow spy hunters to track the activities of their quarry. Technologies are available that can search for patterns in metadata (data disassociated from the identities of its subjects) or that can infer from gathered data any anomalous activity.

This discussion suggests that changes in technology can cut both ways: Hostile intelligence services and terrorists can collect information and send messages in new ways, but they can also be watched more easily—and not just by governments.[28] Whether those responsible for positive intelligence gain advantages over those responsible for counterintelligence depends on their respective wits and creativity. It also depends on the law. Democracies value the privacy of their citizens and are rightfully wary of many of these emerging capabilities; but it is not clear whether citizens will accept governments' efforts to restrict them. Most are displaying some flexibility in legislating state access to private information so long as the search seems warranted and the innocent are left unaffected. This challenge to "do no harm," however, has not been easy to meet. After all, the implications of the emerging era of cyberwar are not yet fully understood but potentially grave: wars triggered in cyberspace; citizen groups battling governments from home computers; and wars terminated by government treaty but continuing in private, where infrastructure might remain at risk. The implications for intelligence are particularly stunning; although some states will be winners and others losers, the results are difficult to foresee.[29]

Ordinarily, rapid technological change would not pose problems for the United States—a country that prizes its entrepreneurs. The American marketplace, which has had a preeminent role in post-WWII application of invention to industry, has helped trigger, and now chiefly sustains, the information revolution on a global scale.[30] Yet complacency would be unwarranted. The same American political culture that prizes invention also places constraints on genius, including its application to information-based wars. The American public expects protection from governmental surveillance of private communications; a significant segment also expects protection from the cosmopolitanism of the entrepreneurial class, which is often perceived as responsible for shipping jobs abroad for profit. Indeed, given U.S. firms' interest in joint ventures and in outsourcing operations to reduce costs, "American" firms are increasingly hard to define and therefore to defend as a national security matter. The course of the information revolution, and the transnational dynamics it generates, suggests therefore that states are on the decline and that the world is, indeed, "flat."[31] Yet this same dynamic has inspired states to fight back—sometimes using the new nationalism of the industrial working class to raise tariffs, tighten borders, and spy on foreigners. The protectionist state is, unfortunately, also likely to be, at least potentially, an antidemocratic one.[32]

Preserving Civil Liberties in an Era of Countersurveillance

In this context, preserving constitutional freedoms is hard; globalization renders distinctions between "us" and "others" increasingly difficult even as it makes such distinctions so necessary. Democracies such as the United States have, in fact, three central problems with counterintelligence. The first is secrecy itself. Protection of state secrets implies the need to control what those outside of government can know or discuss. Classification systems can be abused, however, and their existence in democracies inevitably sets government against the media, who ferret out information for the public so that citizens can hold their leaders accountable. It also sets the media against government, which is expected to protect sources and methods for the common good, such as finding Osama bin Laden and defeating al-Qaeda before it attacks again, for example. Resolving this tension between government and the media falls to citizens who in their daily lives are much more concerned about falling real estate values, lost jobs, and unaffordable health care. In democracies in general and the United States in particular, counterintelligence often has no constituency until things go bad.

Second, offensive counterintelligence, which involves deceiving adversaries to protect oneself, can unintentionally deceive the voting public or even intelligence analysts with security clearances who are nonetheless outside the circle of those "in the know." Even if deception can be directed exclusively toward an adversary, it resembles covert action, which is the secret sponsorship of activity to change political, economic, or military situations overseas. In the United States, offensive CI has not been legally defined nor has its nuanced relationship with covert action been authoritatively described. Unlike covert action, the principal *purpose* of offensive counterintelligence is to disrupt foreign intelligence, but it can have the same *effects* as covert action. This ambiguity renders imaginative counterintelligence activities dangerous for intelligence officials to develop, let alone execute, even when limited to foreign soil.

Third, to the extent that adversaries conduct intelligence and terrorist operations within democracies, effective counterintelligence has often required the joining of secret surveillance to the powers of arrest. In the United States, a healthy legal system has maintained limits on misuse of such powers by the federal government. In wartime, however, the powers of arrest, surveillance, and force tend to merge, and the authorities of those holding these powers tend to expand. Since 9/11, the United States has not only gone to war in Afghanistan and Iraq, it has done so worldwide in what became known as the Global War on Terror. U.S. intelligence agencies have not only ramped up their own efforts against terrorists, they have worked increasingly closely with law enforcement, the military, and allied foreign services to help them do so. Such steps have proven critical to effective disruption of transnational networks for crime and espionage. But they have also turned the intelligence playing field into its own theater of conflict, while testing democratic norms.

For example, fixed on the counterterrorism threat, the American government has believed it necessary to detain foreign nationals in intelligence-run prisons, to use its intelligence service to render foreign operatives to foreign jails, and to use enhanced interrogation techniques by intelligence officers to learn of future plots that threaten American lives and the integrity of the state. Each of these actions has probably been seen by other intelligence services—friends as well as enemies—as counterintelligence challenges to varying degrees, perhaps because the global "war" on terror seems to run parallel to the daily lives of their citizens rather than engaging them in the way traditional wars have done. Italy has, for example, investigated U.S. intelligence activities and charged U.S. intelligence officers with kidnapping for hunting down terrorist suspects and collaborators on Italian soil. Thus, the very rise of transnational threats has led to the empowering and emboldening of state intelligence services, including our own. As these services strengthen their operations, they prompt the strengthening of other state security services.

This intelligence aspect of the security dilemma, so familiar to those who work arms control issues, is dangerous. As intelligence services grow, so do the impulses toward use of them, whether they are good at their tradecraft or not. If intelligence remains a tool with which many Americans, including diplomats and the military, remain unfamiliar, then the likelihood of missteps increases. In any case, the combined powers of surveillance, arrest, and force in the executive are potentially incendiary for vibrant democracies, particularly when moving from war to peace or when suspended somewhere in between. Ending expanded executive authorities has often been difficult; managing them during times of quasi-war, such as the United States is experiencing now, is even more so.[33] Counterintelligence thus appears to present the painful paradox for liberal polities mentioned earlier: roll back civil liberties or accept potentially devastating vulnerabilities. It is, in short, a wicked problem.[34]

Purpose: Clarifying the Debate and Charting a Course

Wicked problems with such long histories generally attract wide-ranging public and scholarly attention; yet the theory and practice of counterintelligence is something of an exception to this rule. Scholars and former practitioners have tended to focus on the history of spy catching and the requirements of deception rather than the principles of the broader policy art. This focus reflects, in part, public interest in the catching of insider spies and heroic and often entertaining stories, such as those from WWII about double, invisible, and "dead" agent exploits.[35] Scholarship on deception stands out as a subgenre of considerable theoretical and policy-relevant work, including recent volumes edited by Loch Johnson and by Roy Godson and James J. Wirtz.[36]

Yet few volumes address the counterintelligence challenge in its entirety or in relation to the broader needs of national security policymaking within democratic states in general or the United States in particular. The most important scholarly treatment of counterintelligence may be Roy Godson's *Dirty Tricks or Trump Cards*, which develops some useful theoretical propositions and analyzes the requirements for successful offensive counterintelligence and covert action in historical perspective. The wickedness of the democratic dilemma is not, however, directly addressed. One central purpose of this volume is to fill this gap—not by covering the counterintelligence challenges in all their dimensions, but by focusing on the ones that must be confronted most directly if the United States is to get its national security policy process in order.

A central thesis of this book is that the "choice" between sound and effective counterintelligence and healthy democracy, including the protection of civil liberties, is a false one. In fact, this zero-sum paradigm is a prescription for paralysis. Public wariness hampers the ability of U.S. intelligence to adapt to technological challenges as much as stiff, unyielding institutions and bureaucratic cultures do. Although this wariness may be justified, it also affects U.S. officials who remain uncertain about how to hone their counterintelligence instruments. Despite reforms, strategic coordination is fitful across disciplines owned by the intelligence agencies (operational security), the Department of State (overseas security), the Department of Homeland Security (domestic security), the Department of Defense (military counterintelligence), and the Federal Bureau of Investigation (law enforcement). This point has been made perhaps most clearly by the former director of National Counterintelligence Executive, Michelle Van Cleave. As she has suggested, true national counterintelligence strategies effectively guide, and not just reflect, current operations.[37]

A national debate on counterintelligence is a necessary first step toward fixing this crucial area of national security policy. By considering counterintelligence strategy in its full theoretical and practical dimensions, we hope to contribute to the dialogue and, more specifically, to the development of innovative counterintelligence strategies that build on our strengths and historical experiences. Although this overarching purpose is rather grand, it includes practical, realistic goals as well. As the director of national intelligence and the U.S. National Counterintelligence Executive work to execute the new counterintelligence strategy for the United States, our aim is to aid them by providing a guide to priorities and a means for leaders to gauge whether, and to what extent, their strategies are succeeding. In doing so, it will discuss and, where appropriate, offer solutions to some of the thorniest problems confronting the modern practice of counterintelligence in democracies, including:

• the dominance of defensive CI, including its emphasis on security, and the resulting disconnect between national security policymakers and the counterintelligence community in the United States;

- the difficulties involved in developing a common approach to counterintelligence among police, federal law enforcement, and intelligence officials, and the benefits and dangers of creating one;
- the continued absence of homes for strategic counterintelligence planning and operations within and across agencies and commands in broader service to national security policy;
- the poor understanding of, and training for, the full range of counterintelligence functions among intelligence officials and federal law enforcement agencies responsible for counterintelligence operations;
- the absence of effective oversight of the counterintelligence community and the new initiatives underway since 9/11.

The Structure of the Book

As with our previous book, *Transforming U.S. Intelligence*, this book is designed to offer constructive suggestions for U.S. intelligence policies and practices. Each author, selected for his or her experience as well as analytic expertise, shares the editors' view that the counterintelligence conundrum democracies face is not a hopeless one. There are answers, and this book offers some. In order to bridge the scholarly and policymaking divide, the editors have asked contributing authors to be both theoretical and policy relevant. They have been encouraged to share their definitions, theories, and beliefs in authors' conferences, informal "salons," and by e-mail.[38] They have not been required to adopt the editors' points of view on any matters of definition, theory, or prescription. The idea has been to engage the debate with a light editorial hand, not to finish it.

That said, in the editors' view, the most critical responsibility of the state is the protection of its people and their chosen way of life; while good counterintelligence poses challenges for democracies, it is not incompatible with it. Good ethics, sound democratic practice, and strong intelligence, including counterintelligence, are not incompatible—even at the operational level. We therefore value counterintelligence oversight as an enabling function of good government. The urgent need is for reasoned discussion of best practices, given the constraints of our system of government and the political culture that underlies it.

The opening chapters of this volume set the stage for exploring counterintelligence issues in the U.S. context, covering crosscutting issues such as history, legal constraints, psychological dynamics, and counterintelligence theory and its implications for strategy. The first chapter expands on the theory of counterintelligence presented above by offering some ideas, many of which are controversial, about how to develop strategies and define success in the twenty-first-century context. In the second chapter, FBI historian John Fox Jr. and DNI historian Michael Warner discuss the development of counterintelligence in the

United States, including the impact of American political culture. Columbia professor Robert Jervis's essay expands his influential ideas on perception and deception in international politics. The section concludes with former defense intelligence officer Austin Yamada's analysis of human rights and civil liberties in American constitutional democracy. Although this section of the book is designed to frame the issues for the volume as a whole, the authors were invited to make recommendations for practical solutions as well. Most of them do.

In the second section of the volume, specific issues and challenges for the United States are addressed in finer detail. Robert Wallace, a former member of the Central Intelligence Agency's Directorate of Operations (now the National Clandestine Service), discusses counterespionage and how technology is changing tradecraft on the human side of the business. Vincent H. Bridgeman, a Marine intelligence officer, considers weaknesses in counterintelligence practices within the military services and the Department of Defense as a whole. Drafts of Bridgeman's paper were shared with senior leaders of the Defense Department, as they reorganized defense CI in 2008. In chapter seven, Dr. Kathleen Kiernan, formerly with the Bureau of Alcohol, Tobacco, Firearms, and Explosives, examines law enforcement's role in and use of counterintelligence, particularly how state, local, and tribal police are cooperating with federal agencies without losing their focus on broad-based community safety. Next, James R. Gosler, a scientist with Sandia National Laboratories, considers the problem of countering digital spies. Finally, Harvey Rishikof, professor of law and national security studies, evaluates U.S. strategy to counter industrial espionage and suggests changes to the current approach.

In its final section, the volume offers strategies for redressing the most pressing weaknesses in U.S. counterintelligence. Rodney Faraon, formerly a security executive with the Walt Disney Company, discusses business counterintelligence. Timothy R. Sample, former staff director of the House Permanent Select Committee on Intelligence, discusses strategies for domestic intelligence. And to conclude, U.S. court of appeals judge Richard Posner analyzes the complex problems attending management of counterintelligence within the U.S. constitutional system.

Throughout all these chapters, the underlying premise is that the 2004 legislation reorganizing the government's intelligence apparatus is just one stage in the ongoing process of intelligence reform. DNI Michael McConnell has already undertaken to update executive orders, surveillance laws, and the IC's strategic "vision." Much more needs to be done. After all, intelligence is an important, indeed crucial, component of state power—one democracies neglect at their peril. Strong states such as the United States can be compromised or lose battles if they have poor counterintelligence; militarily weak states or transnational groups can achieve, and have achieved, their goals with good counterintelligence. This volume is designed to take a hard look at ourselves and to measure the result against a theoretical standard derived from historical practice. The picture of U.S. capabilities, while not pretty, is full of unexploited potential. It is past time to pursue a sophisticated and culturally appropriate counterintelligence strategy for the next century.

Notes

1. In modern practice, the recruitment of an asset inside an intelligence service is considered a counterintelligence move regardless of what intelligence that asset is able to acquire. It is theoretically possible that such an asset will have less access to information on hostile intelligence operations than to important positive intelligence information relating to the adversary's weapons systems and capabilities, in addition to sensitive biographical information on key decision makers.

2. For defense of the connectivity in antiterrorism work prior to 9/11, see Paul Pillar, "Intelligent Design?: The Unending Saga of Intelligence Reform," *Foreign Affairs* 87 (March/April 2008): 138–44.

3. Supplementary Detailed Staff Reports on Intelligence Activities and the Rights of Americans, Book 3, Final Report of the Select Committee to Study Governmental Operations with respect to Intelligence Activities, U.S. Senate, April 23, 1976, 1. Available at www.icdc.com/~paulwolfcointelpro/churchfinalreport3h.htm.

4. Craig R Whitney, introduction to *The 9/11 Investigations*, Staff Reports of the 9/11 Commission, ed. Steven Strasser (New York: Public Affairs LLC, 2004), xxiv.

5. For a law enforcement view of the problem, see Marilyn Peterson, "Intelligence-Led Policing: The New Intelligence Architecture," Bureau of Justice Assistance, U.S. Department of Justice Office of Justice Programs, September 2005 (NCJ 210681); especially 1–4.

6. "Technology Collection Trends in the U.S. Defense Industry" (Alexandria, VA: Defense Security Service Counterintelligence Office, 2006), 4. Available at www.fas.org/irp/threat/2006trends.pdfwww.dss.smil.mil.

7. See testimony of Larry M. Wortzel before the Subcommittee of Crime, Terrorism and Homeland Security of the House Committee on the Judiciary; Hearing on "Enforcement of Federal Espionage Laws," January 29, 2008. See also "Technology Collection Trends," 2.

8. Ibid., 2.

9. In March 1986 the Chinese government launched a national research and development program with the specific goal of enhancing China's long-term high-technology capabilities.

10. Title 18 Section 793 and 794 U.S. Code.

11. Prepared Statement of David G. Major, president, The Centre for Counterintelligence and Security Studies; before the U.S. House of Representatives, Committee on the Judiciary, Subcommittee on Crime, Terrorism and Homeland Security; "Enforcement of Federal Espionage Laws" Hearing, January 29, 2008.

12. Ibid.

13. See for example, the report to the Department of Justice of the Commission for the Review of FBI Security Programs, Chairman William H. Webster, March 31, 2002. Also see the recent cases of Nada Nadim Prouty and Leandro Aragoncillo. See story by Joby

Warrick and Dan Eggen, "Ex FBI Employee's Case Raises New Security Concerns: Sham Marriage Led to US Citizenship," November 14, 2007. Available at www.washingtonpost .com/wp-dyn/content/article/2007/11/13/AR2007111302033.html.

14. According to the DNI, the 500-Day Plan has six areas of focus: 1. Create a culture of collaboration; 2. Accelerate information sharing; 3. Foster collection and analytic transformation; 4. Build acquisition excellence and technology leadership; 5. modernize business practices; 6. Clarify and align DNI's authorities.

15. 50 U.S.C. § 402c (Counterintelligence Enhancement Act of 2002, Pub. L. No. 107–306, § 904,116 /stat.2383, 2434–37 [2002], as amended)

16. See Presidential Decision Directive-75. Available at www.fas.org/irp/offdocs/pdd/ pdd-75.htm. Public Law 107–306. Also U.S. Code Title 50, Chapter 15, Subchapter I, l 402c. Available at www.law.cornell.edu/uscode/50/USC_sec50_00000402—c000-.html.

17. David Kahn, *The Codebreakers: The Comprehensive History of Secret Communication from Ancient Times to the Internet* (New York: Scribner Book Company, 1996).

18. Bruce Berkowitz, *The New Face of War: How War Will Be Fought in the 21st Century* (New York: The Free Press, 2003).

19. George Gruner, "Carbon Nanonets Spark New Electronics," *Scientific American Reports, Special Edition on Nanotechnology*, September 2007, 48–55.

20. See Gary Livick, "If clothes make the man, then sensors make the robot," March 15, 2001. Accessed on April 4, 2007, at www.techgeek.com/subpage/index.phtml?topic= 998&item=1112.

21. Robin Marantz Henig, "The Real Transformers," *New York Times Magazine*, July 29, 2007, 31.

22. Ibid., 55.

23. One program underway is an MIT-sponsored research effort that uses technology to create a functioning and intelligence learning kitchen that responds to context sensors. Accessed on November 30, 2007, at www.media.mit.edu/ci.

24. See Richard A. Falkenrath, Robert D. Newman, and Bradley A. Thayer, *America's Achilles' Heel: Nuclear, Biological, and Chemical Terrorism and Covert Attack* (Cambridge, MA: MIT Press, 2001), 265–66.

25. For example, see Sam Rae, "Holograms to detect photo fraud," June 25, 2005. Accessed on November 30, 2007, at www.world-science.net/othernews/050625_ watermarkfrm.htm.

26. Barnaby J. Feder, "Technology; A Way to Print Detailed Photos for Secure ID's," *New York Times* December 8, 2003. Available at http://query.nytimes.com/gst/ fullpage.html?res=9B01E4D7103DF93BA35751C1A9659C8B63&n=Top/Reference/ Times%20Topics/Subjects/H/Holography.

27. "Photosynth Prototype: What a horrible time to be blind," June 4, 2007. Available at www.collegehumor.com/video:1762315. The combination of Sea Dragon and computer vision research appears to be "doing away with screen real-estate." It allows the viewer to "dive through images." By taking data in the form of common photos from everyone, Photosynth can create a virtual model of any location or building on earth. This model will then grow in complexity as new data is added and meta data is tagged, permitting "cross-modal and cross-user" processing. Similar advances in three-dimensional imaging have been discussed in *The Economist*: "It All Depends on Your Point of View," Economist.com, November 30, 2006 (from print edition).

28. Chuck Prahl notes that the webmaster of haganah.com "tells citizens how to counter the internet jihad with the power of the pen." Available at http://internet-haganah .com/harchives/003133.html. Private communication, May 2008.

29. See Berkowitz, *The New Face of War*; and Alan D. Campen and Douglas H. Dearth, eds., *Cyberwar 2.0: Myths, Mysteries, and Reality* (Washington, DC: AFCEA International Press, 1995).

30. See David C. Mowery and Nathan Rosenberg, *Paths of Innovation: Technological Change in 20th Century America* (Cambridge: Cambridge University Press, 1998).

31. Thomas L. Friedman, *The World Is Flat: A Brief History of the Twenty-first Century* (New York: Farrar, Straus and Giroux, 2005).

32. See Peter Hennessy, ed., *The New Protective State: Government, Intelligence, and Terrorism* (London: Continuum Books, 2007). This volume includes authors who are among the most knowledgeable and prescient British intellectuals—both scholars and practitioners—involved in developing intelligence and counterintelligence policies. Their work underscores the fact that the challenges facing the United States are faced by other democracies as well.

33. For more on these examples see Jeffrey T. Richelson, *A Century of Spies: Intelligence in the Twentieth Century* (New York: Oxford University Press, 1995). In the United States, surveillance where the primary purpose is law enforcement requires either a criminal warrant or a secretly issued warrant through the Foreign Intelligence Surveillance Court. Recent initiatives taken by the George W. Bush administration have suggested that the executive still believes it retains the right under Article II of the Constitution to conduct warrantless secret surveillance of foreign agents for foreign intelligence purposes on national security grounds.

34. "Wicked problems" were the topic of a workshop hosted by Deborah Barger, then associate DNI for strategic planning under John Negroponte. "Wicked Problems, Wicked Opportunities," January 17–18, 2006, *Center for Mission Innovation*. Wicked problems are also mentioned in James Gosler's and Kathleen Kiernan's chapters in this volume, "Counterintelligence and Law Enforcement."

35. In 1953 Ewen Montagu wrote *The Man Who Never Was: World War II's Boldest Counter-Intelligence Operation* (New York: Oxford University Press, 1953), the story of a counterintelligence operation that tricked Adolf Hitler's intelligence service; it was later turned into a movie. Sir John C. Masterman's *Double-Cross System in the War of 1939 to 1945* (New Haven: Yale University Press, 1972) offered details on how the British intelligence services deceived the Axis powers and created quite a stir when it was published. In 1975 Anthony Cave Brown wrote a comprehensive overview of these operations and their role in Allied victories in his *Bodyguard of Lies* (New York: Harper and Row; 1975), which remains entertaining reading despite subsequent scholarship by Thaddeus Holt, Michael Howard, and F. H. Hinsley, whose collective work reveals some of its inaccuracies. See, for example, Holt's *The Deceivers* (New York: Scribner Book Company, 2004); and Michael Howard, *Strategic Deception in the Second World War*, (London: Norton and Co., 1995). Excellent historical works have covered the counterintelligence domain, including works by Nigel West (e.g., *Mask: MI5's Penetration of the Communist Party of Great Britain* [London: Routledge, 2005]) and Christopher Andrew (e.g., *The Sword and the Shield: The Mitrokhin Archive and the Secret History of the KGB* [New York: Basic Books, 1999]).

36. See volumes edited by Donald C. Daniel and Kathryn L. Herbig, *Strategic Military Deception* (Oxford: Pergamon Press, 1982), and on Soviet practice of it by Brian D. Dailey and Patrick J. Parker, *Soviet Strategic Deception* (Stanford, CA.: Hoover Press, 1987).

37. See Gosler's chapter in this volume; Michelle Van Cleave, *Counterintelligence and National Strategy* (Washington, DC: National Defense University, 2007).

38. Burton Gerber and I thank Matthew Walker for cohosting the Georgetown Intelligence Salon, an informal gathering of theoreticians, practitioners, and scholars interested in bridging the gap between theory and practice. Matt is not only a highly successful businessman, he is also a sharp intellect whose tremendous contributions to our thinking, to this volume, and to intelligence theory in general continue to be greatly appreciated.

I

FRAMING THE PROBLEM

1

Jennifer E. Sims

Twenty-first-Century Counterintelligence

The Theoretical Basis for Reform

SIGNIFICANT STRATEGIC victories often turn on intelligence coups, and with almost every intelligence success, counterintelligence rides shotgun. During the American Civil War's battle at Chancellorsville, Union general Joseph Hooker used a spy's report of a gap in Confederate lines to drive his troops fifty-five miles to the enemy's rear; he was able to do so undetected, thanks to a deception effort that "lured Southern cavalry out of position for observing the march."[1] The general had a good plan, but it was a plan that reflected good counterintelligence capabilities tied directly to strategy. Similarly, in the run-up to Germany's naval victory over the British at Coronel in 1914, the German commander Maximilian Graf von Spee used wireless communications from only one ship, the *Leipzig*, to deceive his counterpart into believing the rest of his squadron floated elsewhere.[2] Von Spee's adversary, Admiral Sir Christopher Craddock, and the imperial flagship he commanded went down in the ensuing battle.[3]

When intelligence delivers a winning opportunity, it almost always marries positive intelligence with counterintelligence. During WWII, the British secret services effectively countered the activities of German intelligence by cracking German codes and using the insights for both defensive and offensive purposes. "[W]ith Sigint and the activities of the double agents reinforcing each other as sources of information, the (British) counter-intelligence authorities built up so full a knowledge of the order of battle and the operations of the Abwehr throughout Europe . . . that it presented little threat to British security for the rest of the war."[4]

In contrast, the case of 9/11 reveals what can happen when intelligence and counterintelligence divorce: loss to a weaker enemy.[5] Such losses are not, as it turns out, historical oddities. Generals and admirals well endowed with substantial intelligence capabilities have so often suffered defeat in battle that some distinguished analysts have suggested that intelligence is unimportant to outcomes and that battles are largely decided by superior force of arms.[6] This assertion, though capturing a grain of truth, is nonetheless utterly wrong in its implications. Bad intelligence on both sides of battle will likely throw the victory to the stronger military power. The question is whether *superior* intelligence, used in the context of a particular battle, can overcome relative weakness in arms. If the answer is yes, then a great power, such as the United States was in September 2001, can be defeated in battle by a weaker power if its intelligence weakness is found and exploited.[7] Indeed, 9/11 demonstrated that victory can be achieved by the weaker warrior so long as he fights with superior knowledge at the critical moment—an advantage that can be gained by capitalizing on the opponent's counterintelligence mistakes or by exercising superior capacities for selective stealth and delusion.

Reflexively opposing the adversary's intelligence operations is not, therefore, always the key to success. So what, then, offers that key? This chapter is designed to answer this question. Specifically, I argue that to achieve consistent competitive advantage from intelligence, the United States must apply mission-based counterintelligence planning—an approach that is intuitively understood by most counterintelligence professionals but practiced only episodically. It involves mapping the intelligence practices of the opponent against a theoretical ideal and then exploiting the shortfalls. The purpose is not just to manipulate or frustrate the opponent's intelligence operations, but to capitalize on what he is not doing well or is not doing at all. Because it targets operations before they take place and weaknesses before they are fixed, mission-based counterintelligence requires deep understanding of competitors' intelligence capabilities and strategies as they are linked to the overall contest. Rather than reactive—simply blocking or obstructing hostile operations—mission-based counterintelligence emphasizes the offensive as it exploits gaps in the opponent's intelligence system in order to set up its own side for winning moves.

This approach is, however, counterintuitive to most nonspecialists because it may involve degrading the capabilities of foreign intelligence services by "assisting" the targeted service in selective ways—perhaps causing internal imbalances or reinforcing useful perceptions—a technique described in Robert Jervis's chapter and presented in greater detail below. This idea lies at the heart of the approach. Beyond classic denial and deception, both of which imply actively withholding a highly valued "truth," this approach to counterintelligence may not; it might simply identify idiosyncrasies in a foreign intelligence service and exploit them. The purpose might be to convey information useful to one's own side, to highlight useful facts, or to encourage overreach, such as aggressive collection that might aggravate latent distrust between the service and its overseers.

In this way counterintelligence can help to undermine or influence what an opposing service does in order to achieve favorable results. Because it is done with self-serving objectives and little or no reference to the opposition's "best" strategic choices given the overall strategic context, it is not a benign form of intelligence sharing. The instigator, even when sharing good information, angles for moves that might be inimical to the recipient's broader interests—perhaps feeding a belief that may or may not be valid. For this reason, foreign intelligence liaison can be dangerous as well as useful.[8]

Mission-based counterintelligence operations are not necessarily as grand in scope as they are in impact. Tactical use of them has a long history. Admiral von Spee hid his boats—but he did so at just the right time and only to gain an edge in a battle he foresaw and timed to perfection. In von Spee's hands counterintelligence was not just a way to avoid risk in the face of the British imperial fleet, but an integral part of an edgy and gutsy strategy. His success turned on an often forgotten truth: *predictable* secrecy simply inspires an opponent to ramp up intelligence operations; *selective* secrecy (sudden and unpredictable stealth) confuses or convinces in ways that give the user an edge.

To develop the foregoing arguments, this chapter will begin by discussing traditional counterintelligence operations and their relationship to a mission-based approach. It will then explore the features of a theoretically ideal intelligence capability—an essential first step in discerning an adversary's strengths and weaknesses and thus plotting operations against him. This exploration includes a discussion of specific ways a competitor can operate against an adversary *before* intelligence actions are taken against him. It may be controversial because it presumes some degree of consensus on what intelligence is, what makes it work well, and what spoils it. The analysis assumes that intelligence is best defined as the collection, analysis, and dissemination of information on behalf of decision makers engaged in a competitive enterprise and that its performance can be judged according to some relatively simple measures.[9]

Finally, the paper argues that the concept of mission-based counterintelligence offers an approach that may be less costly and less potentially troubling for democracies to employ than the more traditional, reactive one because it suggests that some hostile operations can and should be ignored and others may possibly even be encouraged.[10] What constitutes an "edge" that needs protection at any moment depends on the nature of the competition and the strategies each side is pursuing.

Traditional Counterintelligence Operations

The idea of mission-based counterintelligence does not make more traditional operational approaches irrelevant—it simply subsumes them within a larger set of options. Counterintelligence is traditionally understood to include operations designed to block, disrupt, or destroy the intelligence operations of an adversary. These counteroperations are generally discussed in terms of four categories: passive or active defense and passive or active offense.[11]

Passive defense, which includes security systems, locks, vaults, and classification rules, is designed to keep valuable information from opponents. The overlap between security and counterintelligence is not complete: Whereas security professionals keep walls secure and patch any hole in them immediately, counterintelligence officers ask how the hole developed, what it may say about any potential intruder's plans, and how long it might be useful to watch it so that his existence can be confirmed and his purposes understood.[12] In any case, the information both seek to protect is of two types: information that might reveal one's own strategy, decision-making processes, and intelligence capabilities, and information that the opponent needs to execute successfully his own strategy, if that is perceived to be threatening.[13] Inferior intelligence systems often confuse the former with the latter or assume the two sets are co-incident, leading to wasteful expenditures of resources or excessive controls on information. The more adversaries with whom a state must contend, the more information that state will likely need to protect. Great powers are particularly vulnerable to pressures for expenditures in passive defense, tying up resources in security at the expense of more active measures and positive intelligence collection.

Active defense involves measures designed to tease out the offensive activities of opponents. Active defense includes surveillance, defector debriefings, wiretapping, interrogations, and the use of "dangles" who, posing as ripe recruits for the adversary's service, aim to learn about the opponent's need for intelligence and thus their strategic intent. Some dangles intentionally do no more than this. If, however, dangles are recruited by the opponent, they can become double agents who may learn about an adversary's intelligence operations before they take place. Similarly, "moles" recruited in an adversary's service can enable defense by warning both of penetrations in the recruiting service and of an opponent's next moves.[14] Moles are usually agents who remain in place in the adversary's intelligence service. Although defectors who leave their countries can provide good counterintelligence information, their usefulness declines as soon as they lose access to their former employers. Moles live in fear of defectors. The 1985 defection of Vitaliy Yurchenko, a senior official in the Soviet KGB, helped lead to the arrest of Ronald Pelton, a former official with the National Security Agency who had divulged critical U.S. secrets relating to technical collection.[15]

In contrast, offensive counterintelligence aims to manipulate an opponent so that he either chooses not to attack or attacks in harmless ways. Almost inevitably, offensive counterintelligence affects not just the opposing intelligence service, but the decision makers it supports by distorting their perceptions and thus influencing their choices. Offensive CI can be passive, involving the use of camouflage, "dummy" weapons, or the masking of military assets inside of innocuous-looking buildings. When Southern troops fooled General George McClellan during the U.S. Civil War by painting logs black and propping them up as if they were artillery, they were using passive offensive counterintelligence. Such techniques work best when the adversary has a reasonably good capacity to collect; after all, he must be able to see what the deceiver intends for him to see. Yet, knowing how the adversary collects and designing camouflage techniques appropriate to his methods are crucial to effectively snookering him. If Northern troops had penetrated Southern lines with spies able to run their hands along the cannon barrels, these passive techniques would not have worked. But knowing that McClellan relied on more distant means, including balloons and telescopes, the Confederates believed, correctly, that the log-laying ruse had a good chance of success.

Active offensive counterintelligence involves duping the adversary by directly feeding false information to him and manipulating his interpretation of it, as opposed to designing a disguise and allowing the opponent to interpret its meaning. Trusted by the targeted service, double agents can feed information specifically designed to twist the minds, and therefore the plans, of the opposing decision makers at just the right moment. The difficulty here is in establishing the bona fides of the doubled spies. It takes a long time to build these agents' credibility—a process that often requires feeding much good intelligence to the enemy. The need to lose intelligence advantages in some lesser battles in order to gain strategically decisive advantages in later ones makes the business of offensive counterintelligence full of peril and risk. Deciding when to use one's double agents for the final and decisive blow, given that the passing of bad information will likely expose these doubles to the wrath of the defeated party, makes the psychological stakes for this kind of game very high indeed. That said, one of the most sophisticated double-agent operations ever conducted, the Double Cross System used by Britain during the Normandy landings in WWII, managed to save many of its agents even as their deceptions were triggered.[16] The Nazis so thoroughly believed in their agents' credibility, including those in Europe who were vulnerable to the Nazis, that they failed to eliminate most of the doubles.[17]

Obviously all types of counterintelligence operations require analytic support. Deciding which assets to defend requires analysis of which targets the adversary is most likely to attack. No counterintelligence enterprise can operate against all contingencies, so analysis of both risk and opportunity is essential. Moreover, if policymakers do not help design counterintelligence operations, the chances are high that these operations will create situations or introduce risks that are counterproductive for policy. For this and other reasons, any separation of counterintelligence operations from foreign and defense policymaking, as has historically been the case in the United States, should be a matter of considerable concern.

Mission-Based Counterintelligence

Counterintelligence analysis has, however, even more important implications for strategic planning than the foregoing description of counterintelligence operations suggests. The research of Ian Walker, a British psychologist at Bath University, makes this point particularly well: Walker, curious about risk proclivities, watched as 2,300 cars overtook him as he pedaled along British roads. When he rode without a helmet, cars gave him a wide berth; when he wore a female wig, they gave him a still wider berth. When he donned a helmet, they zipped close by and at high speeds.[18]

The counterintelligence lessons from Walker's experiment are many, although in-depth analysis would require more data (such as whether the results would be the same in, say, Rome, Italy, or New York City). But these two lessons might be the most useful ones: lowering one's own risks depends on knowing how a competitor will react to what you do; and the results of defensive measures may be counterintuitive and idiosyncratic. These ideas lie at the heart of mission-based approaches to counterintelligence. Important as countering the actual operations of an adversarial service may be, if counterintelligence is not simply to be reactive or mechanistic, it must study an opponent's proclivities, exploit his weaknesses—including what he is not doing but should be—and channel his energies in ways that take advantage of the strengths of one's own service. Such analysis requires a thorough understanding of what successful intelligence entails, which may be summarized as four critical missions: collecting relevant information; anticipating competitors' moves; transmitting useful insights to policymakers (and vice versa); and deceiving competitors or denying information to them.[19] Arguably, a sound counterintelligence effort must identify what an opposing service is and is not doing in these four areas and assist policymakers in exploiting these weaknesses through prioritized means for counterattack. Good knowledge of the opponent's weaknesses can relieve policymakers of the pressure to conduct operations in which costs are likely to exceed expected gains.

If, for example, an opposing intelligence service is not trusted by its masters because it is viewed as incompetent and delivers bad news, greater value may be gained from exacerbating this mistrust than from countering the opposing service's operations at every turn, particularly if its collection capability can be weakened by causing suspicious leaders to redirect resources elsewhere. Agents of influence can be very useful instruments for such initiatives. The British, dismayed by the poor quality of President Woodrow Wilson's intelligence in the second decade of the twentieth century, and noting the president's general distrust of secrecy and stealth, dispatched an agent, William Wiseman, to Wilson's side. Wiseman developed a trusting relationship with both Wilson and his top advisor, Colonel House, and thus helped bring the United States into WWI on Britain's side.

The point is that tactical or defensive counterintelligence operations risk wasting resources against ineffective adversarial service or, at worst, prompting the opposing government to provide greater support to its beleaguered service. Aggravated mistrust, or substitution of trust through agent operations such as Wiseman's, leverages the enemy's core weakness instead. Generating options such as these, which depend for their effective fruition on deep counterintelligence analysis, is the purpose of mission-based counterintelligence.

The Wiseman example also illustrates a rule that is fundamental to all counterintelligence operations: Know the target. Effective degradation of a competitor's intelligence system requires positive intelligence collection and a thorough understanding of the consequences for both sides. Wiseman needed to preempt and control, but not to eliminate, U.S. intelligence, since the strategic objective was to garner an ally. This kind of approach requires manipulating and undermining not just the target's current operations but also his efforts to collect, anticipate, deceive, and influence. After all, the ultimate objective, what sixth-century-BC Chinese strategist Sun Tsu called a "divine skein," is the weaving of strategy, intelligence, and counterintelligence into a winning weapon.[20]

Countering Collection

A successful intelligence service designs and employs collection systems appropriate for targets and terrain; a successful counterintelligence capability undermines or manipulates the opponents' collection in as nuanced a way as possible. The more collection systems employed by an opponent, the richer their collective "take" and the harder the whole system is to deceive. Yet the task of deceiving collection is not always as difficult as it might seem, especially if a state with multiple collectors divides them up against different targets in predictable ways, such as imagery on North Korean nuclear facilities and human intelligence, or liaison primarily against terrorists. Then the opponents' task is clear: defeat or manipulate the critical collector—the liaison service or the appropriate satellite—in other words, the one or two collectors of greatest concern.

Constructive redundancy in collection is therefore useful from a counterintelligence perspective. Indeed, good collection managers array the collection systems they build to gain access to current or anticipated targets as strategy and the overall flow of the contest requires. The task is not unlike conducting a symphony: The manager must know all his instruments and lead them effectively. In intelligence, however, the instruments are endlessly variable and the conductor can rearrange their music. Creating tailor-made collection systems is part of the challenge; doing this well requires information on emerging technologies, considerable engineering skill, and keeping the plans secret. Countering collection requires not just blocking or disrupting the act of collection, but also blocking or disrupting the building, engineering, and orchestrating that underlies it. For this reason, the planning and development of new collection methods are usually kept secret—but not always.

For example, the evolution of photography's role in intelligence was to some extent a public affair in its earliest stages. Innovations in photography during the nineteenth century, led military leaders to consider how these advances might be exploited for intelligence, especially given the Union's use of balloons during the U.S. Civil War. The Prussian General Staff used trained photographers for aerial military surveys as early as 1860. Open publications described experiments that involved tying miniature cameras to parakeets and pigeons.[21] Such openness permitted rapid advances in imaging sensors and creative experimentation in how to deploy as well as to defend against them. During WWI, low-flying reconnaissance aircraft proved valuable, but also vulnerable to ground and anti-aircraft fire.[22] Their use prompted counterintelligence innovations: by 1918 the artist Andre Dunoyer de Segonzac headed a camouflage section of the French Army that numbered about three thousand individuals, many of whom were accomplished painters trained in Cubist deconstruction and visual effects.[23]

Collection managers have to manipulate sensing systems, such as imagery aircraft or human spy networks, to ensure they work well together against their targets. Whether pigeon-based, a satellite system, or a spy network, each collector has five essential components: command and control, platforms, sensors, processing and exploitation, and data exfiltration.[24] In manipulating these components and arraying them against competitors and adversaries, managers seek to maximize the range, depth, and security of the entire collection system, thus optimizing its overall performance.[25] This performance is usually measured in terms of such attributes as productivity, agility, efficiency, and timeliness.[26] To collect against the closed Soviet Union, the United States developed in the 1950s a variety of platforms for intelligence sensors, such as balloons, satellites, and aircraft, including the space-hugging, high-flying jet that later became the SR-71. Some of these platforms weren't operational until the 1960s, but their purposeful diversity helped to ensure that the vulnerability or poor productivity of any one would not blind the United States at a critical juncture. Platforms in space obviously required configuring cameras for that environment and determining how the data would be returned to earth—a set of issues military services had already faced with reconnaissance aircraft between the World Wars. With the rapid evolution of commercial optics in the 1950s, U.S. intelligence had to reach out to the private sector again, building partnerships with commercial firms, such as Kodak, which then became possible targets for foreign intelligence collection.[27]

The ability to find solutions to collection problems, whether they are inherent to the target or created by an opposing intelligence service, depends on having a central manager empowered to fix them. The more that a collector's components are vertically integrated, the easier it should be to adjust its sensors, platforms, and processing and thus maximize its collection against particular targets. When multiple collectors are involved, collection managers can work to balance them so that the overall effort is optimized against the target set. In this way managers provide, for example, coverage that is both broad area (all of Iran) and point-specific (a particular nuclear weapons plant) with tip-offs for when and how to do each.

Managers' efforts to tinker with a collection system's performance can run up against the need for stealth and security. During the Revolutionary War George Washington worried incessantly about the imbalances that might arise among his agents, couriers, and safe houses. The Culper spy ring, which he ran with the assistance of Benjamin Tallmage, used taverns in New York City and Long

Island as platforms to collect against British forces encamped there. Agents employed secret ink provided by Washington to hide their messages. Traders servicing these taverns became couriers; their routes from Long Island to the Connecticut shore were monitored by housewives who encoded warnings by rearranging laundry on clotheslines.[28]

Though this system was crafty and its components initially fit well with one another, it was also only loosely managed by Washington himself, who had limited knowledge and control over what his agents did. A surge in intelligence could not easily be accompanied by a surge in the number of courier runs or laundry loads without raising suspicions. And efforts by some of his exhausted couriers to recruit helpers at periods of heightened vulnerability put existing agents at risk. The Culper example suggests that owning a relatively secure collection system with access to its target is not enough to gain an intelligence advantage over an agile adversary; these components must also respond to a collection manager who is able to adjust them to fit the changing nature of the competition, the targets, and the threat.[29]

Given this description of the collection mission, countering it could simply involve disrupting, fooling, or blocking human or technical sensors by using camouflage and encryption; conducting operations at night; or tracking, distracting, and intercepting human spies. This is the scope of conventionally understood counterintelligence operations, whether they are directed against protecting one's own intelligence service or the larger national security establishment of the country concerned. However, countering collection can also involve stealing, monopolizing, hijacking, or destroying the platforms (such as cars, trees, buildings, or park benches) that spies and other sensors use; breaking down the connections among sensors, platforms, and communications systems; scrambling or slowing down the processing or analysis of the data; or manipulating the messages before they arrive back home. To the extent that collection systems employ commercial technologies, countercollection can involve buying up or threatening the companies that produce them.

Countercollection can also involve influencing, undermining, or owning the principal collection manager—the person or office that orchestrates balance, flexibility, and integration of the collection system itself. Moles can do great damage, not just because they have access to an intelligence system's secrets, but because they can throw small wrenches in the works so that sources become suspect, communications are delayed, and platforms are underfunded.

If an opponent has a strong and effective collection manager, counterintelligence operations designed to block collection assets will tend to trigger innovation by the targeted service. Moscow gained temporary counterintelligence advantage when it shot down airplanes in the 1950s, and later Gary Powers' high-flying U2 in 1960. But the United States had developed an effective system for research and development under Allen Dulles and Richard Bissell. Moscow's efforts, while producing tactical wins, prompted the United States to develop less vulnerable assets such as space-based intelligence collectors. While counterintelligence tactics will always be necessary in such instances, offense (manipulating the adversary's mind) may be preferable to defense (shooting down his reconnaissance aircraft) because, compared with his frustrated counterpart, a confused collection manager will be slower to innovate and adapt and thus more likely to do lasting damage to his own operation. In any case, strategies for countering collection should be tightly integrated with broader intelligence policy so that the systems for collecting against the enemy's adaptive response are in place. Failure to plan in this way may inadvertently deliver advantage to the opponent.

Counteranticipation

The second task of intelligence is to anticipate opponents' moves and warn of surprise. Anticipation is not synonymous with prediction. Providing useful warning involves learning and conveying the plans, strategies, capabilities, and decisions of an opponent (knowable developments) in time for countermoves. It is a tough job but nonetheless one in which it is possible to achieve improvements relative to an adversary.[30] The task involves identifying new, false, or resurgent challengers, gauging their capabilities, learning about their decisions, and understanding their purposes relative to one's own so that options for manipulating, blunting, or stopping them may be generated. Timing is critical.[31] An intelligence service that anticipates an attack and alerts decision makers still fails if it does so too late—that is, when there is no time left for a countermove. *Countering* the warning function involves undermining the opposing service's ability to see the unexpected, perhaps even forcing or luring it into the predictable priorities of policymakers' in-boxes. Performing this counterintelligence task well requires an in-depth understanding of the anticipatory or warning function.

To be good at anticipating, an intelligence service must be successful at collecting against known adversaries and communicating these threats to decision makers in time for them to act. But it should also have a measure of freedom from current decision makers and their agendas—an attribute uniquely important to the warning function. An intelligence service's independence is crucial in two respects: It must be sufficiently free of its own side's cultural and cognitive biases to understand the mind of the opponent, and it must be sufficiently unbound from its own side's policy preferences to collect against the unexpected adversary, the discarded option, and the undesirable outcome. A good intelligence service is thus interested in and capable of directing collection against targets that policy makers undervalue, delivering news policymakers may not want to hear, and directing the data to new decision makers who, though outside the current policymaking "club," may nonetheless be critical to countering the challenger's next move. Pearl Harbor was a failure in this sense; not only was collection poor and analysis skewed, but the commanders in Hawaii were out of the loop for highly classified information. Intelligence officers, embedded in a military chain of command, were limited in their ability to influence the loop or who was in it. An intelligence service must continually seek to strengthen its independence, including its ability to identify those who need its products, or risk that service's being fooled by adversaries who can see both the leash that constrains it and calculate its length. From the opponent's perspective, if an intelligence service is confined within policy requirements and paradigms, there are ways to induce it to be even more so.

Cultural self-awareness and independent thinking require considerable analytic skill distributed across the intelligence enterprise. For example, case officers must judge who is worth recruiting now because he or she will have good access to information in the future when a competition crystallizes or becomes a full-blown war. The "requirement" for such a source may not be backed by current policymakers; indeed the recruitment would be made on behalf of future ones. If case officers are discouraged from deep analysis and from consulting others able to help with such assessments, the warning function will suffer.[32] All source analysts must cultivate a similar detachment from current policy and dominant cultural paradigms as they consider how an opponent is likely to derive meaning from events and act next. In this sense, analysts in the field or at headquarters must join the audience for the opposing conductor's symphony—listening to the music and divining from its melody, crescendos, codas, and rests where the composition is likely to go next and why.

This appreciation of the adversary's next move involves less the search for some evasive "truth" than a perceptual exercise in independent thought. Expertise in it requires cultivating a sense of the other side's vision and preferences—but also his musicality—not one's own. This is not just a matter of cross-cultural understanding, tradecraft, or mind-set management. It is a matter of appreciating the role of intuition and creative impulse in leadership as well.[33] Analysts comfortable with theoretical mathematics, choreography, or other forms of abstraction, *and* with deep knowledge of culture and the key personalities involved, may have the best chance of evaluating the contest from the perspective of their adversaries.

In any case, an intelligence service that limits these intelligence skills by tying collectors or analysts too tightly to policymakers and their priorities weakens its capacity to gather clues of emerging or dissipating threats and makes itself vulnerable to manipulation. This reportedly happened to U.S. intelligence during the run-up to the Iraq war, when agencies backed off intelligence collection on central Iraq, where weapons facilities were located, in order to enhance collection against Iraqi surface-to-air missile sites in the north and south. Although Iraq was clearly threatening U.S. planes patrolling the no-fly zones and Pentagon officials were reasonably confident of Saddam's intent to keep his weapons programs alive, some professionals in the intelligence community believed focusing on support to military operations at the expense of tracking his weapons of mass destruction was shortsighted.[34] The principal collecting agencies were, however, increasingly dependent on the Defense Department for resources, so the pressures to adjust to military officials' preferences were intense. Thus, by 2003, the data on Iraq's weapons of mass destruction had degraded, making the jobs of estimating Iraq's weapons capabilities and warning of changes in them far more difficult than they might otherwise have been. Although Saddam Hussein probably did not threaten U.S. air assets in the north and south *in order to* divert U.S. intelligence from collecting information on his weapons facilities in central Iraq, he *could* have; if he had, such a counterintelligence strategy would have been based on a sophisticated understanding of the power the Pentagon holds over U.S. collection assets under the U.S. system.

If Defense Department officials made the wrong choices in this instance, their error was not uncommon. Even superior commanders tend to focus on their current priorities and to resist evidence of misperception and policy failure. Signs of emerging threats may be perceived as distractions. These sorts of perceptual failure happen even though the best decision makers recognize that the ability to anticipate surprise should be their chief gain from delegating intelligence to others. Similarly, covert action sometimes expends assets such as agents, spies, and analysts, on current policy priorities. Although this kind of expenditure may sometimes be necessary, even successful covert action uses up intelligence assets that might warn of future threats and opportunities in order to gain current policy outcomes—often on behalf of frustrated foreign policy officials. If covert action fails, of course, human assets with access will be lost and the capacity to warn will likely deteriorate. In any case, policymakers err if they place the warning function too heavily on the shoulders of analysts trained to act and think like themselves while restricting these estimators to the data their own vision and requirements generated.

Of course, intelligence officials may take (or be induced to take) their independence from policy too far, becoming so in tune with the adversary that they eventually become distrusted by those whom they are supposed to support. Stalin was so famously suspicious of his intelligence service that he purged it repeatedly. Nevertheless, his spies in Europe and Asia were able to warn him that Nazi Germany was planning to attack in June 1941, despite Stalin's firm belief that Hitler would not and that the threat was concocted by the British. That Richard Sorge, Leopold Trepper, and other Soviet spies were able to collect against the possibility of German treachery had much to do with their complete immersion in the culture they were targeting, maintaining considerable distance from Moscow. That they delivered the warning in time despite the great risk to themselves in doing so reflected in large part the simplicity of their task: They knew their enemies, and they knew to whom they had to deliver their intelligence. Only Stalin, obviously, could order troops to move from the east, where they might deter the Japanese, to the west, where they could counter a German invasion.

In democratic federations, however, defeating an agile adversary may require alerting officials who have never needed intelligence before or who underestimate their own importance to the outcome of battle. In this regard, a fundamental failure on 9/11 was the U.S. intelligence community's inability to connect with those domestic decision makers who could have taken practical steps to counter and defeat the terrorists at each decisive point in their strategy. Trapped in routines of the Cold War, intelligence and counterintelligence professionals were not trained to disseminate "outside channels" and had no procedures for doing so. Even where procedures were in place, they had no clear understanding of what decisions they were enabling and why.[35] The critical decision makers were, in the first instance, consular officers in the Department of State and agents in customs, border security, and FBI field offices, many of whom, because they weren't policymakers or senior enough, had no "requirements profile" in the CIA's directorate of intelligence.[36] By September, the critical decision makers were employees at airports, airlines, and the city fire and police departments. Lashed so closely to the traditional foreign policy and defense establishment, the U.S. intelligence community had no plan or clear authority to help nontraditional decision makers engage an enemy inside the gates. This was an intelligence problem, not just a counterintelligence one. The failure to recognize this gap rests with the division between counterintelligence and intelligence in U.S. practice—a division that lies at the heart of the current U.S. debate over domestic intelligence.

If an ability to anticipate is crucial to gaining competitive advantage by disabling an opponent's capacity to warn, counteranticipation does the opposite. It enables surprise. By diminishing an opposing intelligence service's independence, counterintelligence professionals can make their adversaries risk averse. An opposing service's intelligence operations then become predictable reflections of its master's highest current priorities. By inducing distrust among policy and intelligence professionals, counterintelligence operatives can cause purges of the kind Stalin inflicted on his intelligence service or just restrict the opposing service from taking risks to warn and to collect opportunistically.

Societies that are intrinsically distrustful of intelligence may be most vulnerable to this kind of ploy. In the 1990s the death of an American citizen in Guatemala was linked, albeit indirectly, to a U.S. intelligence asset. The director of central intelligence (DCI) reacted to the growing public outcry by instituting new regulations regarding the recruitment of foreign spies: If they had been involved in human rights abuses or had criminal records, the most senior levels in headquarters had to be consulted before recruitment could occur.[37] Although in this case there was no evidence that a foreign service engineered this result through baits and leaks, this kind of reactive curtailment of espionage capacity is certainly noticed by foreign services, which would see it as a vulnerability. In any case, the curtailment of human intelligence operations was reportedly significant.[38] By knowing an adversary's political system and inducing intelligence "failures" of this kind, an opposing service can stimulate risk aversion, greater oversight of intelligence operations, and a desire to please (and thus not deliver bad news) within the targeted service. Again, the danger of such ploys is that the changes wrought in the targeted service could eventually improve its performance by increasing oversight and trust. But in the interim, the targeted government loses its independence and thus its ability, among other things, to anticipate and to warn.

Even more profitable may be efforts to deceive that play off the cultural or methodological biases of an opposing service's analysts—biases that prevent them from detaching from conventional wisdom. In the U.S. intelligence community, a degree of detachment is encouraged by emphasizing objectivity and rigorous methodologies for analyzing data. Yet, examined carefully, this scientific approach is itself a bias—a way of looking at the world that entraps intelligence analysts and thus provides opportunities adversaries can exploit.[39] For example, to trick U.S. intelligence, a foreign service could advertise the rational while employing the irrational. Al-Qaeda may be doing something similar, albeit probably inadvertently, by releasing videos, tapes, and pronouncements concerning apparently sophisticated political causes while encouraging tactical actions by suicidal or disaffected youth. Although studying an opponent's professed aims may be important for strategic planning, recognizing that his troops may act less on these grand designs than on personal experiences and conspiracy theories is important in actually stopping a terrorist event and thus winning decision advantage.

Countertransmission

Despite its need for a measure of independence, a high-quality intelligence service must also foster intimate relationships with decision makers. In fact, successful intelligence requires the kind of coziness that makes advocates of objectivity and independence cringe. Yet no amount of collection or aptitude for warning can make up for an inability to convey knowledge to decision makers. If policymakers or commanders don't trust an intelligence service, that service will have little influence, and opportunities for gaining decision advantage will be lost. The trick in managing a superior intelligence service is to balance intimacy with distance; the key to *disabling* the adversary's service is to destroy that balance or to undermine the managers whose job it is to sustain it.

History is full of examples of strained relationships between policy and intelligence. Former U.S. director of central intelligence James Woolsey used to joke that the famous incident involving the crash of a light plane onto White House grounds during the Clinton administration was simply his effort to get an audience with the president.[40] An earlier DCI, John McCone, resigned because President Johnson suspected CIA of secretly opposing him; Johnson mistrusted McCone on the issue of Vietnam and began to cut him out of serious discussions of military strategy.[41] Similarly, Robert Blackwill, a senior foreign policy official who has worked at the upper reaches of the State Department and National Security Council, mistrusted the Department of State's Bureau of Intelligence and Research because its focus was, perhaps understandably, on support to the secretary of state, not to him. Blackwill has said that intelligence worked for him only when, once on the National Security Council staff, he had his own set of "analytic hogs"—a reference to the defensive line of the Washington Redskins—who made him their priority.[42] The most recent dustup concerned a Defense Department official, Douglas Feith, who so mistrusted CIA analysis that he, at the direction of his superiors, decided to examine the evidence and generate alternative views on what intelligence sources were saying.[43]

Indeed, trust lies at the heart of what might be called the "transmission function" of an intelligence service. Ideally, policymakers share their strengths, weaknesses, and strategies with their intelligence colleagues to help them gauge threats and conduct net assessment. Intelligence officials, in turn, commit themselves to helping policymakers win. In other words, the objectivity that intelligence needs in order to warn must be melded with an understanding that the purpose of the overall mission is to help one side win. This means intelligence must strive more for relevance to the issues at hand than for factual completeness in some objective sense. Analyzing the attributes of tanks will not help in calculating which side will win an engagement at sea. Persistence in collecting factual data on tanks would soon become infuriating to the naval commander— regardless of how objective and "true" these facts might seem to be. While this example might seem so obvious as to be unrealistic as a modern intelligence problem, it will sound familiar to senators briefed by the Defense Intelligence Agency prior to the Persian Gulf war. These detailed briefings provided accurate facts about Saddam's military assets and emplacements. But, absent data on U.S. capabilities and plans, the picture looked far graver than proved true once forces engaged. Senators subsequently complained they had been misled, while their briefers insisted that their facts were accurate.[44]

If an intelligence service becomes more dedicated to objective "truth" (the number of enemy tanks, for example) than to facts relevant to the winning move (each side's edge under various scenarios), then policymakers will lose confidence that intelligence officers are part of the team, and they will be cut out. Once cut out, an intelligence service will fail—if failure is properly understood to be the loss of an ability to provide decision advantages to one's own side. Alternatively, if policymakers leave their intelligence colleagues in the dark concerning the full scope of the competition as they see it, including strategy, tactics, and related vulnerabilities, intelligence cannot help them. Intelligence oversight by the executive or a third party (judiciary or legislative body) can enhance trust. But the issue is equally one of culture and training for both policymakers and intelligence professionals.

Although logic might suggest that disrupting relations between an adversarial service and its master is good counterintelligence policy, such missions can often be counterproductive. Policymakers often want an opposing government to act rationally to diplomatic pressure or to *correctly* calculate the costs of engagement. Moreover, if one part of an intelligence service has good sources in the upper reaches of an adversary's service and the relationship between that service and policymakers breaks down, the productive "take" from that source will be compromised. If one part of the service is trying to deceive the other, a loss of connection between the deceived intelligence professionals and their policy or military counterparts will make deception more difficult, if not impossible. For these reasons, counterintelligence programs must be strategically linked, work synergistically with positive intelligence programs, and, more generally, connect with overarching policy.

All this said, "countertransmission" efforts can work well if carefully executed. An intelligence service planning a deception can encourage opposing policymakers to distrust certain sources over which the deceiver lacks control in favor of others it does control, thus feeding misinformation through "trusted" channels while encouraging the discounting of contradictory information received by other means.

Counterdenial and Counterdeception

The fourth critical mission for intelligence is, of course, denial and deception. The objective is to degrade or destroy the ability of an adversary to gather and use good intelligence. This strategically defensive mission accomplishes the same objective as positive intelligence—gaining decision advantage—but does so not by enabling one's own side so much as by disabling the opponent. *Countering* denial and deception is the most difficult of counterintelligence missions.

Denial is a straightforward concept insofar as it relates to one's own intelligence and national security processes. Secrets can be protected using secret writing, encryption, classification systems, vaults, and the use of loyalty tests, such as lie detectors or polygraphs, to protect against the risk of turncoats. The more operations, tactics, and intelligence that can be kept hidden from the opponent, the less he is likely to learn about what you are doing. Denying information that an adversary needs to execute his own strategy, however, requires far more creativity. If the adversary plans less to counter your move than to open a new front or outflank you, then just protecting your own assets and plans is fruitless or worse. Terrorists who calculate where they will strike by waiting to see where you defend and, by extension, what remains vulnerable, present the toughest kind of counterintelligence target. One is tempted to try to defend everything and thus to defend nothing adequately. Against opponents who choose to bob and weave, deception can play an important role because it lures as well as defends, increasing one's odds of gaining decisive advantage.

Of course, denial is a necessary adjunct to any effort to deceive an opponent.[45] Successful deception, in turn, involves something akin to a fun-house mirror: reflections that are largely representative, but distorted enough to give the observer a false impression. When, for example, the Allies intended to land in southern Europe during WWII, they planted fake documents on a corpse to deceive Hitler into believing this would happen through Sardinia and Greece instead of Sicily—a relatively minor geographic feint but sufficient to gain strategic advantage.[46] Truth must be *approximated* in order for the deception to be credible; flat-out lies will be too easy for an opponent to discover through information channels that the deceiver cannot control. Deceptions that closely hone to the truth can be seemingly validated by many other sources the deceiver does not control, thus gaining in credibility.

The best way for a deceiver to deliver this false impression is, of course, through the observer's most trusted channel for information. For the relatively naive adversary, trusted collection could simply involve reliance on a news service with a comfortable point of view. More often in international politics, the adversary's intelligence service is his most trusted source. Double agents play crucial roles in these regards since, properly embedded in a foreign intelligence service, they can deliver the distortions. Loyal but overeager or poorly trained intelligence officers can do the job as well, provided they are able to be manipulated and, of course, trusted by their own side. In any case, a good collection capability should be in place to determine whether and when the deception has been successful (or if, instead, it has been spoiled and the double agents turned or controlled by the adversary). As explained earlier, any uncoordinated counterintelligence efforts designed, for example, to break down the relationship between an opposition service and the decision makers it serves just at the point when a stratagem is being delivered, will inevitably *reduce* the opportunities for successful deception. A strong deception capability turns, therefore, on integrating intelligence, counterintelligence, and overall strategy from the tactical through the strategic level.[47]

Countering denial and deception is at once straightforward and the murkiest of counterintelligence tasks. It leads practitioners into the most difficult areas of intelligence policy and practice. Denial can be countered by improved intelligence capabilities—defeating the latest methods of encryption, for example, with improved techniques for cryptanalysis. Countering deception involves both improving collection and such defensive measures as protecting sources and methods (including analytic tradecraft), mole-hunting, and double-agent exposures. It also requires that policymakers understand that counterintelligence officers sometimes have to regard a lack of uncertainty as cause for concern. To be empowered to task collectors against policymakers' firm conclusions requires extraordinary trust between intelligence and policy professionals. It is nonetheless essential.

A paradox here is worth underscoring: The more trusted a targeted service is by those whom it serves, the more likely it is that adversaries will seek to deceive it. This is because an intelligence system that reliably and rapidly conveys intelligence to important officials offers deceivers the most value for their efforts. If a service is not good in this respect, opponents are likely to try to circumvent it by using agents of influence. The latter option was used by the British before WWI and WWII when U.S. intelligence capabilities were minimal. During the Cuban Missile Crisis, the Soviets attempted to deceive U.S. intelligence, then a highly capable service, despite knowing that President Kennedy had lost trust in it following the Bay of Pigs disaster.[48] To cover their bets, they also pursued deception through a back door by sending a Soviet intelligence officer, Georgi Bolshakov, to the White House as an agent of influence.[49]

Both denial and deception can also be countered by changes in tactics and strategy that confuse the adversary about what he needs to protect in order to win. The more wide-ranging a competitor's collection capabilities, the more he can force his opponent to be wide-ranging and reactive in defense—thus trapping and embroiling an opposing intelligence service in irrelevant actions. During the Civil War, for example, Rose Greenhow's reputation as a spy, now apparently overinflated, nonetheless tied up Northern intelligence services in efforts to disrupt her network. Truly inventive and agile adversaries force an opponent to literally lock everything up—a costly choice that can drain the resources of an intelligence enterprise and the state or group it serves, eventually leading to their demise. In this regard, illiberal states may have a disadvantage: Capable of directing resources to protecting the regime, they are likely to overdo it. Even democracies that equate good national security practices with keeping secrets can err in this way. Rigid classification systems are not only poor tools for counterintelligence, they can cripple it and, in so doing, create opportunities for the adversary.

Denial and deception can also be foiled by speed or by counterdeception. Doing either requires a deep knowledge of how the adversaries' operations are run, including the telltale incentives for, and signs of, engineered deceit. It also requires a thorough knowledge of one's own side. Deceivers generally attempt to manipulate the biases and perspectives of their target to enhance the chances that their deceptions will be credible. If good deception thus fits with the expectations of the target; good counterdeception turns on constant revisiting of one's own expectations, testing them for their validity.

• • •

THE FOREGOING discussion suggests that mission-based counterintelligence offers advantages over operations-based approaches because it emphasizes the importance of strategy and generates more options. The following insights seem most significant:

1. The more vertically integrated are the collectors (such as a spy service or eavesdropping capability) of the targeted country, the more effective they will be and the more fruitful may be counterintelligence operations designed to influence or disrupt them, particularly if these collectors are few in number and only loosely managed. *The best protection against such attacks may not be to increase operational security, which can slow down or limit the scope of collection, but rather to increase the number of independent collectors or change their manner of operating*—tactics that have the advantages of increasing the number of trusted "channels" that must be controlled by any opponent planning a deception, while diminishing the likelihood he will understand how to do so.

2. The more independent an intelligence service is, the better it will be able to warn of surprise attacks. The best counterintelligence move against such capabilities may be to increase threats where the adversary expects them (thus drawing collection to expected, rather than unexpected, threats); or to induce suspicion of the service, forcing it to be checked and restrained by those it serves. The former strategy will likely work best when collection management in the targeted government is highly responsive to a single, dominant decision maker; the appropriate "counterintelligence moves" would have to be made by the commander, not the intelligence professionals in this instance. The latter plan involving induced suspicion works best against intelligence services that are not particularly trusted by those they serve in the first place. Democracies are typically good targets for this kind of approach. In either case, *the best way to counter such counterintelligence ploys is to keep oversight effective, to have an independent counterintelligence staff that can collect against targets that are not policymakers' priorities, and to train decision makers to value the resulting insights.*[50]

3. The more engaged an intelligence service is in the policy process it supports, the more opportunity it will have to be influential and trusted. If an opponent has penetrated that service, the service's trusted role may become a benefit to the opponent because of the access it provides; the opponent's best counterintelligence strategy in this case might be to build the trust even more and thus gain more access. Absent a penetration, the opponent's best counterintelligence strategy would be to destroy that trust so the intelligence service is not believed and its access is curtailed. The adversarial service may do so by generating leaks or by creating divergences between the targeted intelligence service's methods and the limits placed on them by the political culture that underpins it. This approach is easiest to execute and works best against liberal societies and democracies and may be executed by the protagonist's policymakers without the involvement of their intelligence services. An alternative approach might be to exploit the targeted service's likely preoccupation with current intelligence and fool it through surprise or deception. The best counterstrategy to most of these ploys has two essential parts: First, *the intelligence service must train officers to understand the difference between relationships of trust, which can involve close interactions on policy, and politicization, in which agents of influence seek to engage.* As the independence of an intelligence service is encouraged for the purposes of warning, *the intelligence service and those policymakers it supports must ensure that operations are lawful and that oversight, which is the predicate for both a long leash for intelligence operations and continued trust in them, is strengthened.* Executive power is, ironically, *weakened* when unlawful intelligence operations break down political consensus and trust in intelligence agencies, causing congressional overseers to tighten their leash on the intelligence community and thus restore trust, but at the price of lost capacity for intelligence agencies to act independently. Similarly, poor oversight that drives wedges between a service and those it supports, either because of latent

mistrust among overseers or their misunderstanding of its purpose, will make matters worse than if there were no intelligence service at all. Bad oversight can literally rob the state of an important instrument of power and cause vulnerabilities that lead to failure.

4. The better a state is at *selective denial,* the better it will be at curtailing the costs of protection and at executing deception. A counterintelligence strategy can exploit weaknesses in this capacity for selective secrecy by generating wide-ranging and ad hoc threats that tie counterintelligence resources to the protection of an ever-increasing number of targets. Over time, an increase in security and surveillance over all these targets will lead to both information overload within counterintelligence agencies and gaps in knowledge among critical decision makers as a growing amount of information is kept compartmented. *The counter to such problems may not be widespread information sharing, which would likely increase the risk of losses as well as the damage from any single penetration, but rather increasing capacities for creating and dissolving compartments, determining "need to know" and for doing collaborative net assessment. The results of net assessment could be used to assist in choosing what to keep secret and what to reveal as befits strategy at any given moment.*

Many more insights could be derived from a mission-based approach, but this brief survey of the methods for countering an opposing service reinforces the counterintelligence axiom that a strong defense rests on a superb positive intelligence capability, including all-source analysis that encompasses sensitivity to counterintelligence missions and their counterapproaches.

Designing a Mission-Based Counterintelligence Strategy for the United States

The basic elements of counterintelligence have not changed over centuries of practice; the foregoing discussion has, however, suggested that practitioners have underestimated the ability of democracies to engage in counterintelligence without putting their societies at risk, provided commanders and policymakers understand the counterintelligence tool and have it available to use. How the United States will fare in the years ahead will be shaped by its understanding of the counterintelligence options discussed above. These options will in turn be shaped both by a political culture that, in its emphasis on freedom and entrepreneurial spirit, infuses Americans' sense of their own security while constraining federal action on their behalf.

While some polities will willingly throw resources into security measures of all kinds, democracies have a competing need to maintain open societies with free press, free speech, and freedom to innovate. Liberal polities have an implicit requirement for openness embedded in their notions of national security itself.

Perhaps nowhere are the challenges of designing effective counterintelligence strategies greater than in the United States, whose political culture is steeped in liberal, capitalist ideas fostered by a vigorous and politically powerful entrepreneurial class. Americans perceive a right to privacy even if its constitutional basis is arguably vague, and they harbor deep suspicion of federal interference in their daily lives. They have a high regard for civil law, but they oppose the use of the federal military for the enforcement of it. And most have a deeply engrained respect for the capitalist values of individualism, pragmatism, and rationalism.[51]

In societies such as the American one, denial strategies can involve more than locks, safes, and secrecy. Some of these approaches, such as information swamping, are less engineered than naturally produced by the liberal political systems involved. Democracies are messy, noisy places. The more parties involved in making foreign policy, defense, and national security decisions, the more complicated the adversary's task of estimating outcomes and identifying deception. The problem is less one of secrets than of confusion—a natural cacophony that a few well-placed disclosures or "leaks" from senior levels can help to exacerbate.

Denial can also involve speed. A competitor can foil an adversary's efforts to anticipate his next moves by simply speeding up his decision making. Companies competing at the cutting edge of technology understand this well. As Harvey Rishikof and Randy Faraon suggest in their chapters in this volume, preservation of proprietary information and therefore profits turns as much on innovation—staying ahead of the market—as on vaults. By going fast, one catches the adversary knowledgeable perhaps, but also seriously flat-footed. Knowledge gained but impossible to use is, of course, useless.

Open societies, especially democracies, often have trouble crafting comfortable and effective counterintelligence strategies. Strategies of denial are particularly difficult to sustain. Hostile intelligence services often have wide-ranging mandates to collect information. If democracies were routinely to withhold all information their competitors seek, they would have to keep an ever-widening range of information from their own citizens, eventually strangling open debate and reducing public accountability.[52] Appropriately balancing public "need to know" with the state's "need to protect" is at the heart of risk management for counterintelligence policymaking.

Liberal, capitalist societies face especially difficult problems with strategies of denial if they regard the security of their economy as a national security priority. If an adversary believes gaining commercial advantage is important, its collection effort may target private industry for the purpose of gathering proprietary information and handing it off to their own firms. Or a competitor may simply encourage its own firms to spy without becoming directly involved. In either case, both legal and illegal means may be employed. Whether the officials in the targeted country choose to help private industry protect its proprietary information has some relevance to industrial policy: Which industries and technologies should be protected by the state—only those targeted by the foreign governments and firms or only those deemed critical to national security? In an era of globalization, what is the definition of a foreign firm? How should state equities in the protection of industry's proprietary information be determined? If a foreign government purchases a significant percentage of a U.S. industry, or a U.S.-based firm chooses to transfer proprietary, advanced technology with defense-related applications to a foreign company—say in the interest of conducting a joint venture or to earn a profit in some other way—should this choice be investigated using intrusive counterespionage tools? Who makes such decisions, and on what basis?

Such questions have been contentious matters of counterintelligence policy in democracies. Although exploring them is beyond the scope of this paper, countering industrial espionage is critically important—particularly if an opponent seems to be targeting weapons-related or intelligence-related firms—and the role the private sector should play in allocating resources for such protection is not clear. The problem is even knottier given that modern militaries and related national security institutions now rely heavily on commercial technologies, although the firms that produce them are increasingly multinational in form and spirit.[53]

Strategies of deception, which rely more heavily on offensive counterintelligence tools such as camouflage and stings are, if anything, even more troubling for liberal democracies. Effective deception would seem to require governments to lie while withholding the truth about what they are up to. Not only is this kind of strategy seemingly contrary to democratic values, it is exceptionally difficult for officials to pull off when confronted by a free press.

Specific Steps and Navigating Minefields

In response to the emergence of newly powerful transnational groups engaged in international organized crime, terrorism, and drug or human trafficking, democracies such as Britain, France, and the United States are using increasingly aggressive counterintelligence techniques. In the United States, officials have argued they must keep detention programs, new methods of domestic surveillance, and harsh interrogation methods secret in order to keep hostile intelligence services and terrorists from knowing who has been captured, what the captives might have revealed to U.S. intelligence, and similar facts.

The analysis above suggests that the debate on U.S. counterintelligence is constrained by an excessively operational focus that misses gains adversaries achieve by inducing us to act in ways that cost us strategically. Thinking in mission-related terms, the following steps illustrate how U.S. counterintelligence officials can advance their agenda without necessarily undermining the civil society they too prize:

1. Change recruitment profiles to seek seasoned experts with deep knowledge of targeted cultures and an ability to perceive as opponents do, including in magical, conspiratorial, religious, and theatrical terms.

The more the United States recruits a youthful, technologically savvy analytic core, the more it will have gathered together people of like minds—that is, with similar cognitive biases. Technologically savvy intelligence officers who work well with others are important for such tasks as information processing and collection management. They collectively cultivate a rational-technical intellectual climate mirroring elite segments within the U.S. society at large. A good cadre of technocrats can reassure upper management that recently procured innovations can be competently used. But in a rapidly changing technological landscape, acquiring a true cutting edge involves obtaining the technology and understanding the inspiration that drove it in the first place and that constantly sharpens that edge. Consider Rodney Brooks, the MIT computer scientist who spearheaded the development of sociable robots mentioned in this volume's introduction. He is described as almost a "cult figure" who, when featured in a documentary "along with a wild animal trainer, a topiary gardener and an expert in naked mole rats," appeared "as a man whose obsessions made him something of a misfit, a visionary with a restless, uncategorizable genius."[54]

Workforce diversity, in short, is not just about recruiting those with varying language skills, ethnic backgrounds, and technical competencies, it is about recognizing, enfolding, and rewarding the artistic and idiosyncratic. Unfortunately, U.S. society has been deemphasizing the creative arts in its approach to education for years, leaving those who specialize in symbolism, derived meaning, and managing individuals toward collective ends (symphonies, ballets, and improvised jazz), either out of the upper levels of professional endeavor or denied recognition for their edgy gifts. Methodological diversity is insufficient for achieving the insights necessary for countering an adversary who recognizes your fascination with puzzles and your ignorance of the sources of inspirational, random, and spontaneous behavior. Cultivated cultural independence, based on understanding how others derive meaning from events, often irrationally, is necessary as well.

Bringing such diversity into an intelligence service and rewarding it through promotions present difficulties. In the first place, diversity is risky. It heightens the risk of apparently irrational behavior, foreign affiliations, and divided loyalties among intelligence employees. Such concerns must be balanced against the gains of countering groupthink and cultural biases that adversaries can exploit. To the extent that a total information-sharing environment minimizes security officials' ability to manage such risks effectively by limiting employees' access to information they don't need, the ability to maximize true diversity in thought is eliminated. What should not be forgotten is the underlying point: Without diversity of thought and a measure of independence, an intelligence service cannot effectively warn.

This recommendation, while challenging in its most extreme interpretation, need not be in its initial execution. For example, the intelligence division of NYPD has recognized that cops on the street, a reasonably diverse collection of nationalities, know their own communities best and can understand the meaning of extremely subtle changes in how those communities work, change, and grow. The New York City Police Department, whose fifty thousand members are 30 percent of foreign extraction, includes thirty-five thousand uniformed officers who walk the streets every day. Working with these officers, NYPD's analytic unit produced the pathbreaking study on terrorist deradicalization—a widely lauded analytic effort designed to help counter the problem of domestic terrorism.[55] The head of the intelligence analysis and his unit in NYPD support these officers both as decision makers dealing with day-to-day law enforcement problems and as collectors able to spot anomalies that may have wider importance to national security. And most of these officers do not need or want security clearances to do their job at the cusp of metropolitan counterintelligence.

2. Recognizing the growing importance of transnational threats, the permeability of borders, and the importance of commercial technologies, create new partnerships with the private sector for collecting against adversaries.

Private firms that conduct surveillance to protect their property, employ environmental sensors for the comfort of their employees, and keep track of lifesaving equipment for emergencies, might benefit from government subsidies to standardize their methods in return for agreeing to share information when a civil or national security emergency arises—but not necessarily before then.

The advances in sensor and energy technologies discussed in this volume's introduction suggest that buildings, bridges, and even cities themselves are becoming platforms for arraying sensors that make these spaces, in many ways, "smart." The public tolerates and even expects such security measures, provided they believe the federal government will not use them for control or influence over their private lives. When attacked, victimized by natural disaster, or at war, however, Americans rightly expect the government to keep them safe and even rescue them.[56] Establishing protocols with private-sector firms that permit "smart" spaces to transfer information to emergency responders about chemical, biological, or nuclear contamination, the location of injured employees, and the stability of damaged structures makes sense and would likely be well tolerated by the public, provided the terms triggering the transfer were established in advance.

3. Increase the federal government's capacity for selective denial.

The choice of what to withhold from an adversary is a matter of considerable importance to policymakers. That matters of classification have not been thought of this way in the United States reflects the widespread notion that counterintelligence is a law enforcement matter. But selective denial is also a matter of intelligence policy and national strategy. Intelligence managers might generally choose to protect sources and methods, but in certain circumstances these might be declassified in order to draw adversaries into the open. More likely candidates for declassification would be items relating to the results of meetings, policy debates, and the like whose collective release would involve little risk but might increase the noise levels for hostile governments. In some circumstances, counterintelligence operations may usefully be broadcast if the release of such information might serve as a deterrent. For example, the Federal Bureau of Investigation's efforts to understand adversaries' uses of open sources—a major source of conflict with libraries and businesses after 9/11—need not always be classified. A mission-based approach might find value in impressing hostile services or terrorists of the FBI's domestic reach and its ability to gain cooperation instead of resistance from local authorities. The NYPD has taken this kind of deterrent approach with its deployment of Hercules teams in Manhattan; they swarm on high-risk sites with heavily armed officers for the purpose of ferreting out terrorists and, if possible, scaring them.[57]

But selective denial is not just about declassifying more; it is also about classifying responsibly and agilely in response to changing threats. Although the U.S. intelligence community has properly focused on employing more "need-to-share" technologies, the dangers of abolishing restrictions on sharing, formerly based on "need to know," are perhaps less well understood. Finding insider spies such as a Robert Hanssen or Aldrich Ames often involves looking for people who want information they don't need in order to do their jobs. State-based threats and foreign penetrations still exist; widespread sharing of intelligence jeopardizes methods for uncovering treachery. Moreover, as James R. Gosler, a scientist with Sandia National Laboratories, has discussed in both our last volume and this current one, cyber technologies permit the embedding of malicious code in the software of intelligence services increasingly reliant on commercial applications and their associated hardware. The more information shared, the more such technical penetrations can reveal through what Joel Brenner, the current U.S. National Counterintelligence Executive (NCIX) has called "electronic undressing."[58] Given that most commercial companies can no longer be tagged "American" or "foreign," because their manufacturing is globalized, the sweeping extent of the counterintelligence challenge becomes obvious. As these technologies spread, the opportunities for foreign penetration go up. With capabilities for aggressive offensive operations distributed widely, the job of protecting intelligence advantage is shifting to the counterintelligence community, where the United States is still weak.

As long as conflict continues, there are only three circumstances in which such an increase in the general burden of secrecy and security (as opposed to a selective approach) need not cause concern: first, if counterintelligence resources are plentiful and easily distributed; second, if policymakers and, by association, their intelligence partners, can compensate by increasing their decision-making speed relative to their adversaries; or third, if it is in the interest of the state to let the adversary think it is gaining good information when it is not—for example, when conducting a deception campaign. Absent these circumstances, any added stress on counterintelligence capabilities will have to be compensated for elsewhere, or the risks of failure will go up. If, for example, everyone has access to all information within the walls of an intelligence enterprise, risk management falls to the gatekeepers who will slow down recruitment and delay acquisitions to ensure that everyone inside is trustworthy. This is not risk management by design but rather by default; it will make a service less agile, not more so.

Risk management is, of course, a crucial element of intelligence policy and may warrant adjusting such general policies in certain areas. However, there is no escaping the fact that acceptance of greater risks in one area—such as internal information sharing—will engender costs elsewhere unless the nature of the competition or the adversary has fundamentally changed. For this reason, a more selective approach is necessary.

4. Consider deception.

The United States has a culture that tolerates tactical deception in areas ranging from the marketing of goods (ridiculously thin department store mannequins) to the creation of Hollywood movies (*Star Wars*). This makes us, whether we like it or not, quite good at conning others. The problem with deception is the possibility of "blowback": What a government does or says to fool others might mislead its own people and institutions. This is a serious concern and may make the execution of deception operations at the strategic level both dangerous and difficult. Yet it is also true that most Americans would prefer to con an adversary into failing than to lose soldiers on a battlefield fighting him. *The Sting*, a movie featuring Paul Newman and Robert Redford, appealed to many Americans not just because of the star power of the actors involved but also because of the satisfying con at the heart of its story of retribution. Americans can admire trickery, cunning, tinkering, and the sneak play when done for a good cause. The trick to any deception in international politics is to convey the lie to the adversary through his most trusted channel—most often his intelligence service, which will protect its insight from public release and thus limit the chances of blowback.

In any case, becoming expert in how to do deception is critical to identifying who is doing it to us. For this reason alone, a highly placed staff under the NCIX should consider deception methods, strategies, and tactics both as others use them and as Americans might tolerate them.

THESE FOUR ideas might be the starting point for discussing a modern, mission-based approach to counterintelligence. The theory presented earlier may well suggest more. Yet none of these initiatives will work unless policymakers recognize their own critical role in effective intelligence, including counterintelligence.

A central theme throughout this chapter has been that counterintelligence, like positive intelligence, must serve the strategy of the overall commander involved at each stage of decision making. The service must investigate opponents to determine how their intelligence is performed, analyze their operations, develop options for shaping them, and estimate the likely effects of restraint. The products of such work will reveal much about adversaries' knowledge of the battlefield and possibly also their intent. Thus, counterintelligence complements and enriches positive intelligence collection at the tactical, operational, and strategic levels. All three must be integrated, however, in support of a strategic plan. The game cannot be played successfully by intelligence professionals alone, for the advantages they can obtain amount to nothing if they do not serve strategy and decisive action.

Notes

1. Edwin C. Fishel, *The Secret War for the Union: The Untold Story of Military Intelligence in the Civil War* (Boston: Houghton Mifflin, 1996), 1–2.

2. Ibid., 2. Von Spee knew the art of operational security as well. He ordered that his ships run silent through the Pacific in order to maximize the opportunity for surprise.

3. John Keegan, *Intelligence in War: Knowledge of the Enemy from Napoleon to Al Qaeda* (New York: Alfred A. Knopf, 2003), 106–26.

4. F. H. Hinsley, *British Intelligence in the Second World War*, abridged ed. (Cambridge, UK: Cambridge University Press, 1993), 119.

5. U.S. foreign intelligence agencies were aware that terrorists might strike the homeland, but they were constrained in their ability to collect domestically. They were unable to work with those local officials and private-sector authorities responsible for countering domestic threats or to deny terrorists the information they needed to implement their strategy, such as flight training, building blueprints, electrical grids, and the like. The problem was not simply a lack of information sharing particular to this attack; it was a lack of appreciation among federal intelligence officials of the counterintelligence needs of the street. The problem wasn't just that FBI field offices and New York City cops couldn't get information to Washington intelligence agencies; even if they had, there was no one in Washington who could effectively act. The fact that open-source information about critical targets was offered on the Internet and remained there for weeks after the terrorists had struck illustrates the essential point: National security decision makers in Washington had not yet conceived of national defense as necessarily involving local authorities, nor had they included them in matters of strategy or ensured that they would be involved in intelligence and counterintelligence flows regarding the al-Qaeda threat. The failure of federal-level decision makers to understand the local dimension reappeared during the flap over Dubai Ports World's prospective purchase of U.S. assets; the mayor of Baltimore noted that neither he nor the governor of Maryland had been advised or consulted on the impending decision.

6. Keegan, *Intelligence in War*. The argument Keegan makes is that weapons and generalship, including force of will, matter more than intelligence, which often fails to offer a decisive edge. My argument is that intelligence is a form of power that can provide an edge in contests; it is the poor execution of intelligence that has led to its spotty history in international politics.

7. In the case of 9/11, U.S. weaknesses included the division of domestic counterintelligence from intelligence functions at the strategic level, fixation on a Cold War concept of state secrecy at the expense of protecting information critical to enemy strategy, an excessively narrow understanding of the counterintelligence mission, and a related inability to understand the importance of open-source information to counterintelligence and thus to anticipate the terrorists' legally conducted surveillance. This last deficiency

was less evident in the FBI, which had long viewed open-source intelligence collection within scientific and academic communities as a principal tool of foreign spies. However, the foreign policy and national security communities, influenced strongly by U.S. political culture, had downplayed the need for tracking foreign interest in open sources prior to 9/11.

8. When sharing occurs without counterintelligence review, good intentions can have unintended consequences. Liaison services have unwittingly shared bad information on citizens suspected of links to terrorists. Subsequent court cases related to the rendition of a Canadian citizen, for example, led to media attention and damaged liaison operations. While there is no indication that any of these problems were induced by a third party, they offer vivid examples of the potential vulnerabilities liaison presents. See my article on this subject: "Foreign Intelligence Liaison: Devils, Deals and Details," *International Journal of Intelligence and Counterintelligence* 19, no. 2 (Summer 2006): 195–217.

9. See Jennifer Sims, "Understanding Friends and Enemies: The Context for American Intelligence Reform," and "Understanding Ourselves," in *Transforming U.S. Intelligence,* ed. Jennifer E. Sims and Burton Gerber (Washington, DC: Georgetown University Press, 2005), 14–31, and 32–59.

10. "Ignored" in this context means "not interdicted or thwarted." It is unwise for any intelligence service to completely ignore another.

11. Counterintelligence experts vary in their classification of operations as passive or active, offensive or defensive. The framework offered here strikes the author as the most useful. Regardless of how operations are described, however, experts generally agree on their purpose and their effects.

12. For this analogy I am grateful to Joel Brenner, current National Counterintelligence Executive (1/2008). When security officials own the counterintelligence mission, they will tend to emphasize the need to build walls and repair breaches as soon as possible, diminishing the capacity for selective secrecy so critical to mission-based counterintelligence (see above).

13. If an opponent's strategy is so ill-conceived that it poses no risk, an intelligence service may choose not to deny the information necessary to execute it. And, obviously, terrorists can often accomplish their strategic goals without stealing government secrets.

14. Moles and double agents are not the same thing. The former are intelligence officers in an opposing service who betray what that service is doing. They might be analysts, collection managers, or satellite designers. Double agents, in contrast, are sources hired to collect on a target—but ones who do so while pretending to collect intelligence for the target as well.

15. Abram N. Shulsky, *Silent Warfare: Understanding the World of Intelligence,* 2nd ed., rev. by Gary Schmitt (Washington, DC: Brassey's, 1993), 124. Shulsky's book is a good primer on both intelligence and counterintelligence.

16. Not all the double agents employed by the British were located in the United Kingdom. Some, such as "Tricycle," were located in or traveled through occupied Europe, as well as Spain and Portugal. At the beginning of his espionage work, "Garbo" convinced the Germans he was spying in the United Kingdom when he was actually in Portugal with a pretend network and a bunch of good tourist maps.

17. John C. Masterman, *The Double-Cross System in the War of 1939 to 1945* (New

Haven: Yale University Press, 1972). See also the official site for MI-5 in Britain for information on Double Cross agents outside of Britain: www.MI-5.gov.uk.

18. "A Hazardous Comparison," *The Economist*, February 28, 2008; accessed at www.economist.com/world/international/PrinterFriendly.cfm?story_id=10766283.

19. My thinking on the utility of deriving insights from CI has been greatly assisted by the work of Vincent Bridgeman, an author in this volume, who has thought deeply about military counterintelligence.

20. See Michael Warner, "The Divine Skein: Sun Tzu on Intelligence," *Intelligence and National Security* 21, no. 4 (August 2006): 483–92.

21. Colonel Terrence J. Finnegan, *Shooting the Front: Allied Aerial Reconnaissance and Photographic Interpretation on the Western Front—World War I* (Washington, DC: National Defense Intelligence College, 2006), 8.

22. Ibid., 54.

23. Ibid., 319.

24. Over time, a sixth element, maintenance and protection, becomes important.

25. Sometimes collaboration in the art of marrying sensors to platforms has led to Rube Goldberg solutions for data exfiltration. Corona, the first U.S. series of imagery satellites, jettisoned film in capsules that had to be retrieved by aircraft equipped with nets.

26. The complete list of performance measures includes productivity (quantity of relevant data), efficiency (productivity over cost), tuning ability (capacity to shift targets without loss of productivity), connectedness (degree to which all components can be adjusted to one another by a central manager), usability (acceptability in battle or in the contest), robustness (resilience and protection), and boosting capacity (ability to contribute to the performance of an allied collection system).

27. The private sector played an important role in the development of imagery intelligence satellite programs and capabilities. See "NRO Honors Pioneers of National Reconnaissance," available at http://64.233.167.104/search?q=cache:iDp-t2Sw50kJ:www.nro .gov/PressReleases/prs_re140.html+Government+collaborates+with+Kodak+in+1950s+ optics&hl=en&ct=clnk&cd=2&gl=us.

28. Alexander Rose, *Washington's Spies: The Story of America's First Spy Ring* (New York: Bantam: 2006).

29. During the Cold War, the United States relied on space-based platforms to collect data on the Soviet Union because entering Soviet territory presented formidable challenges for American spies. Collection managers designed sensors, such as cameras, to accommodate the particular altitudes and orbital characteristics of the satellites on which they were to fly. They also came up with techniques for getting the collected data back from space. Collection managers looked to open-source information on emerging technologies to develop capabilities that went beyond commercial applications. As sensors improved and the bandwidth for communicating the data increased, collection from space became so rich it threatened to overwhelm the systems set up to process and exploit it. The challenge for collection managers was to balance all five components of collection to maximize productivity against Soviet targets at the lowest possible cost and risk and to ensure that no one part of the system undermined any other. Recognition of the importance of integrated collection management of such complex systems led first to the growth of the Central Intelligence Agency's technological endeavors and then to the creation of CIA's Directorate of Science and Technology and the National

Reconnaissance Office (NRO) in 1962. It also led to strong ties between commercial industry and the U.S. intelligence establishment.

30. The classic work on the analytic challenge is Richard K. Betts, "Why Intelligence Failures Are Inevitable," *World Politics* 31, no.1 (October 1978): 61–89. The difficulties of the warning function should not, however, dissuade intelligence managers from trying to increase the odds of beating an adversary who is contemplating surprise.

31. David Kahn, the author of the classic work on codes, ciphers, and encryption, has written: "Surprise is a matter not of insufficient information but of insufficient time. Often, in looking back at the data available at the time of surprise, the indications of the event appear to have been present. But the analysts did not have enough time to under-stand them, to see a pattern in the mass of facts." David Kahn, "Surprise and Secrecy: Two Thoughts," *Intelligence and National Security* 21, no. 6 (December 2006): 1060.

32. Note that this is not necessarily all-source analysis; collectors perform targeting analysis (sometimes referred to as "processing and exploitation") that is as critical to the overall intelligence enterprise as all-source analysis and should receive more attention and resources than it often does. The boxes of "collection" and "analysis" are not mutu-ally exclusive.

33. For more on this art, see Jerome S. Bruner, *On Knowing: Essays for the Left Hand*, expanded ed. (Cambridge: Harvard University Press, 1979).

34. James Simon, Georgetown University Seminar, October 3, 2003.

35. Interview with a staff member of the Joint Committee for the Investigation of 9/11. Interviewed October 11, 2007. One member of the Counterterrorism Center (CTC) apparently knew that she was supposed to pass names of suspected terrorists to the State Department's Tip-off Program, but unaware of this program's connection to consular officers' visa decisions, she decided that handing the information to fellow intelligence analysts was a higher priority.

36. Of course the CIA's CTC, which presumably should have known who the key decision makers were, failed to share the information with the FBI and State Department in a timely way.

37. Statement of Representative Saxby Chambliss, chairman, House Intelligence Subcommittee on Terrorism and Homeland Security; Before the House Armed Services Committee Special Oversight Panel on Terrorism; September 5, 2002. See also the Con-gressional Record: December 12, 2001 (House) Page H9246-H9254.

38. Ibid.

39. It can also simply be wrong. To game what an adversary might do in a state of uncertainty by calculating what would be most in his interest or somehow best for him to do, may get at a conceptual truth but prove wildly off the mark

40. David Halberstam, *War in a Time of Peace* (New York: Simon & Schuster, 2002), 244.

41. Christopher Andrew, *For the President's Eyes Only: Secret Intelligence and the American Presidency from Washington to Bush* (New York: HarperCollins, 1995), 321, 323–24.

42. Jack Davis, "A Policymaker's Perspective on Intelligence Analysis," *Studies in Intelligence* 38, no. 5 (1995): 7–15.

43. Ben Feller, "Ex-Pentagon Official Defends Iraq Stance," Associated Press, February 11, 2007. Available at www.boston.com/news/nation/washington/articles/2007/02/11/ex_pentagon_official_defends_iraq_stance/.

44. Among the senators who felt misled was the chairman of the Senate Intelligence Committee, who was, at the time, my boss. My experience confirmed Senator David Boren's impressions. I was the intelligence staff person for Senator John Danforth, who was initially leaning against authorizing force because of DIA estimates of Iraqi capabilities. Believing that the DIA briefings were inadequate, in part because they did not involve net assessments, I arranged for Senator Danforth to meet with analysts and officers at the National War College. On the basis of these and other briefings, which offered a much different perspective, the senator voted to authorize the use of force.

45. For the best discussion of Allied deception in WWII, see Thaddeus Holt, *The Deceivers: Allied Military Deception in the Second World War* (New York: Scribner, 2004).

46. For more details on this story, see Ewen Montagu, *The Man Who Never Was: World War II's Boldest Counter-Intelligence Operation* (New York: Oxford University Press, 1953).

47. For extended and rich discussions of the theory of denial and deception, see Abram N. Shulsky, "Elements of Strategic Denial and Deception," in *Strategic Denial and Deception: The Twenty-First Century Challenge*, ed. Roy Godson and James J. Wirtz (New Brunswick, NJ: Transaction Books, 2002), 15–39, and Walter Jajko, "Commentary," in *Strategic Denial and Deception*, ed. Godson and Wirtz, 115–22.

48. James H. Hansen, "Soviet Deception in the Cuban Missile Crisis: Learning from the Past," *Studies in Intelligence* 46, no. 1 (2002). Available at www.cia.gov/library/center-for-the-study-of-intelligence/csi-publications/csi-studies/studies/v0146n01/article06.html.

49. Ibid.

50. The importance of gaining insights as part of an optimized counterintelligence process has been highlighted by Vince Bridgeman in his chapter in this volume titled "Defense Counterintelligence, Reconceptualized."

51. For a more complete discussion of U.S. political culture as it relates to national security, see my chapter "Understanding Ourselves," in *Transforming U.S. Intelligence*, ed. Jennifer E. Sims and Burton Gerber (Washington, DC: Georgetown University Press, 2005), 32–59.

52. As mentioned earlier, detailed information on the U.S. defense budget might be of interest to foreign intelligence services, but classifying it would be counterproductive. The United States wisely decided not to keep such information secret during the Cold War; the Soviet Union made the opposite and more expensive choice. Conducting a purely reactive strategy can literally drive a country to ruin.

53. This point was discussed extensively at this volume's authors' conference—a marathon brainstorming session on the problems of modern counterespionage. Discussion of Harvey Rishikof's chapter provoked particularly heated debate, including references to the impact of globalization on economic counterintelligence (Timothy R. Sample) and industrial espionage (Harvey Rishikof). Reference was made to an interesting volume on this topic: R. Vernon's *Sovereignty at Bay: Hegemony of International Business, 1945–1970*, vol. 8 (London: Routledge, 2001). My thanks to those authors who were able to participate in this extraordinary gathering for some of the more gelled ideas in this chapter.

54. Robin Marantz Henig, "The Real Transformers," *New York Times Magazine*, July 29, 2007.

55. Substantial information on NYPD is available on the official website. Explanations of the intelligence analysis unit headed by Samuel Rascoff are available at www.home2.nyc.gov/html/nypd/media/audio/12–08–2006.mp3.

56. As Hurricane Katrina perhaps illustrated best, the public's expectation that government will step in to help includes the entire chain of governance from the local to the federal levels.

57. See Brad Regan, "Meet the New Supercops," *Popular Mechanics*, June 2006. Available at www.popularmechanics.com/technology/military_law/28182/html.

58. Interview and private communications: January 2008.

2

John Fox Jr. and
Michael Warner

Counterintelligence

The American Experience

In 1945 the United States had a world-class counterintelligence capability. A collective of agencies (with much British help) had neutralized Axis intelligence agents around the world. Much of this success stemmed from a pair of wartime innovations that have no current counterparts. The first was the Federal Bureau of Investigation's (FBI) Special Intelligence Service (SIS), which operated in Latin America. The second was the X-2 Branch of the Office of Strategic Services (OSS), which partnered with Britain's secret services to glean Axis message traffic for leads to enemy agents. Together with the efforts of two more-conventional American counterintelligence services—the Bureau's traditional domestic investigations and the Counter-Intelligence Corps of the U.S. Army—these organizations had given the Axis a formidable gauntlet to run.

Within a year of V-J Day, however, both FBI/SIS and OSS/X-2 were gone. A series of decisions—some deliberate, some accidental—ensured that America would employ different instruments in different ways over the course of the Cold War and beyond. Indeed, SIS and X-2 were so radical in comparison with predecessor and successor offices that reviving them today would seem all but unthinkable. And yet their respective demises illustrate several conditions that affect federal efforts to protect Americans from foreign intrigue and safeguard the integrity of intelligence necessary to America's decision-making processes.

This essay considers how those influences have affected the American experience of counterintelligence. Cold War spy stories and armchair psychoanalyses of deceased officials may have their place, but they do not explain which problems the counterintelligence system has solved and which continue to bedevil it. We set aside the personality-driven narratives that have characterized many historical and popular treatments in order to understand how the nation's political culture has affected the evolution of its counterintelligence capabilities since World War I in the Federal Bureau of Investigation, the Central Intelligence

Agency, and the armed services. The institutional and operational patterns for American counterintelligence were set early; for the most part they predated the Cold War and survived it. They endured because they had solved certain fundamental security and counterintelligence weaknesses revealed in the first half of the twentieth century, but their relevance today and tomorrow may be open to question.

No predictions can be offered about the future of American counterintelligence, but a careful reading of the past can offer insights into why certain initiatives have failed and why others have succeeded. These insights can, in turn, help to identify which reforms might actually work. This chapter thus moves beyond the theoretical issues raised by the previous chapter to raise very practical questions for Americans: How has counterintelligence policy been conceived and executed in the historical, legal, and political context of the United States? What do the insights gained from examining the history of American counterintelligence tell us about how the United States might best organize and run its counterintelligence effort in the future?

The Constitutional and Cultural Framework of American Counterintelligence

The Constitution of the United States makes no mention of intelligence or counterintelligence, yet these functions have always been considered essential to an energetic executive and its ability to fulfill its duties. The authors of the Constitution left a place for secrecy in government, but they also took pains to ensure that the executive could not wield its powers for tyrannical aims.[1] The president's authority was checked and balanced through the separation of powers and a Bill of Rights that placed still more strictures on its exercise. Thus the legislative and judicial branches would share in certain aspects of America's counterintelligence, and the very political culture that Americans imbibed would demand respect for liberty, sometimes even at the expense of security.

These features are not unique to the United States, but the resulting combination of offices and authorities has marked the American counterintelligence experience in several important ways. Executive power in the United States is itself divided among cooperating but loosely coordinated departments and agencies. For good and defensible reasons, several cabinet secretaries and agency chiefs need intelligence to inform their own decision making, guard that intelligence from foreign tampering and fulfill their oaths to defend the American people and the constitutional order. Each of these offices wants and needs some share in the responsibility for counterintelligence and some voice in its exercise. Their overseers in Congress do as well—a factor that complicates the task of any president wishing to rearrange duties and resources in the executive branch. Cooperation and competition—not central direction and action—thus mark America's counterintelligence effort. This situation has proven to be beneficial at times, harmful at others, and a conundrum always.

The Constitution's emphasis on rights and liberties has also shaped the American political culture in which counterintelligence must be practiced. Representative democracy as enshrined in the Constitution has (at least since 1865) nurtured long-term political stability, which itself has deprived most native extremist and revolutionary tendencies of political oxygen, eventually enervating their impulses toward radicalism, social strife, and political violence. Americans have by and large settled disputes in the voting booth and the courtroom. Their ability to compromise has sustained the great latitude in speech and association enjoyed by America's manifold political, religious, and ideological persuasions.[2]

And yet this same stability has affected the nation's response to intelligence-related threats—domestic and foreign, real and apparent. Americans, accustomed to stability, can overreact. Danger seems a novelty and thus doubly threatening at first. The democratic competition for public offices has enhanced the harshness of America's responses as partisan spokesmen, at times, vie to look tougher than their rivals. Indeed, many of the official abuses of civil liberties that have marred American history occurred as a result of this unfortunate political tendency.

Such overreactions in turn stimulate the seemingly engrained American distrust of centralized power and distaste for "government intrusion" into citizens' lives. The Constitution reserves to the people powers not specifically entrusted to the federal government; Americans are sensitive about government encroachment on their constitutional rights, and demand that government investigations not even indirectly preempt them. Restrictions and penalties that appear warranted in perilous times grow tiresome as soon as the danger seems to recede. Furthermore, any use on American citizens of methods typically employed against foreign foes smacks of tyranny. It rarely takes long for one major political party or the other (often the one out of power) to find political gain in criticizing official heavy-handedness and calling for reform. Together, these cultural constraints have meant that comprehensive counterintelligence, especially against American persons, is both difficult to implement and ultimately limited in scope.

The Emergence of a Permanent Counterintelligence Capability

How then have these structural and cultural factors emerged and shaped the American experience of counterintelligence? For more than a century after the founding, presidents exercised their responsibility for counterintelligence with virtually unquestioned latitude.[3] Only in the domestic field did Congress or the courts modestly infringe upon presidential freedom in this realm; for instance, by banning the use of the military to suppress strikes; forbidding the hiring of private detectives to target labor activists and radicals; and (after the fact) restricting habeas corpus as a means to quell secessionist sentiments even in a time of domestic rebellion.

As the United States assumed a larger world role at the turn of the twentieth century, it began in an ad hoc manner to institutionalize its intelligence functions. When World War I erupted in Europe in 1914, the United States had several possible counterintelligence guardians. All of them initially failed to prevent attacks by German saboteurs on American soil, or to detect Britain's more subtle compromises of American security and decision making. The small Secret Service focused on counterfeiting and protecting the president, had no formal jurisdiction in the internal security field, and thus only briefly operated in this realm on the ambiguous authority of the secretary of the treasury. The even smaller military intelligence units faced similar issues. The Bureau of Investigation in the Justice Department was larger but more limited in its counterespionage and countersabotage roles. Indeed, the attorney general at the time held the Bureau's agents back from chasing German agents because, as yet, there was no federal statutory ban on espionage or sabotage absent a state of war. When the attorney general proposed such a law, commentators dismissed it as a grab for "spy" powers.

In April 1917 Congress declared war, and the situation changed immediately. The Army created a small Corps of Intelligence Police to handle security and personnel-related CI in the European theater, but the larger changes occurred on the domestic front.[4] The Espionage Act and related amendments were quickly passed, bringing espionage, sabotage, and subversion into the ambit of federal law enforcement. The Act's mandate, in effect, allowed the Bureau of Investigation to elbow the Secret Service out of the internal security field. The security situation soon appeared well in hand, although the extent to which German agents had been neutralized remained a matter of debate. Some policymakers saw a continuing problem; others thought it minimal. Those fearing enemies in the homeland even advocated martial law in response, and popular opinion might have condoned such a step.[5] Indeed, the public had briefly tolerated the privatization of some counterintelligence functions through the Bureau's reliance on a citizen watchdog group called the American Protective League (APL). The initial acceptance of the Palmer Raids in 1919, which aimed to deport suspected radical aliens for their anarchist and Bolshevik activities following a series of bombings, also suggested popular support for restricting civil liberties. Within fourteen months, however, opinion had turned, as Americans recoiled against official abuses that had flowed from these overreactions.

The agencies that grew in World War I shrank in size and responsibility afterward, their excesses hastening their decline. The APL had been disbanded by the Department of Justice soon after the armistice, partly in reaction to its focus on rumor and slander. Army counterintelligence efforts were cut back in light of zealous junior officers investigating labor organizers and pacifist groups on suspicion of espionage or sabotage.[6] Even the Bureau of Investigation had to be overhauled, first after the Palmer Raids, and again following a series of political scandals. Popular repudiation of scattershot counterintelligence methods halted the development of counterintelligence institutions for two decades, but America's first attempt to create such institutions had taught many lessons.[7]

The man who may have learned these lessons best was a young Justice Department attorney named J. Edgar Hoover. Attorney General Harlan Fiske Stone appointed him acting director of the Bureau of Investigation in 1924 and gave him a mandate to clean house. With Stone's blessing, he gradually imposed three cardinal principles on the nation's domestic approach to counterintelligence in the United States; these principles endured for decades:

1. Counterintelligence must be done by professional, federal officers, not delegated to private volunteers or groups like the APL;
2. It must rely on the painstaking cultivation and organization of files and leads under central coordination, preferably in a single agency; and
3. The surest way of insulating counterintelligence from corruption and politicization is to ground it in the investigation of violations of federal criminal law and so tie it to the rule of law and the protections enumerated in the Bill of Rights.

This last principle was the key to the Bureau's long-term survival and effectiveness in the political environment of Washington. Hoover's handiwork proved enduring because he built it on a fundamental feature of national politics: that no party or branch of government will long trust its competitors with a monopoly on the ability to investigate rivals. All parties and branches could agree, however, that alleged violations of criminal statutes should be investigated and criminality thwarted—or at least they would think twice before publicly opposing such probes. This rough consensus provided a safe political space in which the renamed Federal Bureau of Investigation (FBI) could grow.

The association of U.S. counterintelligence activity with law enforcement represents a larger pattern in American intelligence history. Counterintelligence functions have been closely tied to security functions in several agencies; the history of the counterintelligence in the armed services since World War I (when the Army founded its Corps of Intelligence Police) is partly a saga of their repeated attempts to separate themselves from investigative and police duties. The close proximity between investigation and counterintelligence offered some advantages. First, it gave Bureau agents the powerful sanction of prosecution to use in motivating cooperation from suspects whom the Bureau could turn against their employers. Second, access to security files, when granted to counterintelligence practitioners, has usually made their efforts significantly more powerful and effective (albeit often raising civil liberties concerns as well).

At the same time, however, this focus on criminality often kept the Bureau's (and the armed services') analytical capabilities focused on supporting individual investigations; later CIA domestic operations were limited and controversial as the FBI strongly defended its area of influence.[8] The cost of this tactical, case-based approach, at times, was a stunting of counterintelligence gathering and an undernourishment of the analysis of the intentions and capabilities of real and potential enemies. Furthermore, it led these agencies, in some cases, to forgo longer-range penetrations and attempts to control the actions of adversarial intelligence efforts for the more immediate end of prosecution. At significant times, this was not the case: the Bureau can claim strong success in penetrating and neutralizing key aspects of Soviet intelligence at certain points, the Klan during its resurgence in the 1960s, and several major organized criminal enterprises in the 1980s. And yet, these successes did not indicate anything like all-source strategic analysis, and in other periods and against other targets, a more tactical, law enforcement approach was pursued.

The Alliance with Signals Intelligence

A second major pattern emerged along with the FBI's dominance in the domestic application of counterintelligence. While Hoover transformed the Bureau, American counterintelligence was already developing a strong but potentially problematic affinity for signals intelligence, ranging from electronic surveillance to the reading of foreign codes. Indeed, the first duty of the U.S. Army's Cipher Bureau (MI-8) in 1917 was reading the secret messages of German agents in the United States.[9] Monitoring private communications for counterintelligence and law enforcement purposes has rarely sat well with the American public. A prime form of electronic surveillance, the telephone tap, had been in use for more than twenty years and was already controversial; many Americans feared the loss of privacy and the potential for government abuse that could follow from wiretapping. Congress passed the Federal Communications Act (FCA) in 1934, potentially banning most wiretaps. Indeed, the use of wiretaps by law enforcement was challenged in federal courts, leading the Supreme Court in *Nardone v. U.S.* (1937) to restrict the admissibility of wiretap evidence in criminal trials.[10]

The executive branch, though, interpreted its powers differently. Wiretaps (and other signals intelligence techniques) had been used sparingly for national security purposes since World War I, but the growing threat of Nazi and Japanese espionage in the 1930s meant that *Nardone* and the FCA came at a bad time for the administration of President Franklin D. Roosevelt. After internal debate the president's advisors settled on a reading of law and precedent that allowed for wiretaps for intelligence and counterintelligence purposes. Administration spokesmen then defended this interpretation in public by arguing, in effect, that the executive retained the right to use wiretaps in extraordinary cases, such as espionage (and even kidnappings in which saving the life of the victim was paramount to evidence for subsequent prosecution). Wiretapping quickly became a vital counterintelligence tool.[11]

Multiagency employment of a wide variety of signals intelligence techniques supplemented wiretaps as American counterintelligence came of age and built an overseas capability during World War II. Hoover and the armed services persuaded President Roosevelt in 1940 to ratify their preferred division of counterintelligence labor, "delimiting" their roles to give the Bureau primacy in the Western Hemisphere and the military (principally the Army) the leading role overseas.[12] Though clumsy at first as these agencies honed their previously under-used counterintelligence skills, this collective campaign to defend the homeland against the Axis powers grew robust and effective. The military intelligence agencies, the Federal Communications Commission, the Coast Guard, and the Bureau all played roles in intercepting public and clandestine radio broadcasts, especially in the Western Hemisphere.[13] Anglo-American cryptanalysis of high-grade Axis ciphers, moreover, enabled American intelligence to imitate on a smaller scale the British success in identifying and doubling German agents in order to gain intelligence and to spread disinformation.[14]

The FBI and the military intelligence services neutralized Axis agents in the Western Hemisphere, even gaining control of several German intelligence networks. The Bureau's Special Intelligence Service amounted to a counterin-telligence arm deployed overseas by a powerful law enforcement agency, giv-ing it an entrée to constabularies and security services across Latin America. Though Hoover had created SIS reluctantly in 1940 at the command of Presi-dent Roosevelt, he became one of its champions as the organization gained a grudging respect from the Department of State and increasing cooperation from American ambassadors.[15]

In Europe and Asia, the armed services and the Office of Strategic Services helped the British-run campaign that thwarted Axis intelligence and added new dimensions to American counterintelligence. This success relied on perhaps the greatest signals intelligence coup in history: the compromise of German enciphered messages sent by means of the famous Enigma machine and related systems. It handed a priceless advantage to British intelligence and security ser-vices, enabling them to neutralize German agents in the United Kingdom, and it ultimately safeguarded the integrity of positive intelligence operations mounted by British and American agencies. At several points, moreover, this counterin-telligence triumph allowed Allied commanders to deceive Hitler and the Axis about their plans—most notably before the invasion of Normandy in 1944.

The American service that exploited this breakthrough was OSS/X-2, created in 1942 to mirror and support its British liaison partners, but the service soon developed the capacity to run operations on its own.[16] X-2 operated as a secret compartment within a spy service, with secure communications channels outside OSS's normal message traffic and parallel stations beside OSS facilities abroad. Its officers, with their special window into Axis operations, wielded an absolute veto over the recruitment and use of human assets. X-2's most famous alumnus, Rome station chief James J. Angleton, pioneered the feeding of disguised signals intelligence leads to enable other, less-favored agencies to catch Axis agents, and even recruited assets in the secret services of Italy's pro-Allied government after 1943—thus practicing counterintelligence on allies as well as enemies.[17]

The Allies achieved both tactical and strategic superiority in part because of the efforts made by all intelligence components of the executive branch. The War

Department's contribution should not be overlooked; its Counterintelligence Corps (CIC) actually provided most of the "boots on the ground" for American counterintelligence in the war zones and made a significant contribution on the home front as well. CIC agents and units opened thousands of cases and hundreds of operations, and they took on more of a foreign focus once CIC lost many of its security and investigative responsibilities to other Army entities in 1943.[18] Their standards of training and quality did not match those of OSS or the Bureau, but they compensated with numbers, and thus any given Axis agent was more likely to run afoul of CIC than its more elite counterparts.

Army counterintelligence lived on after the war, yet neither SIS nor X-2 long survived V-J Day. The United States demobilized its wartime personnel and capabilities in a chaotic manner and seemed to have no use for the counterintelligence capabilities amassed by a law enforcement agency working abroad or for an overseas service built on the interallied exploitation of signals intelligence. By decree of the White House, SIS lost its role in law enforcement work and was incompletely transferred to the emerging Central Intelligence Agency (CIA).[19] It did not thrive there. X-2 had lost its primary source of leads, the ULTRA decrypts, and with this loss, its original rationale for deference and autonomy. Although it limped along a few more months with the dwindling remnants of OSS in the War Department, X-2 was irrelevant and ignored.[20] It had ceased to exist by the time the CIA took over OSS's remaining stations and personnel.

The Counterintelligence Order in Action

In dissolving SIS and X-2, the Truman administration and the intelligence agencies ratified and reinforced the prewar pattern for the practice of U.S. counterintelligence. That practice had developed four main elements by 1946: First, it evolved in reaction to current threats rather than via strategic planning; second, it was primarily an adjunct of law enforcement, with a sharp division between domestic and foreign roles; third, its capabilities were dispersed across individual executive-branch departments that brooked no central direction or control; and fourth, it exploited signals intelligence to the maximum possible degree. All of these tendencies would continue into the Cold War, reinforced by political and operational developments in the late 1940s.

The National Security Act of 1947, passed within a year of the dissolution of SIS and X-2, implicitly ratified the pattern set by the 1940 Delimitation Agreement by prohibiting internal security work by the new CIA and fostering de facto barriers between intelligence and law enforcement (and between foreign and domestic intelligence). Passing the Act at all, moreover, had required a series of artful political and institutional compromises, made necessary by the deep public distrust of the tools of tyranny and by departmental rivalries that had strangled SIS rather than give it up to the new foreign intelligence agency (and that allowed the War Department enough latitude to neglect X-2 once its ULTRA source dried up).

Ironically, these machinations were occurring at the same time that London and Washington were realizing that their wartime counterintelligence successes were overshadowed by a monumental security failure. Stalin had begun World War II as Hitler's ally, but by the point of America's entry into the war, the USSR was a full member of the Allied coalition. Soviet intelligence used this favored status to great effect, strengthening and deepening its widespread penetration of Allied governments that had begun in the 1930s. The Soviets were allowed to build up diplomatic and liaison establishments in the West—and by implication their associated espionage operations as well—without serious challenge. Soviet networks of ideological spies had burrowed into the U.S. government, and during the war especially they transferred quantities of high-grade intelligence to Moscow, including the secrets of the atomic bomb. The FBI followed some of these activities, even identifying Soviet efforts to penetrate the Manhattan Project, but as a matter of priority, American intelligence focused instead on the Axis threat.[21] This understandable wartime lapse would prove costly as the shape of the postwar peace was debated in the closing months of the war and the outlines of the Cold War emerged.

Weeks after the Japanese surrender, the threat of Soviet espionage had become a concern at the highest levels as Western leaders learned of two Soviet intelligence defectors: Igor Gouzenko and Elizabeth Bentley. Their cases have been discussed at length elsewhere, but their consequences merit emphasis. They set in motion a dramatic counterattack by the Anglo-American security services; indeed, by 1950 British and American cooperation had neutralized many of the Soviets' penetrations. This stunning revelation and swift response had three long-lasting implications for American counterintelligence.

First, internal security efforts within the homeland gained an edge over the Soviets that they never fully relinquished. The signals-derived counterintelligence success against the Axis ended at the close of World War II, but it had a parallel just after the war: "Venona." Army Security Agency cryptanalysts in 1947 learned how to read Soviet diplomatic and intelligence messages sent during World War II between Moscow and its overseas missions. Once fully briefed on these messages (which eventually bore the classification stamp Venona), the FBI and the British services between 1948 and 1951 exploited the breakthrough with the help of Bentley's leads to identify additional spies, including several active ones like Klaus Fuchs, Judith Coplon, and Donald Maclean; the latter's unmasking led to the neutralization of British intelligence liaison officer and Soviet mole Kim Philby as well. A KGB mole in the Army Security Agency, William Weisband, helped Moscow spot the breach and begin to repair the damage to Soviet security, but not before Soviet operations in the United States had been devastated.[22] Despite some significant Soviet espionage successes over the course of the Cold War, the Soviets never again came close to replicating the breadth and depth of the penetrations they achieved in World War II.

The FBI received additional assistance from a favorable Supreme Court decision. For a decade (1948–1957), the Court countenanced an interpretation of internal security legislation (specifically the 1940 Alien Registration Act) that virtually criminalized holding office in the Communist Party. The Soviets had already concluded the party was a poor platform for espionage, and in the 1950s the FBI ensured it could not become one again by driving its leaders underground.[23] The government as a whole, moreover, protected itself more effectively against espionage by finally making security an important part of screening recruits and employees, especially in sensitive positions. The FBI's dominance of the domestic field would be reinforced by the Reagan administration in 1981 via Executive Order 12333, which added to the Bureau's tasks a responsibility to "coordinate counterintelligence activities of other [Intelligence Community] agencies" within the United States (while giving an analogous task to the CIA for activities conducted abroad).[24]

The proficiency of counterintelligence work by American agencies working abroad during the early Cold War is less certain. Much of the documentation needed to assess the degree to which counterintelligence protected American diplomatic, military, and intelligence efforts remains classified. Some assertions can nevertheless be ventured. It goes without saying that counterintelligence overseas proceeded largely without central direction, despite the implied responsibility and authority of the director of central intelligence to coordinate all clandestine activities abroad. The main work was done by the CIA and the Department of Defense. The latter's campaign, moreover, featured a shifting plethora of independent investigatory organizations housed in the individual services and can by no means be viewed as a unified effort. Their accomplishments would appear mixed at best, with some serious setbacks over the course of the Cold War. The American war effort in Vietnam, for instance, seems to have been beset by counterintelligence mishaps.[25] It would seem safe to say that after 1945, American counterintelligence seldom aspired to, and rarely if ever attained, the goal of co-opting enemy intelligence operations.

The second significant implication of the success against the Soviets in the 1940s was that it gave leaders of the FBI the reputation and the belief that the Bureau could handle internal security largely on its own. Director Hoover had won in the National Security Act a virtual monopoly on domestic intelligence work (such was implied in the Act's prohibition on internal security powers for the new Central Intelligence Agency). The National Security Council (NSC) confirmed this privileged position in early 1949, recognizing the "Interdepartmental Intelligence Conference" (IIC) as "responsible for the coordination of all domestic espionage, counter-espionage, sabotage, subversion, and other related intelligence matters affecting national security." The IIC comprised the FBI and the intelligence and investigatory wings of the armed services, and it dated back to 1939, but it did not coordinate actual operations or investigations, and Hoover clearly dominated it.[26] The CIA was not invited to join, despite a 1951 plea from Director of Central Intelligence Walter B. Smith for sharing leads developed in the United States with foreign liaison partners and above all for "a closer coordination of the intelligence on Soviet controlled espionage activities abroad and the intelligence on such activities in this country." Indeed, Hoover rebuffed the CIA's petition to join the IIC and dismissed Smith's plea for greater sharing with overseas partners as a ploy for secrets "for use in bartering with foreign intelligence and security organizations."[27] Precedents set in this exchange and others would last for decades.

Thus was the American counterintelligence establishment split neatly into foreign and domestic spheres of responsibility. Where responsibilities crossed, potential and actual conflicts had to be worked out on a case-by-case basis. Unlike in the field of covert action, where the government in the early 1950s established basic (if initially rudimentary) procedures at the National Security Council level for weighing diplomatic, military, and intelligence claims and equities before approving significant operations, the Bureau's dominance of the counterintelligence sector was not subjected to such an interagency process for pushing competing considerations upward for debate and decision.[28]

Despite this lack of coordination, the system worked fairly well through the Cold War, in no small part because the Soviets had been forced by the allied counterintelligence response to shift much of their espionage efforts to diplomatic posts, and away from ideologically motivated recruits and toward "walkin" volunteers working for money. Soviet case officers supported these agents with "illegals" (nonofficial cover officers) like Rudolf Abel, caught in 1957 as a result of FBI-CIA cooperation.[29] The United States arrested several hundred persons on suspicion of espionage over the course of the Cold War—some of whom did severe damage to our national defense and intelligence capabilities. Nonetheless, it seems safe to say that American counterintelligence capabilities significantly raised the bar for the nations wishing to run intelligence operations in the United States. Nor does the record suggest that any country came close to matching the number and quality of Soviet penetrations of the U.S. government during World War II. Conversely, it should be noted that when new "nonstate" opponents—who by definition worked outside of the ambit of any foreign diplomatic mission—began planning assaults against the United States in the 1990s, this division of counterintelligence into foreign and domestic spheres would prove unsatisfactory. In particular, it left the United States vulnerable to a new threat: foreign-based ideologies whose agents and sympathizers had no ties with governments (or diplomatic posts) and were willing to die in attacks on American citizens.

The third major effect of the early setback to the Soviets was the tainting of the image of counterintelligence with partisanship, thereby making actual counterintelligence organizations and authorities all the tougher to adapt and improve. Much of the American response to the wartime Soviet penetrations—and arguably its most significant part—was handled outside of the public eye, even as elements of it, like the Hiss/Chambers battle in 1948, became public spectacles. In this regard, Venona was part of the problem. Although it had corroborated Elizabeth Bentley's reports on spies in Washington and opened hitherto unseen avenues into Soviet operations, the fact that it remained secret for decades made it easier for those who doubted Bentley and other defectors to dismiss her allegations.[30] The public sensed that Soviet agents had penetrated the U.S. government, but had no way of knowing how many such penetrations there were, nor if and when they had ended. They could only guess whether or not the Truman administration had truly contained the problem. The matter unsurprisingly became a major political issue, and the elusiveness of the truth allowed the emergence of Senator Joseph McCarthy (R-WI) and his allies, whose wild allegations brought the entire counterintelligence cause into disrepute.

Although intelligence community support for "McCarthyism" was at most limited, the public reaction against the community's efforts to deal with domestic unrest would have a similar effect. In an echo of the 1920s, the Bureau, the armed services, and the CIA would fuel public suspicions by employing counterintelligence techniques against domestic dissent in the 1950s and 1960s. Some of these probes and investigations were well intentioned and beneficial. Against the Ku Klux Klan, for instance, the FBI blanketed communities in the South, effectively using electronic surveillance, paid informants, double agents, and basic detective work. Treating the Klan as a domestic insurgency raised few protests in Washington, but the Bureau's counterintelligence programs (COINTELPRO), of which its attack on the Klan was but one example, became increasingly problematic as political leaders began to publicly disavow measures like electronic surveillance while expecting their continued use behind closed doors. This ambiguity led Hoover, the last intelligence leader in Washington holding office since the Jazz Age, to halt much of the Bureau's use of these tools. The Department of the Army followed a similar path; its contemporaneous probes of Vietnam War protest leaders had been facilitated by a powerful conjoining of intelligence and security databases effected in 1965, but that too ended as public and congressional criticism mounted in 1971.[31]

The political reckoning that Hoover had feared when he halted many FBI surveillance programs broke over the entire counterintelligence establishment in the aftermath of the Watergate scandal in the 1970s. Revelations of the various COINTELPROs, warrantless electronic surveillance, and the monitoring of domestic dissent became matters of intense media and congressional scrutiny while the scandals of the Nixon administration unfolded, and the FBI endured harsh criticism for its actions under Hoover.[32] Congressional committees stepped in to assume a permanent oversight role over the intelligence community, eschewing Congress's earlier assent to wider executive latitude. They took an especially strong interest in the intelligence community's domestic activities and the electronic tools used in them.

This oversight had profound effects on counterintelligence. In 1976 the FBI adopted, at the behest of Attorney General Edward Levi, a series of guidelines for domestic intelligence and related activities. As a result, Bureau supervisors grew far more cautious in investigating radical groups (the Army had already retreated, once again, from the domestic security field). The new rules virtually ended "domestic intelligence," but they did not appear to materially affect the classic Cold War struggle against the Soviet Union in the 1980s. Indeed, by providing legal footings beneath the counterintelligence effort, it gave American operatives and prosecutors new confidence.

Thus the battle became in some ways a more public one. Congress's passage of laws like the Foreign Intelligence Surveillance Act (1978), which provided a means to use electronic surveillance evidence in court, and the Classified Information Procedures Act (1980), which allowed some classified material to be used as evidence without compromising it, led the Department of Justice to change policy and embrace the use of prosecution as a tool to neutralize foreign espionage. More than six dozen successful prosecutions of spies were made between 1978 and 1985.

And yet, the number of high-profile espionage cases that came to light during this period, and their severity, was problematic in itself. Edward Lee Howard (CIA), the Walker family spy ring (U.S. Navy), Clyde Conrad (U.S. Army), and Ronald Pelton (NSA) were just four of the most shocking cases that revealed how significant America's losses to espionage had been. It was one thing to catch these spies, but the long-term success of some of them suggested deeper problems. Indeed, at least one congressional panel suggested after these cases that counterintelligence remained a relatively low priority for the community, complaining in 1988 that "[d]espite verbal acknowledgement that some espionage losses have been truly devastating and negated enormous defense investments, top managers remain unwilling to budget relatively modest sums for improved counterintelligence and security measures that would help protect much larger investments."[33] The decade of the 1980s was a period much like the early Cold War in that it highlighted a "Catch-22" of counterintelligence: The successful identification of a spy suggests a failure in security and counterintelligence.

One could draw too gloomy a conclusion from the number and severity of the spies caught in the 1980s. Sophisticated counterintelligence was being pursued as well. For example, the U.S. Army honed its ability to run double agents against the Warsaw Pact's newly aggressive recruitment efforts.[34] While Army operations occasionally ended in well-documented and well-publicized prosecutions, the CIA's record remains largely, even now, hidden behind a high security wall. Enough has been made public through congressional investigations and court filings, however, to suggest the Agency had real success overseas. In a 1986 study the Senate devoted thousands of words to domestic counterintelligence— but less than two hundred to "overseas operations." Nonetheless, the Senate pulled the veil back just a little:

> A major element in counterintelligence is offensive operations, especially efforts to recruit agents-in-place within hostile intelligence services and to induce defections from those services. The strategic payoff of agents and defectors can be immense, as demonstrated by the exposure of Edward Lee Howard and the successful prosecution of Ronald Pelton.[35]

The Justice Department's 1994 affidavit against CIA operations officer Aldrich Ames, moreover, alleged that his 1985 compromise of at least ten "penetrations of the Soviet military and intelligence services deprived the United States of extremely valuable intelligence material for years to come."[36] Hints like these suggest that CIA and the service intelligence agencies by the 1980s had learned to exploit vulnerabilities in the Warsaw Pact's security armor occasionally to spot leads back to moles working in the United States. The 2005 report of the Weapons of Mass Destruction Commission echoed this point by comparing the CIA's current work with its success in the Cold War, "when CIA case officers routinely targeted Warsaw Pact officials, an effort that led to a considerable number of successful counterintelligence investigations."[37]

The dissolution of the Soviet Union led to the further attenuation of counterintelligence as a priority. For a few years in the early 1990s the West seemed to hold a commanding lead over all challengers in the counterintelligence field. But it was not to last. Resources and high-level attention drifted away as the Cold War petered out. Intelligence community budgets and rosters stopped growing; in 1992, for instance, three hundred FBI agents who had worked counterintelligence accounts were shifted to violent crime investigations. In the Pentagon, counterintelligence remained an individual service function and was focused on investigations rather than offensive operations. The need for counterintelligence, however, had not lessened. The rising threat of international terrorism, the numerous, increasing threats posed by a multitude of hostile intelligence services, and the fact that the intelligence community continued to find long-term moles (Robert Hanssen and Aldrich Ames among them), suggested a continuing need for a vigorous counterintelligence program. President William J. Clinton issued not one but two directives (PDD 24 in 1994, and PDD 75 in 2000) to foster increased cooperation, coordination, and accountability across the counterintelligence establishment.

The verdict on the counterintelligence system in the 2005 report of the Weapons of Mass Destruction Commission was harsh: "While our enemies are executing what amounts to a global intelligence war against the United States, we have failed to meet the challenge. U.S. counterintelligence efforts have remained fractured, myopic, and only marginally effective."[38] It is too early to say whether the creation of the National Counterintelligence Executive (2000) and the Counterintelligence Field Activity in the Department of Defense (2002)—or its transfer to the Defense Intelligence Agency (2008)—will provide the long-awaited central coordination of counterintelligence efforts. Similarly, we cannot yet judge whether the creation of the Department of Homeland Security (2003), with its own intelligence duties, will result in a significant augmentation of America's counterintelligence prowess. One significant sign of transformation appeared in the text of Executive Order 13470, signed by President George W. Bush on July 30, 2008. That order amended EO 12333's definition of counterintelligence to "information and activities to *identify, deceive, exploit, disrupt,* or protect against espionage" (emphasis added).[39]

Lessons Learned and Relearned

The short-lived examples of X-2 and SIS, with which we began this essay, suggest that the current division of counterintelligence capabilities and assignments in the United States is neither inevitable nor immutable. Significant and successful alternatives have been tried. That said, the dissolution of X-2 and SIS in 1946 illustrates the difficulty of sustaining such innovations. The past experience and present capabilities of America's response to the threats posed by foreign intelligence services and other groups that employ the tools of intelligence, like terrorists and international criminals, are largely products of America's constitutional order and political culture as it responds to threats foreign and domestic. This reality suggests that the U.S. government's current ordering of counterintelligence functions and doctrine is unlikely to change dramatically in the foreseeable future, for instance, through the addition of a true domestic intelligence agency on the model of Britain's Security Service (better known as MI-5).

The shaping of the American experience of counterintelligence reflects the peculiar genius of the nation's founding and the subsequent evolution of its political system. The American people demand both liberty and security; the counterintelligence community, therefore, must balance these two goals to secure significant measures of both. This balance has been shaped first and foremost by the pervading influence of the Constitution. The American constitutional order contains features that both help and hinder counterintelligence. The fragmentation of powers within the executive branch, for instance, makes it difficult, but not impossible, to sustain a strategic and robust offensive counterintelligence capability both within and outside the nation's borders. Innovation is more likely to occur in times of crisis and, historically, has been highly successful, but it is hard to sustain after the sense of urgency passes. At the same time, however, the enduring stability of the constitutional order has muted domestic radicalism, while simultaneously (and perhaps paradoxically) keeping American institutions and political parties in a permanent state of concern for their civil liberties. Both these latter features of the American political culture help to keep counterintelligence perhaps more successful and less invasive than it has been in other countries. The citizens of the United States appear to accept this state of affairs, oscillating between support for, and criticism of, the government's counterintelligence entities, in part because this maintains the dynamic they collectively want between liberty and security and helps achieve both.

Notes

John Fox Jr. is the historian of the Federal Bureau of Investigation. Michael Warner is the chief historian of the Office of the Director of National Intelligence. The views in this chapter are their own, and do not represent the official opinions of their respective agencies.

1. Alexander Hamilton in *Federalist* 69 argued that the executive was so crafted as to ensure that it could execute the laws and protect national security with energy, the

components of which are "decision, activity, secrecy and dispatch"; *The Federalist* (New York: Modern Library, 2000). Secrecy, of course, has a role in the legislative branch too, as Article I, Section 5, for instance, attests: "Each House [of Congress] shall keep a Journal of its Proceedings, and from time to time publish the same, excepting such Parts as may in their Judgment require Secrecy." In the minds of those who crafted the American government, secrecy was a necessity.

2. The classic expression of this idea may be found in Louis Hartz's book *The Liberal Tradition in America: An Interpretation of American Political Thought since the Revolution* (New York: Harcourt, Brace, 1955). A recent challenge to this thesis is by Seymour Martin Lipset and Gary Wolfe Marks in *It Didn't Happen Here: Why Socialism Failed in the United States* (New York: W. W. Norton, 2001). There is certainly merit in considering the extent to which government action against certain radical movements acted as a revolutionary retardant, although such an argument may beg the question of why other nations with more repressive regimes face greater revolutionary challenges.

3. A succinct summary of the place of intelligence in the early republic can be found in William C. Banks and M. E. Bowman, "Executive Authority for National Security Searches," *American University Law Review* 50, no. 1 (2000): 13–18.

4. James L. Gilbert, John P. Finegan, and Ann Bray, *In the Shadow of the Sphinx: A History of Army Counterintelligence* (Ft. Belvoir, VA: U.S. Army Intelligence and Security Command, 2004).

5. Joan Jensen, *The Price of Vigilance* (Chicago: Rand McNally, 1968), 112–13.

6. Gilbert et al., *In the Shadow of the Sphinx*, 18.

7. Echoes of this first confrontation between counterintelligence and civil liberties still reverberate on the American political stage; see, for instance, the column by Studs Terkel, surely one of the last Americans who can write: "In 1920, during my youth, I recall the Palmer Raids in which more than 10,000 people were rounded up"; "The Wiretap This Time," *New York Times*, October 29, 2007, 19. The Church Committee's report hinted at the longevity and scale of the effort in the Senate Select Committee to Study Governmental Operations, "Warrantless FBI Electronic Surveillance" in *Supplementary Detailed Staff Reports on Intelligence Activities and the Rights of Americans* (vol. 3 of the Committee's *Final Report*), 94th Congress, 2nd Session, 1976. Hereinafter cited as Church Committee, *Final Report*.

8. See, for example, Church Committee, *Final Report*, vol. 2, 96–104.

9. David Kahn, *The Codebreakers: The Story of Secret Writing* (New York: abridged Signet edition, 1973), 169–70.

10. In *Olmstead v. U.S.*, 277 U.S. 438 (1928), the Court had ruled such evidence admissible, but nine years later reversed itself in *Nardone v. U.S.* (1937).

11. Some authors suggest that the Bureau of Investigation was profligate in its use of wiretaps. A succinct summary of this view may be found in Athan Theoharis, ed., *The FBI: A Comprehensive Reference Guide* (Westport, CT: Oryx Press, 1999), 115–27.

12. Robert Louis Benson and Michael Warner, eds., *Venona: Soviet Espionage and the American Response, 1939–1957* (Washington,DC: Central Intelligence Agency, 1996), 34.

13. Larry Valero, "*The State Department, the FCC, and the Latin American D/F Program during the Second World War*," unpublished paper presented at the 2007 conference of the Society for Historians of American Foreign Relations, June 22, 2007.

14. Thaddeus Holt, *The Deceivers: Allied Military Deception in the Second World War* (New York: Simon and Schuster, 2004), especially 442–58.

15. Raymond Batvinis, *The Origins of FBI Counterintelligence* (Lawrence: University of Kansas Press, 2007), 159–86; see also G. Gregg Webb, "New Insights into J. Edgar Hoover's Role," *Studies in Intelligence* 48, no.1 (2004): 51–58.

16. The FBI, too, had access to ULTRA intelligence by 1943, but the extent of its use of this intelligence is an area that has not yet been researched. There are a few comments about this in the FBI's in-house SIS History, written in 1947 and publicly released under the Freedom of Information Act (FOIA) in 2001.

17. Timothy Naftali, "ARTIFICE: James Angleton and X-2 Operations in Italy," in George C. Chalou, ed., *The Secrets War: The Office of Strategic Services in World War II* (Washington, DC: National Archives and Records Administration, 1991), 218.

18. Gilbert et al., *In the Shadow of the Sphinx*, 34–35.

19. Hoyt S. Vandenberg, director of central intelligence, to J. Edgar Hoover, director, Federal Bureau of Investigation, July 3, 1946, in *Foreign Relations of the United States, 1945–1950, Emergence of the Intelligence Establishment* (Washington, DC: Government Printing Office, 1996), 280–81.

20. Timothy Naftali, *Blind Spot: The Secret History of American Counterterrorism* (New York: Basic Books, 2005), 11–12. Louis J. Fortier et al. to Sidney Souers, director of central intelligence, "Report of Survey of Strategic Services Unit under CIG Directive No. 1," in *Foreign Relations of the United States, 1945–1950*, 263.

21. Benson and Warner, *Venona*, viii–xvii.

22. Ibid., xvii–xxvii.

23. For a contemporary view of the success of this internal security effort, see "Status of United States Programs for National Security as of December 31, 1952," Section of NSC 142, February 10, 1953, reprinted in Department of State, *Foreign Relations of the United States, 1950–1955, The Intelligence Community* (Washington, DC: Government Printing Office, 2007), 422–23. Hereafter cited as *FRUS, 1950–1955*; one of the authors of this essay edited this documentary collection.

24. See Executive Order 12333, *Code of Federal Regulations*, sections 1.14(a) and 1.8(d). Section 3.4(a) also defined counterintelligence in broad but primarily defensive terms to mean "information gathered and activities conducted to protect against espionage, other intelligence activities, sabotage, or assassinations conducted for or on behalf of foreign powers, organizations, or persons, or international terrorist activities, but not including personnel, physical, document or communications security programs."

25. See, for instance, Richard H. Shultz Jr., *The Secret War Against Hanoi: Kennedy's and Johnson's Use of Spies, Saboteurs, and Covert Warriors in North Vietnam* (New York: HarperCollins, 1999), 29–31, 90–92, 108–10, and 340–41.

26. National Security Council Directive 17/4, "Internal Security," March 22, 1949, in Benson and Warner, *Venona*, 136–37. For the creation of the IIC, also Attorney General Frank Murphy to President Franklin D. Roosevelt, June 17, 1939, in Benson and Warner, *Venona*, 11–12.

27. See the exchange of notes between Smith (April 17, 1951) and Hoover (May 2, 1951) in *FRUS, 1950–1955*, 137–39.

28. For an interesting contrast, consult the discussions within the Truman and Eisenhower administrations over the issue of squaring covert action operations with national policy. After several years of debate and trial and error, President Eisenhower in 1955 created a forum for arguing out the policy and operational implications of proposed covert actions by decreeing that senior political appointees in the Departments of State and

Defense convene with National Security Council and CIA representatives to approve new operations and review ongoing projects. This basic formula, with modifications, endured for decades. See National Security Council Directive 5412/2, "Covert Operations," [December 1955], in *FRUS, 1950–1955*, 746–49.

29. Abel's true name was William Henry Fisher. The Soviets' ability to mount new operations in spite of the Venona losses fueled worries among James Angleton and others in the intelligence community, particularly in the CIA, which conducted disruptive inquests for Soviet moles in the 1960s. See Robert M. Hathaway and Russell Jack Smith, *Richard Helms as Director of Central Intelligence, 1966–1973* (Washington, DC: Central Intelligence Agency, 1993), 120–26. This publication was recently declassified and made available at CIA's FOIA page.

30. Venona finally reached the public via a series of leaks beginning in the late 1970s. It was not officially declassified until 1995.

31. Gilbert et al., *In the Shadow of the Sphinx*, 131, 138–39.

32. The details, of course, cannot be even summarized here, but there are many sources to further explore these matters. The best starting point is with the hearings and reports of the Church Committee, especially *Final Report*, vol. 3.

33. House Permanent Select Committee on Intelligence, Subcommittee on Oversight and Evaluation, *U.S. Counterintelligence and Security Concerns: A Status Report, Personnel and Information Security*, 100th Cong., 2d Sess., 1988, 19.

34. Gilbert et al., *In the Shadow of the Sphinx*, 148–52.

35. U.S. Senate, Select Committee on Intelligence, *Meeting the Espionage Challenge: Review of United States Counterintelligence and Security Programs*, October 3, 1986, 99th Cong., 2d sess., S. Rept. 99–522.

36. *United States of America v. Aldrich Hazen Ames*: Statement of Facts, United States District Court for the Eastern District of Virginia, Criminal no. 94–64-A; this is reprinted in Frank J. Rafalko, ed., "A Counterintelligence Reader," vol. 3 (Washington, DC: National Counterintelligence Center, 1999), 31. Accessed March 2, 2008, at www.fas.org/irp/ops/ci/docs/ci3/ch4.pdf.

37. Commission on the Intelligence Capabilities of the United States Regarding Weapons of Mass Destruction (the WMD Commission), *Report to the President of the United States* (Washington, DC: Government Printing Office, 2005), 490.

38. Ibid., 486.

39. Executive Order 13470, *Code of Federal Regulations*, Section 4(f).

3

Robert Jervis

Intelligence, Counterintelligence, Perception, and Deception

IF INTELLIGENCE is the neglected child of international politics, counterintelligence is the more neglected—and more misunderstood—stepchild. To most Americans, even experts and scholars, it seems dull because it smacks of police work; excessively defensive because it can only protect, rather than advance, our interests; and unsavory because it calls for mistrust of, if not spying on, members of our own government and society. There is some validity to this impression but also much wrong with it, as explained in other chapters in this volume. In any case, these concerns do not make the subject less important, and they may obscure its broader significance.[1]

Counterintelligence and the Nature of the Regime

One reason for its neglect is that counterintelligence fits uncomfortably within most democracies. Almost by definition, democracies thrive in and foster open societies. The free flow of people and information, widespread discussion, and high levels of trust are greatly valued by these systems and necessary for their functioning. The citizens in a democracy can accept the idea that some information must be withheld from them in order to keep it from adversaries, but there are sharp limits to the forms and the extent of secrecy that can be tolerated. Moreover, it is hard for democracies to function when people mistrust one another, when government officials have to wonder whether every inquiry from citizens or colleagues might be designed to elicit information to be passed on to enemies, and when information and proposed courses of action have to be immediately scrutinized for the possibility that they are of alien design. In an immigrant country like the United States, the idea that newcomers, even from hostile countries, might be spies is particularly corrosive. If the American project is successful, those who come here will become loyal citizens; the very possibility that they will not indicates not only deep personal flaws on their part, but the failure of the American ideal. In the United Kingdom class plays a role similar to Americanism. One reason why the British were slow to develop a system of security clearances, and to investigate the suspicious behavior of people who turned out to be devastatingly effective spies for the Soviet Union, was the sense that those with the proper social credentials could be trusted.

These problems do not arise in dictatorships, many of which are built on betrayal and suspicion. Dictators must foster personal loyalty, but they also must be wary that even their closest associates might turn on them. The idea that others might be spies is second nature to people in these regimes and, indeed, is often useful as a means of internal control. Joseph Stalin's Soviet Union was extreme in its employment of fear and purges, but the basic phenomenon is part of the DNA of dictatorial regimes.[2] These tend toward paranoia, but we should remember that even paranoids have enemies—the fact that the only way to change a dictatorship is through stealth and deception means that nothing can be beyond suspicion. The fact that paranoia comes naturally to most dictatorships does not mean that it is without a heavy price. Although paranoia does not in itself undermine the founding principles of the regime, its operation may well weaken it. Even the most autocratic rulers need loyal supporters; a government without a modicum of trust cannot function; constant purges may enable the dictator to survive and have many of his policies carried out, but they can destroy important instruments of state power. To take only the most obvious example, one reason for the poor performance of the Soviet armed forces in the wake of the German attack in June 1941 was that Stalin had removed most of his best officers in the preceding years.

Intelligence, Perception, and Deception

If the purpose of foreign policy is to advance the national interest (however interpreted), the purpose of intelligence is to provide an understanding of the world on which foreign policy can be based and to support instruments to influence and possibly deceive others. Readers of my previous work will not be surprised to see that I put perception and deception at the center of international politics, and they are surely central to intelligence and counterintelligence. It is tempting to believe that good policy requires a good understanding of the environment, but this is not always the case. The British decision to fight on after the fall of France in 1940 was based at least in part on a picture of the world that was wildly off the mark.[3] As in everyday life, misunderstandings between nations may result in not only comedy, but also success for one actor or the other, and sometimes even mutually beneficial outcomes. This is, however, hardly a formula for the long run. It is also true that despite their constantly saying how much they seek accurate information and analysis, national leaders often find intelligence unwelcome because it tends to increase uncertainty or contradict existing policy.[4] But even the most closed-minded decision maker eventually needs to understand the world in which he or she is operating. Even when they scorn the formal intelligence apparatus, as Richard Nixon did when he famously referred to "those clowns out at Langley,"[5] their perceptions are essential to their behavior, and these can rarely be formed on the basis of first-hand experience.

Deception is central as well. Although self-deception plays a large role in the making of foreign policy because people adjust their perceptions to avoid doubts and remorse, this psychological dynamic will largely be put aside here.[6] More central to intelligence and, especially, counterintelligence, is that actors need both to be on guard against being deceived and often to deceive others. Indeed, the knowledge that deception is possible strongly affects the interpretation of all incoming information and the uses to which it is put. Counterintelligence and deception are closely intertwined. Most obviously, the state must fear that the other side is using its agents to convey a false picture. The other side of this coin is that the state can use the other's intelligence service in order to propagate its own deceptions, as I will discuss further below.

A Wilderness of Mirrors

International politics is characterized and complicated by the fear that things are not what they seem, that apparently solid intelligence is built on sand, and that trusted information is misleading. States often want others to accept a certain picture of the world and an image of themselves that will further their interests. This picture may indeed be an accurate one, but it also may not be, which means that perceivers always must be wary.

This is nowhere more true than in counterintelligence. The state is trying to see whether the adversary (assuming only one for the sake of exposition) is spying on it while simultaneously trying to see whether its own spies are secure and loyal. (We can make parallel analyses of other forms of intelligence, most obviously involving signals and codes.) Since by definition it is very hard to detect a good spy and at least as hard to tell whether one of your spies has been "turned" and is now feeding you false information and betraying secrets to the adversary, a heightened and indeed hypersensitive readiness to perceive deception comes with the territory. But the inevitable cost of this stance will sometimes be to see plots that do not exist, to discount accurate information, to disregard if not jail loyal informants, and to induce a great deal of paranoia within one's government if not country. Because each side knows that the other is trying to play with its senses and prey on its vulnerabilities, counterintelligence inevitably leads one into what James Angleton, the famous (or notorious) Central Intelligence Agency (CIA) chief of counterintelligence, called a wilderness of mirrors.[7]

If the best spy is someone you would never be likely to suspect, then your adversary will try to recruit such a person or have her cultivate the appropriate appearance. This means that the very appearance of being above suspicion should incite suspicion. Of course if the other side understands this, it might recruit people with shady backgrounds because their very unreliability makes you believe that they are less likely to be spies. While this is an exaggeration to a point of caricature, I think that it is good caricature, which means that the features it presents are important and recognizable. The basic point is that in this world it is far from clear what can be trusted, and since both sides are playing the game, indications of trustworthiness are subject to manipulation. The result is that there are no firm guidelines and that anyone who is confident that she has her bearings is lost.

The effects and the disequilibrium this situation creates are best illustrated by the opportunities and dilemmas posed when a member of the adversary's intelligence service offers to provide information or to defect. The obvious question is whether the person is genuine or remains an agent of the adversary; it is equally obvious that there will rarely be a clear answer. Either an unwarranted acceptance or an unwarranted rejection will have high costs. Furthermore, many kinds of evidence have the paradoxical qualities noted above. If everything seems in order, a skeptic will note that this is just what would be expected from a well-prepared enemy agent; gaps or inconsistencies in his story that at first glance seem to indicate that he is a plant could point in the opposite direction because it is unlikely that the adversary would commit such obvious errors. So it is not surprising that offers to provide information often trigger much agonizing by the recipients; many sincere offers are rebuffed,[8] and battles can rage for years about whether the source is genuine or an enemy agent. The most obvious and controversial case is that of Yuri Nosenko, the KGB officer who defected in 1964, bringing with him the story that the Soviets had no ongoing connection with Lee Harvey Oswald and President John F. Kennedy's assassination.[9] Given the high stakes and the inherent ambiguities, these kinds of questions cannot be readily answered and become the center of acrimonious debates.

Indeed, they spill over into arguments about the fundamental integrity of the state's intelligence and counterintelligence systems, debates that can rarely be settled and that exact a high cost. Thus the Nosenko affair gave added urgency to the search for a high-level Soviet agent or mole. For years, Angleton scrutinized CIA, casting doubt on many officials and forcing some out until Director of Central Intelligence (DCI) William Colby decided that Angleton was doing enormous damage and had to be dismissed. Indeed if Colby was correct (and the consensus—which of course could be wrong—is that he was), then by delaying the acceptance of Nosenko's information, displacing valuable officers, and sowing enormous distrust within the organization, Angleton did more damage than most Soviet agents could have. Similarly, some in the United Kingdom believed that the head of MI5, Sir Roger Hollis, was a Soviet mole, and the attempt to show this greatly weakened the organization.

Colby felt that the United States had erred on the side of being too suspicious and rejecting valuable sources: "I never thought that the object of CIA was to protect itself against the KGB. The object of CIA is to get into the Kremlin."[10] Unfortunately, though, CIA could not "get into the Kremlin" if it were penetrated, because the mole would expose our spies, as Aldrich Ames did. These situations make it very hard to know what is sensible. We have to recognize that the most loyal person can indeed turn out to be a spy and the suspicious volunteer from the other side may indeed be a good source. This creates an atmosphere that is hard to cope with. One may not be able to be a good counterintelligence officer without being somewhat paranoid, and the job itself encourages paranoia. Colleagues who thought Angleton had come close to losing his mind by the end of his career may have been right, and perhaps he had overlearned a lesson from the experience early in his career when he worked with Kim Philby, the rising star in British intelligence who turned out to be a Soviet agent. DCI Richard Helms said, "If [Angleton] overdid it, maybe he did, but that's a difficulty inherent in the job."[11] How can one maintain one's balance in an area where almost anything could be true, where appearances are designed to be deceiving, and in which familiar signposts may have been twisted to point in the wrong direction?

Not Taking Deception Seriously Enough

One reaction to this difficult environment is to downplay if not ignore the danger of deception. For many years before and during World War II American authorities refused to take Soviet espionage seriously; this was not a uniquely American failing, as the British were at least as negligent. Although the revelation of the World War II spies led to more careful security checks and a sensitivity to the danger of penetration by Soviet agents, the United States paid relatively little attention to Soviet deception, despite the fact that the Soviets were clearly devoting great efforts to this task. I was surprised by this when I became a consultant to CIA in 1978. My sense is that American intelligence analysts, and probably those in other countries as well, resist taking deception as seriously as they should because doing so would make their already-difficult task even more trying. They work with fragmentary and contradictory information, and if on top of this they had to consider the chance that much of what they were seeing was designed by the other side for this purpose, they could end up paralyzed. The possibility that some parts of the adversary's government are misinformed or are deceiving other parts (as was true in Iraq) is also likely to be ignored, because it too can undercut the validity of what would otherwise be very valuable intelligence.

Deception Comes at a Cost

Another reason for both paranoia and the opposite willingness to accept information from questionable sources is that in order to mount a successful deception campaign, one often must provide the adversary with some valid information of value. One way an agent establishes his bona fides is by providing information that an imposter could not know and that the state would not want revealed to the adversary. For those running a double agent, designing such information is a crucial task. It requires not only knowing the other side's perceptual predispositions in order to understand what information will be seen as accurate, but also difficult choices about what can be divulged that will be seen as valuable enough to be enticing without doing much harm to the state.[12] This "feed" (or "chickenfeed" as it is also called) obviously requires delicate judgments. These are easier to reach the more the state knows about what the adversary knows—or thinks—about the state. Sometimes information can be given up because the state knows that the adversary already knows it (although it is important that the adversary not know that the state knows it). Information that is unknown but about to come out through other sources also can be good feed, and similarly useful is information that is unknown but that cannot be acted on with sufficient speed to harm the state. Furthermore, good feed does not have to be correct, but only seen as correct (or even plausible) by the other side. Even information that is later shown to have been wrong may be usefully employed if the agent can later explain why things did not turn out as he thought they would. Thus an agent who falsely reported that a state was soon going to take a certain action can explain away the fact that it did not do so by pointing to changes in circumstances or personnel that led the decision to be revoked. Of course the adversary is almost always sensitive to the danger that it is being fed, but the judgments it has to make are extremely difficult.

How much the state is willing to give up depends on part of the importance of the deception being designed. The famous case of the Double Cross system in which the British ran the entire German spy network in the United Kingdom throughout World War II involved a willingness to reveal significant information because the ultimate prize of deceiving the Germans about the location of the D-Day invasion was of the utmost importance. Perceivers who understand this then face the added complication that the very value of the information they are getting may indicate, not that the agent is a trustworthy source, but that she is part of a scam of enormous proportions. Perhaps the best prescription would then be to trust the information on all but the most important question. But this would be extremely difficult to do and requires knowing what the state considers to be the vital question for which it is hoarding its capability.

In light of what I said earlier about the necessary paranoia of counterintelligence, one might wonder how these deception efforts could ever succeed. That they can is explained not only by the knowledge that rejecting all reports would be folly, but also by the fact that a service develops a great political, bureaucratic, and psychological stake in its agents. It is very hard for an organization that owes its power—if not its very existence—to its prowess in developing spies to see that they have been turned and that the agency itself is now an instrument of the adversary. The very fact that other agencies within the government try to discredit these agents gives the organization that is running them added reason to stand up for them. Furthermore, it is hard for the individuals most involved to recognize that they may be being made fools of, and in many cases the agency becomes the defender of its agents and overlooks what in retrospect were glaring clues to their true nature.[13] As a Soviet intelligence officer told a nervous double agent he was running, "You'll have no problem. They *want* to believe you."[14]

To Use or Destroy the Other's Intelligence?

The example of Angleton reminds us that a state may employ counterintelligence to cripple the adversary's intelligence service by turning its own counterintelligence against it. The advantages of doing so are obvious: If the state can use the other's counterintelligence to convince the leaders it has moles, the adversary's intelligence will be discredited and shunted aside, and in effect the state will have developed a protective shield. Even if the adversary service has good information about the state, it will not be believed, and so the service will be rendered harmless.

Dictatorial regimes make easier targets than do democracies because of their heightened paranoia. Adversary services have only to play into this, not generate it. Furthermore, intelligence in dictatorships is almost always fragmented, convoluted, and politicized. To bring unpleasant news to the leader's attention is to risk not just one's career, but one's life. So it is no surprise that dictatorships tend to be ill-informed.[15] Much important information did not reach Adolf Hitler in part because his underlings feared him, but the most striking example of a dictator's refusal to believe bad news was Stalin's inability to accept the overwhelming evidence that Hitler was about to attack in the spring of 1941.[16] Fearing that the British and perhaps Hitler's subordinates were trying to provoke him, Stalin assumed that his spies who correctly reported German plans were in fact double agents and dismissed (and then killed) his intelligence chief who kept calling these reports to his attention.[17] The Germans sought to discredit the Soviet intelligence services, and Stalin's misguided faith in his own policy and his enormous suspicions of his own government apparatus made their job much easier.

The possibility of this tactic presents two dilemmas, one for the state sending messages and the other for the perceiver. The perceiver's difficulty is that there is no easy answer to the question of how much paranoia is enough; as we have just seen, too much can disable intelligence, but even paranoids have enemies and there are real reasons for counterintelligence officials to be on guard against penetration and to view officers, agents, and information with suspicion. States have been badly harmed both by being too vigilant and by not being vigilant enough.

The sender's dilemma is that there can be advantages to both using and weakening the adversary's service. It may seem obvious that the state should try to degrade and discredit the adversary's intelligence system and so render it blind.

But this is not necessarily to the state's benefit. In many cases and in many ways the adversary's intelligence may be of value to the state. As I noted at the start, the state wants to project a desired image (sometimes deceptive and sometimes not). This requires a sensitive and respected perceiving apparatus. An adversary that is blind will not be able to gather the information the state is trying to keep from it, but neither will it be able to read the messages the state is trying to send. Of course there are lots of channels for delivering these messages, but a well-functioning intelligence service has the major advantages of being considered reliable by those it serves and having direct access to them. Many signals—either figurative or literal—can be picked up only by an intelligence service, and many messages are much more credible if it is believed that the state is trying to keep them secret.

The adversary's having a good intelligence system is no panacea, of course, and it can miss a great deal. Thus Richard Nixon's elaborate plan to frighten the Soviets into assisting the United States in Vietnam by putting strategic forces on alert in the fall of 1969 failed because Soviet intelligence did not detect the American activities until they were almost completed, and at that point it misinterpreted them.[18] Furthermore, in some cases the state can send credible messages that do not depend on intelligence channels, as when it makes moves that are plain for all to see, even if their meaning can remain subject to debate.

Nevertheless, in many cases the adversary's service is the most important channel by which the state is able to project a desired image. On occasion, the intelligence service can be used as a back channel for communication. This may have the advantage of permitting conversations and feelers that can be disavowed if it becomes necessary because either side can claim that its representatives were speaking without authorization. Indeed, at times the state will mistakenly believe that the agent was speaking officially when in fact this was not the case. Thus at the time, and for years later, it was believed that the Soviet intelligence agent Aleksandr Feklisov's conversations with John Scali during the Cuban Missile Crisis conveyed Soviet positions. Although what he proposed was close to the solution arrived at, we now know that he was acting on his own. Another advantage of using intelligence channels is that the messages are more likely to be kept secret, not only from other countries and the general public, but from wide sections of the government. Of course there is a cost to this, as the history of the Nixon administration shows, but the advantages are not trivial. Third and relatedly, because they are so secret and unusual, messages passed by intelligence agents are often taken especially seriously. This does not guarantee they will be believed, but at least they will receive high-level attention.

Perhaps the most interesting role of the adversary's service is in a double cross: manipulating an adversary's intelligence through double agents or allowing the tapping of communications channels that the targeted state has under counter-surveillance. Here the adversary believes that it has a direct pipeline into important and highly credible information. It thinks it is getting the best possible data on the state's capabilities and is figuratively if not literally overhearing the state's leaders talking about what they plan to do. This seems like pure gold, and of course it can be. The Soviet spies in the United States and the United Kingdom in the 1940s produced information of great value (as we will see below, however, this did not always harm the West). Similarly, well-placed military officers in the USSR and Eastern Europe like Oleg Penkovsky and Ryczard Kuklinski provided the United States with invaluable information on Soviet capabilities, thinking, and war plans. But as counterintelligence is well aware, if these sources are in fact being controlled by the adversary, they can do enormous harm. The classic case is of course the Double Cross system mentioned earlier. By controlling the German spy ring in the United Kingdom, the British were able to mislead the Germans as to the location of the D-Day invasion. Indeed, the credibility of the sources was so high that they were believed when soon after D-Day they reported that the Normandy landings were a feint and the main crossing would be at Calais. It is hard to overstate the importance of Hitler's error: Had he known that the landings were coming at Normandy or had he released his reserve divisions as soon as the Allied troops hit the beaches, he could have pushed the invaders into the sea.

Somewhat simpler and more complex forms of using the adversary's intelligence are also possible. A (relatively) simple method is just to release a message in a way or though channels that you know will take it to the adversary, although the adversary does not know that you know this. For example, during the Berlin Crisis, Secretary of State Dean Rusk apparently urged that certain war plans be transmitted to West Germany because he knew that German poor security meant that they would soon find their way into Soviet hands and that this would bolster the credibility of American threats.[19] More complicated, and even more risky, is the "double bluff," in which true information is released through a channel that the state knows that the adversary believes is being used for deception in the expectation that it will be interpreted as being misleading.[20] What is crucial and difficult is that the state must be one step ahead of the adversary in its knowledge of what is believed.

The previous examples involve the state's manipulation of the other side's intelligence. But sometimes the state can benefit from spies it has *not* discovered. These too can be highly credible sources of information, and sometimes it is in the state's interest to have its secrets conveyed to the adversary. For example, if the state is planning to stand firm in a confrontation, it usually wants the other side to know this, and for this purpose a spy at the highest levels will be extraordinarily useful. In other cases when the state is acting out of fear of the adversary and does not itself harbor aggressive intentions, it may also want this known but be unable to convincingly show this through normal diplomatic channels and behavior. It is not far-fetched to argue that Philby, the great Soviet spy, served the West as well as Stalin extraordinarily well by his great access to the American establishment in the dangerous years of 1949–1951. What he was hearing was that the United States would forcibly resist further Soviet incursions but that it did not plan offensive actions of its own. If this is what was conveyed to Moscow and believed, this would have both restrained Stalin from pressing harder and reassured him that he did not need to act preventively to forestall Western aggression. Philby may then have influenced history, and he could do so only because of the strength of the Soviet intelligence system and the failure of Western counterintelligence.

In closing I want to return to the crucial nature of perceptions and their links to deception. To have their desired impact, messages have to be interpreted in a way that the sender intends. This is far from automatic. People's perceptions are strongly driven by their needs and expectations, which are difficult for senders to comprehend, let alone manipulate. Attempts to project images, accurate or not, will work only if the receiver is receptive. One might think that the appropriate way to design a deception plan is to first decide what you want to do and then to develop ways of convincing the adversary that you are going to do something else. In fact, this is not likely to work. The adversary will interpret the evidence in light of what he expects you to do, and it will be very difficult to change his mind. So you have to first know what he expects you to do, and then plan to do something different and develop a deception plan that will reinforce what he already believes. The Allied deception plan would not have convinced Hitler that the invasion would take place at Calais and/or Norway if Hitler had not believed this for reasons of his own. This returns us to the close links between intelligence and counterintelligence. Attempts to use the adversary's intelligence system to convey a desired message require a good understanding of how the adversary sees the world. Counterintelligence, then, is much more than passive defense and can fulfill its potential only in close coordination with other instruments.

Notes

1. See William Odom, *Fixing Intelligence* (New Haven: Yale University Press, 2003). As Odom makes clear and as many of the essays in this volume stress, counterintelligence is not, or not only, about catching spies. It is intelligence about other countries' intelligence. Like intelligence, it is about gathering and analyzing information, and what is done with the information varies according to the circumstances. Preventing the penetration of one's own society and government is only the most obvious response. The alternatives and their resulting complications are much deeper.

2. For the argument that tyrants are different from normal people, see Stephen Rosen, *War and Human Nature* (Cambridge: Harvard University Press, 2005), chapter 5.

3. David Reynolds, "Churchill and the British 'Decision' to Fight on in 1940: Right Policy, Wrong Reasons," in *Diplomacy and Intelligence During the Second World War*, ed. Richard Langhorne (New York: Cambridge University Press, 1985), 147–67.

4. I have discussed this further in the concluding chapter of my forthcoming book *The Politics and Psychology of Intelligence and Intelligence Failure* (Ithaca, NY: Cornell University Press, forthcoming).

5. Quoted in Rhodri Jeffreys-Jones, *The CIA and American Democracy*, 2nd ed. (New Haven: Yale University Press, 1998), 177.

6. For further discussion see Robert Jervis, "Understanding Beliefs," *Political Psychology* 27 (October 2006): 641–64.

7. David Martin, *Wilderness of Mirrors* (New York: Harper & Row, 1980).

8. For one example, see Barry Royden, "Tolkachev, A Worthy Successor to Penkovsky," *Studies in Intelligence* 47, no. 3 (2003): 5–34.

9. For the latest in a long stream of books about the case, see Tennent Bagley, *Spy Wars* (New Haven: Yale University Press, 2007).

10. "Reflections of DCIs Colby and Helms on the CIA's 'Time of Troubles,'" *Studies in Intelligence* 51 (Summer 2007): 19.

11. Quoted in Martin, *Wilderness of Mirrors*, 206.

12. This means that deception planners have to know what their own state is planning to do: "It is impossible, or at any rate highly dangerous, to tell a lie until you know what the truth is going to be." M. D. Foot, "Conditions Making for Success and Failure of Deception and Denial: Democratic Regimes," in *Strategic Denial and Deception: The Twenty-first Century Challenge*, ed. Roy Godson and James Wirtz (New Brunswick, NJ: Transaction, 2002), 120.

13. In fact, in some cases the agent does not have "a true nature," or at least a true loyalty, and may be providing both accurate and inaccurate information to both sides.

14. Quoted in Bagley, *Spy Wars*, 274.

15. Ralph White, "Why Aggressors Lose," *Political Psychology* 11 (June 1990): 227–42.

16. Zachary Shore, *What Hitler Knew: The Battle for Information in Nazi Foreign Policy* (New York: Oxford University Press, 2003).

17. David Murphy, *What Stalin Knew: The Enigma of Barbarossa* (New Haven: Yale University Press, 2005); for a different version see Geoffrey Roberts, *Stalin's Wars* (New Haven: Yale University Press, 2006), 61–81.

18. William Burr and Jeffery Kimball, "Nixon's Secret Nuclear Alert: Vietnam War Diplomacy and the Joint Chiefs of Staff Readiness Test, October 1969," *Cold War History* 3 (January 2003): 113–56.

19. Marc Trachtenberg, *A Constructed Peace: The Making of the European Settlement, 1945–1963* (Princeton: Princeton University Press, 1999), 295n39.

20. Robert Jervis, *The Logic of Images in International Relations*, 2nd ed. (New York: Columbia University Press, 1989); Thaddeus Holt, *The Deceivers: Allied Military Deception in the Second World War* (New York: Scribner, 2004).

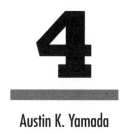

Austin K. Yamada

Counterintelligence and U.S. Strategic Culture

> We the People of the United States, in Order to form a more perfect Union, establish Justice, insure domestic Tranquility, provide for the common defence, promote the general Welfare, and secure the Blessings of Liberty to ourselves and our Posterity, do ordain and establish this Constitution for the United States of America.
>
> —Preamble to the U.S. Constitution

THIS SIMPLE prologue introduces the United States Constitution and explains its purpose. The preamble neither empowers the federal government nor inhibits its actions, but serves to outline its raison d'être. There is a distinct, and some would argue intentional, absence of guidance on how to best balance competing elements of liberty and security, or when—or even if—trade-offs between the two should be made. Reducing the argument to a zero-sum choice between liberty and security does not accurately frame the issue—it is not a question of whether national security trumps civil liberty in times of national crisis (or vice versa) but rather how best to achieve a balance between them. This dynamic balance can be achieved only by recognizing the need for pragmatic policy and institutional arrangements that make domestic intelligence and its effective oversight practical, even if imperfect.

American citizens enjoy personal freedoms and privacy rights envisioned by the Founders and suitably crafted and protected by constitutional provisions that have withstood the test of time and the folly of Man. Americans ardently believe in civil liberty arising from a freedom-inspired revolution that took place over two centuries ago and that has been codified in the Constitution and Bill of Rights. Wars have been fought and countless lives lost to protect these freedoms and the American way of life. The struggle to ensure that this culture is nourished and passed on to future generations requires constant vigilance and the willingness to confront any and all threats to our freedoms. The tension between the core values of liberty and the provision of security is especially strained in the post-9/11 era when threats to our national security—and to our civil liberties—have both taken new and potentially ominous forms.

Civil liberty is generally understood to mean the freedoms that protect the individual from coercive or invasive government actions, and it sets the limits of government power when it comes to the private lives of its citizens. As discussed in Judge Richard Posner's chapter in this volume, the concept of personal privacy centers on the ability of individuals to keep information about their private lives and personal affairs to themselves. National security turns on the territorial integrity, sovereignty, and international freedom of action of the United States and includes intelligence activities relating to military, economic, political, scientific, technological, and other aspects of foreign developments that pose actual or potential threats to U.S. national interests. Civil liberty and security are essential elements of a democratic society and must coexist in harmony, but the exact formula for balancing these elements is fluid, shifting emphasis from one element to another as international conditions change and society evolves.

The historical chapter by Michael Warner and John Fox Jr. in this volume makes clear that the tension between liberty and security is most apparent in times of national distress. Almost every historical instance of national emergency has been accompanied by a setback to civil liberties. Notable examples include the Palmer Raids conducted in 1919–1921 on radical left-wing political groups after a series of bomb attacks on court buildings, police stations, churches, and homes attributed to immigrant anarchist groups. President Woodrow Wilson himself promulgated the real or imagined threat posed by some foreign-born residents and warned of "hyphenated Americans who have poured the poison of disloyalty into the very arteries of our national life . . . such creatures of passion, disloyalty and anarchy must be crushed out."[1]

Perhaps the best-known example of ethnic profiling in the name of national security is the internment of over 110,000 Japanese Americans during World War II in response to the Japanese attack on Pearl Harbor. Lieutenant General John DeWitt, who commanded the Western Defense Forces, led the internment effort and testified to Congress, "I do not want any of them [persons of Japanese ancestry] here. They are a dangerous element. There is no way to determine their loyalty. . . . It makes no difference whether he is an American citizen, he is still a Japanese. American citizenship does not necessarily determine loyalty. . . . But we must worry about the Japanese all the time until he is wiped off the map."[2]

Just as the domestic bombings of 1919–1921 and the Japanese attack on Pearl Harbor on December 7, 1941, drastically altered the balance between civil liberty and security, the terrorist attacks of September 11, 2001, may alter our lives more dramatically than we now realize, as we stand barefoot in security lines at airports, clutching quart-sized plastic bags containing toothpaste and contact lens solution. We have lost more soldiers, sailors, airmen, and Marines in Iraq and Afghanistan—ostensibly fighting the terrorist threat—than the number of citizens who died on 9/11;[3] we have accepted legislation allowing more invasive application of intelligence collection capabilities that impact our civil liberties and privacy; and we have seen the indefinite detention of terror suspects without formal charges or legal hearings. How fixed is the balance between national security and civil liberty? How should this balance be calibrated, and who should fine-tune the calibration in a political environment that is becoming increasingly more polarized? The answers to these questions will drive us toward the establishment of policies, institutional processes, and procedures that will improve our ability to establish, adjust, and manage the balance between security and liberty.

The question of whether security takes precedence over liberty in time of national crisis is not a new one. Even the framers of the Constitution were not exempt from the debate. Thomas Jefferson himself wrote: "[A] strict observance of the written law is doubtless one of the high duties of a good citizen, but it is not the highest. The laws of necessity, of self-preservation, of saving our country when in danger, are of higher obligation. To lose our country by a scrupulous adherence to the written law, would be to lose the law itself, with life, liberty, property and all those who are enjoying them with us; thus absurdly sacrificing the ends to the means."[4]

Arguably one of the most eloquent expressions of the belief that constitutional restrictions on governmental power must give way to urgent practical needs was made by Supreme Court Justice Robert H. Jackson in his dissent in the 1949 case of *Terminiello v. Chicago*, where he wrote, "The choice is not between order and liberty. It is between liberty with order and anarchy without either. There is danger that, if the court does not temper its doctrinaire logic with a little practical wisdom, it will convert the constitutional Bill of Rights into a suicide pact."[5]

However, the notion that the Bill of Rights should be open to contemporary logic and practical wisdom in light of the post-9/11 security environment has not yet resulted in the establishment of coordinated authorities, policies, and doctrine for domestic intelligence, counterintelligence, and counterterrorism. Nor have we seen the implementation of sound strategies that ensure the safety of our civil liberties as dutifully as they protect life and property. While it is imperative that prudent measures be taken to better protect lives and property from legitimate threats, the personal freedoms and civil liberties that our Founding Fathers so masterfully cosseted from potential abuse and abrogation must be protected with equal fervor.

The Need for a Pragmatic Approach

Much has been written recently about how the asymmetric nature of terrorism and the dramatic advances in technology require a pragmatic interpretation of the scope of constitutional civil liberties and creative strategies for the implementation of more effective security measures that defend civil liberties as energetically as they protect people and property.[6] Richard Posner posits in *Not a Suicide Pact: The Constitution in a Time of National Emergency* that the interpretation of constitutional rights should be adjusted in a pragmatic but rational manner in response to the terrorist threat to our national security. Posner categorizes the terrorist threat as "sui generis"—not fitting neatly into legal categories of acts of war or crime—and requiring a tailored regime that affords terrorist suspects fewer constitutional rights than ordinary criminal suspects. Posner argues that the damage to personal liberty must be weighed against the improved security provided by increased security measures in a sort of cost-benefit analysis. Posner, a judge himself, raises the question in this volume of whether the courts should be the primary guardians of our civil rights or if the executive branch is best positioned to make pragmatic judgments regarding liberty and security in times of national crisis.[7]

Posner presents an approach in which constitutional rights of personal liberty, privacy, and public safety are of equal importance, and that marginal adjustments must be made to such rights when they come into conflict during times of national emergency. He contends that constitutional law is intended to be adaptable to changing circumstances and responsive to the flux and pressure of contemporary events. A Constitution that does not bend, Posner contends, will most likely break.

American culture is fickle. At times of national emergency, when we feel vulnerable to a threat—real or imagined—Americans tend to be nationalistic. During times of relative calm and self-assuredness, Americans tend to become contemplative and more liberal in their thinking. But whether they feel threatened or safe, Americans demand pragmatism in policy, procedure, and in their everyday lives.

A pragmatic approach to balancing liberty and security requires several important elements. First, there must be some credible substantiation of the threat that clearly identifies its nature and potential consequences. Second, a comprehensive approach must be developed, based on careful review and, where necessary, amendment of the legal structure for domestic intelligence, counter-intelligence, and oversight. Last, there must be clear leadership in framing the goal for the American people—the achievement of a dynamic balance between civil liberties and national security that provides mechanisms for recalibration as required over time.

However, taking the "not a suicide pact" idea too far and tinkering with the Constitution may jeopardize enduring democratic values and principles of freedom to achieve the somewhat limited short-term benefit of increased security. Is terrorism so great a threat to our national security as to consider bending the Constitution? Some say yes—some say no.

Is the Threat of Terrorism Real?

They that can give up essential liberty to obtain a little temporary safety deserve neither liberty nor safety.

—Benjamin Franklin, 1759

Threats to our national security are numerous and complex. Traditional strategic threats are usually ascribed to peer or near-peer nation-states with the capability and intent to conduct some form of large-scale attack on the United States or its interests, but the events of 9/11 have focused attention on terrorism, which may be conducted by subnational or nonnational groups unhindered by the nation-state construct. Terrorist groups such as al-Qaeda represent strategic threats to the United States due to their demonstrated ability to strike U.S. and other targets worldwide with strategic effect. Other threats to national security include natural and man-made disasters, crime, and the conduct of espionage and sabotage. During World War II the mere presence of a large number of Japanese Americans (citizens and noncitizens alike) inside the United States was interpreted to constitute a strategic threat because it was feared that they were potentially a "fifth column" for the Japanese. The situation today is no less threatening, with over ten million undocumented persons estimated to be inside the United States.

However, there is no universal agreement that the terrorist threat presents a real crisis for national security. Contemporary critics of our current reaction to the events of 9/11 include John Mueller, who, in his recent book *Overblown*, maintains that most of what we hear today from the government and in the media regarding the threat of terrorism is a wild overestimation. Mueller and others contend that there is a tendency to impart undue relevance to extreme events by envisioning them as harbingers rather than as aberrations. Pearl Harbor and the terrorist attacks of 9/11 are examples, Mueller maintains, of just such miscalculations.[8] Mueller and others argue that there is little reason to believe that threats to our national security are any different now than prior to the attacks on the World Trade Center and the Pentagon on September 11, 2001. They maintain that the rhetoric we hear today about the threat of terrorism is largely unjustified, akin to the fearmongering arguments for the internment of Japanese Americans during World War II. Is today's terrorist threat limited in scope and overinflated, or does it represent an existential challenge to our security and way of life so onerous that we should consider tinkering with the fundamental principles of democracy?

The current U.S. intelligence structure was developed in the post–World War II era and has evolved over the last sixty years. And while our national security condition has evolved in response to the dynamic nature of world events since that time, our national security policies, procedures, and organizational structures have not necessarily kept pace. Organizational and procedural changes post-9/11 include the establishment of the Department of Homeland Security

(DHS), the creation of the Office of the Director of National Intelligence (ODNI), organizational changes in the Federal Bureau of Investigation (FBI) and other government organizations, and the passage and reaffirmation of the USA PATRIOT Act—all ostensibly improving the domestic security of the United States. However, it is still unclear if the country is any safer—or if, in fact, our constitutional rights have been unnecessarily eroded and governmental accountability unacceptably diluted by these changes. The debate continues about how best to detect and deter further attacks while preserving the civil liberties and personal freedoms upon which our democracy is based. Finding and maintaining this balance is our greatest domestic security challenge.

Lessons from History

We have been down a similar road at least once before. In late 1941, as war with Japan loomed, the State Department conducted a special study of Japanese Americans to assess the potential threat they might pose as saboteurs, spies, or agents of Japan. Curtis Munson, commissioned by President Roosevelt to prepare the report, concluded that Japanese Americans posed little threat to security. In fact, Munson said he found a remarkable, even extraordinary degree of loyalty among Japanese Americans. The report, however, was closely held and provided only to the State, War, and Navy Departments, and the government never revealed Munson's report when the issue of imprisoning Japanese Americans was discussed.[9]

In contrast to Munson's findings, several key political, military, and public figures of the day contended that people of Japanese ancestry (both citizens and aliens alike) posed a genuine and serious threat to national security, and plans were developed to forcibly remove Japanese Americans from the West Coast and intern them in "Relocation Centers." Supporters of the internment concept included General John L. DeWitt, who had command of the West Coast Defense Forces; Secretary of War Henry Stimson; Treasury Secretary Henry Morgenthau; popular columnist Walter Lippmann; and California Attorney General Earl Warren.[10]

Opposing the internment approach was, among others, Federal Bureau of Investigation Director J. Edgar Hoover, who dismissed the notion that Japanese Americans posed a threat to national security and described the internment as a capitulation to public hysteria. Hoover, who had a prominent role in the Palmer Raids of 1919–1921, told Morgenthau that arrests should not be made unless there was probable cause upon which to justify the arrests. Hoover contended the rights of American citizens should be protected, and he protested the dragnet-type procedures used to remove these individuals from the West Coast.[11] Attorney General Francis Biddle also opposed the internment concept and pointed out that since a large number of Japanese Americans were citizens, any forced removal would violate their constitutional rights. Ultimately, Biddle, like Hoover, was unsuccessful in turning President Franklin Delano Roosevelt against the internment policy and later regretted he had not fought harder against it.[12]

Despite the general lack of evidence that Japanese Americans posed a significant threat to national security, Roosevelt, in response to pressure from the military and general public sentiment, authorized the internment by signing Executive Order 9066, allowing military commanders to designate certain areas as military exclusion zones from which any or all persons could be excluded. The order did not specify the West Coast of the United States as the specific region or Japanese Americans as those targeted for exclusion, but the authority was used to declare that all people of Japanese ancestry would be excluded from the West Coast, including California and parts of Oregon and Washington.[13]

To effect the internment, President Roosevelt set up the War Relocation Authority (WRA) to oversee the forced removal and detention of Japanese Americans from the West Coast, and he appointed Milton Eisenhower, brother of Dwight D. Eisenhower, to head the WRA. The dozen or so internment camps were located in remote parts of the western United States, mostly on Native American land, behind barbed-wire fences replete with armed guards and watchtowers. Milton Eisenhower resigned after several months and would later write: "How could such a tragedy have occurred in a democratic society that prides itself on individual rights and freedoms? I have brooded about this whole episode on and off for the past three decades."[14]

The internment authority established by Executive Order 9066 was later upheld by the Supreme Court of the United States. In hearing the case of Fred Korematsu, a Japanese American who refused to obey the military order to evacuate his home in California in compliance with the order, the Supreme Court upheld the constitutionality of the exclusion, removal, and detention, arguing that it is permissible to curtail the civil rights of a racial group when there is a pressing public necessity.[15] In that case, the "pressing public necessity" was based not upon a documented threat to national security, but essentially on the say-so of the president.

Many years later, however, Congress commissioned a study of the rationale behind the internment, and the Commission on Wartime Relocation and Internment of Civilians (CWRIC) concluded in 1983 that the incarceration of Japanese Americans was not justified by military necessity, but rather was based on race prejudice, war hysteria, and a failure of political leadership.[16] George P. Fletcher writes: "History has been unkind to the Supreme Court's decision in Korematsu. Few, if any, would be persuaded today that safeguarding the equal rights of Japanese Americans would have brought us close to national suicide. Similarly, a huge outcry would occur if the government were to create detention camps for Iraqi Americans now, based on the same reasoning."[17]

However mollifying Fletcher's statement may be, his "lesson has been learned" argument may not hold true if the tragic events of 9/11 are followed by another terrorist attack on the United States resulting in substantial loss of life and property. It is not too difficult to imagine a call, following such an attack, for the detention of identifiable "enemy combatants" and members of potential "sleeper cells" in the United States akin to the call for internment of Japanese Americans during World War II. The lack of a huge public condemnation of the detention of unlawful enemy combatants in Guantanamo Bay after 9/11 casts doubt on the premise that an outcry would occur if the government were to impose sanctions on Iraqi Americans (or other identifiable elements) similar to those imposed in 1942.

The internment of Japanese Americans during World War II raises the question of whether constitutional restrictions on government power give way to urgent practical needs in times of national crisis. There is no easy answer. Patriots on both sides of the argument have debated whether security concerns trump restrictions on governmental power. Despite the widely accepted notion that the internment during World War II was driven less by national security concerns and more by racial bigotry and fearmongering, it should not be overlooked that the nation was at war, the enemy was formidable, the consequences were great, and there was little room for error. In her recent book, Michelle Malkin argues that the internment was a sound military judgment that Franklin Roosevelt and his top advisers made based on intelligence that Japan had organized Japanese resident aliens and their American-citizen children into a vast network of spies and subversives.[18]

One explanation as to why there have been no terrorist attacks in the United States since 9/11, says John Mueller, may be that there are very few, if any, terrorists in the United States and that the terrorists that do exist are far less capable and/or less motivated than we have been led to believe. Mueller's summary argument is that terrorism does not pose the existential threat that we have been led to believe it does, and that we should therefore spend less time, attention, and money defending against worst-case scenarios and concentrate instead on better intelligence, more effective law enforcement, and the disruption of radical foreign groups overseas.

Despite Mueller's argument that terrorism is not as serious a threat to our security that many believe, there is compelling evidence to the contrary. The National Intelligence Estimate (NIE) released in July 2007 on terrorist threats to the homeland judges the United States will face a persistent and evolving terrorist threat. It also assesses that al-Qaeda, the most serious terrorist threat to the U.S. homeland, will focus on targeting the political and economic infrastructure in the United States with the goal of producing mass casualties, visually dramatic destruction, significant economic aftershocks, and/or fear among the U.S. population. Furthermore, the NIE judges that al-Qaeda terrorists will continue to try to acquire and employ chemical, biological, radiological, or nuclear material in attacks to achieve their goals.[19]

Director of National Intelligence Mike McConnell, our top intelligence professional, testified before Congress that the national security threats we face are real and serious. He urged every American citizen to read the unclassified portions of the NIE judgments to dispel the notion that there is no substantial threat to our nation that would justify any additional intelligence collection authorities beyond that which already exists. In his prepared remarks, McConnell expressed his professional belief that while the first responsibility of intelligence is to achieve understanding and to provide warning, there is a dual responsibility to protect American citizens, both in their privacy and against foreign threats. McConnell further stated that the threats to our national security are not limited to terrorism, but extend to clandestine intelligence activities conducted by foreign powers and agents of foreign powers, most notably China and Russia, and the risk of weapons of mass destruction being obtained by transnational terrorist networks. [20]

While the NIE on the Terrorist Threat to the U.S. Homeland concedes that only a handful of individuals with ties to al-Qaeda senior leadership have been discovered in the United States since 9/11, the collective assessment is that the radical segment of the West's Muslim population is expanding in the United States and that al-Qaeda will intensify its efforts to put operatives here. The NIE concludes with the judgment that we will need a greater understanding of how suspicious activities at the local level may relate to strategic threat information, and of how best to identify indicators of terrorist activity in the midst of legitimate activities of law-abiding citizens.[21]

The State Department's *Country Reports on Global Terrorism* provides a strategic assessment of trends in terrorism and the evolving nature of the terrorist threat, and identifies three notable trends: first, the emergence of "micro actors" resulting from U.S. and allied successes in killing, capturing, or isolating much of al-Qaeda's leadership in Afghanistan and in reducing its centralized command and control capability and operational capacity, restricting it to more of an ideological role; second, a trend toward improved sophistication across many areas of operational planning, communications, targeting, and propaganda; and third, an increasing overlap of terrorist activity with international crime with respect to supply, transport, and moneymaking networks.[22]

The Congressional Research Service (CRS) assesses the threat from radical jihadists as more widespread, diffuse, and increasingly homegrown, often with a lack of formal operational connection with al-Qaeda leaders such as Osama bin Laden or Ayman al-Zawahiri. The CRS also identifies emerging trends that may require enhanced policy focus, including attacks that cause economic damage (e.g., attacks on transportation infrastructure, tourism, and oil installations and facilities); the growing number of unattributed terrorist attacks; and the growing power and influence of radical Islamist political parties in foreign nations.[23] If, as the State Department's *Country Reports on Terrorism 2005* indicates, the threat from small terrorist groups or lone terrorists is increasing, then so is the potential for these microactors to inflict deadly harm and costly economic damage. This assessment is consistent with other research and analyses.[24]

Many other organizations and analysts have studied trends in terrorist activity, and in many instances, their analyses are consistent with the trends identified by the State Department. A 2006 report by the Netherlands Central Intelligence

and Security Services cites increasing homegrown terrorism; decentraliza-
tion and implantation of international jihad; radicalization and emergence of
local networks; and incitement of jihad through the Internet, including self-
radicalization, possibly of lone operating terrorists.[25] A 2005 study by the RAND
Corporation also reported trends that indicated an increased focus on civilian
targets; an ongoing emphasis on economic attacks; a continued reliance on suicide attacks; a desire to attack with weapons of mass/complex effects; increased
homegrown attacks; and the possibility of future attacks from the far right, an-
archists, and radical environmentalists.[26]

Some critics question whether the diverse nature of individual terrorists and
terrorist networks allows for meaningful analysis, and others lament that using
past trends as future predictors is inherently problematic. Furthermore, an overreliance on *quantitative* indicators should not be made at the expense of their
qualitative significance. However difficult and subjective, identifying trends as
indicators of terrorist activity can help disrupt future attacks and effectively
prioritize and apply counterterrorism resources.

Balance and Compromise

Achieving a dynamic balance between the imperatives of securing civil liberties
and the safety of Americans will involve three critical elements: adequate mapping and management of domestic intelligence functions; ample planning and
resource allocation; and effective oversight and governance.

The adequate mapping and management of domestic intelligence functions is
a complex task. The Office of the Director of National Intelligence, the Office of
Intelligence and Analysis (OI&A) within the Department of Homeland Security,
the National Counterterrorism Center, the National Security Branch of the Federal Bureau of Investigation, and numerous other elements of the counterterrorism, intelligence, and law enforcement communities have been evolving since
9/11 to more effectively meet the growing threats facing our nation. The success of the domestic response capability depends on progress in the analytical
and organizational domains, including collaboration at all levels of government,
requiring fair and open information-sharing within the appropriate legal and
procedural constraints. And any discussion of domestic security must include
not only the federal government, but also state and local governments as well
as the private sector.

There are several key issues that must be addressed in mapping and managing domestic intelligence functions. Federal, state, local, and tribal authorities,
domestic intelligence responsibilities, and missions must be clearly delineated;
legal authorities should be reaffirmed, established, or modified as appropriate;
policies and procedures that facilitate and optimize domestic intelligence capabilities should be developed and implemented; counterproductive redundancy
should be eliminated; and requisite resources should be identified and assigned.

While these key elements are basic to many similar efforts, the risk associated with counterterrorism makes these urgent and abiding necessities.

Adequate planning and resource allocation depend on a well-developed and coordinated national strategy. Some parts of the collective domestic intelligence community, notably the FBI's National Security Branch and the DHS Office of Intelligence and Analysis, have relatively clear domestic intelligence authorities and responsibilities, as do numerous other federal, state, local, and tribal authorities. What is problematic is the definition and structure of domestic intelligence as a coherent, efficient, and effective national endeavor with appropriate operational parameters; oversight from the executive, legislative, and judicial branches of government; and the understanding and approval of the American people.

During the Korean War, J. Edgar Hoover apparently had his own plan to arrest and imprison over twelve thousand American citizens he suspected of disloyalty. In a recently declassified letter to President Harry Truman's Special Consultant Sidney Souers dated July 7, 1950, Hoover outlines his plan to suspend the writ of habeas corpus and apprehend all individuals potentially dangerous to national security identified in an index that contained approximately twelve thousand individuals, 97 percent of whom were U.S. citizens. Hoover's plan was to respond to four types of emergency situations: attack upon the United States; threatened invasion; attack upon U.S. troops in legally occupied territory; and rebellion. While there is no evidence to suggest that President Truman approved any part of Hoover's plan, the United States has experienced at least two of the four emergency situations described in Hoover's plan, either in the 9/11 attacks or in other terrorist attacks against U.S. interests overseas.

The recent declassification of Hoover's 1950 plan sheds some light on the type of planning and forethought that precedes actions that may have deleterious effects on civil liberty and personal freedoms. Are similar plans in place today to deny U.S. citizens of their constitutional rights (e.g., the right to seek relief from illegal detention) to protect the country against treason, espionage, and sabotage? Should Iraqi Americans or Muslim Americans be fearful of losing their civil liberties or their personal freedoms?

Effective oversight and governance may be the most critical ingredients to achieving a dynamic, healthy balance between security and liberty—especially in planning and execution. Congressional intelligence committees were established in the mid-1970s precisely for this purpose and long enjoyed a reputation for effectively performing bipartisan oversight functions. The committees provide an outside check on actions by the executive branch and are often in a position to bring about necessary change—something that is not easily achieved within the executive branch itself. However, since 9/11, political infighting within Congress has resulted in diminished bipartisanship and has reduced the overall effectiveness of the two intelligence committees. Public confidence is eroding at a time when the American people need to have faith that the balance between national security and civil liberty is being objectively and professionally considered, and that oversight by the Congress actually works. As Britt Snider aptly states, "[U]ntil the committees reestablish themselves as credible, authoritative voices, their role as overseers and producers of change within the intelligence community is going to suffer."[27]

Our three branches of government have taken somewhat different approaches to the question of how far the national security versus civil liberty pendulum should swing. President George W. Bush issued an order after the terrorist attacks of 9/11 that effectively allowed the United States to hold suspects indefinitely without a legal hearing, access to a lawyer, or formal charges. Congress passed a law suspending the writ of habeas corpus for anyone deemed an "unlawful enemy combatant," and the Supreme Court has affirmed the right of U.S. citizens to seek a writ of habeas corpus. In June 2008 the Supreme Court ruled that persons detained at Guantanamo Bay have the legal right to access the United States courts.

Effective oversight may be the key to countering the belief that national security decisions rest primarily with the executive branch and there is little need for either cooperation or coordination among the branches of government. Jack L. Goldsmith, former head of the Justice Department's Office of Legal Counsel, writes, "I was astonished, and immensely worried, to discover that some of our most important counterterrorism policies rested on severely damaged legal foundations." Goldsmith testified before Congress that he could not find a legal basis for some aspects of the National Security Agency's terrorist surveillance program and that Justice Department legal opinions on the NSA program were fundamentally flawed. Goldsmith, referring to David Addington, Vice President Richard Cheney's Chief of Staff, writes that "he and, I presumed, his boss viewed power as the absence of constraint. They believed cooperation and compromise signaled weakness and emboldened the enemies of America and the executive branch."[28]

Adding to the growing concern for the legitimacy of terrorism legislation, U.S. District Judge Ann Aiken ruled that two provisions of the USA PATRIOT Act are unconstitutional and permit the executive branch of government to conduct surveillance and searches of American citizens without satisfying the probable cause requirements of the Fourth Amendment. In her opinion, which at the time of this writing is under judicial review, Judge Aiken wrote that "for over 200 years, this Nation has adhered to the rule of law—with unparalleled success. A shift to a Nation based on extra-constitutional authority is prohibited, as well as ill-advised."[29]

The debate is becoming more polarized, and the prospects for crafting a compromise that will satisfy both intelligence community officials concerned about conducting surveillance against terrorists and civil libertarians who demand robust protections for American citizens are not encouraging. There seems to be a growing divide between the two camps, fueled by seemingly partisan politics that stems from the handling of ongoing NSA surveillance efforts under the legal framework of the Foreign Intelligence Surveillance Act. A compromise that would allow aggressive surveillance of terrorists (and others who pose threats to national security) while providing an effective oversight mechanism that would protect American citizens and their constitutional rights may be out of reach at the moment.

Conclusion

A plan without action is daydream; action without a plan is nightmare.

—Japanese Proverb

There are at least three key elements of any strategy for the future if the nation is to be prepared for threats to liberty and security. These elements, involving each of the three branches of our government, must find a way to work toward a common goal with commitment and integrity. There is no room for partisan politics or gamesmanship—the stakes are too high. The ultimate goal is to protect the core values of liberty and security with equal vigor, and to do so in a way that earns the confidence of the American people.

The executive branch of the federal government must develop a comprehensive approach to intelligence that includes the interrelated aspects of foreign intelligence, counterintelligence, law enforcement intelligence, and domestic intelligence. This approach must be designed not only to meet the needs of the current environment, but to be a lasting architecture upon which future adjustments can be laid. The executive branch must be willing to find a compromise between the extremes in order to reach a dynamic balance between civil liberty and security. It may take trial and error, and a number of iterations, before a comfortable solution is achieved. Effective political leadership is key to success, and the executive branch must demonstrate the willingness to take the lead in developing a comprehensive structure and strategy for intelligence in the twenty-first century.

We should carefully consider past events that have taken this country down similar paths. Are there lessons to be learned from the Palmer Raids of 1919–1921 and the internment of Japanese Americans during World War II? How do we determine the proper balance between civil liberty and national security, and do we have adequate procedures in place to help implement our policies?

We must ensure that our intelligence policies are updated to accommodate the rapid technological changes that have transpired in recent years. Many of our fundamental intelligence policies are based on outdated technologic foundations. A comprehensive review of intelligence is needed to ensure that our capabilities and strategies are aligned with the priorities and intent of their use.

The National Security Act of 1947 identifies the intelligence discipline as consisting of foreign intelligence and counterintelligence. The Act defines foreign intelligence as information of potential intelligence value concerning the capabilities, intentions, and activities of any foreign power, organization, or associated personnel. Counterintelligence is defined as information gathered and activities conducted to protect against espionage, other intelligence activities, sabotage, or assassinations conducted by or for foreign governments or elements thereof, foreign organizations, foreign persons, or international terrorist activities. There is no mention of domestic intelligence or other types of intelligence. It is becoming less clear how traditional foreign intelligence and counterintelligence disciplines interface with emerging counterterrorism and domestic intelligence functions in the post-9/11 era, as Jennifer Sims suggests in her introductory piece.[30]

The United States possesses the most robust intelligence collection and analysis capability in the world. The good news is that we can apply the full measure of these capabilities to focus on foreign threats to vital national interests; the bad news is that if these same capabilities are applied internally, they jeopardize the personal freedoms and civil liberties that are the foundation of our democratic society. We must update our intelligence lexicon to address new functions related to counterterrorism and domestic intelligence, and we must assess the impact of a nontraditional adversary—the transnational terrorist organization—on our policies, organizations, processes, and strategies. Unless and until a comprehensive approach is taken to maintain a balance between liberty and security, we will likely continue to experience the knee-jerk approach that frequently results in a giant step backward for civil liberty in order to achieve marginal improvements to national security.

The executive branch must not operate on a "trust me" basis when it comes to decisions that tilt the balance between civil liberty and security. Collaboration with the other branches of government is necessary to maintain the effectiveness of the separation of powers. The solution cannot be dictated by the executive branch but must involve the totality of government to most effectively establish a framework for the future that respects the concept of checks and balances and the theory of separated powers.

The need for adequate and appropriate oversight of intelligence activities is essential. Past abuses of intelligence are well documented. Future abuses may well be unavoidable, but a strong oversight apparatus will scrutinize policy and procedure and minimize abuse. By its very nature, our intelligence community operates at the edge of legality and public acceptance, so strong oversight is necessary to protect us from ourselves. We need to be creative in our ability to apply the legal authorities and procedural frameworks to successfully navigate in an increasingly complex world against players who show no compunction about not playing by the rules. We must find ways to streamline, simplify, and professionalize intelligence oversight so that we can improve our ability to collectively defend our nation, our freedoms, our privacy, and our civil liberties. These must not be mutually exclusive objectives.

The key elements of oversight in our separation-of-powers approach to democracy involve all three branches of government. The executive branch must put in place effective mechanisms for self-oversight on the operational end, while the judicial and legislative branches must exercise external checks-and-balance functions. In times of national crisis, when the executive branch generally exerts more power, it is incumbent on the other oversight bodies to ensure that our civil liberties and personal privacy are not needlessly sacrificed in the name of national security. Strong leadership is essential.

The legislative branch is frequently responsible for granting the executive branch more power in the first place, but it can also check the power by incorporating sunset provisions that nullify the legislation after a certain date. The Protect America Act is a case in point—Congress granted the executive branch broad authorities for intelligence collection, but included a six-month sunset clause that requires further debate if the authorities are to be continued. The legislative branch can also exercise oversight through effective use of legislative committees (for example, the Homeland Security Committee or the Intelligence Committee) and special commissions like the 9/11 Commission. Ultimately, however, the effectiveness of legislative oversight will rest on how dutifully it performs its legislative functions and whether it allows the executive branch to circumvent its direction.

The judicial branch also has an important oversight role to play when liberties are threatened in times of national emergency. The judicial branch can check those actions of government that affect basic liberties—like the right of habeas corpus and the right to trial by jury—by declaring violations of civil liberties unconstitutional. Ultimately, in order to perform its oversight function effectively, the judiciary must be ready, willing, and able to challenge executive branch actions and powers from a bipartisan perspective.

It is incumbent on each of us to understand the true nature and magnitude of the threat and to ensure that our government and elected officials take the actions necessary "to establish Justice, insure domestic Tranquility, provide for the common defence, promote the general Welfare, and secure the Blessings of Liberty" in a balanced approach that protects our constitutional rights as effectively as it protects people and property.

While the professionals who analyze the intelligence and sift through the chatter tell us that the terrorist threat to our national security is real and potent, we should be cautious and prudent in our response—especially when our actions may threaten the very institutions of democracy that we hold so dear. In light of recent debates in Congress and in the media regarding the new rules for domestic intelligence that may be required by the war on terror to balance the equation between civil liberties and national security, we must ensure that necessary and prudent steps are taken to protect people and property from legitimate threats to security while ensuring that privacy and civil liberty protections and the American way of life are not compromised.

A plaque at the site of the former World War II Relocation Camp in the desert outside Poston, Arizona, is engraved with this prophetic epitaph: "May it serve as a constant reminder of our past so that Americans in the future will never again be denied their constitutional rights and may the remembrance of that experience serve to advance the evolution of the human spirit." While we debate how best to balance civil liberties and national security, let not the cost of security be the freedoms we intend to secure.

Notes

1. David M. Kennedy, *Over Here: The First World War and American Society* (New York: Oxford University Press, 1980), 24.

2. Testimony of John L. DeWitt, April 13, 1943, House Naval Affairs Subcommittee to Investigate Congested Areas, Part 3, 78th Cong., 1st Sess.), 739–40,cited in http://caselaw .lp.findlaw.com/scripts/getcase.pl?court=US&vol=323&invol=214#fff1.

3. In addition to the 19 hijackers, 2,974 people died as an immediate result of the attacks on the World Trade Center and the Pentagon on September 11, 2001. There were 4,186 U.S. military fatalities in Iraq and 613 in Afghanistan as of October 20, 2008. Available at www.defenselink.mil/news.

4. Paul Brest, Sanford Levinson, Jack M. Balkin, Akhil Reed Amar, and Reva B. Seigel, *Processes of Constitutional Decisionmaking: Cases and Materials*, 6th ed. (New York: Aspen Law & Business, 2006), 65–67.

5. In *Terminiello v. Chicago*, the Supreme Court overruled the disorderly conduct conviction of a priest whose pro-Nazi speech at a rally had incited a riot and found that Chicago's breach of the peace ordinance violated the First Amendment. The Oyez Project, *Terminiello v. Chicago*, 337 U.S. 1 (1949), available at www.oyez.org/cases/ 1940-1949/1948/1948_272/

6. Richard Posner presents a case for strong action in *Preventing Surprise Attacks: Intelligence Reform in the Wake of 9/11* (Lanham, MD: Rowman & Littlefield, 2005) and in *Uncertain Shield: The U.S. Intelligence System in the Throes of Reform* (Lanham, MD: Rowman & Littlefield, 2006); David Cole and James X. Dempsey warn that civil liberties are being sacrificed without effectively protecting national security in *Terrorism and the Constitution: Sacrificing Civil Liberties in the Name of National Security* (New York: New Press, 2006); and M. Katherine B. Darmer, Robert M. Baird, and Stuart E. Rosenbaum present a collection of opinions on the trade-offs between national security and civil liberties in *Civil Liberties vs. National Security in a Post-9/11 World* (Amherst, NY: Prometheus Books, 2004).

7. See Richard A. Posner, *Not a Suicide Pact: The Constitution in a Time of National Emergency* (Oxford, UK: Oxford University Press, 2006).

8. John Mueller, *Overblown: How Politicians and the Terrorism Industry Inflate National Security Threats, and Why We Believe Them* (New York: Free Press, 2006).

9. Michi Weglyn, *Years of Infamy* (New York: Morrow Quill Paperbacks, 1976), 33–53.

10. Earl Warren was elected governor of California in November 1942 and later became Chief Justice of the United States. Some believe he backed the internment of the Japanese Americans to promote his candidacy for governor.

11. W. Ray Wannall, *The Real J. Edgar Hoover* (Paducah, KY: Turner Publishing Co., 2000), 69.

12. *Personal Justice Denied: Report of the Commission on Wartime Relocation and Internment of Civilians*, Washington DC, 1982. Available at www.nps.gov/history/ history/online_books/personal_justice_denied/index.htm.

13. See Executive Order 9066.

14. Michi Weglyn, *Years of Infamy* (New York: Morrow Quill Paperbacks, 1976), 299.

15. See *Korematsu v. United States*, majority opinion by Justice Hugo Black. Available at www.findlaw.com.

16. *Personal Justice Denied: Report of the Commission on Wartime Relocation and Internment of Civilians*, Washington DC, 1982.

17. George P. Fletcher, *The Cliché That "The Constitution Is not a Suicide Pact": Why It Is Actually Pro-, Not Anti-, Civil Liberties*, FindLaw Legal News and Commentary, January 7, 2003. Available at http://writ.news.findlaw.com/scripts/printer_friendly .pl?page=/commentary/20030107_fletcher.html.

18. See Michelle Malkin, *In Defense of Internment: The World War II Round-Up and What It Means For America's War on Terror* (Washington, DC: Regnery, 2004).

19. See National Intelligence Estimate, *The Terrorist Threat to the U.S. Homeland*, July 2007. It should be noted, however, that caveats and explanations of the estimative language that accompany the NIE cover a lot of ground. The caveats state, for example, that the NIE is trying to convey an analytical assessment based upon incomplete or fragmentary information; may be based directly on collected information or may be founded on previous judgments; and is not intended to be interpreted as fact, proof, or knowledge.

20. See Statement for the Record of J. M. McConnell, Director of National Intelligence, before the Judiciary Committee, House of Representatives, September 18, 2007. Unclassified portions of the NIE are available at www.dni.gov.

21. National Intelligence Estimate, *The Terrorist Threat to the U.S. Homeland*, July 2007.

22. See *Country Reports on Terrorism, 2005*, United States Department of State Publication 11324, Office of the Coordinator for Counterterrorism, released April 2006.

23. Raphael Perl, *Trends in Terrorism*, Congressional Research Service Report for Congress RL33555 (2006).

24. See *Terrorism Future: Tactics, Strategy, and Stealth*, by Peter Probst in Hi-Impact Terrorism: Proceedings of a Russian American Workshop, National Research Council (Washington, DC: National Academies Press, 2002), 260–67.

25. See *Violent Jihad in the Netherlands: Current Trends in the Islamist Terrorist Threat*. Available at http://English.nctb.nl/images/Violent%20jihad%20in%20the%20 Netherlands%202006_tcm127–112471.pdf.

26. See *Trends in Terrorism, Threats to the United States and the Future of the Terrorism Risk Insurance Act*, by Peter Chalk et al., RAND, Center for Terrorism and Risk Management Policy, 2005.

27. See L. Britt Snider, "Congressional Oversight of Intelligence after September 11," in *Transforming U.S. Intelligence*, ed. Jennifer E. Sims and Burton Gerber (Washington, DC: Georgetown University Press, 2005), 239–55.

28. Jack L. Goldsmith, *The Terror Presidency: Law and Judgment Inside the Bush Administration* (New York: W.W. Norton, 2007).

29. Dan Eggen, "Patriot Act Provisions Voided: Judge Rules Law gives Executive branch Too Much Power," *Washington Post*, September 27, 2007. See also R.R. 3162, "Uniting and Strengthening America by Providing Appropriate Tools Required to Intercept and Obstruct Terrorism (USA PATRIOT ACT) Act of 2001."

30. See the National Security Act of 1947, Pub. L. No. 235, 80th Cong., 61 Stat. 496, which realigned and reorganized the United States' armed forces, foreign policy, and the intelligence community.

II

TOOLS AND TACTICS

5

Robert Wallace

A Time for Counterespionage

The General to the American Ambassador: Incidentally, they know your code.
American Ambassador: We know they know our code. Sure, we only give them things we want them to know.
(Later) The General to the Soviet Ambassador: Incidentally, they know you know their code.
Soviet Ambassador: We have known for some time that they know we know their code.
(Still later) The General to the American Ambassador: They know you know they know you know

  . . .

American Ambassador: Are you sure?
The General: You mean you didn't know?[1]

THESE LINES from Peter Ustinov's award-winning Cold War comic spoof illustrate for many the game of competing intelligence services trapped in a seemingly endless, meaningless espionage cycle. The exchange between the general and the ambassador conjures up the image of two players permanently immobilized in contorted positions on a Twister mat. In addition to being good theater, the dialogue is at once humorous and instructive. One need not be a counterintelligence professional to recognize the humor and futility of such endless, open-loop spy-versus-spy sequences.[2] Even government treasuries would tire of paying for such foolishness. Yet the Twister analogy offers another, more subtle, insight for intelligence officers. There can be a winner—it will be the contestant who is able to walk away from the mat at the time of his choosing after freezing the opponent in a position from which he cannot recover.

Intelligence organizations face a never-ending challenge of protecting their own secrets while developing capabilities and operations to obtain the secrets of their adversaries. The emerging twenty-first-century issues confronting U.S. intelligence agencies include a reassessment of counterintelligence strategies. This article will address the need for counterespionage to play a larger role in the nation's counterintelligence strategy.

In its broadest form, counterintelligence (CI) encompasses all elements required for developing and executing a strategy to protect a nation's secrets. For most Americans, one aspect of CI is captured in the U.S. Oath of Citizenship with the words "I will support and defend the Constitution and laws of the United States of America against all enemies, foreign and domestic." In this context CI is understood as a combination of law enforcement activity and military defense implemented through institutions granted analytical, security, investigative, and protective authorities.

Under the Executive Order governing U.S. intelligence activities, counterintelligence encompasses information gathered and activities conducted to protect against espionage and other specified intelligence activities of foreign powers, but it excludes most security programs.[3] Other definitions of counterintelligence emphasize the protection of classified or sensitive information and the security of facilities and persons holding such information.[4] Counterintelligence objectives are served using both offensive (running double agents) and defensive (document classification, personnel background checks, security investigations, fences and safes) means to safeguard the nation's secrets.[5] Published counterintelligence analysis and discussions emphasize the defensive and protective elements of the profession, with offensive counterespionage usually occupying a boutique status.[6]

While counterintelligence and counterespionage sometimes appear interchangeable, this essay will characterize counterespionage as the covert and clandestine measures directed against opposition intelligence services to understand, penetrate, and thwart their operations. In our Twister analogy, counterespionage successes arise from CI-directed offensive actions that immobilize the opponent and preserve the ability of the victor to walk away at the time of his choosing. Players of the counterespionage "game" are unlikely to be satisfied with a draw.

The American Target: Strengths and Vulnerabilities

Other contributors to this volume have made the persuasive case that U.S. classified information and industrial proprietary data are under persistent, directed attack by foreign governments and other adversaries. Americans, quite reasonably, have a problem believing what they cannot see. So the point bears repeating: Foreign economic, political, and military espionage against the United States is as old as the nation and has intensified in the past century.

The successes of these foreign spies are instructive. In the late 1920s, for example, nearly two decades before Soviet spies drained atomic secrets for Stalin from his World War II American "ally," the Russian musical and technical genius Lev Theremin became the toast of New York. Theremin arrived in the United States with "a little extra assignment" from his covert sponsor, the GRU Fourth Department (Soviet military intelligence) to report on U.S. military technology and industry.[7] Over the next ten years, the internationally acclaimed entertainer distracted the population with captivating music and worked to "pick their pockets clean."[8] In 1938 Theremin voluntarily returned to the Union of Soviet Socialist Republics (USSR) and soon thereafter was imprisoned. For years as a prisoner and then after being released, he continued his secret scientific work for a succession of Soviet intelligence organizations, until his retirement in 1964.[9]

Theremin was accompanied by many "fellow travelers" and agents who were doing secret work for the Soviet Union during the 1930s and 1940s. German agents also infiltrated the United States to serve the interests of Hitler's Germany through the same period. The FBI, with it national responsibility for counterintelligence, conducted counterintelligence investigations of suspected Soviet and German agents, and most German spies were caught before they could do much damage. There was less success against the Soviet agents, as the FBI focused primarily on the Communist Party (CPUSA) and its agents until after 1945, when U.S. perceptions of the USSR began shifting.[10] Throughout the 1930s and during the war years, Soviet spies penetrated the U.S. nuclear weapons program, and others, like Theremin, worked for years before being discovered, retiring, or fleeing the country.[11] In a foreword to the declassified Venona documents, William P. Crowell observed, "There can no longer be any doubt about the widespread and successful Soviet espionage operations against the United States and Great Britain during the 1940s."[12]

This scenario, catching the spy after the damage was done, would be repeated throughout the Cold War most spectacularly in 1985, 1994, and 2001 with Navy, National Security Agency (NSA), Central Intelligence Agency (CIA), Federal Bureau of Investigation (FBI) and Defense Intelligence Agency (DIA) moles John Walker, Larry Wu-Tai Chin, Ronald Pelton, Aldrich Ames, Robert Hanssen, and Anna Montes. The arrest of four other individuals in February 2008 on charges of spying underscored China's continuing espionage operations against the United States[13]

One lesson from these cases is that as long as counterintelligence is primarily reactive, U.S. defenses will continue to be overwhelmed. The Defense Personnel Security Research Center (PERSEREC) has documented and analyzed more than 150 cases of espionage by U.S. citizens since World War II, including those of Walker, Pelton, Ames, and Montes.[14] According to PERSEREC data, with only two exceptions since 1974, one or more arrests for espionage were made every year. Other counterintelligence successes that remain secret are known to national security policymakers and the intelligence oversight committees of Congress.

Successful espionage operations, whether those of the United States, its allies, or its adversaries, are prima facie evidence that the security systems of the nations involved have exploitable gaps. In 2003 the FBI stated that there are more foreign spies operating in the United States today than at any other point in our history.[15] Spies from more than two dozen countries have penetrated most U.S. national security agencies, including all branches of the military and the frontline intelligence organizations, in the thirty years between 1975 and 2004. These penetrations included the CIA, the NSA, the FBI, and the Department of State's Bureau of Intelligence and Research (INR), as well as major defense contractors.[16] The damage from these known spies has been significant, and the number of ongoing investigations suggests that adversaries are continuing to initiate new espionage operations.[17] These statistics represent, however, only arrests. Hundreds of cases remain under active investigation, and many others have been closed due to lack of sufficient evidence to prosecute.

We face the reality that persons convicted for espionage represent a tiny percentage of the American citizens and foreign nationals who operate as either agents or intelligence officers in the United States. No counterintelligence professional would assert that even a majority the spies operating in the United States have been caught or even identified. Given the reality that many spies are never identified, coupled with a relatively small annual number of significant arrests over the past forty years, the evidence seems compelling that our security strategy is inadequate. In an interview with a U.S. espionage historian following the collapse of the Soviet Union, a senior KGB clandestine photography officer said, "The spy cases [in America] you have known are from arrests of my former students who made mistakes. My best students you have never heard of because they paid attention, learned their tradecraft lessons well, and returned home successfully and quietly."[18] The inescapable conclusion is that foreign intelligence services are consistently finding and exploiting seams in our counterintelligence armor.

Sources of Weakness

The level of damage caused by foreign spies operating against the United States suggests that there are persistent weaknesses in U.S. counterintelligence. The problem is broader than the theft of classified documents alone; the U.S. government policy has failed to address the strategic significance of the layered attacks against it. A former colleague at the CIA, James R. Gosler, observes in a companion chapter in this volume that during the height of the Cold War and despite billions of dollars spent on satellites, sensors, signal intercepts, and human operations to gather intelligence, U.S. policymakers did not comprehend the Soviets' overall intelligence strategy or the breadth of their operations. He suggests that this indifference to strategic counterintelligence may be attributed to an American political culture accompanied by arrogance and naiveté toward the capabilities of our adversaries.

United States leadership has generally been reluctant to sanction "high-pain" actions against the spy and his sponsor unless a "smoking gun" of espionage has been produced.[19] One example is the Cold War Soviet program focused on acquiring advanced Western technology by every possible means, legal and illegal. U.S. companies represented the primary target. CIA analyst Gus Weiss asserted that his warnings of Soviet technology espionage were downplayed by

the Nixon, Ford, and Carter administrations during the years of SALT negotiations and détente. In 1981, however, Weiss's analysis was vindicated when
the French provided reporting that revealed strategic KGB and GRU targeting
of U.S. technology and clandestine operations to acquire design, components,
and entire systems since the 1960s. A KGB officer spying for the French service revealed details of a Soviet intelligence program that had been only partly
understood by U.S. intelligence for more than a decade.[20] The Reagan administration responded to this threat and other intelligence provocations in October
1986 by ordering eighty Soviet diplomats out of the USSR's UN mission, the
Washington embassy, and the San Francisco consulate.[21]

A third reason for U.S. weakness has been, quite simply, our adversaries'
strengths. Technology theft was only a portion of the full Soviet intelligence
attack on the West in general and the United States in particular. Sustained KGB
propaganda and disinformation operations sought to undermine and discredit
U.S. officials and policy through four decades beginning in the 1950s.[22] Throughout the Cold War Soviet intelligence organizations conducted worldwide signals
and communications collection (SIGINT/COMMINT) using the best technology of the time. These operations were backed by a high level of sustained funding and the support of Kremlin leadership.[23] The U.S. embassy in Moscow was a
continuous target. When foreign embassies in Moscow were evacuated in 1941
as the German army approached the city, Lavrentiy Beria instructed the NKVD
to hardwire the vacated buildings with microphones. After the buildings were
reoccupied in 1944, 120 hidden microphones were found in the U.S. facility.[24]

The Soviets never stopped. Four decades later CIA technical imagination conceived, built, tested, and deployed a collection system whose results proved the
Soviets had penetrated the construction system by lacing the concrete pillars
with electronic bugs and collection devices. So serious was the problem that
in 1985, President Reagan ordered construction stopped.[25] Decades of SIGINT
collection from the antenna-congested roof of the USSR's embassy in the low-
lying downtown area of Washington was enhanced when the Soviets built a
new compound on Mount Alto, one of the highest hills of the city. Soviet "business" and "scientific" enterprises such as Aeroflot, AMTORG, the State Committee for Science and Technology (GKNT), Intourist, Technopromexport, and
Eksportkleb, all of which negotiated, traded, and promoted exchange visits with
American commercial and research firms, were laced with intelligence officers
and operatives. The USSR's UN mission, its San Francisco consulate, and the
Washington embassy were staffed with personnel—many of whom were KGB or
GRU—far beyond the numbers actually required for diplomatic functions.

Finally, the Soviets were not reluctant to support and use cooperating allies,
including Cuba, East Germany, Czechoslovakia, Hungary, Poland, and others,
in pursuit of intelligence goals. Cuban double agents in the 1980s provided the
Soviets with information about the CIA's advanced covert communications
gear. Karl Koecher, born in Czechoslovakia and trained as an intelligence officer,
"defected" in Austria in 1965 and immigrated to the United States that same

year. He acquired U.S. citizenship in 1971 and eventually became a translator for the CIA. In reality Koecher was a spy and provided information that was eventually given to the KGB and led to the arrest in 1977 of a top CIA agent in Moscow, code-named TRIGON. The East German spymaster Markus Wolf enjoyed the professional and personal respect of top Soviet officials because of his many contributions to the KGB.[26] Among the intelligence jewels Wolf claimed to have offered were U.S. embassy and CIA communications between Europe and Africa. According to Wolf, these messages, intercepted by a West German listening post in Spain, were clandestinely acquired by East German agents who "let the West Germans do the dirty work [for us] of spying on their American Allies."[27]

Fourth, the United States has had trouble sustaining active and offensive counterintelligence strategies during periods of either strategic détente with a major adversary or heightened tensions with "hard target" states. Soviet and Eastern Bloc illegal acquisition of Western technology during the Cold War took advantage of American business interests and the policy of détente. Coordinated, worldwide operations began in the 1960s, well over a decade before reporting from *FAREWELL*, the KGB officer spying for the French, confirmed the specifics of the program to acquire restricted and classified technology.[28] During the 1980s the discovery of compromised Selectric typewriters in the U.S. embassy in Moscow revealed the KGB's sustained and sophisticated technical attacks against U.S. diplomatic installations.[29]

With respect to hard targets, Cuba, Iraq, and Iran have been high on the U.S. list over the past half century. Yet reportedly all of the CIA's Cuban agents before 1987 were doubled and operated for years under the control of Cuban Intelligence Service handlers. Soviet intelligence operated a modern intercept station at Lourdes, Cuba, directed against U.S. satellite and telephone communications.[30] The 9/11 aircraft hijackers spent months on U.S. soil preparing for the operation before taking action.[31] More recently, the existence and status of weapons of mass destruction (WMD) programs in Iraq, Libya, North Korea, and Iran were effectively masked by their respective governments' propaganda and deception operations.

Keeping a Balance Sheet

Rampant as Soviet spies and hard-target deception operations may have been since WWII, it is important to consider three related questions when balancing gains and losses: Which side used its advantages more effectively, elevated tactical advantages into strategic ones, and timed its exploits more productively for policymakers?

By these measures, the U.S. counterintelligence record during the Cold War is mixed. A number of spies were identified, imprisoned, or expelled from the country. These actions temporarily disrupted Soviet collection programs, and the KGB's propaganda, or "active measures," efforts in the United States were exposed.[32] Yet, despite these achievements, a counterespionage gap remains at the strategic level between what we confidently know about individual foreign espionage operations and our understanding of the adversaries' intelligence strategy and the scope of their operations. Too often the United States has failed to discover, anticipate, and neutralize the clandestine activities of foreign services, whether those be collection, sabotage, or deception.

Discovering why these failures occur is difficult. Most assessments of U.S. defensive counterintelligence capabilities, both success and failure, are Soviet-centric and filtered through a cloud of the twenty-year history of the late James Angleton's domination of CIA's counterintelligence operations.[33] Three decades after Angleton's forced retirement and the dismantlement of his CI empire in 1975, Sam Papich, Angleton's ally at the FBI, asserted that the CIA's "counterintelligence capability has never been reconstructed."[34] While this is overstatement, a judgment that Angleton's nearly singular focus on defense through mole hunting within the CIA stymied the maturation of the Agency's offensive counterespionage operational culture seems accurate.[35] Angleton's confidence in Anatoli Golitsyn and his growing obsession with finding the CIA mole to the exclusion of other Soviet operations points to two persistent challenges facing counterintelligence analysis—the need for independent validation of judgments and the difficulty of integrating inconsistent information from multiple sources.

Yet perhaps more important to counterintelligence success than restraining overzealous officers is the ability to identify which are the most important intelligence services to counter, and to recruit spies in them. The task of recruiting one source inside an adversary's intelligence structure can be monumental, and in most instances, more than one is necessary for assured continuity and validation of reporting. Overreliance on a single source and the accompanying mixture of factual and interpretative information for both counterintelligence and policy analysis becomes dangerous. There is neither a means of independent corroboration nor a capacity to refresh his reporting as time passes, and the adversary adjusts operations to compensate for the defection.

After Angleton's departure, new CIA leadership opened more windows into counterintelligence as a core mission and included aspects beyond countering Soviet operations. Case officers received greater encouragement to integrate CI into all operations. However, work and reporting on counterintelligence targets often did not receive the same cachet as recruiting agents who reported on foreign policies and intentions or military subjects. Over time, officers concentrating on CI cases usually recruited fewer agents, and the distribution of CI reports was, for good reason, sharply limited. Although high-value foreign intelligence did come from recruited foreign intelligence officers, the stream of CI information they produced was less likely to appear in the president's daily briefing book. When a CIA officer became involved with a counterespionage operation, the compartmentation of the activity, with a few exceptions, often precluded the officer from ever seeing it "count" as a step to promotion. For the majority of case officers the path to career success was seen in recruiting and handling assets who could regularly report on policy, plans, and intentions, rather than pursuing counterintelligence and counterespionage targets.

Double-agent operations are, in any event, very tricky to manage. One tragic example concerns the case of a jointly run FBI-CIA double agent named Nicholas Shadrin.[36] Shadrin, a Soviet naval captain who had defected to the United States, was recruited as a double agent. Shadrin led several years of a double life before accepting an assignment to meet his Soviet handlers in Vienna in December 1975. He was never seen again. Within counterintelligence lore, the case remains a persistent reminder of human risks generated by aggressive counterespionage and, in particular, double-agent operations.[37] Shadrin's tragic end has been traced to an essential and sometimes overlooked element of sound tradecraft—the necessity of operational testing. The KGB, acting either prudently or because of suspicion, developed an operational test of Shadrin by requesting a meeting in Canada. Through the reporting from a penetration of the Canadian service, the KGB calculated they would learn if the Americans informed the Canadians of the meeting and thus be able to confirm that Shadrin was a double agent.[38]

Professional intelligence services conduct operational testing of this kind because they recognize that agent motivation, loyalty, courage, and circumstances may change over time. Permanent reliability cannot be assumed. Discreet countersurveillance can detect where an agent goes after a meeting and whether instructions are followed. Phone and communications intercepts can reveal an agent's contacts that might have been kept secret from his handler. Agents may be given requirements to obtain information that is already known to determine if he has access or is accurately reporting. In cases where one agent is the sole source of intelligence that might drive national policy, the necessity for testing and validation becomes an operational imperative.

Today U.S. counterintelligence faces multiple adversaries with new technological means of acquiring sensitive information, targets that extend beyond government institutions and an increased presence within the United States. As adversaries continue to adapt their operations to exploit seams in our security, their presence can go largely unnoticed. The National Counterintelligence Executive (NCIX) has warned against ignoring our vulnerabilities by believing that "since they can't be seen [like microbes], then they don't exist."[39] Counterespionage operations can contribute significantly both to creating a broader awareness of "the microbes" and to reducing their damaging impact. The United States needs to focus on improving its capacities to find insider spies, recruit its own, and validate all through operational testing.

America's Counterespionage Challenge

The extent and the successes of Soviet spying during the Cold War, the number of nations conducting espionage in the United States, plus terrorist capabilities to inflict substantial damage on the homeland as outlined in the 9/11 Commission report, suggest two twenty-first-century counterespionage challenges for the United States. First, we must eradicate any remaining notions of our own invincibility and naiveté toward their intentions. Second, to meet the new types of threats we face from terrorists and technology-enabled espionage, we will need to attend to the challenges of conducting counterespionage operations consistent with law and regulations governing organizational authorities and citizen rights—a challenge covered in detail in other chapters in this volume and so only briefly discussed below.

The successes foreign services have had operating against the United States reflect not just U.S. weaknesses, but the growing professionalism of adversarial services. History illustrates that over time, intelligence services adapt their tradecraft to defeat counterintelligence measures. For nearly a century, the Soviet, and now the Russian, services have conducted sustained clandestine operations against the United States based on the tradecraft standards, experience, and training that are characteristic of professional espionage organizations. Such professionalism is taught, learned, practiced, and passed on by successive generations of intelligence officers in all services—German, Cuban, French, Israeli, Russian, Chinese, British, Pakistani, or Korean. Each develops officers with skills and uses its asset base and technical devices as needed to operate securely in hostile (to them) environments. We should not be surprised that those who target the United States are successful—they are constantly adapting and changing in response to our improving defenses.

The United States has made similar efforts to develop its professionalism in this area. Beginning in the late 1960s, the CIA began building the capability to handle some agents and conduct technical operations in Moscow despite the KGB's pervasive surveillance and counterintelligence apparatus and difficulties with Angleton. These operational successes multiplied in the 1970s but only after two decades of setbacks, experience, and learning. Between 1975 and 1985, one-of-a-kind technical collection systems and more than a dozen agents were successfully run in the USSR under the nose of the KGB. These operations remained undetected by the massive KGB's defensive counterintelligence network of technical countermeasures, security investigations, and surveillance until American traitors who knew about the clandestine activities reported that information to the Soviets.

U.S. professionalism has been largely honed, however, against adversaries that have either disappeared (for example, the USSR) or changed dramatically. As foreign intelligence services grow in number, sophistication, and boldness, their differing operational approaches and varied targets make each a different threat. All services will integrate available techniques, human, technical, and combinations of these, to conduct operations best suited to their individual targets and style of penetration.[40] The result is that each espionage operation is one of a kind, a custom-designed attack planned in detail and executed to maximize success. To penetrate a target, the operational planner will select and mix the best tools available. For professional services these resources include human agents, surreptitious entry, audio and visual surveillance, software implants, open-source information, commercial cover companies, co-opted businesses, false identity, communications intercepts, bribery, common ethnic and religious affiliations, computer exploitation, and liaison relationships with other services.

Variations within espionage operations are numerous, and the best services will always play to the target's weakest point. Nations like China and Russia have multiple objectives, including collection, influence, and deception, while countries like Taiwan, Iran, and Cuba may focus more narrowly on specific bilateral diplomatic, economic, or military policies. However, when one considers that counterintelligence must pay attention to protecting national secrets from attacks by adversaries, rivals, competitors, nonstate organizations, terrorists, criminals, and even "friends," curtailing espionage "one spy arrest at a time" is like fighting fires without a corresponding fire prevention program.

That foreign professional services can successfully conduct secret operations inside the United States should be, however, cause for neither astonishment nor despair. The failure to understand the scope of Russian espionage (and that of other hostile services) in the United States points to our limited ability to learn about the adversaries' plans, assets, and tools. The infrequent arrests of spies, given the extent of foreign intelligence arrayed against us, suggests that we have only a small window into, and too little advance information about, the adversaries' attack strategies, methods, planning, and ongoing operations. The time-consuming damage assessment that follows a spy arrest, like an arson investigation, is useful in determining who started the fire, but the building is still in ashes.

Stronger counterespionage strategies, including offensive operations, can be effective in catching spies earlier. Walker, Wu-Tai Chin, Ames, and Hanssen operated for years, sometimes decades, before being stopped. Often we catch spies only after we have failed to preempt or prevent their spying. A lesson from the Ames and Hanssen cases is that by initially betraying all of his own country's penetrations of a foreign intelligence service, a wise spy protects himself first. Hanssen took an additional step in self-protection: He did not reveal his identity to his handlers although he established his bona fides through the breadth and quality of the information he provided. One of Robert Hanssen's covert communications, quoted in the FBI's arrest affidavit, points directly to his fear of betrayal and the value of offensive counterespionage operations. Hanssen wrote, "I am loath to [meet in the United States] not because it is risky but it involves revealing my identity. That insulation has been my best protection against betrayal by someone like me working from whatever motivation, a Bloch or a Philby." As a trained FBI counterintelligence officer, Hanssen understood better than most spies that his greatest risk of exposure lay in betrayal by another human spy within the Soviet intelligence system—a fear that ultimately proved accurate. A counterespionage penetration at the right level of the KGB's American section might have alerted U.S. counterintelligence to the existence of new spies, even if not their identities, within weeks of Hanssen's and Ames's initial activities. The irony of counterespionage success is that recruiting an agent inside a hostile service often leads to the sad news that our own service has been penetrated.

That counterespionage sometimes delivers bad news should not, however, dissuade senior managers from designing aggressive operations. The scope of counterintelligence responsibilities has broadened since the FBI chased communists and fascists under Soviet or German direction in the 1930s and 1940s. Former KBG major general Oleg Kalugin boasted that Soviet agents infiltrated every major federal agency in Washington during the 1940s, then added that "spying on America by foreign countries . . . increased [after the Cold War] especially in the area of economic and technical espionage."[41]

U.S. counterintelligence faces foreign threats that directly undermine at least four categories of our national interest in a multipolar world: partnerships and alliances, military capabilities, civil security, and economics. With respect to the first, the United States relies increasingly on cooperative foreign liaison to conduct sensitive intelligence operations, especially against terrorists and narcotics trafficking, and these new "friends" will continue to spy on us.

The Cold War ended, but the Russian SVR still bugged a State Department's seventh-floor Conference Room in 1999; the Israeli collection operation involving Jonathan Pollard is an even starker example of the problem.[42] International institutions that serve important diplomatic purposes in curtailing nuclear proliferation and the acquisition of the ability to build weapons of mass destruction can themselves become tools used by our adversaries to conduct deception operations. This was evident during the 1980s when the Soviets repeatedly denied the existence of their secret bacterial warfare research program conducted at Voz Island, despite being a signatory to the 1972 International Biological Weapons Convention that banned such activity.[43] Deception targets diplomats as well as warriors. The consequences of Saddam Hussein's deception regarding Iraq's weapons of mass destruction continue to be played out in war in Iraq.

Multiple regions of U.S. military engagements overseas highlight the importance of preventing espionage against military capabilities. For eighteen years beginning in 1967, John Walker and, later, his spy ring provided the Soviets with information about communications and cipher systems that enabled them to read more than a million intercepted U.S. military and intelligence messages. The Chinese government obtained advance weapons information from Peter Lee, a Los Alamos National Laboratory physicist, in 1985. As he was about to depart the United States in 2001, Brian Regan was arrested while carrying missile site information on Iraq and was found to have offered to sell the information to foreign governments.[44]

Similarly, with respect to civil security, the dangers have intensified since the Cold War. President Richard Nixon declared a "War on Drugs" in 1972, and the intelligence community responded with new tasking for collection and analysis on narcotics. In the years that followed, other nontraditional intelligence topics such as international crime, climate change, and human trafficking were added.[45] The CIA established a Crime and Narcotics Center and played a lead role in an eight-year environmental research project in the 1990s known as MEDEA.[46] After September 11, 2001, terrorism dominated America's national security agenda. The intense public debate over military strategy and intelligence tactics to combat religiously driven terrorist ideology and its accompanying acts of violence against civilians continues to consume major portions of the intelligence community's attention and drives its allocation of resources.[47]

On the economic front, reports from the FBI and the NCIX have pointed to increasingly aggressive and widespread espionage directed against the United States by foreign governments, enterprises owned or directed by foreign governments, and foreign-owned private companies.[48] Proper apportioning of responsibility for counterintelligence between the private sector and government is beyond the scope of this paper, but the progressive blurring of distinctions between "sensitive military technology" and "civilian consumer technology" requires a rethinking of national security classification processes and new collaborative government–private sector mechanisms to address this issue. The current national CI structure and resources are inadequate for the task.

Espionage practices are adapting to modern information and rapidly evolving communications technologies that are available to all intelligence services and terrorist organizations. Director of National Intelligence (DNI) Mike McConnell's Senate testimony on February 5, 2008, discussed the vulnerability of critical U.S. information technology (IT) infrastructure. McConnell asserted that foreign threats arise not only from nations like Russia and China but also from nonnational organizations including al-Qaeda, Hamas, Hezbollah, and "criminal elements." The DNI offered that in January 2008 a classified directive had been issued that "directs a comprehensive national cyber security initiative . . . to help deter hostile action in cyberspace by *making it harder to penetrate our networks*."[49] (italics added) Setting aside the question "What took the intelligence community so long?" if the January directive does not go beyond emphasizing deterrence by making networks harder to penetrate, in coming years we will read one headline after another of successful foreign "cyber attacks," "IT infrastructure penetrations," and "computer spying." Evidence is abundant that already the number and sophistication of the attacks require a strategy that aggressively encourages burglars to avoid the neighborhood, not just a program that puts better locks on windows and stronger chains on doors. Such a strategy must be preemptive and offer assured unacceptable consequences to the attacker. Counterespionage operations can play a key role in accomplishing these objectives.

The Counterespionage Technology Challenge

The combination of computing power, digital communications, data storage, and universal access to the Internet is disruptive, permanent, and influencing every element of espionage. The way potential human assets are assessed and the way tradecraft is practiced are changing.[50] Information technology, properly used by our adversaries, can make recruiting agents easier and handling spies less risky. Personal information about hundreds of thousands of employees and contractors for U.S. companies and agencies of interest to foreign intelligence services is universally available on the Internet. Individuals with potential access to secrets can be "spotted" through data aggregation and key-word searches; the "potentials" can be assessed based on profiles, credit scores, interests, ethnicity, and attitudes revealed in blogs and chat rooms. Contact can be made through e-mail or text messaging. All of this can be done without ever actually meeting the target or revealing the hand of an intelligence service. It can be done from five miles or five thousand miles distant, and the hostile recruiter never needs to be in the United States or even meet the target.

High-quality espionage equipment is no longer the monopoly of top-tier intelligence services. Pretty good spy gear (PGSG), similar to pretty good privacy (PGP) encryption, is readily available. Two hundred dollars will purchase a commercially available cigarette-sized key logger that when attached between the keyboard and a computer in a five-second plug-and-play operation, will record every keystroke for weeks and eventually expose passwords and other sensitive information. For nearly a decade advances in commercial, easy-to-use steganography programs have offered opportunities for anyone to hide messages in any file format—data, video, graphic—for covert communications.[51] Miniaturized, high-fidelity audio and visual surveillance equipment, once the exclusive providence of a handful of intelligence services, is available over the Internet or from a local "spy shop" for the home nursery as well as for concealment in the lamp on a target's desk. Not two decades after intelligence services invested tens of millions of dollars to create a small digital camera for spies, camera phones available in every part of the world perform nearly the same functions. Oleg Penkovsky's clandestine face-to-face debriefings by U.S. and British officers in European safe houses in 1961 seem prosaic compared to the multiple technical options now available that will allow a spy to steal weapons blueprints, policy papers, economic plans, or shift schedules of nuclear plant guards and communicate them to his handler.

Digital technology changed virtually every process in the creation, storage, transmission, and securing of secrets. Spies and counterintelligence defenders both recognize that technology presents the greatest potential for electronic copying and exfiltration of previously unimaginable amounts of data. Secrets by the gigabyte can be almost instantly copied onto storage devices smaller than a stick of gum. All of the information passed to the KGB by John Walker during his eighteen-year spy career could be stored on a memory card small enough to be concealed inside an MP3 player or a digital camera.

An adversary's options for successfully performing clandestine acts are dramatically multiplied when technology presents viable alternatives to risky face-to-face meetings or lengthy device-to-device radio communications. Videocasting means the spy can see and talk to his handler without being in the same city, the same country, or even on the same continent. Device-to-device communications with data hidden within data can occur in milliseconds. Technical penetrations no longer require a professional technical installer with advanced knowledge and training. Among other advantages that digital technology and the Internet offer the attacker are the ability to conduct remote target assessment and to operate from the safety of other geographic locations. Attackers can create anonymous digital identities, break through classification compartmentation, and conduct data exfiltration through software Trojan horse implants. All of these measures can enhance clandestinity and, obviously, cause new security nightmares for defenders.

Technology is introducing options that alter the definition of "personal meeting" as ubiquitous videoconferencing, digital-image phone transmissions, text messaging, and electronic funds transfers become a part of daily life. Intelligence services will find the means to conduct clandestine "virtual personal meetings" with assets attuned to that environment. They will "recruit" technology and technical systems, as well as humans, "to spy." Critical national security information, whether classified, proprietary, or unclassified can be targeted for collection and aggregation by malicious "bots" and crawlers operating inside data networks.

The impact of these technological challenges may be best understood through hands-on experience. For the past four years I have been part of a team presenting seminars about how sophisticated intelligence services plan offensive operations; our audiences are made up of people responsible for defending U.S. communications and weapons systems. The two-day seminar discusses the power of combining technical capabilities, social engineering, surreptitious entry, and patience with imagination and cheating to conduct espionage. Seminar students represent premier talent in their respective defensive fields, yet few have had previous exposure to all elements of an integrated attack.

During the seminar's final session participants are divided into groups, each representing a different foreign intelligence service such as China, Iran, Russia, France, Israel, and India. The groups are asked to plan an attack on a contrived, but realistic, target in their U.S. facility. The results of these "planning" exercises are as disconcerting as they are consistent. Virtually every group develops an operational scenario that they assert with confidence could penetrate their organization and obtain the targeted secrets. For the students, new insight lay not in realizing that they or their organization could be a target—they already knew that. Rather their perspective on what constitutes an effective defense strategy is dramatically altered by a new awareness of the breadth of resources available to foreign services and the likelihood of success when those resources are applied in a "no rules" operating environment.

The global availability of commercial spy technology is leveling the espionage playing field. Foreign attackers, including nontechnical, poorly financed services, are likely to seize on this technology to exploit espionage opportunities. Internet capabilities are already in the hands of terrorists and "second tier" services as well as "first world" countries. Much of the "intelligence information" useful to terrorists resides outside the formal classification systems, and commercial spy gear provides "good enough" security for their operations. Our counterintelligence agencies will be outmaneuvered if these new dimensions of operations are not recognized and countered. The classic spy who reports secrets he has heard or copies classified papers represents only one side of the emerging espionage triangle. Intelligence services will increasingly take advantage of technology to launch human-enabled technical attacks like the 1999 bug in the State Department's conference room chair rail that was remotely activated by a Russian technical officer from a parked car or to collect from, and potentially disrupt, information systems by deploying virtually autonomous "software spies." The more effective and possibly the least expensive component of future counterintelligence may be more and higher-risk offensive counterespionage operations aimed at revealing our adversaries' planning and intentions before spies, whether human or technical, are dispatched.

With more Americans working in national security disciplines having more access, more often, to more information than ever before, the pool of potential spies is multiplied. Career advancement in intelligence is enhanced by serving in multiple agencies and moving across programs, all of which requires and provides access to more secrets. The emerging intelligence culture emphasizing "career-broadening assignments," broad collaboration, fusion centers, and information sharing remains in tension with traditions of need-to-know and compartmentation. The digital environment offers attackers rapid access to tools for clandestine collection and communication options that make detecting covert messaging far more difficult. In an environment where intelligence operations can be quickly launched and executed, counterespionage may offer the greatest potential for detecting and preempting the adversaries' attacks.

Adopting an Aggressive Counterespionage Strategy

Counterespionage is distinct from, and value added to, counterintelligence. Counterespionage assists counterintelligence in preventing hostile penetrations and manipulation of U.S. intelligence services and exposes the operations of foreign services. At its best, counterespionage penetrates and manipulates foreign intelligence services to monitor and potentially control the actions of hostile nations. Three illustrations contrast CI and CE:

CI: A U.S. scientist is briefed on elicitation techniques used by Chinese engineers attending an international conference.

CE: The U.S. scientist is directed to make himself attractive to an intelligence-affiliated Chinese engineer as a first step in a double-agent operation.

CI: A preliminary investigation is conducted on a foreign official who extends an unsolicited dinner invitation to a CIA officer under unofficial cover.

CE: Following determination that the foreign official has an intelligence affiliation, the CIA officer is directed to develop a relationship and begin eliciting information against counterespionage requirements.

CI: The relationship of a foreign telecommunications manufacturer with its intelligence service is assessed.

CE: A recruitment operation is directed against an individual who can influence the design of telecommunications equipment being manufactured for a target foreign intelligence service.

These examples are illustrative of CE as "that branch of CI which penetrates and manipulates [the] alien spy apparatus; it is aggressive."[52]

Deficiencies in our counterintelligence posture are rarely found in investigative inattention to espionage once we know it is occurring; rather our failures begin with not knowing or not confidently predicting the intent and plans of hostile services early enough. It is a gap that can be closed only by dramatic improvements in collection and analysis driven by aggressive offensive counterespionage operations against foreign intelligence organizations.[53] For such improvements to occur, changes in our counterintelligence practices are necessary, including a shift of resources from enforcement and defensive security to the bolstering of counterespionage. Former deputy defense secretary John Hamre's concise observation that "the goal should not be to catch the spy after he is [here]; we've got to stop him before [arriving,]" points in the right direction.[54]

America's twentieth-century economic, technical, and military strength, combined with its geographic distance from most of the world's trouble spots, provided security advantages that no longer exist. Despite Walker, Ames, and Hanssen, America's intelligence losses in recent years are discussed as episodic spy cases without presenting the foreign sponsor's strategic intelligence objectives or the extent of its existing agent network. A danger presented by focusing on arrests is the potential of using case statistics to overestimate the effectiveness of our counterintelligence capability and underestimate the scope of continuing Russian, Chinese, Cuban, and other adversary espionage. Another dimension of our counterintelligence misalignment became apparent in the failure to preempt the 9/11 operations of al-Qaeda, a nongovernment organization that shattered any remaining self-perception of invincibility from attack against the U.S. mainland.

In many respects, America takes pride in being a society that, from a foreign intelligence service perspective, is an inviting espionage target—and few of us would wish for or advocate a change in the sources of that attractiveness. We treasure cultural openness, ethnic diversity, ease of travel, foreign students and visitors, the presence of international organizations, H-1 visas for talented professionals, our rule of law, and our personal privacy. Because each of these valued characteristics limits to varying degrees the methods and reach of any internal security and investigative agency, America remains more hospitable than most other countries as an operating ground for hostile intelligence services. This is particularly true for the human agent who as a spy can move freely, blend in, exploit laws, and have his privacy respected.

Due to the relative openness of the nation and the espionage-enabling technology available to our adversaries, if our future vision of counterintelligence is confined primarily to catching more spies, more information losses and security breaches can be expected. Four major contemporary vulnerabilities include the varying accessibility of America's strategic military, economic, and policy secrets; the difficulties of managing the consequences of terrorist attacks in a federal system of government; the prevalence of well-organized criminal activity and narcotics trafficking; and U.S. dependence on vulnerable classified and national security information networks.

Identifying and catching spies in the act of delivering classified information to dead drop sites or cutouts is only a part, and possibly a diminishing piece, of the future U.S. counterintelligence challenge. To be sure, classical agent-handler personal meetings provide an invaluable venue to read body language, quickly clarify misunderstandings, exchange physical goods, and "take the measure of the man." However, as comfort with technically based social interaction grows, fewer members of the next generation of spies will require regular meetings with their case officer—they can be remotely recruited and handled using methods similar to those of Hanssen.

An offensive counterespionage strategy offers the potential for markedly improved security and a strengthened counterintelligence posture. Offensive operations present the potential for learning what we do not presently know about our adversaries' intelligence designs against us. It opens the strategic window from which practical, tactical results flow. The new strategy will require operations using and integrating human assets, technical capabilities, information technology, liaison relations, and private as well as government resources. These operations must be conducted where the target can be reached, most likely in hostile territory under the scrutiny of the target's own security service. They must have the clear objectives of acquiring advance knowledge of the adversaries' intent and plans and destroying their confidence of operational success against us. The nature of the operations will require special training for officers and new incentives for working in this discipline. Evaluation and screening of candidates from which the counterespionage cadre will be selected and trained are critical. The cadre will require strong analytical and targeting support and an agile security process capable of managing the inherent ambiguities of the activity. It must begin with the IC leadership's commitment to making offensive counterespionage a counterintelligence "delta force."

Such a force is not just muscle; it requires training, integrated analytic capabilities, and, perhaps most important, a high tolerance for risk. It will require developing an understanding of our adversaries' intelligence strategies and thus their larger designs against us. Such a strategy would allow us to anticipate their moves, neutralize their technical capabilities, and identify their spies. With this greater knowledge of the playing field, we would be able to develop options for optimizing the security of our own operations and for controlling the playing field through the use of disruption, deception, and disinformation. In this way, homeland defense becomes less a front line for engagement than a line of defense woven into the course of offensive operations—much as a "castling" move might be considered in a game of chess. And with this more intimate knowledge of the adversary, defensive counterintelligence would have greater options for response. In addition, should attacks occur, we could attribute them to the perpetrators and punish accordingly.[55]

In addition to the historical and political difficulties discussed earlier, counterespionage is difficult to manage programmatically. First, similar to other critical intelligence programs such as influence, propaganda, deception, and covert action, counterintelligence must withstand the constant criticism of the bureaucracy's metric mavens. For such programs, managers find it is often insufficient to articulate clear strategic goals underpinned with specific actions. In these areas statistical measures of success are virtually impossible, and those who insist on such metrics are unlikely to be supportive. Yet political support of counterespionage within the intelligence community and the Congress is imperative. Offensive operations require sustained funding and a willingness to accept the inevitable periodic failures and compromises. In the past, aggressive operations usually begin with a great sense of adventure and expectation, but when messy problems arise, too often the last officer holding the operational bag takes the blame and the criticism.

A second management problem concerns the requirement for secrecy in counterespionage. Management of compartmentation to protect the ultrasensitive information required to conduct counterespionage operations may be particularly vexing as the intelligence community expands information sharing and collaborative analysis. Because opposition services understand the importance of protecting their internal intelligence capabilities from counterespionage attacks, unintended leakage of source identity or collection targeting becomes devastating.

Both the political and operational risks of aggressive counterespionage operations must be calculated and managed. National counterintelligence resources are limited, and there will be deep skepticism about the wisdom of shifting resources from home-based defensive security measures to counterespionage programs whose future benefits are promising, but not assured. Counterespionage advocates must be wary of conveying unrealistic expectations of these operations, particularly in the initial learning stages, when failure rates are potentially high. The areas and types of success will be unpredictable, specific successes will not necessarily be repeatable, and "progress" may require years of effort.

Operationally, to obtain and maintain access to counterespionage targets, we will be exposing our officers to the opposition's best, in effect placing them in situations where they themselves will be assessed, developed, and likely "pitched." All information collected will be suspect until vetted and validated through independent processes requiring exacting analysis and skepticism. Intense conflict among policymakers over the use of counterespionage intelligence for diplomatic, law enforcement, public, or clandestine actions is inevitable.

Secrecy is essential since success, if revealed, will be used by the adversary to revise its now compromised operational methods and plans.

With these realities understood, there are, nevertheless, sound reasons for optimism that the obstacles can be overcome and the risks mitigated. Both the CIA and the FBI have experience in running counterespionage operations. Overseas CIA stations regularly employed counterespionage to protect their unilateral operations in the host country.[56] A former head of CIA's European operations observed that he could not be confident about any agent unless he had an independent penetration of that agent's counterintelligence organization, and he insisted that such operations be undertaken. The FBI's internal counterespionage authorities and mission are clear. Double-agent operations by the FBI and military services have been successful. Nevertheless, much of this activity, overseas as well as domestic, remains tactical and case focused. In the future, the need for strategic counterespionage must be incorporated into all targeting and reporting with the objective of upgrading such cases to address the opposition's higher-level plans and intentions. Whenever a counterintelligence operation is launched, a potential counterespionage window can be opened by asking, "How can we leverage this to increase visibility into what else the adversary is doing and has planned against us?"

In 1996 a presidential commission chaired by former secretary of defense Harold Brown and former senator Warren Rudman issued a report, "Preparing for the 21st Century: An Appraisal of U.S. Intelligence." Among the report's conclusions were that counterintelligence had been "a weak sister" within the CIA during the previous decade. Addressing the deficiency, the commission argued that counterintelligence needed to become "integral to the entire intelligence process."[57] However, in its subsequent discussions of the topic, the report confined counterintelligence to defensive measures such as improving personnel threat awareness and security practices, validating of foreign intelligence reporting, and enhancing investigations and enforcement. The term *counterespionage* appeared only once, in an appendix reference to responsibilities of the FBI. No specific recommendations were made for aggressive counterespionage actions.

More recently, language in the Director of National Intelligence (DNI) strategy paper "Transformation through Integration and Innovation," prepared in October 2005, indicates that U.S. counterintelligence policy may be taking a more proactive turn.[58] Moving beyond the Brown Commission's effort to raise the status of counterintelligence in the intelligence community, the DNI's strategy advocates an offensive approach. Although the term *counterespionage* did not appear in the paper, action statements such as "deploy effective CI measures," "assess the intelligence capabilities and actions of our adversaries to . . . penetrate hard targets and understand their leadership," and "enable aggressive counterintelligence activities," point toward continued movement beyond a reactive, defensive policy.

A necessary first step toward more aggressive counterintelligence activities is recognizing the strategic challenges that confront the counterintelligence community and have been discussed above, such as foreign cyber attacks, vulnerabilities in foreign-manufactured critical systems, and achieving interagency collaboration in countering espionage.[59] Aggressive operations can accomplish four primary tasks in meeting these challenges: understanding the full scope of collection, deception, and sabotage operations directed against U.S. sensitive information, installations, infrastructure, and information networks; second, undertaking covert and public information campaigns that discourage adversaries from launching operations; third, catching spies—human and technical—much more quickly; and fourth; attributing espionage to the hostile actor with a punishing response.

To achieve practical results of disrupting and mitigating our adversaries' operations and maintain public support, counterespionage concepts must be consistent with U.S. law and executive orders and receive political commitment from executive leadership and congressional oversight. National counterintelligence resources will need to be reallocated, and professional incentives increased for those who would undertake such work. Similar to other elements of intelligence, when leadership sets clear counterespionage policy and establishes a sound strategy and incentives, innovative officers will devise effective tactics to execute the operations.

When friends express skepticism about the value of our imperfect intelligence to American policy, I readily concede that good intelligence does not guarantee wise or successful policy. I then add that in contrast to no intelligence, sound intelligence will markedly improve the odds. An aggressive counterintelligence posture will not eliminate espionage against the United States, but greater emphasis on a counterespionage offensive strategy can provide higher confidence that our secrets are secure, our operations are clean, and vital national security is maintained. Done well, aggressive counterespionage will convince many bad guys that this neighborhood is simply best avoided.

Notes

The following individuals provided valuable assistance to the author in preparing this article: Burton Gerber, James Kirkman, Henry Schlesinger, Chuck Prahl, H. Keith Melton, Don Arabian, David Robarge, and Hayden Peake.

1. Scene from Peter Ustinov's *Romanoff and Juliet*, which opened on Broadway's Plymouth Theater in New York on October 10, 1957.

2. The concept of double agents is firmly established in the public consciousness by a popular television shows and movies. Notable film portrayals include the "James Bond" character as featured in *Casino Royale* (1967 and 2006), *GoldenEye* (1995), and *The Living Daylights* (1987). Other films include Alfred Hitchcock's *North by Northwest* (1959) and *The Ipcress File* (1965), adapted from the Len Deighton novel on the theme of counterespionage. The television appeal of double-agent heroes is evident in response to long-running series such as *I Spy, Mission: Impossible, The Man from U.N.C.L.E., Alias,* and *24.* Danny Biederman's *The Incredible World of Spy-Fi* (San Francisco: Chronicle Books, 2004) describes these and other pop-culture fictional spy icons.

3. Executive Order 12333, United States Intelligence Activities, December 4, 1981.

4. Leo Carl, *The International Dictionary of Intelligence* (McLean, VA: International Defense Consultant Services, Inc., 1990), 83. The relationship of counterintelligence to security practices and programs remains a matter of professional discussion. The National Counterintelligence Executive, Joel Brenner, commented in an October 24, 2007, speech to the NRO/National Military Intelligence Association Counterintelligence Symposium, "Addressing counterintelligence as a strategic capability is automatically challenging because we don't all have the same idea of what it is."

5. Loch K. Johnson, ed., *Strategic Intelligence 4: Counterintelligence and Counterterrorism: Defending the Nation against Hostile Forces* (Westport, CT: Praeger Security International, 2007), 5.

6. The specialized role counterespionage holds in counterintelligence writings is evident from a Google search of the two words. *Counterintelligence* yielded 1.2 million hits, while *counterespionage* generated only 7 percent of that total.

7. Albert Glinsky, *Theremin: Ether Music and Espionage* (Urbana: University of Illinois Press, 2006), 76.

8. Ibid., 49

9. Ibid., 300.

10. Robert Louis Benson and Michael Warner, eds., *Venona: Soviet Espionage and the American Response 1939–1957* (Laguna Hills, CA: Aegean Park Press), xix.

11. Ibid., vii–ix. After 1945, information derived from the Venona code-breaking program, supplemented by debriefings of Igor Gouzenko, a defector and GRU code clerk in the USSR's Ottawa Embassy, Elizabeth Bentley, who served as a courier for passing information to the Soviets, and Whittaker Chambers, enabled the FBI to identify and apprehend a number of Soviet agents.

12. Ibid., v. At the time of *Venona*'s publication (1996), Crowell was the deputy director of the National Security Agency.

13. Jerry Markon, "Defense Official Is Charged in Chinese Espionage Case," *Washington Post*, February 12, 2008, 1. CIA employee Larry Wu-Tai Chin spied for China for more than thirty years before his 1985 arrest.

14. Espionage Cases, Summaries and Sources, Defense Personnel Security Research Center, Monterey, California, December 2004. Katherine L. Herbig and Martin F. Wiskoff, "Espionage Against the United States by American Citizens 1947–2001," published by PERSEREC, Technical Report 02–5, July 2002.

15. "FBI Tries to Tackle Growing Espionage Threat," *Fox News*, quoting Associated Press report, August 3, 2003.

16. Herbig and Wiskoff, PERSEREC, Technical Report 02–05, July 2002. According to the PERSEREC report, countries that received U.S. classified information from agents or cooperating sources included the Philippines, Cuba, the USSR, South Africa, Poland, East Germany, France, Israel, Bulgaria, Greece, Taiwan, Russia, China, Hungary, Czechoslovakia, Libya, Ecuador, Japan, North Vietnam, South Korea, Iraq, Saudia Arabia, Ghana, Jordan, El Salvador, and unspecified "West African countries," as well as al-Qaeda.

17. Associated Press, "FBI Tries to Tackle Growing Espionage Threat," August 3, 2003.

18. Author correspondence from H. Keith Melton, reporting on his interview with the KGB officer, February 23, 2008.

19. See James R. Gosler's companion chapter "Counterintelligence: Too Narrowly Practiced," for a discussion of the roles of sanctions and punishment in counterintelligence.

20. Gus W. Weiss, "The Farewell Dossier," *Studies in Intelligence* 39, no.5 (1996): 121–26.

21. See report by George J. Church, "Bang! Bang! You're Out!" *Time*, November 3, 1986.

22. See testimony by Richard Helms, U.S. Senate Committee on the Judiciary, "Hearing Before the Subcommittee to Investigate the Administration of the Internal Security Act and Other Internal Security Laws," 87th Cong., 1st sess., June 2, 1961; and testimony by John McMahon, U.S. House of Representatives, "Hearing Before the Subcommittee on Oversight of the Permanent Select Committee on Intelligence," 96th Cong., 2nd sess., February 19, 1980.

23. See Viktor Sheymov, *Tower of Secrets: A Real Life Spy Thriller* (Annapolis, MD: Naval Institute Press, 1993), for a description of the USSR's commitment to intercept operations. Following his defection in 1980, Sheymov warned the U.S. intelligence community against making the mistake of believing that the low level of quality and technology found in Russian refrigerators reflected in any way the country's SIGINT capabilities.

24. This and other Soviet-sponsored clandestine technical operations against its U.S. ally are described in Gary Kern, "How 'Uncle Joe' Bugged FDR," *Studies in Intelligence* 47, no. 1 (2003): 19–31.

25. Christopher Andrew and Vasili Mitrokhin, *The Sword and the Shield: The Mitrokhin Archive and the Secret History of the KGB* (New York: Basic Books, 1999), 338.

26. See Norman Polmar and Thomas B. Allen, *Spy Book: The Encyclopedia of Espionage*, 2nd ed. (New York: Random House, 2004), 361–62; for Koecher case and more on Markus Wolf, see Wolf's book *Man Without a Face: The Autobiography of Communism's Greatest Spymaster* (New York: PublicAffairs, 1997), especially chapter 11, for Wolf's description of East German intelligence liaison with the KGB.

27. Wolf, *Man Without a Face*, 162. Whether Wolf's assertions about the specific operation are accurate is secondary to the point that Soviet intelligence benefited greatly from the operations of East European and other allies. Counterintelligence must guard not only against "the main enemy," but all other services cooperating with it.

28. Weiss, "The Farewell Dossier," 121–26.

29. Jay Peterzell, "The Moscow Bug Hunt," *Time*, July 10, 1989.

30. Polmar and Allen, *Spy Book*, 165.

31. *9/11 Commission Report: Final Report of the National Commission on Terrorist Attacks upon the United States*, U.S. Government Printing Office, July 22, 2004.

32. Details of some Soviet "active measures" programs are presented in U.S. House of Representatives Permanent Select Committee on Intelligence, *Soviet Active Measures*, 97th Cong., 2nd sess., July 1982; and David A. Spetrio, "Aids Disinformation," *Studies in Intelligence* 32, no.4 (1988): 9–14.

33. David Robarge, "Moles, Defectors, and Deceptions: James Angleton and CIA Counterintelligence," *The Journal of Intelligence History* 3, no. 2 (Winter 2003): 49.

34. Ibid., 48.

35. Ibid., 47.

36. The Shadrin story is detailed by Henry Hurt in *Shadrin: The Spy Who Never Came Back* (New York: Reader's Digest Press, McGraw-Hill Book Company, 1981).

37. Author interview with retired CIA senior officer Burton Gerber, February 6, 2008.

38. See Tennent H. Bagley *Spywars: Moles, Mysteries, and Deadly Games* (New Haven: Yale University Press, 2007), 299n4, quoting Oleg Kalugin, *The First Directorate* (New York: St. Martin's Press, 1994), 95–96 and 152–58.

39. Joel F. Brenner, "Counterintelligence in the 21st Century: Not Just a Government Problem," speech delivered to the AFCEA (Armed Forces Communications and Electronics Association) Counterintelligence Conference, December 4, 2007.

40. Jay Peterzell, "When 'Friends' Become Moles,' *Time*, May 28, 1990. The article observed that French intelligence, in addition to running a ring of agents to obtain sensitive U.S. high-technology research and marketing information, "routinely intercepted electronic messages." Robert Courtney, a former IBM security official, is quoted as saying, "There's no question that they have been spying on IBM's transatlantic communications and handling the information to Compagnie des Machines Bull for years." (CMB was the French computer competitor to IBM.)

41. Kellie Lunney, "Spy tour brings government employee espionage to Light," *Government Executive*, January 19, 2001. Joel Brenner, National Counterintelligence Executive, defines counterintelligence as broader than traditional espionage against government, indicating that it would also include corporate secrets regardless of whether they are classified. See AFCEA remarks delivered December 4, 2007.

42. See David Johnson and James Risen, "U.S. Expelling Russian Diplomat in Bugging of State Department," *New York Times*, December 10, 1999; and Steven Erlanger, "Israeli Found Spy's Data Irresistible," *New York Times*, March 3, 2006.

43. The secret research program is detailed by Ken Alibek and Stephen Handelman, *Biohazard: The Chilling True Story of the Largest Covert Biological Weapons Program in the World—Told from Inside by the Man Who Ran It* (New York: Dell Publishing, 1999).

44. PERSEREC, "Espionage Cases 1975–2004," 49, 29, 40.

45. The CIA established a Crime and Narcotics Center and coordinated the eight-year-long MEDEA research project in the 1990s.

46. One of the most significant Medea projects is described by Dan Belt, "An Arctic Breakthrough," *National Geographic*, February 1997, 36–57.

47. Adoption of the 9/11 Commission Report's recommendations on priorities and government organization will require long-term commitments of new resources to both foreign intelligence and homeland security programs.

48. Annual reports by the Office of the National Counterintelligence Executive on this issue are available at: www.ncix.gov/publications/reports/fecie_all/index_fecie.html.

49. George Hulme, "National Intelligence Director: Cyber Risks Rising," Information Week.com, February 6, 2008.

50. See James R. Gosler, "The Digital Dimension," in *Transforming U.S. Intelligence*, ed. Jennifer E. Sims and Burton Gerber (Washington, DC: Georgetown University Press, 2005), 96–114; Gosler argues that technology and technical systems can be "recruited" to provide secret information. For a discussion of the impact of digital technology on operational tradecraft, see Robert Wallace and H. Keith Melton, *Spycraft* (Dutton: New York, 2008), Section 6, 363ff.

51. See Eric Cole, *Hiding in Plain Sight* (Indianapolis: Wiley Publishing, Inc., 2003), 5–7.

52. William R. Johnson, *Thwarting Enemies at Home and Abroad: How to Be a Counterintelligence Officer* (Bethesda, MD: Stone Trail Press, 1987), 2. A 1976 Senate report

offered a similar definition emphasizing the proactive element of counterespionage: "As an activity, CI consists of two matching halves: security and counterespionage. CE is the offensive, or aggressive, side of counterintelligence." See Appendix A, "CIA Counterintelligence: An Excerpt from the Church Committee Report," in *Strategic Intelligence 4—Counterintelligence and Counterterrorism: Defending the Nation Against Hostile Forces*, ed. Loch K. Johnson (Westport, CT: Praeger Security International, 2007), 186.

53. The author's concept of "offensive counterespionage" is similar to that of "strategic counterintelligence" as outlined in Michelle Van Cleave's 2007 article "Strategic Counterintelligence," *Studies in Intelligence* 51, no. 2. Available at www.cia.gov/library/center-for-the-study-of-intelligence.

54. Ibid.

55. Duane R. Clarridge, *A Spy for All Seasons: My Life in the CIA* (New York: Scribner, 1997), 336–37, describes a 1987 successful counterespionage operation that virtually destroyed the Abu Nidal terrorist organization.

56. In the 1970s the CIA developed a body-worn intercept device with camouflaged antennas and earpieces that allowed officers to secretly listen in on the communications of KBG surveillance teams that might be following them. Another CIA audio operation in Moscow targeted a fixed KGB surveillance site to covertly collect counterespionage intelligence. See Wallace and Melton, *Spycraft*, 106–8, 228–29.

57. Harold Brown and Warren Rudman, "Preparing for the 21st Century: An Appraisal of U.S. Intelligence," *Report of the Commission on the Roles and Capabilities of the United States Intelligence Community*, March 1, 1996.

58. Office of the Director of National Intelligence, "The National Intelligence Strategy of the United States of America: Transformation through Integration and Innovation," October 2005. See www.dni.gov/publications/NISOctober2005.pdf.

59. Joel F. Brenner, presentation to the NRO/National Military Intelligence Association Counterintelligence Symposium, October 24, 2007.

Vincent H. Bridgeman

Defense Counterintelligence, Reconceptualized

FOLLOWING THE attacks of September 11, 2001, and in particular since the establishment of the Counterintelligence Field Activity (CIFA) in 2002, the Department of Defense (DoD) has invested much money and effort in its counterintelligence (CI) program. Unfortunately, until very recently, these investments were made without consideration of how DoD's structure, division of labor, and missions drive CI needs. Instead, DoD invested in the status quo and missed the opportunity to address fundamental problems. By the summer of 2007, when General James Clapper assumed the post of undersecretary of defense for intelligence, he found Defense CI poorly prepared to mount a strategic, offensive effort or to provide the full spectrum of CI advantages to operational decision makers, making it more difficult to defeat adversaries, current and future.

This need not have been the case. Though counterintelligence is much maligned, generally misunderstood, and frequently sidelined—even within the intelligence community—it is straightforward in concept. As Jennifer Sims has stressed in her prior work and explains in her chapter on mission-based counterintelligence in this volume, the function must be understood in terms of the competitive advantages it conveys to the supported decision maker.[1] Since large competitive enterprises such as the Defense Department involve a division of labor, there is a division of decision making that accompanies it. Specialization is a hallmark of the division of labor, so inevitably different decision makers will have different information—and intelligence—needs. It also happens that counterintelligence advantages come in different flavors, and that some specialists will need one flavor, while others will need another. This chapter, then, will start with the following proposition:

> Aligning the acquisition of counterintelligence advantages with competitive needs is a necessary (but not sufficient) condition for a sound counterintelligence program supporting multiple decision makers and their division of labor.

125

Working on this foundation, this chapter will identify the specific types of competitive advantages that counterintelligence can provide and will describe the process by which those advantages are developed. I will then apply this refined theory of counterintelligence to the Department of Defense, relating the types of advantages that can be obtained, or counterintelligence "modes" and processes, to the major decision makers and the competitive needs they represent.

The case study will illustrate two serious and related flaws in the counterintelligence program as General Clapper found it in mid-2007: first, that it was poorly prepared to provide competitive advantages that were relevant to the specific needs of the senior decision makers, in particular the combatant commanders, and second, that the Defense Department's separation of the management of its clandestine human intelligence collection and its counterintelligence activities hampered both missions, while also complicating departmental management of clandestine activities in general.[2] Although General Clapper is taking significant steps to alleviate these problems and eliminate their causes, at the time of this writing it is unclear how deep and lasting these changes will be. For these reasons, this chapter will discuss defense counterintelligence as it existed at the start of 2008 and derive recommendations for remediation based on these findings, with some additional commentary on recent significant changes.[3]

The flaws confronting the undersecretary of defense for intelligence in early 2008 stemmed from two interrelated issues. First, the three counterintelligence agencies within the military departments played a difficult role in providing support to combatant commanders' operations. Second, two of these three agencies and the central operations manager, the Counterintelligence Field Activity (CIFA), have treated counterintelligence as "law enforcement." Even with a super-empowered CIFA as recommended by the WMD Commission Report, the counterintelligence agencies of the navy, the air force, and the army—the primary operational counterintelligence elements of the defense establishment—will still be struggling against major structural and organizational flaws. After I explore these problems in detail, I will discuss common defenses of the status quo. Finally, I will comment on changes that have taken place during 2008 and offer further recommendations for improving Defense counterintelligence.

Context: Definitions, Misconceptions, and Organizational Tensions

Three elements of the Defense Department's approach to CI and intelligence in general must be discussed at the start because they provide context for the discussion that follows. One element is definitional, rooted in a narrow conception of intelligence; the second is a natural consequence of the first; and the last is a misunderstanding rooted in historical practice. Bearing all three in mind will help illuminate the analysis to follow.

The first point to consider is the Defense Department's definition of intelligence. As illustrated by intelligence historian Michael Warner, the department (and consequently much of the intelligence community) has long defined intelligence as providing secret information to decision makers and eschewed the broader, more historically apt, definition of intelligence as a clandestine quest for competitive advantage.[4] The narrow DoD definition causes some serious difficulties for counterintelligence, which is legally a subset of intelligence but conceptually is capable of providing operational advantages beyond what a simple decision-making model would suggest. The narrow DoD definition thus results in an artificially limited focus on secret decision support. This makes it difficult for defense officials to properly understand (and thus properly organize for and execute) the counterintelligence mission. In just one example of this misunderstanding, the department's primary doctrinal publication for intelligence incorrectly lumps counterintelligence in with the other intelligence collection disciplines, such as human intelligence, imagery, measurement and signature intelligence, and so forth.[5] Whoever authored this intelligence doctrine seems to think of counterintelligence primarily in terms of collection; the remainder of the publication offers no explanation of the mission's potential operational advantages. For the student of intelligence, this is startling.

This conceptual problem explains why many activities that historically (and at the national level) have been considered intelligence-related are explicitly considered *not* so by the Defense Department. For example, special operations may involve clandestine activities that come close to the functional definition of covert action;[6] the debate over how close rests not upon subtle differences in functions but upon the intended purpose.[7] Some in the Defense Department have applied similar logic to counterintelligence: that it is neither intelligence nor covert action but law enforcement "operations."[8] These parsed definitions are an understandable outcome of organizational tensions within the executive and the department, but that will not change the perception of the nation against whom these activities are directed. This makes for complicated management and oversight, as there is no single party responsible for managing the breadth of clandestine activities of the department. The direct implications for defense counterintelligence will be discussed later in this chapter.

The final problem lies in the U.S. military's persistent treatment of counterintelligence as a law enforcement function. While the Pentagon's definition admittedly does not make enforcing laws the primary purpose of counterintelligence, in practice two of the three primary counterintelligence agencies (and the central operations manager) treat the mission as an explicitly law enforcement function.[9] As noted in more detail in the theory presented below, such a system has serious trouble operating strategically or providing the full spectrum of counterintelligence advantages against military competitors.

Counterintelligence Theory: A Review

For Americans, counterintelligence is a polarizing word, spoken with either distrustful contempt or faintly justified awe. Sadly, much of the U.S. intelligence community has a similarly shallow understanding of the subject. The problem is partly a result of the additional secrecy required for counterintelligence, partly the negative (and skewed) popular narrative of counterintelligence in American culture, and partly the definitional problems noted above. Perhaps most significantly, as noted by one particularly well-informed observer, American counterintelligence lacks a unifying conception, as it is conducted by numerous parts of the executive branch with differing needs and approaches to counterintelligence and no central leadership.[10]

It need not be so. Counterintelligence is the broad subset of intelligence focused on the intelligence efforts of a competitor.[11] The core of the mission is about understanding and exploiting a competitor's reliance on intelligence. As Sims has illustrated in previous work, like its counterpart positive, or foreign, intelligence (FI), one "does" CI to provide advantages to a decision maker engaged in a competitive enterprise.[12] For this, a sound counterintelligence effort must meet many of the same basic criteria as foreign or positive intelligence. It must recognize which decision makers require the different types of advantages offered by this discipline; it must accurately identify those decision makers' information needs and the nature of their decision-making cycle; and it must consider the above two points for the competitor(s).[13] Understanding what advantages counterintelligence can offer *beyond* the decision advantages offered by positive intelligence and how those operational advantages are developed is critical.

By engaging a competitor's intelligence effort, our decision maker can draw advantage in three ways. First, he can engage in *passive* denial by better securing key information or other assets to prevent them from being obtained and exploited by a competitor, or *active* denial by tying up the competitor's intelligence and decision-making effort with useless "operational games."[14] Either way, denial is about preventing the competitor's intelligence service from conveying a decision advantage to the competitor's decision cycle. Second, our decision maker can aggregate knowledge of the competitor's intelligence effort, and especially *insight* gained by accessing the competitor's intelligence cycle into his broader intelligence knowledge base, and then apply that advantageously in an operational decision.[15] This added insight will not otherwise be available to an intelligence effort without a focused "counter" intelligence effort against the competing intelligence service. Third, the decision maker can choose to *manipulate* his competitor using the competitor's own intelligence channels as a means to achieve an operational outcome through deception.[16] Counterintelligence involves at its core an ongoing intelligence cycle focused narrowly on the competitor's intelligence efforts and decision making, plus additional activities conducted to degrade the competitor's intelligence capability or manipulate the competitor's decisions to achieve a policy outcome.[17]

These three potential advantage areas (or modes) of counterintelligence—denial, insight, and manipulation—are not mutually exclusive. They overlap because the means for developing and exploiting them are often identical, and so priorities and operations must be balanced by the decision maker at all times to leverage the right form of advantage at the right time.[18] To do so, our decision maker must make some initial judgment about who his competitors are and in what arena they are competing; his goal must be to gain as complete an understanding of the competing intelligence effort as possible so he can develop options for exploiting it, including but not limited to the classic double agent. This process is critical to the development of CI advantage.

Counterintelligence as Process

The process of gaining understanding of a competitor's intelligence effort—and ultimately exploiting his reliance upon it—involves three steps. First, the decision maker must detect some previously unknown portion of the competitor's intelligence activity even though the competitor will attempt to secure and conceal it. Second, the activity itself must be studied as fully as possible, and the fruits of that study must be considered in the context of what counterintelligence analysts already know about that competitor's intelligence efforts and how they relate to his decision making. The access to the competitor's intelligence cycle developed during this step will enable counterintelligence advantages during the next step; the need for secrecy during these first two steps is critical to the preservation of potential advantage. Finally, from this new understanding, our supported decision maker can choose which mode of counterintelligence advantage might be drawn from the particular activity, and then move to draw that advantage.[19] This process of "detect, study, act" must be continuously at work in an effective CI system and will require the supported decision makers to remain constantly involved in order to draw maximum advantage from the potential offered by CI.[20] The key point about this process, one required of counterintelligence every bit as much as of its positive counterpart, is that the appropriate decision makers must be involved in guiding the process even if they have delegated the actual management of the effort to a subordinate. For any competition the decision maker weighing trade-offs between CI modes should be the same person responsible for the conduct of the competition, or the relevant portion of the competition; this should be common sense. As noted at the outset, this is not the case for counterintelligence in the Department of Defense and is the fundamental flaw of its system.

A more difficult problem concerns when and where the counterintelligence manager should bring options for gaining counterintelligence advantages to the attention of the decision maker, usually driven by a concern for keeping the operation a secret. While effective counterintelligence often demands secrecy, any decision maker entrusted with the outcome of a given contest is implicitly trusted with the outcome of the decisions therein. For this reason engagement should be continuous, especially considering that decision cycles on the whole tend to get shorter at critical junctures in a contest, or as the competitive arena becomes more tactical. An important caveat, however, is that extraction of CI advantage that might also affect the outcome of contests of a higher order of magnitude—strategic versus tactical, or global versus local—would necessarily be entrusted to the decision makers at the highest level affected. A useful analog might be the noninterference principle employed in the Defense Department's information operations doctrine; this allows for multiple components to employ information operations to further their missions with the caveat that the operations not interfere with the operations of other components.

In sum, the counterintelligence process for a given decision maker must be tasked to a single CI manager who will control all steps in the process, who has access to all required collection and operational assets, and who understands the needs of decision makers with respect to the timing and types of advantages they seek. The manager must have a dedicated analytic capability to drive his own counterintelligence process. The process must be integrated with operational planning and execution, intelligence collection and production, and deception or information operations. It must also drive and receive feedback from accompanying security efforts.[21]

As described at the outset, decision makers operating under a division of labor have different operational priorities and, as is clearly the case within the Defense Department, different and sometimes divergent needs for counterintelligence and the advantages it can provide. Supporting a division of labor requires developing "local" advantages for different decision makers, arbitrating differences in priorities between decision makers, and balancing those local needs against "global" development and preservation of advantages for higher-level decision makers. This is a prime task for a central counterintelligence manager in the Defense Department. Before covering the theoretical needs of the Defense components, however, we must first clear up a common misunderstanding and expose another key source of weakness in the Defense counterintelligence program.

Counterintelligence Is Not Law Enforcement

A persistent misunderstanding of counterintelligence, no doubt a result of the long-standing role of American law enforcement agencies in the counterintelligence business, is that it is inherently a law enforcement function. This is unfortunate, because it severely limits the perspective of both the supported decision maker and the counterintelligence agencies involved.

*Counter*intelligence is by definition directed against the intelligence activities of foreign nations (or groups). In conducting intelligence activities against the United States, those foreign nations have revealed themselves as competitors who subordinate respect for American sovereignty and law to self-interest. The single act of espionage, even when committed by Americans, is but one part of any such competitor's overall intelligence efforts. To make the primary aim of an espionage investigation a conviction ignores this fact and may nullify most of the potential operational advantage CI has to offer. Counterintelligence is, of course, a responsibility of the FBI as well as other government agencies;

espionage conducted against the United States is clearly codified as a crime under U.S. law, a clear deterrent to those who might commit it. But the crimes are incidental to larger purposes that a comprehensive counterintelligence effort can help to identify, analyze, and defeat.

Catching and punishing Americans and foreigners who commit espionage is clearly a part of a comprehensive counterintelligence effort, and a way of reaping denial-mode advantage, including that of deterring would-be spies by punishing others. Conversely, there might be instances where competitive advantage is gained by not prosecuting even the guiltiest of spies. Either way, the supported decision makers generally have larger interests than those of each specific case. Counterintelligence is thus correctly viewed as a strategic international relations tool rather than a domestic law enforcement mission.

A counterintelligence effort that has apportioned some of its duties to law enforcement agencies, whose measurements of success generally revolve around arrests and convictions, presents at least two important challenges. First, the system must have a means by which the decision makers involved may extract advantage from espionage "cases" in the most beneficial way. This might mean forgoing many prosecutions in favor of a strategy of observing from a distance, feeding misinformation at key times, and turning double agents. Second, law enforcement agencies charged with counterintelligence responsibilities must be organizationally cognizant of the fundamental difference between these responsibilities and law enforcement, and sensitive to these sometimes divergent tasks. For example, investigations must seek to satisfy counterintelligence analysts' specific collection requirements in addition to looking for evidence, and the conduct of investigations must preserve other modes of advantage for decision makers.

A better conceptual model, based upon the discussion outlined above and one implicitly favored by the proponents of the MI-5 model over the current FBI model, is a system that separates a counterintelligence "investigation" from the criminal investigation relating to espionage and intended to support prosecution. Under this model the supported decision maker and counterintelligence manager, in conjunction with legal authorities, handles any criminal-related espionage issue in "CI" channels until the determination is made that there is more value to be had in the prosecution of the individual. This completely separates the criminal investigative organization from the intelligence organization and allows the manager to develop advantages free from the denial-biased organizational imperative to convict. This is how the Department of the Army handles its counterintelligence investigations, and it is an exception within the large Defense Department counterintelligence agencies; the Departments of the Navy and Air Force and CIFA all consider such investigations to be a law enforcement function. It is worth noting here that there is nothing in U.S. law and no executive order that currently compels the Defense Department to treat counterintelligence as a law enforcement function.[22]

Division of Labor and Counterintelligence Needs

We will first consider the needs of the Defense Department in the context of the modes of counterintelligence advantage presented above. The key ideas here are threefold. First, and as already discussed above, an effective effort can provide advantage in three distinct modes: denial, insight, and manipulation. Second, for counterintelligence to be effective, an adversary's intelligence efforts must be detected and studied in a way that builds and preserves the right kinds of advantages for the supported decision makers. This process of "detect, study, act" should be iterative, continuous, and additive in an effective system. Finally, building and extracting advantages through this process requires tight integration with positive intelligence, operational planning and execution, and security. These three concepts rest beneath the overarching proposition that no counterintelligence system is perfect; as with any other type of risk, there must be some trade-off between risks and operational gains during a mission. The decision maker responsible for the contest is the only appropriate arbiter of this risk.

An enterprise as large as the Department of Defense manages its wide array of activities and responsibilities through a clearly delineated division of labor. This division of labor was formally and forcefully mandated by the Department of Defense Reorganization Act of 1987, also known as the Goldwater-Nichols Act. In general there is a departmental leadership and staff (Office of the Secretary of Defense), a military advisory staff (Chairman and Joint Chiefs of Staff), a military capabilities-building effort (military departments and services), a military planning and operations effort (combatant commands and assigned forces), and several specialized support agencies that provide common services across the department. Though perhaps oversimplified, this roughly approximates the Defense Department's division of labor. Identifying the competitive advantage needs of each of these decision makers is a simple function of comparing specific counterintelligence advantages to particular missions.

For example, the foremost decision maker in the department is the secretary of defense. The president's primary executor of defense policy holds responsibility for contributing to foreign policy development and execution, development and implementation of military strategy, weapons systems and force development, and defense budgeting. The secretary competes at the strategic level, and on a time scale extending to decades. These decision-making responsibilities require insight-centered counterintelligence advantage, oriented toward competing decision makers in adversary countries. The secretary needs to know the scope, the capabilities, and the aims of intelligence threats directed against the department. The secretary's counterintelligence staff should provide forewarning of adversaries' military strategies and courses of action and give added insight into the strategic direction of competing policymakers. Since the secretary participates in a contest that is relatively inseparable from the geopolitical and economic facets of state-level relations, it is assumed here that any departmental-level counterintelligence advantage should be developed and exploited toward national level goals. The defense secretary has no direct need for what I have termed manipulation-mode counterintelligence advantages—that is, deceiving adversaries—but rather should bring the department's capabilities to bear in support of national efforts to do so.[23]

The three military departments and their four services are the Defense Department's primary force developers, and they organize, train, and equip the vast majority of the nation's combat forces. The primary counterintelligence needs of these organizations are denial-oriented. To preserve the military advantages that they are responsible for developing, their counterintelligence programs must deny competitors' intelligence services access to those advantages. These efforts must help to protect, among other things, advanced weapons and information systems, research and development efforts, and the personnel accession process.

The unified combatant commanders serve as the operational planners and executors of defense policy; the president issues his orders directly to them. These commanders' responsibilities are either geographic or functional in nature, and their counterintelligence needs differ according to their roles. The functional combatant commanders provide common operational support functions to the geographic combatant commanders. For most, this supporting role indicates a need for emphasis on the denial mode of counterintelligence. For example, airlift support provided by the U.S. Transportation Command requires operational security.

Denial is not the rule for the functional combatant commanders; some support functions require or benefit from the other kinds of operational advantages counterintelligence can provide. The strategic command's specialized global strategic roles, particularly for information operations (IO) and strategic deterrence, demand the full spectrum of advantages counterintelligence can offer. Worth noting here is that the Defense Department's denial bias shows up clearly in information operations doctrine; the department limits counterintelligence support to information operations as simply "a critical part of guarding friendly information and information systems."[24]

As the primary executors of military planning and operations, the geographic combatant commanders clearly require the full spectrum of advantages counterintelligence can provide. Denial allows the commander to keep his capabilities and intentions from being uncovered or exploited by his adversaries. Insight gives the commander a glimpse into the intentions and operational priorities of his competitors. Perhaps most beneficial to military contests, manipulation allows the commander to influence the decision making of his adversaries to his advantage. Two critical reminders here are that the counterintelligence process must build potential advantages during the earlier planning phase, and extraction of advantages must be closely integrated with operational decision making or execution and incorporated into intelligence estimates and feedback.

The Defense agencies, such as the Defense Information Systems Activity (DISA), provide common services across the department. Similar to the functional combatant commanders, a role as a provider of support rather than as an operational competitor points to DISA's need for primarily denial-mode counterintelligence. Specialized needs exist in places such as the Defense Intelligence Agency, but we will rest in general on the idea that the Defense agencies require denial-mode advantage as they are not directly engaged in military contests.

Finally, there is the special case of the Special Operations Command (SOCOM). This combatant command has the unique responsibility to organize, train and equip special operations forces (SOF), to provide those forces in support of the other combatant commanders, and to perform as a supported commander, particularly as the lead for the war on terrorism. Clearly, the full spectrum of counterintelligence advantages is needed here, for all the reasons cited for the military departments and the operational commanders, with the added requirement to support unique SOF missions.

Two disclaimers about the analysis presented here are, first, that the above analysis does not presuppose a division of CI labor; it is simply intended to illustrate the basic counterintelligence needs of the department's components in order to better understand the current defense system for this intelligence mission, especially for supporting military contests. One central organization could conceivably provide counterintelligence advantages for the entire department, or every component could resource their own CI program independently. Regardless, a central manager remains critical to developing and extracting advantages at the right time and place for a given contest and decision maker, and for arbitrating divergent needs between them. A second disclaimer is that the analysis to follow does not pretend to explore how every last bit of counterintelligence advantage is gained and used throughout the Department. In one example, the Defense Department has a complex system of security policies, ranging from classification to communications security, which represents the systematized extraction of denial-mode counterintelligence; rigorous discussion of this topic alone might exceed the length of this book. The following analysis seeks to illustrate that the department's CI program is hindered from providing advantages beyond denial (an organizational development and culture problem) and from providing the right advantages to the right decision makers (an organizational structure problem).

The Status Quo

Currently, most Defense CI is conducted by the three counterintelligence agencies of the military departments, with the Counterintelligence Field Activity (CIFA) acting as a central manager. The Naval Criminal Investigative Service (NCIS), the Air Force Office of Special Investigations (AFOSI), and the army's Intelligence and Security Command (INSCOM) provide the vast majority of the counterintelligence support to the DoD, including support to the combatant commanders and deployed military forces. These agencies have been in place in one form or another since long before the Goldwater-Nichols Act was passed, and as noted, two of them use the "CI is law enforcement" approach. In the Department of Defense, they alone have the authority to conduct the full spectrum of counterintelligence activities, from investigations to offensive CI operations.[25] These agencies provide the bulk of support to the rest of the components through a "lead agency" system in which the military department counterintelligence agencies are assigned responsibility to provide "general counterintelligence support" to the eleven Defense agencies and the ten combatant commanders.[26]

The Counterintelligence Field Activity (CIFA) was established in 2002 to act as the central manager of defense counterintelligence, initially for only planning, programming, and budgeting.[27] There was no intent to convey operational authority, but loose policy writing in the CIFA charter left enough ambiguity for exploitation. Equally unfortunate, CIFA was given the role for policy interpretation and for managing the Defense-wide counterintelligence budget. Due to a combination of lax oversight in the Defense Department and the Congress and generous post-9/11 funding, CIFA's "central manager" role grew into several hundred contract employees, a huge investment in new infrastructure, and a vastly self-expanded mission. Still, the creation of CIFA acknowledged the need for a central manager for counterintelligence, and it filled that need. Following changes made by the undersecretary of defense for intelligence, CIFA's organizational goals have been somewhat curtailed, but the organization retains its "central manager" role.[28] Included within this role is the ability to levy operational "mission tasking" upon the counterintelligence agencies within military departments.[29]

The Defense Intelligence Agency (DIA) is assigned under Executive Order 12333 the role of providing the "defense contribution to national CI products," but under Defense counterintelligence policy the DIA does not have authority to conduct either "offensive" counterintelligence activities or investigations beyond those of its own employees.[30] Since 1991 the DIA has also been the central manager for the department's human intelligence (HUMINT) activities.[31] Various other Defense agencies have small offices, which are generally responsible for educating the workforce on counterintelligence awareness, establishing agency-specific policy in this area, and coordinating investigative support from the agencies in military departments assigned to support them. Intelligence agencies such as the National Security Agency (NSA) have more comprehensive CI efforts, but they are still limited in scope.

At first glance, all seems in order. There is a central operations manager for counterintelligence (CIFA). There is a place for centralized analysis and contribution to the national effort (DIA). There are capabilities and a system in place to provide counterintelligence support to most decision makers. The military departments have their own agencies chartered to provide the full spectrum of advantages that decision makers need and that counterintelligence can provide, the secretary and Joint Staff get support from DIA, and the combatant commanders and Defense agencies can receive the full spectrum of counterintelligence advantages they need from the counterintelligence agencies of the military departments.[32] This is not a bad first impression. The establishment of CIFA seems to have been warranted, and the WMD Commission's recommendation for further strengthening of CIFA appears to have been sound.

This impression, however, holds only at first glance; we (and the WMD Commission) have breezed right past a fundamental flaw. The current arrangement, in which the military departments provide counterintelligence support to the Defense agencies and especially the combatant commanders does not work. The problems, which are organizational and doctrinal, are serious ones. The department also separates management of counterintelligence activities from HUMINT activities, which handicaps both. These problems are part historical legacy and part conceptual, reflecting a misunderstanding of the nature of the counterintelligence mission. In any case, they represent a profound weakness in the Defense Department's program.

Organizationally Deficient

Of primary concern is the overall organizational problem, which counterintelligence theory eloquently highlights. As previously noted, "act" phase counterintelligence, especially that which either seeks to degrade the intelligence capability of a competitor or seeks to manipulate the decision-making process of the competitor in a deception, must be integrated with the operational planning and activities of the supported decision maker. Identifying the supported decision maker(s) is critical to integrating intelligence and counterintelligence in a way that provides the most advantage to them. In the case of military operations conducted to further U.S. policies, the primary Defense Department decision makers vary depending on the stage of the competition, but they always lie within the "operational" chain of command. When viewed in the context of the theory presented in this chapter, one might argue that counterintelligence efforts should be managed at different levels within the operational enterprise, or that this kind of support might best be provided by outside specialists with relevant expertise; one would have a very difficult time arguing that the CI effort should be run by someone engaged in an entirely different enterprise altogether. But this is currently the case for the Department of Defense. Further, counterintelligence efforts are managed by the military departments, while positive foreign intelligence (FI), including human, signals, and imagery intelligence, is managed by the Defense Intelligence Agency and the combatant commanders' joint intelligence centers (JICs); FI and CI are completely separated.

Setting aside intelligence theory, it seems unreasonable to expect the head of a military department based in Washington, DC, such as the air force, to ensure that his counterintelligence agency meets, or even understands, the needs of the combatant commanders or the Defense agencies. Military department-level decisions are driven by priorities far removed from military operations and planning, and the last thing a department head contemplating future capabilities, budget cycles, and congressional testimony ought to be concerned with is whether a combatant commander is happy with the counterintelligence support he is receiving.

That there are not one but three such agencies providing support to ten combatant commanders and eleven Defense agencies, all with radically divergent missions, operational environments, and hostile intelligence threats further undermines the effectiveness of the system. That these three CI agencies all have explicitly "worldwide" missions with no one in the lead confuses the matter yet again. Asking CIFA to centrally manage such a poorly organized system is a lofty, perhaps unreasonable, order.

A second organizational problem is the Defense Department's policy of completely separating human intelligence collection (HUMINT) from counterintelligence. Central management of Defense HUMINT collection lies with the Defense Intelligence Agency.[33] Defense HUMINT is operated as an enterprise, with authorities for the conduct of human intelligence collection spread throughout the department. These diverse HUMINT operations are centrally managed within the Defense HUMINT Management Office (DHMO) of the Defense Intelligence Agency.[34] The DHMO, in turn, is the department's point of contact for the similar responsibilities of the national clandestine service (NCS, formerly the CIA's Directorate of Operations). This seemingly well-rationalized arrangement falls apart when one notes that counterintelligence operations are excluded from central management within the Defense Department; the military departments coordinate directly with the CIA's national clandestine service for their counterintelligence efforts. Indeed, it is entirely probable that NCS knows more about the sum of HUMINT and counterintelligence operations conducted by the Defense Department than is known by any one office within the department itself, including the office of the secretary or his deputy for intelligence.[35]

While it is clear that for security reasons, counterintelligence operations and related information should be handled in separate, more restricted channels from positive intelligence, completely separating the management of these missions is problematic. History tells us that penetrations of opposing intelligence services are a key part of an effective counterintelligence effort. The U.S. national counterintelligence strategy emphasizes this type of aggressive, offensive approach. Separating the Defense counterintelligence agencies from the centralized Defense HUMINT manager nullifies a broad collection capability that might provide useful leads or actual penetrations of competing intelligence services.[36] The role of the Defense HUMINT manager in evaluating training, establishing and enforcing operational standards, reviewing operations, and establishing common communications architecture is also a critical one; that the Defense Department does not include counterintelligence operations or the agencies that conduct them in any of these important efforts means that these agencies will likely lose out on any benefits derived from them.

Doctrinally Inconsistent

These organizational flaws challenge defense doctrine because the Defense Department makes unity of action a fundamental goal of all military efforts. Given the structurally divergent priorities of the military departments and the combatant commanders, provision of counterintelligence support by the former to the latter is difficult at best. Policy within the department provides control of counterintelligence activities to the military departments, with exceptions on a case-by-case basis.[37] Some spectacular fights have erupted at the level of the Joint Chiefs of Staff (JCS) when the subject of combatant commander control of counterintelligence forces during military operations has been discussed. With few exceptions, the departmental counterintelligence agencies have prevailed.

These tensions are not unwarranted and are often acutely manifested at the tactical level. Just before the current Iraq war, a Marine infantry unit training on Faylaka Island in Kuwait was attacked by a small group of Kuwaiti jihadists; Marine Military Police shot and killed two assailants. Marine Corps tactical counterintelligence personnel, who are dedicated to supporting ground maneuver units, rushed to exploit the scene for information that might prevent additional, imminent attacks. At the same time, a special agent of the Naval Criminal Investigative Service persuaded the ground commander, against his instincts, to prevent the intelligence exploitation on the basis of the investigative prerogative of the departmental counterintelligence agency. Thus, a ground commander attempting to protect his forces while operating under the full authority of the combatant commander was prevented from gaining the counterintelligence advantage he needed (insight) by an agency investigator, an employee of the secretary of the Navy, who had a different priority—an after-the-fact criminal terrorism investigation.[38] In terms of the counterintelligence theory presented here, there was no system in place to balance tailored counterintelligence support among decision makers with vastly different requirements. Nor is there ever likely to be. Developing organizational coordinating mechanisms for a lengthy and slow-moving contest such as the "Cold War" might once have proven effective; but rapid-paced and multiparty competitions require fundamentally different solutions.

This tactical example seems relatively minor, but it is not isolated. In the case of the 2003 ground invasion of Iraq, these problems got played out at the strategic level. During this period, DoD participated in a global "CI campaign," nicknamed Imminent Horizon, mounted against the Iraqi Intelligence Service (IIS) in the months before the war. The campaign was reactive rather than deliberately planned, and the main reason any campaign was even attempted was because the order originated at the highest levels of government.[39]

This is a direct indictment of the military departments' role in providing counterintelligence support to the geographic combatant commanders. Though hostilities had been ongoing for some twelve years, and the war planning effort went on equally as long, there was no offensive counterintelligence plan on the shelf. No consideration had been given to how a comprehensive effort might provide counterintelligence advantages during the execution of the war plans; few preparations had been made to provide those advantages. Though the after-action report reads like the mission was a smashing success, it is important to note that it was written by the counterintelligence agencies involved. The majority of the operations were ad hoc, reactive, and not at all guided by a strategic understanding of the Iraqi Intelligence Service. The Defense Department's failure to systematically develop counterintelligence advantages to complement or support war plans is at least partly—probably mostly—attributable to the military departments' inherently circumscribed ability to provide such support to the combatant commanders.

Organizational Culture and Development

Last is the organizational culture and development problem, and here the greatest challenge is the "CI is law enforcement" approach favored by the Department of Defense.[40] The evidence is quite clear, as the Naval Criminal Investigative Service (NCIS), the Air Force Office of Special Investigations (AFOSI), and CIFA are all formally law enforcement organizations, with agents trained at the Federal Law Enforcement Training Center in Glynco, Georgia, and carrying badges and guns.

As noted in the theory above, treating counterintelligence as law enforcement predisposes those responsible for the former to a narrow, defensive, and tactical worldview. This is a result of the institutional emphasis on the single act of espionage as a crime rather than the sum of the espionage effort as a manifestation of a competitor's foreign or defense policy. Many observers have noted this as a key source of pre-9/11 weakness in the FBI's counterintelligence program; some in Congress are still doubtful that the problem of organizational culture there can be overcome. [41]

To be fair, there is a broad range of additional training provided to Defense Department counterintelligence personnel by CIFA's Joint CI Training Academy, but this training is heavily focused on specific skills and does essentially nothing to communicate the fundamental difference in concepts between law enforcement and counterintelligence, meaning that leadership is ill-prepared to think "CI" and execute it in a meaningful, strategic way. Undoing a career's worth of paradigm takes more than skills-based training. That, combined with the fact that naval and air force counterintelligence personnel move between law enforcement and CI postings, often without receiving any training on the difference, makes for less than ideal counterintelligence force development. The National Counterintelligence Executive acknowledged this in a 2006 report, observing that "there is a gap—with strategic implications for national security—between counterintelligence performance requirements . . . and the current capacity to train and develop a professional CI cadre."[42]

Another organizational development problem arises from these agencies' positions outside of the "organize, train, equip" machinery of the military services. As part of their responsibilities under the executive agency system, these agencies provide counterintelligence personnel to support the combatant commanders in combat zones like Iraq and Afghanistan, and in unpredictable environments like Haiti or Côte d'Ivoire. In effect, they are performing as supporting commanders, or combat support agencies, for the combatant commanders. This might not be a problem during peacetime, but with a largely civilian workforce, no formal mechanism to build and evaluate military-compatible infrastructure, and no mechanism (or formal requirement) to ensure combat training or education in either service or joint military doctrine, these agencies have placed their personnel at organizationally irresponsible risk by deploying them into these environments.

One recent example: In 2003, the department rushed counterintelligence personnel from military department CI agency offices around the globe to Iraq to help stem the growing insurgency. During that time, the Naval Criminal Investigative Service's headquarters was buying "combat gear" from mail-order outlets and military surplus stores, and the Air Force Office of Special Investigations was spending tens of millions of supplemental dollars on brand-new weapons, vehicles, and tactical communications gear, which its agents had never trained with or even seen, to be used for the first time in Iraq. To be fair, the personnel of these two agencies have performed creditably, but they have done so in spite of the current arrangement.

Defending the Status Quo

Status quo advocates have successfully defended the current arrangement on the grounds that the counterintelligence agencies are fulfilling explicit responsibilities of military departments. These responsibilities include their role in enforcing the Uniform Code of Military Justice (law governing military members), the need to meet specific Title X responsibilities to control intelligence activities, and the need to comply with section 162 in the same code exempting the assignment of certain military department personnel to the combatant commanders. These arguments are badly flawed, and in any case are trumped by the secretary of defense's authority to establish additional intelligence capabilities as deemed necessary.[43] Still, the bureaucratic effectiveness of these arguments warrants a closer look at them.

The first argument is that military department heads are ultimately responsible for enforcing the Uniform Code of Military Justice for their respective service personnel, and since espionage is after all a crime, all defense counterintelligence investigations involving military personnel must remain under the purview of military department CI agencies. This argument reverts to the narrow view of counterintelligence common to law enforcement organizations. This view is in no way prescribed by U.S. law, and it poses a considerable hurdle to the development and exploitation of the advantages counterintelligence offers beyond simple denial. It ignores the full spectrum and sum of intelligence threats directed at the department in favor of a structure focused on the criminal convictions of the few spies who are caught red-handed.[44] It is also an incomplete argument; assuming counterintelligence investigations are best conducted by law enforcement agencies, it explains why investigations would need to be the purview of the military departments, but not why the spectrum of other related activities ("offensive CI") that the military departments conduct should remain within their purview.

Related to the law enforcement argument, the CI agencies of military departments have historically fought the assignment of their forces to combatant commanders by citing a line in current defense counterintelligence policy which states that the military departments are responsible for retaining command and control of counterintelligence in U.S. code.[45] This mistake is perpetuated by the WMD Commission's understanding that "counterintelligence is assigned, under Title X of U.S. law, to the military services as their responsibility, controlled and conducted by them."[46] This is not the case; the juxtaposition of two lines of exceptions in Title X cited by the Defense Department's policy appears to convey legal responsibilities for departmental control which simply do not exist. It is incorrect to maintain, as does current defense policy, that U.S. law proscribes the assignment of military department counterintelligence personnel to the combatant commanders as with the remainder of military forces. Indeed, after clearing up the spectacular errors in the current policy, it seems that U.S. code would actually require it.[47]

This issue has been discussed repeatedly at the highest levels of the Defense Department. Two recent studies, conducted by the Institutes for Defense Analysis and a for-hire consulting company, have concluded that there is no problem with command and control of Defense Department counterintelligence.[48] These studies share three flaws. First, neither study made even a cursory examination of the department's policy and its inaccurate reading of Title X as outlined above. Second, each study simply asks, "Is there a command and control problem with respect to CI?" while omitting the important context of what an optimal counterintelligence system might look like as a benchmark. As noted before, the Defense Department's doctrinal understanding of counterintelligence leaves much to be desired. With no reference to the spectrum of advantages this mission area offers, and no challenge to the implicit assumption that counterintelligence is just about catching spies, the resulting research is quite shallow and reaches a predictable conclusion. Finally, since most combatant commanders know relatively little about counterintelligence theory (most are drawn from the combat arms), each would have had little basis for answering the research question. They most likely referred these questions to their staff officers, which by Defense Department policy are representatives of the counterintelligence agencies of military departments who remain happy with the status quo. Allowing the assigned agency representative to answer these research questions invites the bureaucratic impulse to protect one's home-agency turf. At a minimum, these three problems call into question the objectivity and relevance of the data collected by these studies, if not their conclusions outright.

Recommendations and Conclusion

The preceding analysis does not discount the military departments' need for certain counterintelligence advantages. Clearly, they and their services have vast resources to protect. Counterintelligence plays a very important conceptual role in denying adversary intelligence collection, driving the security efforts of military departments, and providing insight-mode contributions to the assessment of the department's foreign competitors. Protecting the "organize-train-equip" function preserves military advantage and contributes to the military and decision advantage available to the nation in a time of war. What this analysis points out is that the continued vesting of authority for counterintelligence activities intended to support military operations in the hands of the military departments, when those departments have no other role in the planning or execution of the military operation, makes little sense.

Central management by CIFA under the current construct might help ensure that military operational needs are met, but then the military departments and their counterintelligence elements are still in the tough position of executing operations in support of two (or seven or ten) divergent missions; this is complicated by the additional organizational and cultural problems noted above. Finally, the vast artificial gulf between human intelligence activities and counterintelligence operations within the Defense Department ignores potentially advantageous operational capabilities inherent in the Defense HUMINT enterprise and unnecessarily complicates management and oversight of both CI and HUMINT within the department and the U.S. government. More effective coordination and support mechanisms than currently exist might be provided for, but why be satisfied with additional rules and procedures to fix a complicated organizational problem when theory hints at more eloquent solutions?

The basic steps are clear. At the minimum, the Defense Department must get the military departments out of the business of providing counterintelligence support to the combatant commanders; the current arrangement does not align the acquisition of CI advantage with decision-making needs. Goldwater-Nichols was clear about the division of labor in the Defense Department, and the current arrangement of CI responsibilities is in clear contradiction to sound theory. Likewise, the department must formally separate CI from law enforcement. The last thing on any counterintelligence agency's agenda should be an espionage conviction, particularly when that agency is chartered to provide the full spectrum of counterintelligence support to a war effort.

Beyond these basic steps, there are multiple organizational reforms that could solve some of the problems raised in this chapter. The author's view, supported by CI theory, current national-level policy and law, and historical practice, is that counterintelligence, an inseparable subset of intelligence, should be integral to the existing intelligence capabilities of the major components and have a properly empowered and positioned central manager. Like the component counterintelligence capabilities, that manager should be integral to the appropriate intelligence agency, the Defense Intelligence Agency. The logical choice would be the Defense HUMINT manager, who would then be more appropriately dubbed the "clandestine operations manager."[49]

In fact, this seems to be the solution chosen by the Defense leadership. On August 4, 2008 (just as this chapter was being completed), the department announced the creation of the Defense Counterintelligence and Human Intelligence Center, which essentially merged the DIA's existing HUMINT function with many of the roles once held by CIFA. The awkward separation of operations management and CI analysis under CIFA and DIA respectively appears to have been eliminated. More important, the department's problematic separation of HUMINT and CI operations management has been rectified (at least on paper). The importance of these two changes cannot be overstated. What remains to be seen is whether the DIA will prove an effective provider of CI operations in support of the combatant commander. In the positive column, DIA is a combat support agency and has both the experience and a formal system in place for ensuring that the support it provides is combat capable, interoperable with joint military forces, and responsive to the commander.

Also unclear and probably more significant for defense CI is whether the military departments will continue to play a key role in this effort. Of concern is the institutionalized mistake of treating CI as a law enforcement function. Notable is how explicitly the department's press release states that "CIFA's designation as a law enforcement activity did not transfer to DIA." But the Departments of the Navy and Air Force, respectively, still assign CI to their law enforcement agencies. Continued conduct of CI by departmental law enforcement agencies (NCIS and AFOSI) will likely remain a major hurdle to an effective, offensive strategic counterintelligence effort. And since the military department CI agencies still have global missions including offensive counterintelligence operations, and will inevitably be continuing to support service components in wartime, how well will they coordinate those missions with DIA's new CI and Human Intelligence Center? Has DIA been given enough authority to perform as *the* central manager, as sound theory recommends?

Clearly, defense counterintelligence is receiving attention at the highest levels of the U.S. government, as evidenced by the establishment of CIFA, recent investment in related programs, and the attention it received from the WMD Commission. None of these efforts have delved deeply enough into the Defense Department's conceptualization of counterintelligence to recognize the significant problems with the current program. Until the Defense Department fully embraces counterintelligence as a strategic means of gaining competitive advantages over adversaries instead of a reactive, defensive security effort, it will continue to misunderstand both the intelligence threats posed by adversaries and the operational advantages offered by counterintelligence. And until senior Defense Department leaders, in and out of the counterintelligence community, abandon the bureaucratic impulse to guard their "rice bowls" and divide authorities and missions along rational lines—lines in concert with counterintelligence theory, Goldwater-Nichols, and the way the Defense Department fights today—defense counterintelligence will continue to be unprepared to support anyone's needs in an effective manner.

Beyond a more detailed reconceptualization of the system than that presented here, and the accompanying policy revision, there are other real challenges to be faced. Organizational sea changes always raise the question of a capability gap during the transition. Senior officials whose entire worldviews have been shaped under the old system are often ill-prepared to adapt to a new one and so may be expected to resist actively. Damaging leaks, and public and partisan political infighting, are the historically predicted outcomes. The simple cost of making such changes can by itself be prohibitive, especially since in its five years of existence CIFA has invested vast sums on information technology infrastructure based upon the "CI as Law Enforcement" model.

None of these challenges justifies inaction. Preserving and extending the DoD's advantage over the nation's military competitors is an integral part of our national security, and it cannot be accomplished without a sound counterintelligence program. Outside of ongoing war and security policy issues, completing the overhaul of Defense Department counterintelligence should be the first order of defense-related business for the next administration.

Notes

The views expressed in this chapter do not necessarily represent those of the U.S. Marine Corps or the Department of Defense.

1. The core theory of intelligence used in this formulation is taken from Dr. Sims's Georgetown University course *Theory and Practice of Intelligence.*

2. The serious problems with separating clandestine HUMINT, CI, and covert action management are lucidly explained in the IC21 report "IC21: The Intelligence Community in the 21st Century," Staff Study Permanent Select Committee on Intelligence House of Representatives, 104th Cong., Chapter 13, Intelligence and Law Enforcement. Available online at www.access.gpo.gov/congress/house/_intel/ic21/ic21009.html. I will only briefly discuss these problems in this chapter.

3. Earlier drafts of this paper were provided to senior leaders in the Department of Defense prior to their decisions on counterintelligence reform. This paper is left largely unmodified from the earlier drafts.

4. Personal e-mail correspondence with Michael Warner, November 5–7, 2007.

5. Joint Publication 2–01 Intelligence. Available at www.dtic.mil/doctrine/ jel/new_pubs/jp2_0.pdf.

6. See Richard A. Best Jr. and Andrew Feickert, *Special Operations Forces (SOF) and CIA Paramilitary Operations: Issues for Congress,* Congressional Research Service, December 6, 2006, 2.

7. Jennifer D. Kibbe, "The Rise of the Shadow Warriors," *Foreign Affairs* 83, no. 2 (March/April 2004): 2–3.

8. Readers familiar with 2002–2004 Defense-level CI working groups will recall the push to make CI an explicit function of the combatant command J-3 (operations officer)

instead of the J-2 (intelligence officer). The supporting argument was that CI is "not intelligence;" Title 50 defines intelligence as including both foreign intelligence and CI.

9. The DoD dictionary defines CI as "information gathered and activities conducted to protect against espionage, other intelligence activities, sabotage, or assassinations conducted by or on behalf of foreign governments or elements thereof, foreign organizations, or foreign persons, or international terrorist activities." Available at www.dtic.mil/doctrine/jel/doddict/data/c/index.html.

10. Michelle Van Cleave, "Strategic Counterintelligence: What is it and what should we do about it?" *Studies in Intelligence* 51, no. 2. Available at www.cia.gov/library/center-for-the-study-of-intelligence/csi-publications/csi-studies/studies/v0151n02/index.html.

11. Many practitioners and authors have narrowly defined CI as security and counterespionage; CI's "triad of three essential functions is: protecting secrets, frustrating attempts by foreign intelligence services to acquire those secrets, and catching Americans who spy for those foreign intelligence services," from Frederick L. Wettering, "Counterintelligence: The Broken Triad," *International Journal of Intelligence and Counterintelligence* 13, no. 3 (2000): 265–300. Some have commented on the need to define CI as being inherently multidisciplinary: "The CI threat must be redefined as the composite human and technical threat that it is, and appropriate cross-disciplinary countermeasures must be developed to defeat and exploit this threat," from George T. Kalaris and Leonard V. McCoy, "Counterintelligence for the 1990s," in *Intelligence Requirements for the 1990s: Collection, Analysis, Counterintelligence, and Covert Action*, ed. Roy Godson (Lexington, MA: Lexington Books, 1989), 130. The theoretical formulation presented here assumes a multidisciplinary approach.

12. Dr. Jennifer Sims defines intelligence as "information collected, analyzed or disseminated on behalf of a decision maker engaged in a competitive enterprise;" the linkage of advantage, whether from intelligence or CI, to the correct decision makers in the competitive enterprise is critical.

13. Jennifer Sims, class notes from her course "Intelligence: Theory and Practice," given at Georgetown University, fall 2003, supplemented by e-mail dated April 6, 2005.

14. "Exploited" applies broadly; a competitor may obtain information that could benefit his decision making, such as a war plan, or his operational capability, such as a weakness in U.S. tank armor. I first heard the term "operational games" at the excellent CI Centre seminar on denial and deception. According to former KGB major General Oleg Kalugin, "operational games" was the primary mission of the KGB.

15. Most CI officers associate this concept with double agents or penetration agents; agents are one example of the penetration of a competitor's intelligence cycle. A multidisciplinary CI approach should seek penetration by whatever means to support the information or operational advantage requirements of the decision maker.

16. Deception, as noted by many authors, requires a competing decision maker to make decisions based upon an altered presentation of reality, or ruse. This requires a combination of denying access to information that would discredit the ruse and a channeling of information—real or otherwise—that supports the ruse. Thus, effective denial is a critical component to manipulation. See J. Bowyer Bell, "Towards a Theory of Deception," *International Journal of Intelligence and Counterintelligence* 16, no. 10, (2003): 244–79; and Roy Godson and James Wirtz, "Strategic Denial & Deception," *International Journal of Intelligence and Counterintelligence* 13, no. 4 (2000): 424–37, for discussions of the topic.

17. This subtle but powerful explanation is paraphrased from Bernard E. Victory, ed., "Modernizing Intelligence: Structure and Change for the 21st Century" (National Institute for Public Policy, January 2002), 99. Available at www.nipp.org/Adobe/_ rev%20intel%20complete.pdf. It also appears in similar formulation in Roy Godson, *Dirty Tricks or Trump Cards: U.S. Covert Action and Counterintelligence* (Transaction Publishers, 2000), 184–85.

18. A prime example of this is the British Double-Cross system of World War II. The massive double-agent operation simultaneously provided denial by helping to identify new German agents entering England, insight by providing access to German information requirements and leadership intentions, and manipulation by channeling false information that was then confirmed by other German intelligence means as part of a larger deception operation. The point is that those advantages were balanced depending on the operational needs of the decision maker at any given point in the competition. See J. C. Masterman, *The Double-Cross System: 1939–1945* (London: Sphere Books Limited, 1973).

19. The CI manager or supported decision maker may have "red lines." Whether based upon a previous body of CI analysis or the current priorities of the decision maker, "red lines" may short-circuit the previously described CI process, taking a detected activity more rapidly from the detect phase to the prescribed act phase.

20. The Cheka's TRUST Operation is a good example of "detect-study-act." The Soviet intelligence service detected, studied, and penetrated the exiled resistance movement worldwide; it then spent several more years using deception to lure key leadership back to the USSR, where the resistance was destroyed.

21. As Sims discusses in chapter 1 of this volume, security is at essence part of CI; in terms of the theory presented here, it is the systematized extraction of denial-mode CI advantage through a system of rules, access control, and personnel vetting.

22. Title 50 defines CI as a subset of intelligence, and Executive Order 12333 makes no mention of CI being law enforcement. Confusion creeps in when convictions become the final goal of espionage cases.

23. This is explicitly recognized by the authority of the National Clandestine Service to manage all U.S. government clandestine intelligence activities, including CI.

24. Joint Pub 3–13, App B, page B-3. Available at www.dtic.mil/.

25. DoD Directive 5240.2 para 5.2.3 refers to "CI operations" and explicitly assigns authority to the military departments.

26. DoD Instruction 5240.10, May 14, 2004. Available at www.dtic.mil/whs/_ directives/corres/rtf/524010x.rtf.

27. CIFA's charter is DoD Directive 5105.67, dated February 19, 2002. Available at www.cifa.mil/Library%20and%20References/documents/CIFA%20Charter.pdf.

28. "Clapper Approves Sweeping Reorganization of Pentagon Counterintelligence," *Inside Defense Newstand*, June 28, 2007. Available at http://defense.iwpnewsstand .com/.

29. The WMD Commission Report recommended giving CIFA operational authority; the DoD response fell short of new operational authority and instead conferred the ability to task operational requirements through mission tasking authority (MTA). See Memorandum for Public Release. Available at www.cifa.mil/Library%20and%20References/_ documents/_Mission%20Tasking%20Authority.pdf.

30. DoD Directive 5240.2, Defense Counterintelligence, May 22, 1997.

31. DoD Directive 5200.37, Central Management of Department of Defense HUMINT Operations, December 18, 1992.

32. DoD Instruction 5240.10, Counterintelligence Support to Combatant Commanders.

33. DoD Directive 5200.37. Furthermore, actual conduct of HUMINT collection operations was centralized there (minus tactical collection) in 1993; Memorandum from Defense Secretary William Perry to the DoD Components, titled "Consolidation of Defense HUMINT," November 2, 1993. Available at www.gwu.edu/~nsarchiv/NSAEBB/NSAEBB46/document19.pdf.

34. See 2006 Senate Intelligence Committee Report. Available at http://intelligence.senate.gov/report%20_ia2006.pdf.

35. Coordination is required under EO 12333 and pertinent intelligence directives; DoD Directives 5200.37 and 5240.2 place these coordination requirements on the DIA and the military departments, respectively.

36. The 2006 Senate Intelligence Committee Report explicitly supported including Departmental CI efforts under the rubric of DHMO coordination: "The Committee supports the creation of the Defense HUMINT Management Office (DHMO) as a means of executing DoD objectives under the DoD HUMINT Enterprise, including the intelligence activities of the military department counterintelligence agencies." Available at http://intelligence.senate.gov/report%20_ia2006.pdf.

37. DoD Directive 5240.2 Defense Counterintelligence, paragraphs 4.4–4.6.

38. Is exploiting pocket litter on a dead terrorist CI, or is it positive intelligence? This example shows that at essence, CI and positive intelligence are inseparable and often indistinguishable. Their similarity is especially apparent when networked competitors can conduct their own intelligence to support their actions. The organizational need to divide labor for control, efficiency, and specialization brings about the distinction; at the end of the day CI is all about information-driven advantage in a competition.

39. Van Cleave, "Strategic Counterintelligence."

40. This problem has been noted before. See "IC21: The Intelligence Community in the 21st Century." Available at www.access.gpo.gov/congress/house/intel/_ic21/ic21013.html. Also, Victory, "Modernizing Intelligence," 99–101.

41. Senate Select Intelligence Committee Hearing on the FBI's National Security Strategic Plan. See video transcript at www.c-span.org.

42. NCIX, "The Universal Counterintelligence Core Competencies," vol. 1, 12. Available at www.ncix.gov/publications/_reports/index.html.

43. Executive Order 12333, paragraph 1.12(e), explicitly authorizes the secretary to establish other offices within the Department of Defense appropriate for conduct of the intelligence missions and responsibilities assigned to the secretary of defense.

44. Some agencies spin this argument further, stating that as law enforcement agencies conducting CI, they can "dual hat" their investigators, with one investigator switching from a law enforcement role to a CI role as needed during an investigation. The result, they maintain, is a speedier resolution of a case and a faster transition to indictment and trial. The author maintains that the speed at which an indictment is reached is a poor measure of effectiveness for CI investigations. This argument was being used (to great effect) on Congress's intelligence committee staffers as recently as 2004.

45. DoDD 5240.2, paragraph 4.4. Actually, the exceptions provided for in subsection (c)(7) of the applicable departmental sections (3013, etc.) refer to "departmental intelligence activities," not just CI.

46. Walter Jajko, "The State of Defense Counterintelligence," *Journal of U.S. Intelligence Studies* (Winter/Spring, 2004): 7–9, quoting from footnote 19 of chapter 11, WMD Commission Report.

47. 10 USC 162(a)(2) makes explicit exceptions for the assignment of forces to the combatant commanders only for those military department forces noted in subsection (b) of the respective Military Department sections (3013, etc.), and makes no mention of excepting the assignment of forces under subsection (c) whatsoever. Subsection (b) concerns personnel involved in the "organize-train-equip" mission and makes no mention whatsoever of intelligence or CI personnel. The juxtaposition of the exception wording in DoD CI policy makes 10 USC 162(a)(2) appear on the face to apply to subsection (c)(7) of the pertinent Military Department sections. It does not. The author credits Jack Butler, lieutenant colonel USMC (Ret.), for this keen observation.

48. The Institutes for Defense Analysis and Bearing Point, respectively, conducted reviews of command and control of DoD Counterintelligence support to the combatant commanders in 2002–2004. The results of these reviews have not been published; however, the author participated in both.

49. This would begin to align DoD with the CIA's approach to categorizing and managing intelligence collection as "clandestine collection" rather than the DoD methodology of breaking them down by discipline, i.e., HUMINT vs. MASINT vs. CI.

7

Kathleen L. Kiernan

Counterintelligence and Law Enforcement

The cause is hidden. The effect is visible to all.

Ovid (43 BC–AD 17)

THE INSIDIOUS nature of deliberate compromise once exposed—be it with people, networks, or technical capabilities—always seems to surprise the affected organization. Within law enforcement or intelligence agencies compromised by a trusted insider, damage can be particularly deep. Trust among and between colleagues is fundamental to operational efficiency, but it can be a vulnerability unless accountability standards are applied consistently and without considerations of rank, seniority, or affinity. Damage assessments have frequently revealed that spies hide in plain sight, suggesting that serious damage could also easily be averted if procedural safeguards, including routine polygraph screening, employee oversight, and access to critical data, are established and then enforced to identify such activity.[1]

Historically, counterintelligence in local law enforcement has largely been absent, and collaboration between police departments and federal agencies with regard to national intelligence has been weak at best. Prior to the September 2001 terrorist attacks, law enforcement's focus on terrorism was related to domestic threats by so-called single-issue groups, such as violence-prone animal rights, ecology, and antiabortion groups. The primary law enforcement mission involved public safety accomplished through community policing. Intelligence and counterintelligence functions were limited largely to combating organized crime, street gangs, and drug trafficking. Most cooperation with federal agencies involved the Federal Bureau of Investigation (FBI), the Drug Enforcement Administration (DEA), and the Bureau of Alcohol, Tobacco, Firearms, and Explosives (ATFE). Cooperation between local police departments and federal agencies was limited largely to the investigation of specific criminal activity, initiated in many cases to optimize the increased penalties for criminal violations at the federal level. While professional relationships invariably developed, missions were viewed as separate and distinct and were often complicated by interagency rivalries. Any mission creep was viewed with suspicion and, at times, animosity.

The events of 9/11 and the subsequent war on terrorism have had a dramatic impact on law enforcement at virtually every level, resulting not only in legislative action and reorganization, but also in the recognition that local law enforcement can and should be an important resource for the national counterintelligence effort. This realization involves an important paradigm shift at a time when new threats challenge police departments' ability to manage their resources. Policing now is more than public safety; it is a national security function. Both organizational acceptance and adoption of this shift at the state, local, and tribal level will require that federal authorities demonstrate tangible benefits from collaboration and offer a clear nexus for operating jointly with traditional policing. Unfortunately, increased responsibilities in the counterintelligence arena by state, local, and tribal law enforcement could have the opposite result, causing tension with mission partners at the federal level and exacerbating organizational tensions.

Given that 9/11 and subsequent attacks against Western democracies demonstrate that the level of threat continues to increase in severity and sophistication, it stands to reason that existing national level capabilities must be enhanced. Of course federal authorities must meet the challenge of identifying foreign intelligence activities directed against U.S. interests; but other individuals and agencies are now responsible for standing watch at all levels. The increased sharing of information and intelligence-derived products runs counter to the basic principles of counterintelligence, including those identified in the National Counterintelligence Strategy. Broader access and information sharing often require extending an increased number of national security clearances to the public and private sector, while the National Intelligence Strategy warns that "the more readily available one makes classified information, the more likely it is to be somehow compromised, and the easier it is to steal."[2] The newly released National Intelligence Sharing Strategy clearly establishes the role of state, local, and tribal law enforcement in protecting the nation against terrorist and criminal activity in a proactive way and one that is inseparable from national level imperatives.[3] Emphasis is rightly placed on the need to share information that is timely, credible, and actionable through the structuring of all-source, all-crime, and all-hazard multidisciplinary fusion centers.[4]

How that tension is minimized while agencies cope with decreasing appropriations and increasing requirements levied at the national level is a challenge at the center of the fractious relationship between national-level intelligence agencies and state, local, and tribal law enforcement. The field of counterintelligence is just one of the disciplines in conflict; others include counterterrorism and relationships between law enforcement agencies and the Department of Homeland Security (DHS). Sincere, yet awkward, attempts at partnership development on both sides invariably confront the issue of access; however the perceptions regarding resolution are dramatically divergent.

At the national level, the focus continues to be on limiting access to critical sources, methods, and information while maintaining the strategic advantage of the United States against foreign adversaries. The shield carriers at the local level, charged with the historical responsibility of homeland security and burdened with increased terrorism-related requirements, perceive deliberate exclusion, based on a lack of trust in their ability to safeguard secrets, anathema to the profession. Access to national-security-level clearances is not only misunderstood, but also perceived to be an artificial barrier that hinders law enforcement preparedness and response. The lack of access to timely and credible data related to specific events and threats is characterized by Chief William Bratton of the Los Angeles Police Department: "The frustration is that intelligence gathering and sharing networks at the federal level are not working for local chiefs of police. . . . We're used to things breaking very quickly and have to respond quickly. We don't have the luxury of waiting."[5] A similar sentiment, expressed by Charles Ramsey, former chief of the Metropolitan Police Department in Washington, DC, illustrates the principal difference in mission responsibilities: "The FBI is worrying about who might have done it, but what I care about is that there was an attack on a transit system and I have rush hour coming up. . . . I don't need a threat analysis. I need to know what I can do proactively to strengthen the security of our transit system. Terrorism always starts as a local event. We're the first responders."[6]

This divide and the collective failure to bridge it satisfactorily constitute a classic "wicked problem," a term mentioned in the introduction of this volume and originally coined by Horst Rittel to describe a problem that is strongly stakeholder dependent, ill-defined, and inextricably intertwined with complex contextual and professional issues, and further, one for which solutions may in fact yield additional complex problems.[7] In this case the development of solutions would reveal that the clearance system process as it currently exists is already completely overburdened and inefficient. Adding thousands of police officers into the process will hobble it entirely and contribute to the further erosion of its credibility at the national level. Moreover, the use of lifestyle polygraph examinations is controversial and has occasionally limited access by state and local law enforcement to national task force efforts and training. The potential negative career impact of a failed polygraph examination with no apparent appeal process has prompted some police unions to push back against the requirement.

Traditional counterintelligence missions (in the national security sense) are the shared responsibility of members of the intelligence community and the FBI, as well as the Defense Department agencies. State, local, and tribal law enforcement agencies are not equipped, staffed, funded, or trained to engage in traditional counterintelligence missions against national security threats or foreign intelligence and security services. When nonfederal agencies have engaged in national security and related counterintelligence roles, as when the FBI enlisted local and campus law enforcement officials to perform counterintelligence activities against domestic groups in the 1960s and 1970s, these actions often ended in scandal, federal or congressional investigations, sanctions, and sometimes criminal prosecution against the responsible officials.[8]

That said, state, local, and tribal law enforcement agencies often engage in a form of counterintelligence in their daily criminal investigative and internal affairs activities. This chapter addresses the counterintelligence activities inherent in policing and investigative procedures and draws parallels where appropriate to traditional notions of counterintelligence for national security. Currently, the United States lacks an effective structure for developing and sharing information between local law enforcement and federal agencies that fully addresses issues related to counterintelligence. The problem is further compounded by scarce literature and research on counterintelligence as it relates to law enforcement.

This chapter focuses on these issues and puts forth recommendations for future approaches to address a problem that is not insurmountable, but one that will require a comprehensive review of traditional perceptions and a greater emphasis on nonconventional partnerships. The preservation of a degree of friction between the various elements of law enforcement is acceptable and even healthy as it provides protection against the potential of a national police force, which conjures up images of a wholesale erosion of civil liberties.

The Law Enforcement Mission

Law enforcement in the United States is made up of approximately 65 federal agencies, 49 state agencies, and more than 17,800 state, county, local, special jurisdiction, and tribal agencies.[9] The total number of sworn (full-time) police officers in the United States was estimated in 2004 as 836,737, approximately 87.5 percent of which are at the state and local level maintaining public order and enforcing the law.[10] The Bureau of Justice Statistics completed its most recent survey of training academies in 2002 and identified 626 state, local, and tribal law enforcement academies in the United States. State commissions govern law enforcement training standards and length of training, so there is a degree of variance from state to state. However, all training academies are consistent in their requirements of criminal law and procedure, ethics, tactical and physical proficiency, use-of-force guidelines, criminal investigations, civil rights, and equal opportunity guidelines. For example, a basic academy for the Boston and Los Angeles Police Departments consists of twenty-eight and thirty-two weeks of training respectively. Basic-level training is followed by probation with an assigned training officer for a period of time, on average of one year, before the individual operates without constant oversight. With the exception of the FBI, law enforcement personnel at the federal, state, local, and tribal levels do not receive any standardized counterintelligence training.

The profession of law enforcement is oriented around the core value to "protect and serve" a community by reducing crime and preserving a quality of life for its citizens. In the law enforcement world, the action of "deliberate compromise" is a technique used to disable criminal enterprises; its tools consist of collecting and exploiting information, turning informants, penetrating organizations, running sting operations, and collecting evidence for prosecutorial action. Successful police work requires the ability to see what is invisible to the untrained eye and to discern anomalies that indicate deception or potential criminal activity. Traditional law enforcement culture depends heavily upon *streetcraft*, or the operational art of law enforcement. Streetcraft is neither codified in any standard operating procedure nor taught in a police academy, but it is earned on the street through dealing with the extremes of human behavior, learning to detect the traces of deception, and quickly adjusting to changing tactics and technologies. The very life of a police officer will depend on his or her ability to assess a potential threat and react to it quickly, often without immediate backup from colleagues and in situations in which the adversary may have a tactical advantage with superior weapons and no concern for innocent bystanders.

This skill set also includes the honed ability to question the obvious. Arthur Conan Doyle made this technique somewhat famous when his literary protagonist, Sherlock Holmes, solved a case by noticing that a family dog did not bark at an intruder; Holmes surmised correctly that the dog, not considering the "intruder" a threat, most likely knew him.[11] A key precept of law enforcement training is the refinement of observation skills, including the ability to notice changes, however subtle, in behavior and the surrounding environment. Seasoned veterans are not always able to articulate the combination of factors or indicators that signal the "just does not look/feel/smell right" reaction that leads to further questioning of a subject or of his information.

This professional sense is more than intuition; it is part training, part experience, and part instinct—arguably all areas that are relevant in the practice of counterintelligence. It is enhanced by receptivity to unsolicited information gained in the course of routine police activity, which may yield important information beyond the scope of an initial inquiry or response. Without an understanding of the potential value of this information, an officer may not record or act upon it. The ex-wife of John Walker repeatedly told law enforcement officers responding to complaints of domestic abuse that her husband was selling secrets to the Russians—which he was. To a police officer focused on the original complaint, such an accusation probably sounded spurious, coming from an aggrieved individual in an emotionally tense situation. This information was later reconstructed when she became a key source for the FBI and helped build a case against him. The gap in formal reporting, however, permitted Walker to continue his espionage activities.

Law enforcement officers regard the manipulation of individuals, absent the use of force or illegality, as fair play and engage in the practice to "turn" criminals against one another in order to target the leadership in a criminal organization. Techniques include "shaking the tree," a slang reference for exciting a network through arrests or provoking individuals to observe their immediate responses, which are monitored and recorded and may serve as the basis for further investigative or prosecutorial action. Achievement is measured with statistical data, and both success and failure are open to public scrutiny.[12] Safeguards are in place to protect sensitive information, including the identity of undercover agents, witnesses, victims, and informants. In all police operations, officer safety is a primary issue. The threat is generally viewed as coming from outside the organization, and it is usually more concerned with thwarting an investigation or prosecution than with exerting control over, or deliberately weakening, the entire organization itself.

The idea of a foreign intelligence service infiltrating a domestic law enforcement organization to influence, compromise, or otherwise disrupt it is, in fact, an unfamiliar concept, but one that must now be considered in light of current threats. Most police departments have an internal affairs component that in effect is responsible for policing the police—looking for indications of corruption, excessive use of force, unprofessional behavior, or criminal activity. This mission is a necessary element and, under the best of circumstances, a difficult assignment in a closed environment in which individuals literally place their lives in the hands of their colleagues. Ironically, this closed environment, not dissimilar to those that exist in intelligence community agencies, may also shield potential malicious activity, as colleagues are reluctant to voice suspicions against fellow officers. Accusations against police officers related to violations of civil rights are referred for action to the FBI and form the basis for much of the traditional and historical animosity between state and local law enforcement and the FBI.

In the criminal world, the scenario involving the deliberate compromise of an adversary or a member of one's own organization is played out over and over, based principally on competition and motivated by profit and domination of illegal markets. Tools usually involve intimidation, exploitation, manipulation, and violence—often in the extreme to extract hidden knowledge of supply chains, distribution networks, caches, stashes, enforcers, and leadership hierarchies. Information is power, and it is protected by a variety of means ranging from the use of rudimentary codes to the employment of sophisticated encryption technology and an enforced "need to know" operating principle. Complex cellular structures, in which senior leaders are both isolated from and protected against exposure to lower levels in the organization, are not unusual within organized criminal networks. Street justice is exacted upon traitors and infiltrators, and in some cases, brutal punishment extends to other family members—the knowledge of which keeps individuals in line.[13]

The Traditional Counterintelligence Mission and the Role of Police

Michelle Van Cleave, who served as the National Counterintelligence Executive (NCIX), has framed the modern challenge of counterintelligence, including the financial dimension the mission implies: "Each of the major challenges confronting America's security—defeating global terrorism, countering weapons of mass destruction, ensuring the security of the homeland, transforming defense capabilities, fostering cooperation with other global partners, promoting global economic growth—has an embedded counterintelligence imperative."[14] While she did not specifically identify a role for law enforcement, Van Cleave implied the importance of protection of the homeland, which is a key aspect of the responsibilities of law enforcement officers.

Gaining a strategic and tactical advantage while hardening one's own intelligence operations against disruption by hostile nations or their intelligence services is vital to the counterintelligence mission. John MacGaffin perhaps makes the closest tie to a complementary skill set of law enforcement in his characterization: "Counterintelligence is not activity apart from human intelligence—it *is* human intelligence and it is separated from HUMINT at the peril of collector and consumer alike."[15] Unlike the resources available to the intelligence community, law enforcement has almost exclusively relied upon the ability to collect information unaided by any national technical means and has over time developed a deep level of expertise.

One of the first uses of police for counterintelligence began, not with public law enforcement, but rather with the Pinkerton Detective Agency during the Civil War, when agents were employed by the government to both spy on the Confederacy and to root out spies working against the Union. Historical analyses of police in the United States showed that even in the mid-nineteenth century the melding of police functions, criminal investigation, and intelligence operations aroused great public suspicion.[16]

Local law enforcement's counterintelligence function during World Wars I and II was minimal, although there was suspicion that some police officers of German descent were likely to be sympathetic to their country of origin. However, during this period local law enforcement did play a key role in gathering intelligence on immigrant groups. As Mitchel P. Roth notes, "Fear of communist subversion at home and rising juvenile crime and the battle for civil rights presented the criminal justice system with new challenges in the 1940s and 1950s.[17] Austin Yamada's chapter in this volume discusses the internment of Japanese citizens on U.S. soil in World War II. Law enforcement officials participated in identifying, evacuating, interning, and interviewing these individuals.

During the Prohibition era and the emergence of organized crime, police departments in the larger cities were faced with notorious levels of corruption and experienced both infiltration by and cooperation with criminal organizations—developments in keeping with decades of political malfeasance during the so-called spoils era. The efforts of Eliot Ness and a squad of local and federal officers in Chicago may have been one of the few counterintelligence operations during this period. The Untouchables, as they came to be called, employed counterintelligence tradecraft to identify corrupt law enforcement officials working in Chicago, protect their unit from infiltration, and eventually bring down Al Capone and his organized crime machine. Ironically, it was a federal statute related to income tax invasion that brought about Capone's demise.

Following Prohibition and World War II, law enforcement found itself coping with the emergence of the growing proliferation of illegal drugs and the emergence of youth gangs, particularly in minority communities. Black and Hispanic gangs began to move in on the Italian and Irish mobs that controlled much of the trade in drugs, gambling, and prostitution. Webs of corruption had a stranglehold on local government in many of the inner cities of America. Public officials had been corrupted through bribery, compromise, and the threat of potential public exposure. Local law enforcement's intelligence function during this period was weak at best, and most major corruption or infiltration investigations fell to federal agencies, and particularly to an FBI that was motivated, says Ronald Kessler, largely by press scandals.[18]

The turbulence of the 1960s and 1970s prompted major reforms in law enforcement, brought upon largely by the Report of the President's Crime Commission, *The Challenge of Crime in a Free Society*, and a series of task force reports. The emphasis on education and training began what many view as the inception of police reform and the beginning of a professional law enforcement model. With these changes came a three-decade effort to cope with a changing world in which the localization of police problems would slowly give way to international concerns about drug trafficking, organized crime, and global terrorism.[19]

As local law enforcement in the United States has evolved to meet these new challenges, the infiltration of police departments by individuals for criminal purposes has been rare. Many departments have developed a high level of expertise in the use of undercover operatives, informants, and unwitting sources in efforts to combat organized crime and drug trafficking, and there have evolved systems for the compartmentalization of information to protect the identity of the undercover officers and the informants who assist them. Organized crime and drug cartels have had reasons for accessing law enforcement information, but they have usually done so by bribing officers or clerks rather than infiltration. Background investigations, polygraph examinations, drug screening, and the rigors of police training academies have also helped to limit potential bad actors from attempted assimilation into police organizations. The expertise developed by law enforcement in identifying rogue officers and in gaining access to the inner workings of criminal groups has been an important asset in countering the efforts of terrorist groups trying to infiltrate law enforcement or gain access to computer systems and other forms of electronic information.

Emerging Threats and the Law Enforcement Response

Most American citizens do not realize that law enforcement officials regularly encounter, in the course of routine policing activities, known or suspected terrorists. For example, the state of Wisconsin released the following data on its Department of Justice website giving a snapshot of the volume and types of interactions resulting primarily from routine traffic stops.[20] For 2006–2007 Wisconsin registered 178 total encounters with individuals in the Terrorist Screening Data Base. Fifteen of these individuals had multiple encounters during the period; 44 were encountered only once. The Terrorist Screening Center identified individuals belonging to or affiliated with the following terrorist groups during this period: Hamas (45%), Sunni extremists (25%), al-Qaeda (18%), and individuals from other groups (13%).[21] Of these 178 encounters, nearly 85% were ground encounters (the remaining 15% were flight encounters), meaning that the encounters likely were the result of law enforcement interventions rather than security screenings. One can appreciate the significance of the domestic presence of extremist and terrorist organizations, which law enforcement must be prepared to identify and interdict, when one extrapolates the Wisconsin experience to the rest of the country. According to Donna Bucella, then the director of the FBI's Terrorist Screening Center (TSC), in the first twenty-eight months of the TSC's operations, police and other government workers in the United States came in contact with terrorists or people suspected of foreign terror ties more than six thousand times.[22] Arguably this law enforcement activity has critical offensive and defensive potential for identifying individuals who may have escaped other official scrutiny and may intend harm to U.S. interests, and it can contribute to national level counterintelligence efforts.

Analysis by researchers outside the law enforcement community substantiates the threat of domestic extremism. For example, open-source research conducted at the Institute for the Study of Violent Groups (ISVG) at Sam Houston State University between 2002 and 2007 identified nearly 200 extremist groups operating in the United States. The study defined such groups as those espousing rhetoric supporting violence or destruction of property for a political, social, or religious cause. All states except Alaska, Delaware, Hawaii, Maine, North Dakota, South Dakota, Rhode Island, and Vermont have had at least 10 instances of extremist activity since 2002, with California leading the states with 523 incidents. During the same period ISVG also identified 37 terrorist groups, which are distinguished from extremist groups in that they have actually attempted or carried out acts of violence or destruction of property for a political, social, or religious cause within the country. These violent attacks have occurred in thirty-two states since 2002.

In many cases gangs use bribery, cyberhacking, and other methods to infiltrate police departments for information or intelligence. They constitute a real and potential resource for terrorist groups planning attacks inside the country.

The 2004 National Youth Gang Survey, which represents the latest national-level survey of street gangs in the United States, estimated that there were more than 760,000 gang members and 24,000 gangs active in more than 2,900 jurisdictions in the United States. Phil Cline, superintendent of the Chicago Police Department from 2004 through 2007, commented at a conference in 2007 that over the past eighty years the Chicago Crime Commission had recorded 1,000 homicides by members of the Mafia, or traditional organized-crime families, whereas in just the last five years there have been 1,300 killings by street gangs in Chicago.[23] "The street gangs of today are worse than organized crime ever was," he said.

Following the attacks of 9/11, numerous organizational and legislative changes have strengthened the role of law enforcement in the domestic arena, giving police expanded intelligence powers that fall within the counterintelligence domain. The Uniting and Strengthening America by Providing Appropriate Tools Required to Intercept and Obstruct Terrorism (USA PATRIOT) Act of 2001 extended the reach of law enforcement in part through the strengthening of the criminal laws with respect to terrorism-related crimes, enhancing the electronic surveillance and interception authorities to include the use of roving wiretaps, increasing the domestic law enforcement focus on international money laundering, and strengthening efforts against illegal immigration.

The complexity of the task of building bridges between the intelligence and law enforcement communities for counterintelligence purposes is illustrated by the number of executive orders (EOs) and presidential decision directives (PDDs) that govern the relationship between them, particularly with respect to information sharing. Potential incursion on the constitutionally protected civil liberties and civil rights of U.S. citizens has fueled a continuous debate and resulted in some organizational entrenchment. The executive orders that have a direct impact on the issues raised in this collective work include:

Executive Order 12333: *United States Intelligence Activities.* Originally codified in 1981, this legislation limits the intelligence community's ability to collect and retain information on the domestic activities of U.S. persons. The sixtieth anniversary of the National Security Act of 1947 prompted reexamination at the national level of the need for broadening exceptions to this order.

Executive Order 12958: *Classified National Security Information.* This executive order implements directives for the handling of classified information with the goal of declassifying national security information wherever possible. It includes the "originator control" (ORCON) provision, which allows originating agencies to "control" the dissemination of intelligence to secondary agencies. This in effect impedes the sharing of classified information with law enforcement partners. Efforts are underway on the national level to eliminate the ORCON designation. Strict guidelines remain in effect, however, for the sharing of classified data.

Executive Order 13388: *Further Strengthening the Sharing of Terrorism Information to Protect Americans.* Executive Order 13388 supersedes Executive Order 13356 and supports the Intelligence Reform and Terrorism Prevention Act of 2004, as amended. It reaffirms the importance of exchanging "terrorism information" among agencies. However, law enforcement agencies, especially at the state, local, and tribal levels, struggle to identify and differentiate terrorism information from all other information and often deal in an "all crimes, all hazards" environment. In many cases there is no initial difference between criminal and terrorist-related information. The principal difference may well reside with the intended end result of the activity: criminal profit or funding for terrorist activities.

In addition, Directive 6 (HSPD-6) on September 16, 2003, gave U.S. law enforcement a new tool for identifying suspected terrorists through expanded intelligence and enforcement powers.[24] The Terrorist Screening Center maintains the U.S. government's consolidated terrorism watch list, which contains the names and identifiers of known or suspected terrorists.[25] The data is contained in a repository, the Terrorist Screening Database, which is accessible to federal, state, local, and tribal law enforcement entities, as well as to a small number of allied governmental partners. The U.S. Department of State uses the database for processing passport and visa applications. The Customs and Border Protection Agency, the Immigration and Customs Enforcement, and the Transportation Security Agency use it for screening activities related to domestic flights. Additionally, the Terrorist Screening Center has made information on terrorist identities accessible through the National Crime Information Center, a database used daily by law enforcement.[26] In practice, this means that when a law enforcement officer makes a traffic stop or has another encounter, any information related to potential terrorist activity can be provided in real time. A range of responses may follow, from additional questioning of the individual to an immediate referral to a Joint Terrorism Task Force (JTTF) capable of responding to the location.

The TSC is a unique entity implemented post-9/11 to support terrorist screening and law enforcement operations. According to the center's first director, Donna Bucella, "The TSC ensures that government investigators, screeners, federal agents and local law enforcement officers have ready access to the most thorough, accurate, and current information that they need to respond quickly when a known or suspected terrorist is encountered in the United States, at our borders, and at our embassies. For the first time, a comprehensive U.S. terrorist watch list is accessible to all who are engaged in preventing terrorism. The fact that a local police officer has access to the same list as the intelligence community is an invaluable and significant step to real information sharing."[27] While law enforcement officers may not know which intelligence community agency might be interested in the information they provide, the recognition that their activities can make a valuable contribution to U.S. national security has led police departments to include the TSC process within their standard operating procedures across the country.

Indeed, since 9/11 American law enforcement agencies have undergone a paradigm shift that has affected virtually every aspect of their traditional operating models, from resource allocation to strategic initiatives and budgetary allocations. Virtually all federal law enforcement agencies have undergone significant changes, many stemming from the creation of the Department of Homeland Security. It has taken a number of years to develop a process for informing police executives on the credibility of threat information that in turn affects decisions on resource distribution. Unspecified or general threat information broadcast by DHS created significant financial burdens on police departments responding to the information, often discovering later that the threat was either deemed not credible or did not have any potential impact on their jurisdictions. The disconnect between local law enforcement's failure to react and their perception of overreaction on the part of the federal authorities increased the level of mutual distrust and did little to allay the early fears of the citizenry regarding additional terrorist attacks on domestic soil.

At the local level and before 9/11, most police chiefs considered terrorism to be a remote possibility, something handled almost exclusively by the FBI, and not a high priority for resource allocation. The 9/11 attacks, the growing number of terrorist-related cases, and evidence of common criminal involvement in terrorist activity have changed perceptions, training, deployment, and focus. For example, the International Association of Chiefs of Police immediately moved forward with recommendations on the improvement of intelligence capabilities within law enforcement and convened the first summit on intelligence sharing in March 2002. The summit's express purpose was to develop a process for the collection and analysis of information gathered by law enforcement officers in the course of their regular duties; this information, when viewed with a different contextual lens, might contain elements critical to both homeland and national security. The overall loss of life as a result of the attacks of 9/11, including the lives of 71 police officers and 343 firefighters in New York, was an additional catalyst.

The British model of intelligence-led policing was examined and championed as a useful model for policing operations in the United States. The concept originated in the Kent Constabulary in Great Britain as a means to prioritize response efforts and proactively target the most serious crimes.[28] This model emphasizes an analytical approach to the use of information/intelligence as a means of strategic deployment of resources, pattern and geospatial analysis, forecasting, prediction, and suspect identification. As a direct result of that effort the Department of Justice initiated the Global Intelligence Working Group (GIWG), which developed the actual architecture for implementation, known today as the National Criminal Intelligence Sharing Plan (NCISP).[29] In 2004 Attorney General John Ashcroft approved the implementation of NCISP's twenty-eight recommendations on standards for intelligence sharing, including a mechanism to access relevant classified data, minimum training standards from street level officers to command level, and a seamless technology architecture that leverages existing systems to share data. The Department of Justice emphasized the protection of civil liberties and civil rights in the formation of the recommendations and on lawful collection and storage of data.

Federal and local interests have merged in the creation of intelligence-related fusion centers at the state and local levels—a development encouraged by the Department of Homeland Security. Fusion centers bring a multiagency, all-crime approach to criminal investigations; this approach involves the investigation of potential terrorist activity for which the commission of crime is the common denominator. Such activity might include activities related to the illegal acquisition of firearms and explosives; money laundering; the use of fraudulent documents; narcotics trafficking; and the diversion of legal commodities such as tobacco to obtain funding to support terrorist groups. For example, the Los Angeles Police Department revamped the Anti-Terrorism Division into a Counter Terrorism and Criminal Intelligence Bureau (CTCIB) with dedicated resources to identify, detect, and interdict the next terrorist threat. A terrorism intelligence investigative function has remained within the Anti-Terrorism Intelligence Section (ATIS), and it includes all intelligence investigators as well as the LAPD personnel assigned to the Joint Terrorism Task Force and the Drug Enforcement Administration. Lieutenant Stephan Margolis described the evolution of the unit under his command and commented that the life force of the unit is the focus on optimization of investigative capacity against low-frequency, low-signal, and high-consequence events. "Chief Bratton recognized that the bifurcation of investigations and analysis was a post–World War II model that lacked the speed, fluidity, and real-time insight gathered by the practitioners. The uniqueness of the unit is the fact that the detectives assigned to the investigative section are all cross trained as analysts, effectively creating a hybrid approach that seamlessly blends operational experience with critical thinking skills."[30] This results in a methodologically based approach to crime solving and investigative prioritization. The emphasis on an all-source response is formally reinforced monthly with a rigorous case review by a board of supervisors, which prioritizes investigative efforts with the investigating officer.

As Michael Downing, assistant commanding officer of the Counter Terrorism and Criminal Intelligence Bureau, points out: "Local law enforcement has had a long history in investigating individuals and groups while developing and handling human and electronic intelligence. No agency knows their landscape better than local law enforcement; it was designed and built to be the eyes and ears of communities."[31]

Law Enforcement Counterintelligence?

Intelligence has long been seen as a strong asset to law enforcement in their struggle to cope with crime, and a tremendous vulnerability for the want of it.[32] From a historical perspective, one need only consider the 1967 Organized Crime Task Force of the President's Crime Commission, which discussed an urgent need for law enforcement to improve its use of intelligence in its investigative and crime control efforts. The commission specifically recommended that police agencies in every major city in the United States should have a special intelligence unit dedicated solely to uncovering and interdicting organized criminal intelligence activity. The fact that the law enforcement community is only now rediscovering the importance of standardizing intelligence into law enforcement operations shows how little progress has been made in integrating the two disciplines. Only about 15 percent of state, local, and tribal law enforcement agencies, often from major urban areas, have a dedicated intelligence capability that regularly collects, coordinates, and shares information across states and with federal intelligence partners. These early adopters include the police departments of Los Angeles, New York City, the District of Columbia, Houston, Seattle, and the New York State Police. Both the New York and Los Angeles Police Departments have deployed officers to overseas locations, embedding them with foreign law enforcement partners to better understand cultural influence on crime and terrorism and to develop direct access to threat information and the tools, techniques, and procedures required to counter or otherwise respond to the threats should they emerge on domestic soil.

The nonfederal law enforcement community remains an excessively limited sensor network for counterterrorism when terrorist activity is viewed as separate and distinct from criminal activity. When terrorism and crime are viewed as interdependent, the significant role for uniformed law enforcement may be appreciated but also recognized as underused, particularly in large urban areas. The majority of law enforcement agencies in the United States have fewer than twenty-five sworn personnel, lack access to sophisticated technology, and do not have personnel dedicated to either analyst- or intelligence-related duties.

Further, law enforcement's lack of understanding about intelligence necessarily prevents it from understanding the discipline of counterintelligence, which is increasingly becoming a matter for local law enforcement. This is especially egregious, as many of the threats that state and local law enforcement face, namely international organized crime groups, terrorist organizations, and trafficking cartels, conduct hostile intelligence or intelligence-like operations. Outlaw motorcycle gangs, militia organizations, hate groups, cults, radical environmentalists, animal rights activists, antiabortion extremists, anti-immigrant groups, "traditional" organized crime groups, and regional-national street gangs are known to run intelligence operations *against* law enforcement agencies. [33] These activities include probing operations and surveillance and countersurveillance, as well as rigorous vetting practices to discover attempted penetration by law enforcement or paid informants.

While the need for incorporating counterintelligence into the law enforcement discipline can be easily demonstrated, the efficacy of such a union is a point of contention. Perhaps its fiercest critic is the late Lieutenant General William Odom (Ret.), a former NSA director during the Reagan administration and the author of *Fixing Intelligence*. Odom recognizes that while law enforcement and counterintelligence are inextricably linked (counterintelligence cases often result in prosecutions in the American criminal justice system), he cites several points as reasons for *not* integrating counterintelligence into the law enforcement discipline. First, catching spies and uncovering foreign technical collection capabilities within the United States are more complicated activities than catching domestic and transnational criminals. Second, the motivations and resources backing criminals are different from those backing foreign intelligence services, and thus, criminal investigation skills often work poorly in counterintelligence operations. Third, says Odom, counterintelligence and law enforcement are only currently combined in the FBI, in the U.S. Air Force's Office of Special Investigations, and in the U.S. Navy's Naval Criminal Investigation Service. And while strong arguments can be made for mixing offensive human intelligence and counterintelligence in single organizations, the arguments for mixing counterintelligence and law enforcement against ordinary criminals are not compelling.

Dr. Roy Godson, professor of government at Georgetown University and a longtime scholar of intelligence issues, echoed Odom's criticisms when he discussed the incompatibility of law enforcement and counterintelligence in his book on U.S. covert action and counterintelligence. Godson argued that "[l]aw enforcement agencies have little impetus to develop the skills and knowledge for long-term, high-level strategic penetration and neutralization of secret adversary infrastructures, particularly foreign organizations that may or may not be threatening."[34]

There are, however, contrary points of view. Lawrence Sulc, a former CIA case officer and author of *Law Enforcement Counterintelligence* (which to date is the only such text on the topic) argued forcibly for the integration of counterintelligence into the law enforcement discipline. He observed that if one were to replace "foreign intelligence services" with "domestic anti-law enforcement organizations" in traditional definitions of counterintelligence, the concepts would fit equally well. Sulc assessed law enforcement operations against emerging transnational threats, extremist organizations, and traditional organized criminal activities and concluded that law enforcement was ill-prepared to counter the hostile intelligence activities of these organizations directed against it. Twelve years later the hostile intelligence threat to law enforcement has not subsided. As discussed above, U.S. law enforcement is challenged by a whole new host of extremist and terrorist groups, including widely dispersed yet interconnected transnational criminal organizations, and street gangs that actively work to infiltrate law enforcement. The competing arguments of the efficacy of integrating law enforcement and counterintelligence aside, most law enforcement agencies—and especially the police agencies for the major U.S. cities—perform counterintelligence-like functions, although they are rarely identified as such. Defensive counterintelligence functions are usually performed under the auspices of a police agency's internal affairs unit and consist mainly of anticorruption operations across various units within a department. Offensive functions are less common and are usually performed by specialized investigative units through confidential informants and undercover operators.

Despite some key improvements, there is still a major problem in the lack of coordination between the vast majorities of local law enforcement agencies. Stephen Martin notes that there is the lack of a "coordinating entity to ensure that domestic intelligence is strategically utilized, both horizontally through the federal government, and vertically among federal state, and local entities."[35] L. J. Jordan further notes that "although discovering and thwarting domestic terrorists depend critically on the alertness of local police, they have not been told what to look for," which means indicators are likely to be missed or misinterpreted.[36]

A New Role for Law Enforcement in Counterintelligence: Recommendations and Warnings

Many of the intelligence abuses committed by American law enforcement in the 1960s and 1970s, ostensibly under the guise of offensive counterintelligence, led to the estrangement of the intelligence and law enforcement disciplines in the 1980s and early 1990s. It was not until advances in information technology in the 1990s and the recognition of an expanded intelligence role for law enforcement in the post-9/11 United States that counterintelligence practices have reemerged.[37] The adoption of the evolutionary intelligence-led policing (ILP) construct has established the crucial relationship between the mandates of homeland security protection and the role of the nation's law enforcement officers in that process.

The importance of the ILP concept to the following recommendations warrants a review of its central features. ILP extends beyond the traditional law enforcement role of collecting and processing information to involvement in the rigors of analysis and the development of all-source intelligence end products. These end products, in turn, inform management decision making related to resource deployment and the administrative choice between proactive versus reactive enforcement. While currently underused at many state and local law enforcement agencies, strategic intelligence improves the law enforcement officers' understanding of the intelligence community and respect for the role of analysts. Implementation of the ILP model is supported by policies such as the 2007 National Strategy for Homeland Security and the National Criminal Intelligence Sharing Plan, which is endorsed by the Department of Justice and the International Association of Chiefs of Police. However, at this writing, there is no consensus on the practical implications of intelligence-led policing on police agencies' mission, structure, and processes.

In 2005 the Department of Justice, through the Bureau of Justice Assistance, published a study titled *Intelligence-Led Policing: The New Intelligence Architecture*, which examined the role of intelligence in policing in a post-9/11 world.[38] It argues for the integration of an intelligence discipline within all law enforcement organizations and emphasizes the need for collaboration across the public and private sectors, changing in the process the traditional hierarchical model of information management to a more fluid model that moves the information to the appropriate end user, from street-level practitioners to key decision makers, in an expedient way. At the time of publication, fusion centers were just beginning to emerge as a new way of doing business for law enforcement. Acknowledging that there are different levels of capability across law enforcement agencies, the report categorizes four levels of intelligence capability, offering some insight into the difficulties of imposing new requirements.

Level 1 applies to fewer than three hundred agencies in the United States, each of which employs either hundreds or thousands of sworn personnel, embeds an intelligence cycle within its operating principles, and produces both tactical and strategic intelligence products. Level 2 applies to fewer than five hundred agencies in the United States and differs from Level 1 in the production of tactical and strategic products that support investigations rather than drive operations. They have an intelligence-based structure and use analysis to support the investigations of complex criminal enterprises and conspiracies. Level 3 is identified as the most common level of intelligence function in the United States, and it includes thousands of small and midsized departments, most of which do not employ full-time analysts. These departments are often involved with partner agencies, fusion center efforts, and federal intelligence centers. Level 4 includes the majority of police departments in the United States, many of which have fewer than twelve sworn personnel and do not have any full-time resources dedicated to analytical or intelligence functions.[39]

The issue for those implementing an intelligence-led policing architecture is to design a new counterintelligence role for law enforcement and to implement it among diverse law enforcement entities that are both unequal in their capabilities nationwide and, at this writing, lacking standardized fusion centers. Until such a design is crafted, imaginative leaders such as Chief Bratton in Los Angeles will continue to hone law enforcement officers' skills in collection and analysis through the establishment of specific training requirements and the execution of multidisciplinary and all-crime analysis applied to criminal cases. Initiatives such as Chief Bratton's lead the way for intelligence-led policing while also expanding the gaps between the top and bottom tiers of capability within the law enforcement community nationwide.

Such gaps should not, however, slow initiative or innovation in this important new arena of counterintelligence. Perhaps the best argument for integrating counterintelligence and law enforcement in a new framework for the twenty-first century is the third commandment in James Olson's *Ten Commandments of Counterintelligence*: to "own the street." In his original essay this charge referred to the need for counterintelligence officers to take back the streets in foreign capitals and make the necessary human and financial commitments to have a professional, reliable, full-time, local surveillance capability. This commandment also applies on the domestic front, especially in the modern era of transnational criminal threats to the homeland. Building a construct for the vertical and horizontal integration of counterintelligence capabilities needs become a priority at the national level, perhaps beginning within the nationally funded fusion centers.

Critics will argue that yet another set of requirements levied upon already overburdened police officers will dilute the delivery of mission-related services upon which communities depend. Others will proffer that police departments are both unwilling and unable to expend resources protecting one another's jurisdictions, a premise that belies the ethos of policing and shared concern for officer safety, regardless of the color of the uniform or configuration of the shield. One need only reflect on national disasters such as Hurricane Katrina in New Orleans in which off-duty law enforcement officers from around the country responded not because they were part of the organized response, but because they were driven to do so by a deep sense of commitment to their fellow officers. Instead of examining the issue strictly in terms of new requirements, one may frame it in the context of education and training, as well as in the context of information sharing that benefits overall security, not just individual organizations.

The issues surrounding a greater role for law enforcement in national counterintelligence are indeed complex and have historically been regarded as inimical to sustainable change. Yet a strong case can be made that with four steps, several of which are already underway, real improvements can be made without damage to the country's political culture and societal norms. The first step is to recognize the importance of information sharing both among law enforcement entities and with the federal government's national security agencies. As Lee Hamilton, vice chair of the 9/11 Commission, stated in testimony: "We have made minimal progress toward the establishment of a seamless information sharing system. You can change the law, you can change the technology, but you still need to change the culture; you need to motivate institutions and individuals to share the information."[40]

The place to begin is within and among police departments themselves. Historically, the larger police departments have had success in the use of undercover operatives and informants in combating organized crime and drug trafficking. Undercover operatives working in other areas, particularly narcotics, organized crime, or gunrunning [as well as illegal immigration] frequently will have information on potential terrorists. For this reason it is important to maintain good contacts with other units within the police organization, as well as with federal and state authorities working in this area.[41] As indicated earlier in the domestic violence case, an increased level of situational awareness for law enforcement may yield indicators related to counterintelligence activities.

Familiarizing local law enforcement with the tactics and techniques of subversive groups must also be a high priority. Programs such as the training offered in the State and Local Anti-Terrorism Training (SLATT) program, sponsored by the Institute for Intergovernmental Research, is but one example of the types of training required by those on the front lines of policing. Information and intelligence can be acquired in the course of investigating corruption and organized crime, through prison intelligence, and from resources within the private sector that have developed safeguards for potential loss of sensitive data, insider threat, and manipulation for competitive advantage. With the growth of understanding among local law enforcement officers of the importance of their work to national security, more effective information sharing can take place through the approximately 101 Joint Terrorism Task Forces, coordinated by the FBI at the national level, and the Field Intelligence Groups, one of which operates in each of the fifty-six FBI Field Offices.

The second step is to reinforce the core mission of police: law enforcement, not counterintelligence. On the domestic front only law enforcement is positioned to effectively own the street and challenge the hostile activities of foreign intelligence services and domestic anti–law enforcement organizations. Challenging, however, does not require that every law enforcement officer become a counterintelligence specialist, which is neither a realistic nor a preferred solution for law enforcement or the national counterintelligence structure. Each community has its specific responsibilities and authorities and these, however complementary, are still separate and distinct from one another. Training for counterintelligence operations should underscore the distinction between counterintelligence for national security and more traditional policing. In this light, it makes sense for states with multiple fusion centers to designate one center as the primary statewide coordination point to interface with the federal government and coordinate the gathering, processing, analysis, and dissemination of homeland security information, terrorism information, and law enforcement information on a statewide basis.

Increasing the situational awareness and training of law enforcement collectors who are well positioned to see what may be hidden in plain sight and provide early warnings of potential offensive counterintelligence activity will naturally lead to better domestic collection against terrorist threats—the third step in improved performance. The idea of "every cop a sensor" is axiomatic and already a part of the law enforcement culture. Educating these professionals on the potential indicators of counterintelligence activity and insider threat provides an ability to conduct a finer screening of information as it is collected in routine policing activity as well as in dealings with foreign national informants, illegal immigrants, and ethnic-based organized crime organizations. Understanding the tradecraft of offensive counterintelligence activity may also yield early warning of threat if suspicious materials or technologies are uncovered in legal criminal searches or fall within the purview of licensing requirements.[42] Law enforcement officials are the first people acting in an official capacity to observe individuals who may pose a potential threat as they attempt border crossings, travel domestically and internationally, assimilate into neighborhoods, and experience routine encounters with police, from traffic stops to their involvement in criminal activity.

The fourth step must be to insist on strict accountability for the effectiveness of counterintelligence operations within the law enforcement domain. It is of paramount importance that abuses and mistakes be kept to a minimum and promptly corrected in this new era; appropriate oversight authorities should especially scrutinize offensive counterintelligence activities by law enforcement. Any information developed should be provided to the appropriate authority through established channels such as the Joint Terrorism Task Forces or the Field Intelligence Groups. Fusion centers may also share law enforcement information for intelligence purposes directly with the Department of Homeland Security Office of Intelligence and Analysis. The scope for such exchanges should, however, be subject to careful review and oversight. The "Federal Fusion Center" of the National Counterterrorism Center (NCTC) will continue to have primary responsibility within the federal government for analysis and integration of all intelligence and information pertaining to terrorism and counterterrorism and should support the Department of Justice in these regards, as well as Department of Homeland Security and other agencies responsible for disseminating terrorism-related information. Housed at NCTC, the newly established Interagency Threat Assessment Coordination Group (ITACG) is designed to ensure that classified intelligence products issued by federal entities within the intelligence, law enforcement, and homeland security communities are not only "federally coordinated," but also that they are fused, validated, deconflicted, and approved for dissemination to state, local, and tribal officials.

The counterintelligence mission is far too important to the national security of the United States and to the investigative missions of its law enforcement agencies to continue to be conducted in isolation without the potential benefit of hundreds of thousands of trained law enforcement professionals standing watch. The national efforts underway at this writing by the Information Sharing Environment (ISE) Program Manager, in particular the adoption of the recommendations contained within the National Strategy for Information Sharing (NSIS) by state and local law enforcement, will enhance operational efficiency in traditional policing activities and broaden the aperture of collection relevant to countering terrorist activity as well as any activity that would qualify as counterintelligence efforts by foreign intelligence services and nonstate actors on domestic soil. As illustrated within this chapter, law enforcement officers are uniquely positioned to recognize anomalies at both a macro and micro level because the sheer nature of their job requires close contact with the populace. Intelligence is no longer just about gathering and analyzing foreign secret information; it also encompasses a wide variety of facts, presumptions, and conditions. The most valuable information, particularly open-source, may not be secret at all, but rather merely hidden from the analyst who is unaware of where and how to look for it.

Notes

1. A key example is that of Robert Hanssen, formerly a special agent with the FBI who was convicted of espionage. Hanssen held a senior position within the FBI and worked

counterintelligence issues—ironically being initially assigned to the investigation of a suspected penetration which in fact was him. Hanssen spied for the Soviet Union for over twenty years and avoided detection as a result of a less-than-optimal enforcement of employee oversight, procedural safeguards, and routine polygraph screening. Although anecdotal information indicated Hanssen was considered "different" by his peers, there was no unusual scrutiny applied as a result.

2. Office of the National Counterintelligence Executive, *National Counterintelligence Strategy of the United States, 2007* (Washington, DC, 2007), 3.

3. Available at www.ise.gov/.

4. See U.S. Department of Justice (DOJ), U.S. Department of Homeland Security (DHS), Global Initiative, Fusion Center Guidelines: Law Enforcement Intelligence, Public Safety, and the Private Sector. Available at http://it.ojp.gov/topic.jsp?topic_id=209.htm.

5. John M. Broder, "Police Chiefs Moving to Share Terror Data." *New York Times*, July 29, 2005. Available at www.nytimes.com/2005/07/29/national/nationalspecial3/29bratton.html.

6. Ibid.

7. See Jeff Conklin, *Dialogue Mapping: Building Shared Understanding of Wicked Problems* (West Sussex, England: John Wiley & Sons Ltd., 2006).

8. See James Kirkpatrick Davis, *Spying on America: The FBI's Domestic Counterintelligence Program* (Westport, CT: Praeger/Greenwood, 1992), and David Cunningham, *There's Something Happening Here: The New Left, the Klan, and FBI Counterintelligence* (Berkeley: University of California Press, 2005), for comprehensive accounts of the FBI's counterintelligence operations in the 1960s and 1970s, the FBI enlistment of local law enforcement in these counterintelligence activities, and the resulting investigations, sanctions, and legislation created to prevent such activities from occurring in the United States again.

9. B. A. Reaves, *Federal Law Enforcement Officers, 2004* (Washington, DC: Bureau of Justice Statistics, 2006); and Reaves, *Census of State and Local Law Enforcement Agencies* (Washington, DC: Bureau of Justice Assistance, 2007).

10. See www.ojp.usdoj.gov/bjs/lawenf.htm.

11. See Arthur Conan Doyle, *The Memoirs of Sherlock Holmes*, "Silver Blaze" (Garden City, NY: Doubleday & Company, 1893), 346–47.

12. Although crime statistics have always been an unwelcome metric for law enforcement, the advent of COMPSTAT (Computer Statistics) by Commissioner William Bratton and Deputy Commissioner Jack Maple at the NYPD in 1994 brought the use of crime statistics to a whole new level, as the NYPD increased accountability for crime occurring in the city by pushing the responsibility to control crime to the patrol level. The precipitous fall in New York City's crime rate during the implementation of COMPSTAT became a de facto validation of the practice, and the COMPSTAT paradigm has been widely adopted by police agencies across the United States. See Vincent Henry, *The Compstat Paradigm* (Flushing, NY: Looseleaf Law Publications, 2002), for a descriptive history of COMPSTAT and an analysis of it as a law enforcement management strategy. Annual publications such as the Uniform Crime Reporting (UCR) developed by the International Association of Chiefs of Police (IACP) in 1930 reflect the types and the frequency of certain violent crime and other criminal activity by jurisdiction. Reporting is voluntary, although a survey in 2003 indicated law enforcement agencies participating in the UCR represented 93 percent of the nation's population. The FBI now produces this publication.

A comparable publication entitled the National Crime Victimization Survey (NCVS) published annually by the Department of Justice estimates the number of unreported serious crimes, and in tandem, law enforcement administration and management use both reports. See www.fbi.gov/ucr/ucrquest.htm.

13. For instance, the traditional tactic of street justice for Colombian cartel members was the "Colombian necktie," which involved slicing a person's throat and pulling his/her tongue through the open wound. Another example of street justice is the extreme violence of MS-13, an El Salvadoran street gang that is infamous for its brutal tactics including beheading, mutilation, and amputating limbs of victims and rivals. Available at www.ndu.edu/inss/books/2007snss.pdf.

14. Michelle Van Cleave, "Counterintelligence and National Strategy," National Defense University Monograph (April 2007), 14.

15. John MacGaffin, "Clandestine Human Intelligence," in *Transforming U.S. Intelligence,*ed. Jennifer E. Sims and Burton Gerber (Washington, DC: Georgetown University Press, 2005), 79–85.

16. Mitchel P. Roth, *Crime and Punishment: A History of the Criminal Justice System.* (Belmont, CA: Wadsworth Publishing, 2004), 128.

17. Ibid., 255.

18. Ronald Kessler, *The Bureau: The Secret History of the FBI* (New York: St. Martin's Press, 2002).

19. "President's Commission on Law Enforcement and the Administration of Justice" (Washington, DC: Government Printing Office, 1968).

20. See Terrorist Screening Center brief posted by Wisconsin Department of Justice. Available at www.doj.state.wi.us/dles/cib/conf_08/WisconsinTerroristscreening.pdf.

21. Percentages are of total number of encounters and are approximated.

22. Mark Sherman, "200,000 people in U.S. terror suspect database, director says," *Associated Press Newswires,* March 14, 2006. Available at http://archive.southcoasttoday.com/daily/03–06/03–15–06/22world-nation.htm.

23. The conference was cohosted by the FBI and the Los Angeles Police Department to examine the impact of violent street gang activity on society. Invited participants included eleven police chiefs from major cities throughout the United States and the special agents in charge from the FBI in those cities. Efforts were directed at defining the size and scope of the gang problem, developing a framework for response to it, and coordinating the response capabilities between federal, state, and local law enforcement.

24. See www.fas.org/irp/offdocs/nspd/hspd-6.html.

25. Defined as "known or appropriately suspected to be or have been engaged in conduct constituting, in preparation for, in aid of, or related to terrorism."

26. See www.fbi.gov/terrorinfo/counterrorism/tsc.htm for additional background information on the Terrorist Screening Center, including information related to the protection of privacy and civil liberties.

27. Interview with Donna Bucella on January 31, 2008.

28. Marilyn Peterson, "Intelligence-Led Policing: The New Intelligence Architecture" (Rockville, MD: Bureau of Justice Assistance Clearinghouse, September 2005), 5, 9.

29. See www.it.ojp.gov/documents/NCISP_Plan.pdf.

30. Interview with Lieutenant Stephan Margolis via telephone on January 23, 2008.

31. Michael P. Downing, assistant commanding officer, Counter-Terrorism/Criminal Intelligence Bureau, Los Angeles Police Department, "Statement Before the Committee

on Homeland Security Subcommittee on Intelligence, Information Sharing, and Terrorism Risk Assessment United States: House of Representatives," March 22, 2007.

32. See Department of Justice Report to the Deputy U.S. Attorney General re the February 26, 1993, raid on the Branch Davidian Compound in Waco, Texas. Available at www.usdoj.gov/05publications/waco/wacotocpg.htm. This serves as an example of a law enforcement intelligence failure.

33. National Youth Gang Center, *2004 National Youth Gang Survey* (Washington, DC: Office of Juvenile Justice and Delinquency Prevention, 2006).

34. Roy Godson, *Dirty Tricks and Trump Cards: U.S. Covert Action & Counterintelligence* (McLean, VA: Brassey's, 1995), xxvii.

35. S. Martin, "Using Intelligence to Protect Homeland Security," *International Journal of Intelligence and Counterintelligence* 18, no. 3 (2005): 549, 557.

36. L. J. Jordan, "New Mission for Law Enforcement Groups: Looking Homeward for Terrorists," *Chicago Daily Law Bulletin*, August 30, 2006, 1, 24.

37. The technological advances of the 1990s included the emergence of COMPSTAT and the integration of software applications into both crime analysis and criminal intelligence analysis.

38. Peterson, "Intelligence-Led Policing."

39. Ibid., 13–14.

40. Testimony of Lee H. Hamilton before the Subcommittee on Intelligence, Information Sharing, and Terrorism Risk assessment, Committee on Homeland Security, U.S. House of Representatives, November 8, 2005, 2. Cited in Todd Masse, *Homeland Security Intelligence: Perceptions, Statutory Definitions, and Approaches*, Congressional Research Service (August 18, 2006).

41. James W. Osterburg and Richard H. Ward, *Criminal Investigation: A Method Reconstructing the Past* (New York: Lexis Nexis, 2007), 574.

42. By way of example, the criminal investigators for the Department of Commerce have the responsibility to monitor the acquisition process for export of materials or technology in the United States that may have a dual use and could pose a threat to national security.

8

James R. Gosler

Counterintelligence
Too Narrowly Practiced

EFFECTIVE COUNTERINTELLIGENCE (CI) is an essential element in combating foreign technical threats to the United States. Unfortunately, these threats are increasing in sophistication, and their impact on compromised U.S. systems has already reached dangerously unacceptable levels. The American counterintelligence apparatus is struggling to culturally adapt and establish its role in this fight. This struggle is compounded in part by the absence of a uniform communitywide understanding of the technical threat facing U.S. systems, competing elements vying for funding, and ambiguous terminology used across the often warring factions.

The terms *information dominance, information superiority, information warfare, information operations, cyberwarfare,* and *net-centric warfare* are often used interchangeably and with little precision. These terms have evolved, been in favor and out of favor, shaped new organizations, and been the focus of heated debate. In fact, these debates have resulted not just in the formation of cults, but in unnecessary fragmentation and dysfunction within government.

In the end, what matters is developing, organizing, and using the capabilities underpinning all these activities to support national security objectives. In spite of the confusion and ambiguity the lexicon generates, several common ideas are deeply embedded in the overarching concepts of information operations. First, the key to modern war fighting is the innovative use of information technology (IT). The technical foundation of net-centric warfare is built upon the information technology (IT) infrastructure.[1] Computing, networking, and sharing of information, when done well, provide significant military advantage. Second, today U.S. military strategy and projection of military force are critically dependent on capitalizing on advantages the United States maintains in information technology. As a result, the IT itself will become the game-changing target for our opponents. They will want to exploit these systems and steal information. They will want to corrupt the information within the systems, leading to breaches in their integrity and loss of user confidence.[2] They will want to deny our use of our own systems. Thus, defending these capabilities is fundamental if we are to take advantage of the benefits of net-centric concepts in an adversarial environment. Third, we want to have the capability to inflict the same negative impact on the IT systems of our opponents.

U.S. experts have written thousands of papers and briefings, both classified and unclassified, over the last twenty years explaining and debating these three aspects of modern warfare, and today there appears to be general agreement on these tenets. In fact, there is growing evidence that China recognizes that IT is the U.S. center of gravity (game-changing target) not only in military operations, but in economic and political power as well. China's leaders appear to be positioning themselves to compete or surpass the United States in utilizing advanced IT, protecting their investment from opponents, and, should China ever directly confront the United States, to arm themselves with the capabilities to strike where we are most vulnerable.

Unfortunately, the United States has invested "superpower" resources in developing advanced architectures, systems, components, strategies, and tactics without the corresponding investments necessary to effectively defend these systems against a sophisticated opponent. This gap is surprising, given the abundant evidence that these complex systems are inherently fragile. For example, Boeing's new Dreamliner seems to suffer from its own complexity.[3] Against even an average adversary, these systems are too vulnerable, and our dependency upon them much too great.

There are options available to correct this imbalance. We can choose to decrease our military dependence on these advanced IT systems that have increasing foreign provenance, decrease our opponent's offensive capability to exploit these vulnerabilities, decrease our opponent's willingness to exploit our weakness (deterrence), or significantly increase our ability to protect these systems. Once we finally recognize this imbalance, a strategy that includes a combination of the four approaches stated above must emerge, allowing the United States, with confidence, to fight and win in a Net-Centric-based war. Counterintelligence, in its broadest definition, which is significantly broader than merely finding spies, must play a much more substantial role in this strategy if we are to successfully mitigate our current weakness.

In March 2004 Vice Admiral Mike McConnell, USN (Ret.), then a senior vice president at Booz Allen Hamilton, agreed to an hour-long interview during which he shared his candid thoughts and views on information operations (IO).[4] This was familiar territory for him. During his tenure as director of the National Security Agency (NSA), McConnell's understanding of the spectrum and effectiveness of offensive IO had deepened and broadened. In this interview he emphasized the defensive challenges facing the nation. When asked what he would do if he had the opportunity to be king, his response was quick and succinct: "I would ratchet up the defensive parts significantly." His knowledge was impressive, and his passion for the issues appeared to be genuine. In fact, in his view, if the nation does not come together in a bipartisan manner to address this defensive problem, "we have a train wreck coming."[5] On April 21, 2005, the Office of the Director of National Intelligence (ODNI) was established, and on February 20, 2007, McConnell was sworn in as the nation's second director of national intelligence (DNI). He now has his second chance.

If the National Counterintelligence Strategy of the United States of America 2007 is any indication of DNI McConnell's direction and intent, then we are headed on a positive course toward change.[6] The definition of CI adopted by the ODNI is "information gathered and activities conducted to protect against espionage, other intelligence activities, sabotage, or assassinations conducted for or on behalf of foreign powers, organizations or persons, or international terrorist activities, but not including personnel, physical, document or communications security programs."[7] Of particular importance is that this definition addresses the nation's need for a broad spectrum of capabilities, intelligence, and operations conducted to support the defensive mission of the United States. While the definition excludes key elements of a defensive strategy, the document in its entirety conveys the need for CI to partner with other defensive elements, such as personnel, and physical and communications security. By including these other elements, we can eliminate seams within our defensive strategy that an opponent could exploit.

Unfortunately, we have barely begun to implement this defensive strategy. Enacting change will require cooperation among the country's diverse security disciplines. The government's limited appreciation for this necessity is partly responsible for its inaction. Even with increased awareness, however, significant cultural obstacles must be overcome. Today, the dominant culture within the counterintelligence community remains focused on "finding the spy." We are only beginning to appreciate the importance of technical CI. Thus while we have a useful definition of CI, it is simply too narrowly practiced. In an earlier work titled "The Digital Dimension," this author presented a characterization of a sophisticated offense and the associated ramifications to the defense.[8] The principal purpose of this chapter is to build upon and expand on these concepts and relate them to challenges facing the CI community in the United States.

The issues presented are becoming increasingly important to the security of the nation. Fortunately, awareness of the impact of the growing gap between offense and defense has increased within the senior ranks of government and industry. Additionally, advances in our defensive tool kit have been made. As we will see, a proactive, as opposed to a purely reactive, CI community is necessary to provide the country with the tools, operations, and policies needed to perform effective risk management. It is reassuring to note that the 2007 national counterintelligence strategy states that the United States is positioned to become much more aggressive in using offensive techniques to thwart the activities of foreign intelligence services. Operationally penetrating these opponents through both human and technical means will be necessary in order to better understand their full spectrum of technical and operational capabilities, operational requirements, and their limitations. The gap between the need for more offensive measures and the public tolerance for them must be addressed.

The Threat

While the United States gives significant attention and resources to dealing with the terrorism threat, the United States is developing blind and deaf spots relative to threats from hostile nation-states. These states are concerned primarily with those issues deemed important to their self-interests. To the extent the United States is aligned with those interests, we are friends. When our interests are not aligned, there is potential for conflict. In most cases, these disputes can be resolved through both formal and informal diplomatic means. In instances where the issues escalate and diplomacy fails, the possibility of military conflict becomes real. If, in the mind of the hostile states, military action is possible, then they must be prepared to deal with the conventional military strength of the United States. For any country within the foreseeable future, this forces them to adopt asymmetric strategies. The most effective means to both conceive and execute these strategies is the hostile nation's intelligence service(s).

Implicit in this discussion is the recognition that many of our friends (with a few notable exceptions) employ their intelligence service(s) against the United States to gain advantage, to our disadvantage. Stimulated by global economic competition, this trend appears to be on the rise. What friends and adversaries have in common is an understanding of the enormous advantage a capable intelligence service provides. The return on intelligence investment is substantial.

One of the best unclassified examples to illustrate this point is the Soviet strategy during the Cold War to exploit U.S. and European technological strength. In the "Farewell Dossier," Gus Weiss provides a riveting account of Soviet efforts to shake loose U.S. technological secrets, Americans' unwillingness to believe they were being exploited, the exploits of a Soviet KGB officer spying for the French, the finding of an unambiguous smoking gun, and the development of a brilliantly conceived and executed U.S. response.[9] The Soviets understood the security implications of significantly trailing the United States in technology. Roald Sagdeev, Gorbachev's science advisor, indicated in his book *The Making of a Soviet Scientist* that in two key technological areas, microelectronics and computers, the Soviet Union lagged behind the United States by fifteen years.[10] Imagine for a moment the colossal effort that would be required within the Soviet system to legitimately gain technological parity with the West. But by tasking the Soviet intelligence apparatus to narrow the gap, what seemed initially impossible became highly probable. By creatively capitalizing on détente, the Soviets developed overt and clandestine human and technical access to our technology treasure chest. They regarded our regulations and policies as exploitable weaknesses. They exploited the competitive nature of U.S. companies, such as Lockheed and Boeing, and pitted them against one another in order to gain valuable insights. They created cover companies to circumvent export controls on key technologies. This was an integrated, highly coordinated, very compartmented, and impressively executed strategy designed to narrow the U.S.-Soviet technological gap.

That the Soviets were able to operate for over a decade with little U.S. comprehension of their strategy, the scope of their operational activity, and the magnitude of their impact, is a testament to U.S. arrogance, naïveté and lack of sound CI practices. In the 1970s a few U.S. individuals were suspicious of the Soviet intent to "steal us blind." They would provide examples of alarming Soviet behavior, timelines that attempted to piece together the puzzle, and coincidences that would seemingly be difficult to explain away. However, man's ability to rationalize away uncomfortable issues is truly amazing. According to Weiss, "In the style of Sherlock Holmes, the clues could almost speak for themselves: the USSR was behind in important technologies, their intelligence was accomplished at collection, and détente had opened a path."[11] Senior government officials would repeatedly defuse the "alarmists" with responses like "There is no evidence to support your claims," "Your anecdotal clues are easily explained away," or "We must have a smoking gun." Weiss concludes, "It seemed to have escaped these authorities that having no evidence does not mean it is not true. The system defied movement."[12]

From the CI perspective, what is the threshold of proof necessary to force decision and movement? Clearly in this case the preponderance of evidence was insufficient. Fortunately for the United States, proof beyond a reasonable doubt was established in 1981. The Soviet KGB officer spying for the French, Colonel Vladimir I. Vetrov, codename "Farewell," photographed and delivered about four thousand KGB documents associated with the Soviets' technology exploitation operations against the West. Vetrov was in the perfect position. He was an evaluator of the intelligence the Soviets were collecting. He knew the names of the Soviet case officers. He knew the collection requirements, and most important, he knew which requirements had not yet been satisfied. Weiss's article details the scope and impact of the Soviet activity. "Since 1970, Line X had obtained thousands of documents and sample products in such quantity that it appeared that the Soviet military and civil sectors were in large measure running their research on that of the West, particularly the United States."[13] Weiss continues, "Our science was supporting their national defense. . . . Line X had fulfilled two-thirds to three fourths of its collection requirements—an impressive performance."[14] The Soviet return on investment in this case was astounding; yet today the cost to the adversary is even lower and the gain is significantly higher.

With senior government officials no longer able to deny or rationalize away this comprehensive Soviet operation, the technology transfer issue became a top priority. A brilliantly crafted U.S. counterstrategy was initiated. In January 1982 Weiss met with the director of central intelligence, William Casey, to discuss the plan. Based upon knowledge of the KGB's unmet technology requirements and of several KGB officers involved in the Soviet collection effort, the United States would "help" the Soviets satisfy their remaining objectives. However, these designs and products would be enhanced. The designs/parts would appear to be authentic, but the subtle enhancement(s) would cause the system/part to fail. If successful, this strategy would cause delays, confusion, and cost overruns within the Soviet technology enterprise. Even if the highly compartmented U.S. program was compromised—either through a double agent, a technical penetration, or the "enhancement" was discovered—the Soviets would have to question all of their "special" procurements.[15] Thus the added work factor for the Soviets would be enormous. As Weiss points out, "This would be a rarity in the world of espionage, an operation that would succeed even if compromised."[16]

The Soviets' own clandestine collection effort would be used against them. If they started to discover evidence or ponder observed coincidences, the Soviets would have to deal with the same cultural problems the United States struggled with a decade earlier. It is not career enhancing for an individual within a foreign intelligence service to be duped by the opponent (the United States in this instance). In these cases, there exists great personal and organizational motivation to creatively pretend the problem away.

According to Weiss, "The program had great success, and it was never detected."[17] Ironically, Thomas Reed, former secretary of the air force, recounts that the project proved so sensitive that records were not kept due to security concerns associated with the new, computerized, internal National Security Council communication system.[18] In the intervening decades our sensitivity to the inherent security issues related to IT-based systems appears to have eroded. In this author's view this story provides an outstanding and now unclassified illustration of how a competent, world-class, intelligence service can utilize the full spectrum of offensive capabilities to meet their national security objectives. It also conveys the impact on national security if you are the target of such an operation. Finally, the story illustrates the importance of a proactive CI capability in reducing the likelihood and the impact of such operations conducted against U.S. interests.

It may be safe to assume that the historical approaches of Soviet intelligence provide useful insights into the character and approaches of current Russian intelligence. "The Digital Dimension" pointed out the difficulty involved in changing large organizations; they tend to deeply embed, in unchallengeable dogma, those elements that made the institution preeminent. Whether the organization is IBM, Intel, NSA, CIA, or the KGB, this social dynamic seems to be a constant. Two other constants seem to emerge out of the "Farewell" account: Intelligence organizations develop defensive measures designed to protect against how they exploit/attack, and intelligence organizations are very reluctant to admit failure.

As we will see, the current environment defined by globalization increases these operational opportunities. When KGB defector Viktor Sheymov was asked what surprised him the most about U.S. defensive strategy and tactics, he responded by identifying four areas that should be of ongoing concern: the inadequacy of protecting the isolated nodes (end points) of critical systems, the weakness of perimeter security at overseas facilities, the use of local workers in these facilities, and the susceptibility to supply-chain attack.[19] His response suggests that Vetrov and Sheymov had the opportunity to participate in and observe the same world-class intelligence organization in action. Should one be tempted to believe that the effectiveness of the Soviet intelligence community was diminished with the end of the Cold War, one only need study the paper of Alferov, Baranov, and Markov to appreciate that Russia's technical excellence, coupled with its exceptional operational strength, is still world-class in every respect.[20]

Indeed, we appear to be at a tipping point with respect to the perception of cyber threats. High-profile cyber-related offensive activity is routine in the news today. The alleged Russian denial-of-service attack against the IT infrastructure of Estonia, the detection of espionage programs in computer systems in the German chancellor's office, and the Office of the Secretary of Defense's unclassified e-mail system taken off-line as a result of a detected cyber penetration, all serve to illustrate the pervasiveness of these attacks.[21] These and countless other detected penetrations over the past decade have significantly increased the visibility and importance of cyber security issues within the minds of many senior U.S. government officials. Today policymakers are hard-pressed to deny the existence and seriousness of this operational activity.[22] Indeed, it is arguable that without these foreign cyber operations, we might likely find ourselves in the "pre-Farewell" era, denying the scale and potential impact of foreign technical operations, of which cyber is a subset.

The activities mentioned above are those for which we have tangible proof. These technical and operational approaches are a far cry from the level of sophistication and stealth revealed in the "Farewell" story. It is the strong view of this author that the lack of evidence indicating the occurrence of more sophisticated operations is not indicative of their absence. Counterintelligence specialists, in partnership with the rest of the intelligence community, must provide the needed insight to detect and thwart this currently unseen operational activity.[23] Otherwise, we might see a return to the "seniors in denial" syndrome that played such a major role in the Farewell story.

The Response: More Than Finding Human Spies

The defensive elements of the United States must form a seamless coordinated partnership to effectively counter the various threats to our nation and regain advantage over our adversaries. Counterintelligence should be a more proactive and integrated player within this union. It is imperative that we move beyond the predominant bias of just looking for spies. While the definition of counterintelligence discussed earlier in this chapter is sufficiently encompassing, the practice and the culture of the discipline are simply too narrow within U.S. institutions. Furthermore, it is vital that the various security disciplines excluded from this definition of counterintelligence work collaboratively to eliminate seams.

The 2007 national counterintelligence strategy for the United States conveys a heavily weighted bias toward dealing with spies.[24] The document is emphatic: "When necessary, we will disrupt these activities through arrest and expulsion." Such a straightforward approach is more feasible with a spy than with an enhanced microprocessor. While this document does convey the intent to expand their capabilities into cyberspace, the strategy's extension into cyberspace is weak, insufficiently weighted, and much too narrow in scope.

Michelle Van Cleave's "Counterintelligence and National Strategy" serves as an outstanding reference for the CI professional.[25] It is thought-provoking, well documented, and written by an individual who, as former director of NCIX, has been on the inside. Her emphasis on the importance of taking CI to the opponent is on target. She states, "The ultimate goal of offensive CI is to penetrate the opposition's own secret operations apparatus: to become, obviously without the opposition's knowledge, an integral and functioning part of their calculations and operations."[26] Our views appear to diverge relative to the emphasis placed on human intelligence. While it may be true that most of the world's governments principally collect through human espionage, it is perhaps misleading. Compared to the United States, Russia, and China, most of the world's governments have modest intelligence organizations. It would be very dangerous to assume that potential opponents such as Russia and China are not well resourced and experienced in full-spectrum technical collection. Furthermore, technical collection will likely become much more important to these organizations. They have a ten-to-twenty-year advantage in applying their technical operational capabilities against high-tech targets.[27]

To develop a deeper appreciation of what is needed for a balanced counterintelligence strategy, one only need ask and answer the following question: Is it "the who" or "the what" that has greater access and closeness to our secrets and mission-critical applications and systems? We understand and accept the importance of trusting someone who will be given access to important secrets. As the importance of the secret increases, a greater degree of trustworthiness is required of the individual. Because we cannot depend upon a person's integrity, we take potential candidates through a gauntlet of tests designed to increase our confidence in them. The tests include background investigations, financial disclosures, polygraphs, and the personnel reliability program. But if the assertion of increased foreign use of technical collection is well founded, what gauntlets is the technology subjected to? Is it possible that the microprocessor, power supply, printer, disk drive, operating system, firewall, antivirus software, BIOS, or word processor has been recruited by a foreign intelligence service to spy on its behalf?[28] It is difficult to polygraph a printer. As hard as it is to find a human spy, it is even more complicated to find a cleverly hidden spy embedded within the technology—software or hardware. Moreover, our tendency to dismiss oddly behaving technology as "nothing to worry about—normal problem—sorry, I forgot to remove the diagnostic software that transmits the crypto key" manifests itself with great regularity. The "seniors in denial" syndrome discussed in the "Farewell" story is still alive and thriving.

There are at least two schools of thought on the relative weighting between human and technical operations as conducted by a foreign intelligence service. An unnamed defense department official has reportedly said, "There appears to be a systematic underestimation by the U.S. intelligence community of the Chinese offensive cyber-warfare threat that is only now being understood."[29] In contrast, Van Cleave's view is that "[f]oreign emphasis on human collectors over other means of collection is the single most distinctive asymmetry in modern intelligence structures, and it has profound implications for U.S. CI."[30] While each view has strong and credible support, such seemingly divergent views could lead to very different national strategy implementations with corresponding differences in investment strategy. It is vitally important to debate and resolve this apparent dichotomy. To the degree an opponent utilizes technical collection, the CI community must answer with an appropriate mix of technical and human CI.

The Technical Game

This chapter will neither discuss the fundamentals of human espionage nor technical operations in support of human operations. Many other books have been dedicated to these important topics, including *Spycraft*, which discusses technical support to agent operations.[31] Instead, this chapter will focus on an important subset of technical operations as conducted by sophisticated intelligence services that utilize a full spectrum of human and technical capabilities. In addition, the next section will present promising technical advancements in detecting covert organizations and people operating in an alias persona.

To appreciate the defensive challenge of balancing utility, affordability, and security in a globalized market for information technology, a deeper understanding of the methods of offensive attack is needed. In general, the objective of a technical operation is to steal information from a target, to deny the owner the use of the system, or to corrupt the integrity of the information. If the target system is connected to a global network, such as the Internet, a remote attacker can exploit the target by taking advantage of an inherent vulnerability.[32]

A common vulnerability is a buffer overflow within either an application or the operating system.[33] Exploiting this vulnerability is particularly attractive to hostile actors, because the attacker never has to develop clandestine life-cycle access to the target.[34] For low-level threats, such as hackers, the combination of a connected target and an inherent vulnerability is sufficient to exploit targets. Since the utility of attacking the target is highly dependent upon its degree of connectivity, the primary defensive approach is to deny the adversary the use of the inherent vulnerability in the target in the first place. This defensive strategy relies on rules for hardware and software vetting, acquisition, and maintenance and is therefore principally compliance-based; its effectiveness is therefore limited. In fact, today, U.S. targets are routinely exploited using this approach. In the recent past, U.S. adversaries have collected and exfiltrated several terabytes of data from key Department of Defense networks. The apparent inability to patch U.S. systems in a timely manner provides opponents with ample opportunity for access to our information systems. While we are aware of these operations, we do not appear to have the technical ability to close the access holes or to clearly attribute these operations to the perpetrator(s). More important, despite recent improvements, we continue to lack the will to respond aggressively. Tackling these operations is particularly important because they help conceal more sophisticated attacks, which are discussed below.

The second method of attack is less obvious. If a target is either not connected to a global network such as the Internet or has no known exploitable inherent vulnerability, the intelligence service must find a way to get close to the target or to introduce a vulnerability (the "Farewell" enhancement concept introduced earlier in this chapter) through a life-cycle operation. It is this approach or vector that separates the hacker from the sophisticated adversary. It is this vector that provides abundant operational opportunity for the sophisticated adversary who can take advantage of the global market for information technology. The keystone of a foreign information operations strategy would be to aggressively leverage increasing market share in software and microelectronics in order to operationally introduce exploitable vulnerabilities into the critical systems of the target.

An excellent example of leveraging the global supply chain was uncovered in a recent article from the *Taipei Times*.[35] It appears that a U.S. hard-drive company manufactures some of its hard drives in Thailand and that the Thai company subcontracts part of the manufacturing process to a Chinese company. While the drives are in the hands of the Chinese company, a Trojan horse is installed on the drives that when executed will exfiltrate the contents of the drive to one of two websites in China. These drives were sold in Taiwan and are typically used in various government agencies. After an internal Taiwanese investigation exposed the Trojan horse, a Russian antivirus company offered its assistance to the customers of the infected drives. As the world gets flatter, the intelligence opportunities increase dramatically.

Today, it is apparent to Internet users that the hacker community is thriving, requiring even the individual consumer to acquire and configure commercial defensive products. Based upon the omnipresent nature of this overt and low-level threat, the antivirus, antispam, and firewall business has become very lucrative. Since a sophisticated adversary may take advantage of an inherent vulnerability (it is very difficult to impossible for a hacker to engage within the life-cycle realm), the noise introduced by the hacker activity provides added stealth and nonattribution benefits to the sophisticated attacker. More important, it appears that the U.S. has become defensively fixated on this hacker level of threat and correspondingly has applied a significant percentage of its defensive resources, both people and dollars, to combat it. While the United States clearly understands the characteristics of a sophisticated IO adversary and operates at this level, it has been unable to effectively incorporate this knowledge into its defensive mission and broader strategy. Even so, great forward movement is on the verge of being initiated.

It is this everyday "patch and pray" activity that leads many to believe that this is the entire spectrum of the defensive game. In fact, such mundane approaches make up only a small portion of the arrows that the high-end adversary has within its quiver. A common but incorrect perception is that the only way to prosecute a cyber target is with cyber tools.[36] While negatively affecting the confidentiality, integrity, or availability of the cyber target is the operational objective, the offense has a rich array of tools at its disposal. That array includes surreptitious entry, spies, SIGINT, clandestine technical collection, cyber, foreign partners, and the use of cover companies.[37] A critical first step in operational planning is to conduct a targeting assessment. One of the first questions asked is this: How can we meet the operational requirements and reduce the costs and risks of the operation to acceptable levels? Once this assessment is completed and a high-level plan developed, the gears of the intelligence service shift into overdrive. Operational access options are examined; partners are approached; special technology is developed; and legal and policy constraints are examined. The adversary gets to pick the time, the place, and the combination of methods conducted within a veil of secrecy to achieve its objectives (see figure 8.1). The synergistic and mutually supportive nature of these tools and approaches can yield powerful offensive results. In the case of the United States, this offensive paradigm is often ignored, dismissed as not real, or deemed too difficult to handle. For mission-critical applications, this conclusion may well turn out to be a deadly mistake; the result would then be similar to what the captain in *Cool Hand Luke* famously found, "What we've got here is a failure to communicate."

Figure 8.1, "The Ambiguity of Computer Network Defense (CND)," attempts to convey two competing perspectives of the threat and the associated defensive ramifications. The first threat, depicted within the oval of figure 8.1, is best characterized by the hacker or criminal. This opponent uses straightforward and usually known cyber tools in an attempt to compromise a connected computer or network. The common perspective of CND is based upon this level of threat. The defensive strategy associated with this type of threat includes installation and optimum configuration of hardware/software firewalls, utilization of anti-spyware software, utilization of antivirus software, and utilization of an intrusion detection system (IDS). A more informed strategy would also investigate the provenance of the defensive tools in order to increase confidence that the security tool had not been compromised by an adversary. This common and very limited perspective tends to see the opponent attempting to compromise a network, such as SIPRNET—DoD's secret network, with just cyber-related tools. The more sophisticated threat is depicted at the bottom of figure 8.1 as a

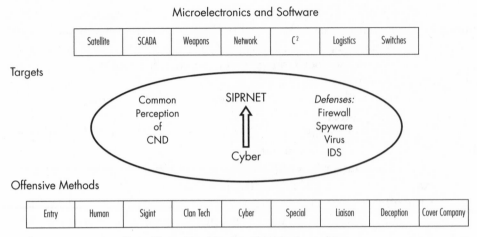

Figure 8.1 The Ambiguity of Computer Network Defense

collection of capabilities. While the list is not intended to be comprehensive, it does illustrate that the high-end threat has a variety of capabilities that when effectively used in combination pose a very serious challenge to our national security systems for which our current defenses are inadequate. The array of capabilities include surreptitious entry, spies, SIGINT, clandestine technical collection, cyber, foreign partners, deception, and cover companies. These formidable capabilities are woven into an operational framework that plays out over time, in various parts of the world, and in combination to target a very broad spectrum of targets, not just computer networks. This spectrum of targets is depicted at the top of figure 8.1, where the common denominator between targets is the use of microelectronics and software.[38]

If the United States is to develop a more effective and balanced counterintelligence strategy, the people and organizations working within the oval of figure 8.1 must have an enhanced level of awareness of the full-spectrum threat characterized at the bottom of figure 8.1. If a system is of sufficient value to a sophisticated adversary using this full-spectrum offensive approach, world-class defensive efforts within the oval of figure 8.1 will do little to impede this opponent from compromising the confidentiality, availability, or integrity of his target. Strangely enough, the defensive efforts within the oval could well enable the attack vector of the opponent.

In March 2007 this author was invited to speak at the Unrestricted Warfare Symposium.[39] In this talk I presented what I strongly believe to be true: that the discounting of foreign governments' innovative operational capabilities with judgments like "They would never do that" is, essentially, insane. This thought, which I stand by today, is captured in my comments as recorded in the conference proceedings: "Last summer, a senior General Officer briefed the Defense Science Board (DSB) Summer Study on Information Management for

Net-Centric Operations.[40] He reported that many systems are being developed in this domain, but it appears that many of the program managers responsible for developing these systems seem to be taking the view that they are not going to be subject to attack. That phenomenon is pervasive throughout our government. It is insanity to continue to design these mission-critical systems as if they were going to operate in an adversary-*free* environment."

What Do We Do about This Situation?

First and foremost, we must develop a balanced and integrated counterintelligence strategy that effectively addresses the issues discussed above. We are, and will increasingly be, operating in an adversary-*rich* environment. We have illustrated the operational effectiveness of an opponent's utilizing, in a mutually supportive fashion, both human and technical operations. A sound offensive strategy will be to attack the defense at its seams. Thus, any successful defensive strategy must minimize these seams, present a uniformly strong in-depth defensive implementation, penetrate the opposing offense, and be sufficiently agile in its approach to adjust as the opponent evolves its strategy. This is a never-ending challenge, and effective risk management is the ultimate goal. The role of CI in characterizing the foreign intelligence service, identifying the case officers, identifying the liaison partners and the nature of their relationship, identifying the human and technical recruitments, and conducting operations to counteract their operational activity is both fundamental and vital. These CI operations will also use the full spectrum of offensive capabilities discussed above. These are the same capabilities, when in the hands of our opponents, against which we are defending.

Despite the enormous challenges of countering sophisticated attacks, there have been some promising advances over the past few years in identifying anomalous behavior in people and organizations. These advances suggest that open-source work will be of increasing importance to effective counterintelligence in the future. For example, "The Digital Dimension" introduced the topic of big-data challenges. Although that chapter addressed the challenges associated with counterterrorism, its findings are also applicable to counterintelligence. One important finding discussed in "The Digital Dimension" is best captured by the following quote: "[I]t has been demonstrated that the extent to which covert networks can operate clandestinely is fundamentally limited, and that by adopting increasingly sophisticated communication and operation security procedures the terrorist network potentially increases its profile."[41] This is true not only of terrorist networks but any clandestine network. Thus, if you are a case officer, a spy, or a supporting organization such as a cover company, it will become increasingly difficult to maintain the secret life.

To introduce the basic ideas behind this claim, it may be useful to start with the familiar example of promptly locating information on the Web using Internet search engines such as Google.[42] Essentially, a search engine like Google consists of Web crawlers that continually and automatically explore the Web by following hyperlinks from one Web page to another, and indexing programs that parse the Web pages, sort them according to content, and then index and store the pages in a manner that enables efficient future retrieval. In addition, a sophisticated search engine like Google estimates the quality of each Web page, by, in part, examining the patterns of hyperlinks in the page's Web neighborhood. When a user submits a query, the search engine parses the query, scans its index of stored Web documents in an attempt to find relevant matches, and returns those documents that are estimated to be query-relevant and of high quality.

It is clear that Google is able to successfully address the Web search Big Data Problem (BDP): There are presently billions of websites containing every imaginable form of content. Google is able to consistently return relevant, high-quality results to most queries. Perhaps more subtle is that a key reason Google is successful is that it is able to exploit the *evolving structure* of the Web itself when it conducts searches. The Web is continually evolving, adding and removing pages and hyperlinks through the unsupervised and biased actions of Web-page creators. Google uses the resulting network of hyperlinked Web pages to efficiently find and assess information on the Web. For instance, rather than attempt to automatically "read" and digest every Web page to determine relevance and quality, Google leverages the enormous collective expertise and efforts of millions of Web-page authors by using the information that is present in the hyperlink structure created by these authors. Thus Google turns the Web-search BDP into a Big-Data Opportunity (BDO) by harnessing the "latent" information encoded in the evolving Web's network structure.

Recent research in the field of complex networks offers evidence that this situation, in which an evolving system generates structure that can then be exploited to turn BDPs into BDOs, is ubiquitous in nature and society. Systems as diverse as electric-power grids, the Internet, genetic and metabolic networks, and networks of terrorists and weapons of mass destruction proliferators all evolve to increase their robustness and reliability by correcting previously observed defects and failure modes. Recent work suggests that such evolution inevitably makes these systems "robust yet fragile" (RYF): They are able to perform reliably for extended periods despite external disturbances and internal flaws, but they are susceptible to catastrophic failures in response to unexpected perturbations.[43]

Consider, for instance, the sophisticated protection logic systems that enable power grids to reliably deliver electricity to entire continents in the presence of widely varying customer demand and significant natural disturbances. This very same protection logic also introduces grid fragilities in which small but unexpected perturbations trigger continent-spanning cascading power outages. Similarly, the "protection logic" provided to us by our amazingly effective immune system also increases the vulnerability we have to autoimmune diseases. And such RYF behavior is not limited to technological or biological systems. Terrorist networks that implement good communication security practices will strive to reduce the number of redundant communications between agents. This typically improves their ability to operate covertly. However, such behavior also *generates* an unintended signature—a suppressed number of "triangles" in network representations of their communications—and this signature can be exploited to efficiently identify terrorist networks even in very large data sets.[44]

Both the Google and terrorist network examples provide overwhelming evidence that the structure of evolved networks may allow us to obtain deep information from limited observations (DILO) of system behavior.[45] While a detailed mathematical description of the relationship between RYF and DILO is beyond the scope of this chapter, the basic idea is straightforward. RYF implies that system evolution makes most system "features" robust but causes a few of these features to be fragile. As a result, the overall system becomes robust in the face of common perturbations but fragile in encounters with certain rare disturbances. Thus, roughly speaking, the behavior of the system can be understood with only a limited appreciation for its many robust features, provided that its few fragile features are well understood. In the case of Google, good search results are obtained in a scalable manner by focusing on key structural features of the Web, such as hyperlink topology, because these features provide reliable feedback. For example, if one wants to find an authoritative source of information on hedge funds, it is better to focus on those pages that are "pointed to" (via hyperlinks) by many other reliable sources rather than to simply trust a Web page that proclaims itself to be a hedge fund authority.

While it is clear that currently available approaches to the BDP, such as Google, are able to perform well, there are crucial differences between the queries typically submitted to Google and questions of interest to national security analysts. Perhaps the most important difference is that the typical user of Google wishes to quickly find information that *someone* already knows and has documented in some form. On the contrary, the vast majority of interesting intelligence questions are of interest precisely because either they have not been crisply documented or in some cases because *no one* actually knows the answer.

As an illustrative example, consider the problem of identifying scientific research activities and trends among scientists involved in covert programs using openly published scientific data. At first glance it may seem that open publications would be of little value in assessing clandestine research among target scientists—it is clearly unlikely that, for instance, biological warfare (BW) researchers will publish a paper detailing their latest approach to weaponizing anthrax. However, research indicates that publication databases contain genuine, if distorted, information regarding the activities of authors even if denial and deception (D&D) tactics are being employed.[46] Intuitively, while it is straightforward to avoid publishing information that is directly informative regarding a covert program, it is virtually impossible to suppress all indirectly related information. Of course, the challenge is to detect these indirect signatures in massive publication data sets and extract from them a quantitative, reliable assessment of a target's research activities.

Consider the problem of deducing information about research at a target facility through analysis of one high-potential source of information: the network of interconnected authors, papers, and concepts in a scientific database. Richard Colbaugh, professor at New Mexico Tech and a staff member at Sandia National Laboratories, and his colleagues applied this basic approach to a study of the Institute of Applied Microbiology in Obolensk, Russia.[47] This laboratory was ostensibly conducting research on infectious diseases of importance to the USSR (e.g., tuberculosis) during the period under study (1970 through the mid-1990s). However, it is now known that for a portion of this period the laboratory was involved in BW research.[48] For example, the institute was working to genetically engineer antibiotic-resistant strains of plague and tularemia and to develop bacteria-toxin combinations (e.g., myelin toxin and plague). Indeed, around 1980 an aggressive program was initiated at the institute to pursue a BW mission, and this program continued until about 1992, when then-Russian president Boris Yeltsin decreed that the BW program would cease. An application of the network analysis methodology to the Obolensk laboratory was able to identify this BW research activity easily despite the aggressive D&D program implemented by the Soviets during this period.[49]

As discussed above, the availability of vast data collections makes it much more difficult for individuals and organizations to implement and maintain a compelling deception. This counterintuitive idea is valid because such collection has become so pervasive and because it is so difficult for adversaries to ensure that their behavior does not generate "second and third order" signatures (indirect and unintended signatures) that are inconsistent with the deception being undertaken. Moreover, RYF/DILO indicates that many of the data sets of interest are sufficiently structured so that such inconsistencies in adversary behavior are detectable in a robust and scalable manner.

To provide a concrete illustration of one way advanced analytical methods can be applied within a CI context, consider the problem of detecting interesting behavior by observing the way individuals use computers and computer networks in a workplace setting. More specifically, consider the problem of detecting deception in e-mail and of identifying abnormal behavior in the way individuals navigate Web pages. To be practically useful, any analytical methods proposed as solutions to these problems must be scalable to vast collections of e-mails or sequences of Web-page navigation clicks. Thus, for example, the analysis of e-mail collections should involve only very shallow, automatic processing of message content and/or the metadata associated with e-mail communication (e.g., "from-to" or "bcc" fields).

An interesting pilot study exploring what can be achieved along these lines was recently conducted for the Office of the National Counterintelligence Executive by researchers at Sandia National Laboratories and New Mexico Tech.[50] The investigation of deception detection in e-mail used the Enron e-mail corpus, a publicly available collection of approximately five hundred thousand e-mails exchanged between Enron employees and others over a three-year period. Both message content and e-mail metadata were analyzed. For the message content portion of the study a very simple "bag of words" model was used, so that the message was considered to be simply a set of words, and all other syntactic and semantic structure was ignored. The deception model employed was also quite simple. It was assumed that individuals engaged in deceptive informal communication exhibit reduced usage of first-person pronouns and exclusive words and increased usage of negative emotion and action words. Analysis consisted of building very large network representations of the message content for the entire Enron e-mail corpus, with messages linked to key words from the four classes of words hypothesized to be relevant for deception. Automated analysis of this network successfully identified both deceptive messages and individuals who were particularly prone to engaging in deception (as independently verified via court transcripts and other information sources). A detailed analysis of the Enron e-mail communication patterns, such as who sends e-mail to whom and who is cc'd on the message, produced interesting and useful results. For example, analysis found the use of "bcc" fields during periods of crisis particularly revealing.

Recent research in complex networks and other domains suggests that advanced analysis methods can turn "big data problems" into "big data opportunities," and several new projects are being started to investigate this exciting possibility. For example, Sandia National Laboratories has initiated a three-year, multimillion-dollar internal Grand Challenge effort entitled "Network Discovery, Prediction, and Disruption" to study this problem in the context of national security. This project adopts the perspective that isolated individuals and events pose only a limited threat to the United States, and that it is *networks* of enemies and actions that pose a real threat. To ultimately defeat an adversarial network, the project will focus on discovering networks within the context of much larger networks with uncertain and deceptive information, and using predictive methods to facilitate adversarial network disruption. This presents an enormous challenge, requiring high-performance informatics and computing methods for fusing and analyzing vast quantities of heterogeneous data from disparate sources such as intelligence reports, cyber traffic, communications, financial transactions, and more.

The technologies to be developed will support analysts and decision makers as they explore various network disruption options, predict consequences, and anticipate side effects. The project is a close partnership between Sandia researchers and analysts, who will be engaged in defining the innovative analytical methodologies. Major distinguishing features in the proposed approach include a focus on temporal dynamics of networks, systemic consideration of the challenges of uncertainty, and the leveraging of advanced methods for analysis and prediction.[51]

In addition to the more traditional approaches of revealing spies and front companies, the advanced techniques briefly discussed above are showing great promise in reducing the advantages of the opposing offense. While the challenges of discovering technical modifications and operations remain daunting, there are certain classes of technical operations that require regular human intervention. For this class of operation these advanced analytic techniques help to uncover the human link, a connection that provides useful clues leading to the discovery of technical activity. A perfect illustration of this approach was the discovery of the Russian "bug" in a conference room on the State Department's seventh floor.[52] Stanislav Gusev, an attaché at the Russian Embassy in Washington, was under FBI surveillance. The surveillance of his activities in the vicinity of the State Department revealed that Gusev was remotely servicing a listening device in the State Department utilizing special equipment hidden within his official embassy car. This led to the discovery of the audio device concealed within the conference room.

At the Unrestricted Warfare Symposium, four key and related factors were identified to be at the heart of the defensive challenges related to countering the more sophisticated foreign technical operations.[53] First, the probability of detecting improperly behaving components, such as software and/or microelectronics is low. In fact, if the component has been "Farewell"-enhanced by a sophisticated opponent, the probability of detection is close to zero. Experiments conducted in the mid-1980s support this assertion.[54] During these experiments very small security critical components were intentionally subverted to assess the likelihood of subversive constructs being detected. The outcomes of these experiments confirmed that even for extremely small systems it would be difficult to maintain confidence in the security of the system when an opponent has had this level of life-cycle access regardless of the level of evaluation conducted. In the intervening twenty years, this situation has worsened. Our ability to evaluate security critical components has not come close to keeping up with the increase in the complexity of the components.

Second, it appears that the likelihood of correctly attributing detected bad behavior to its perpetrator is even lower. Glenn Gaffney, deputy director of national intelligence for collection, expands on the challenges of attribution: "The hooks a foreign intelligence service implants in a U.S. target for exploitation (stealing information) can suddenly and simply be turned to disrupt and destroy the target. The hooks installed by one adversary (foreign intelligence service) for intelligence gathering can be discovered by another adversary (other foreign intelligence services) and used for more destructive purposes. This scenario makes attribution without effective counterintelligence impossible."[55] Without the ability to attribute, deterrence strategies will be hard to develop.[56] This leads to the third factor. If we detect an adversary's penetration of one of our systems and we are able to attribute, with sufficient confidence, the attack to a particular opponent, today there is no significant consequence to the attacker. Without appropriate and substantial penalty to the attacker, there can be no deterrence even with attribution. Political will and a corresponding national policy must be developed before rules of engagement and effective consequences emerge.

The fourth factor is the impact on the owner of the system when the system is compromised. By mitigating the impact of a system's compromise, the advantage to the adversary is reduced. As discussed below, the "impact if compromised issue" and "these systems are not subject to attack issue" are related. By addressing these four factors (detecting bad behavior, attributing bad behavior, increasing consequence to the attacker, and reducing the impact of a compromise) in combination, we can significantly improve upon the current situation. Factors one and two are research issues. It is essential that we identify and invest in research areas that will increase the probability of detecting and attributing bad behavior in mission-critical components. There are numerous studies that have identified research areas to consider. The recent National Academy of Science reports "Toward a Safer and More Secure Cyberspace" and "Hard Problem List" are two such examples.[57] The third factor requires legal and policy support. Within this realm, what does proportional response mean? Is a proportional response sufficient? What level of confidence is required before imposing a penalty on the adversary? If a U.S. person is involved or suspected of being involved, what legal constraints exist? What is the range of retribution available to the United States? Questions like these need to be identified and addressed. The fourth area is a function of system architecture and training. Several recent Defense Science Board reports have identified the need for mission-critical systems to incorporate a war reserve mode. Additionally, since these systems are subject to attack, it becomes essential to frame military exercises in which these systems are degraded, corrupted, or destroyed. By exercising and training with these systems in various stages of degradation, we are better positioned to identify problem areas, increase our confidence in fighting through a problem, and decrease the opponents' confidence that its "Farewell" enhancement(s) will have its intended effect. The old adage of "One test is worth a thousand expert opinions" has a lot of merit in this area.

Summary

Against an adversary employing the full spectrum of tools depicted in figure 8.1, most of our mission-critical applications are vulnerable—very vulnerable. Retired Admiral William Studeman's talking points for the first meeting of the 2006 Defense Science Board Summer Study on Information Management for Net-Centric Operations set the stage for the Information Assurance perspective of the year-long study.[58] In the beginning of the study, the magnitude of the threat, the susceptibility of the systems, and the impact of compromise were not well received or well accepted. His stated position that the challenge of information assurance may be the biggest single problem facing DoD and the national security establishment today was seen as an overstatement by most. As the debates and discussions developed over the year, the membership's views appeared to soften in this regard. If Studeman is correct and we do little to mitigate this threat, then the consequences are dire. If he is wrong or has significantly overstated the threat and we act, we have improved our security awareness and posture at the expense of working other important national security challenges. A principal objective of this chapter is to augment the body of un-classified knowledge to support Studeman's assertion.

Even though the "Farewell" story and the current national security challenge are separated by almost thirty years, they have many aspects in common. The most intriguing common element may be the social dynamic preventing senior policymakers from accepting the preponderance of evidence and decisively act-ing. A book by Bazerman and Watkins sheds some light on this quandary.[59] In examining why leaders fail to act in the face of problems that could develop into disasters, they have zeroed in on six distinguishing characteristics of a predict-able surprise:

- Leaders knew the problem existed and that the situation would not go away.
- Individuals understand that the situation is expanding (getting worse) with time.
- An easy fix does not exist, and significant resources are required to address the problem. The benefits of current efforts will not be realized until later.
- Addressing the problem requires a large down payment right away, while the benefit involves avoiding a potential disaster in the future.
- Addressing the problem requires both organizational and personal change, and human nature seeks status quo.
- Competing interests will benefit from not addressing the problem and will subvert actions to address the problem.

The issues addressed within this chapter appear to correspond closely to these six criteria. Therefore, any strategy to address this problem must take into ac-count the social complexities described above.

Significant progress has been made since the publication of "The Digital Dimension" in 2005. There is a critical mass of seniors within the intelligence community and DoD with a clear understanding of the gravity of this situation. Partnerships, strategies, and implementation plans are being developed, and re-sources made available. One of the biggest and most urgent challenges facing leadership today is ensuring that these plans and actions not only survive the change in administration, but are quickly adopted by the new team. The nation cannot afford to lose the momentum recently generated.

Within the counterintelligence community there is still debate over the rel-ative importance of catching spies as compared to discovering and thwarting foreign clandestine technical operations. Both are critically important, but the culture within counterintelligence is still focused on arresting and expelling bad actors. In a recent conversation, Art Money, former assistant secretary of defense for command, control, communications, and intelligence (ASD C3I), said, "While foreign intelligence services have always depended upon techni-cal operations, the rapidly escalating use of this approach by our opponents is alarming. Based upon the pervasive U.S. dependence of commercial technol-ogy with foreign pedigree, the national security impact of compromise could be staggering. The U.S. counterintelligence strategy must adjust to this growing threat."[60] We must move beyond our current reactive and investigative posture. The counterintelligence culture must adapt and become more proactive to meet these national security imperatives. There is growing agreement within the community that counterintelligence specialists should conduct operations against opposing forces. The innovative application of offensive capabilities to address defensive objectives shows great promise.

It is, however, not surprising that three chapters in this volume discuss counterintelligence as a "wicked problem." John Kao, in his book *Innovation Nation*, makes clear the linkages between complex problems, culture, innovation, systems engineering, and national security. "The wicked problems of our time rarely have clear-cut solutions that can be unlocked by a single discipline," Kao writes. He goes on to say, "They are complex and ambiguous. Issues such as climate change, health care, and national security are, at once, political and psychological, financial and technological. They require breakthrough business models and new ways of thinking about how to change the status quo. Above all, they require integrative approaches that blend necessary perspectives into a new way of doing the actual work of innovation.[61]

We are critically dependent on advanced technology for almost every aspect of U.S. national security. Trust in these systems is very hard to measure or guarantee, and the consequences of misplaced trust in this arena is growing and frightening. The path that we have traveled for the past twenty years has failed to provide the necessary tools for risk management. We must find a new path, a Kao path.

Notes

The views expressed in this chapter are solely my own and are not intended to represent the views of any organization with which I am associated, including Sandia National Laboratories, the DOE, the NSA, the CIA, or the DoD. I would like to acknowledge the contributions to this chapter of Richard Colbaugh, Trudy Blake, Glenn Gaffney, Rick Proto, James Babcock, Larry Contrella, Rick Wilson, Bob Wallace, and Al Romig. Finally, this chapter is dedicated to the memory of Rick Proto, who passed away during the publication of this book. His friendship and counsel will be deeply missed.

1. Network Centric Warfare (NCW) is a key component of DoD planning for transformation of the military. NCW relies on computer-processing power and networked communications technology to provide a shared awareness of the battle space for U.S. forces. Proponents say that a shared awareness increases synergy for command and control, resulting in superior decision making, and the ability to coordinate complex military operations over long distances for an overwhelming war-fighting advantage.

2. Glenn Gaffney, private communication, January 19, 2008. The adversarial objective of corrupting the information and applications within the IT system is somewhat counterintuitive. In recent discussions with Glenn Gaffney, deputy director of national intelligence for collection, he conveyed special concern over integrity breaches. He maintains, "In fact, you don't have to corrupt any information to corrupt all of it. The nasty side of the integrity breach is that all the code/data contained within the system is

rendered suspect. Just the fact that an adversary has been present in your system makes the entire system suspect. The depth of the risks associated with the integrity issue and the potential costs for recovery are frightening. It is much more insidious than it appears on the surface and could put our confidence in the systems developed within these trusted networks at serious risk. And it is just the tip of the iceberg."

3. "The 787 Encounters Turbulence," *Business Week*, June 19, 2006. Available at www.businessweek.com/magazine/content/06_25/b3989049.htm.

4. Interview with J. M. McConnell, vice admiral, USN (Ret.), private communication–oral history, Tysons Corner, Virginia, March 22, 2004.

5. Ibid.

6. Office of the National Counterintelligence Executive, *The National Counterintelligence Strategy of the United States of America, 2007* (Washington, DC, 2007). Available at www.dni.gov/ncix_strategy_2007.pdf.

7. Executive Order 12333, "United States Intelligence Activities," December 4, 1981, 46 F.R. 59941.

8. James R. Gosler, "The Digital Dimension," in *Transforming U.S. Intelligence*, ed. Jennifer E. Sims and Burton Gerber (Washington, DC: Georgetown University Press, 2005), 96–114.

9. Gus W. Weiss, "The Farewell Dossier," *Studies in Intelligence* 39, no. 5 (1996): 121–26.

10. Roald Z. Sagdeev, *The Making of a Soviet Scientist* (New York: John Wiley & Sons, 1994), 298–301.

11. Weiss, "The Farewell Dossier," 123.

12. Ibid.

13. Line X: A separate department within major Soviet Residencies (KGB offices abroad) specializing in collecting scientific and technical information.

14. Weiss, "The Farewell Dossier," 124.

15. This "questioning effect" is a perfect illustration of a source of Gaffney's anxiety relative to integrity breaches.

16. Weiss, "The Farewell Dossier," 124.

17. Clearly the Soviets determined that they had been duped after reading Weiss's paper in the journal *Studies in Intelligence*.

18. Thomas C. Reed, *At the Abyss: An Insider's History of the Cold War* (New York: Ballantine Books—Presidio Press, 2004), 268.

19. Viktor Sheymov, KGB defector, former member of the highly secretive Eighth Chief Directorate, responsible for ensuring secure Soviet worldwide cipher communications and author of the book *Tower of Secrets: A Real Life Spy Thriller* (Annapolis, MD: Naval Institute Press, 1993). Richard Proto, former director of research at NSA, conversations with author relative to lessons from the Cold War, Fort Meade, Maryland, November 11, 2007. The Gunman operation discussed in my chapter "The Digital Dimension" in *Transforming U.S. Intelligence* certainly fits this mold. In 1984 the electric typewriters in both the U.S. Embassy in Moscow and the U.S. Consulate in Leningrad were seized in a "no notice" secret operation conducted by the U.S. government. Based upon the suspicion that the Soviets intercepted and modified the typewriters in transit to the U.S. facilities, a comprehensive investigation was initiated to discover the implants. The investigation revealed that the innovative design of the implant concealment made discovery through visual inspection next to impossible. This Soviet operation indicates that

they placed a high priority on technical operations targeting U.S. facilities. There are numerous indications that the utility of the technical operations of the mid-1980s have not been forgotten by the Soviets, and now the Russians.

20. Alexander Alferov, Alexander Baranov, and Alexander Markov, "On Designing of Cryptographic Algorithms with a Short Synchronization Sequence," *Eurocrypt '95 Rump Session,* May 23, 1995.

21. "Estonia: A cyber-riot," *The Economist,* May 10, 2007. Available at http://globaltechforum.eiu.com/index.asp?layout=rich_story&doc_id=10726&title=Estonia %3A+A+cyber-riot&channelid=4&categoryid=29. "China Promises Germany to Crack Down on Alleged Cyber-Spying," *AFX News Limited,* August 27, 2007. Available at www.technewsworld.com/story/59029.html. "China denies hacking into Pentagon," *CNN.com/asia,* September 5, 2007. Available at www.cnn.com/2007/WORLD/asiapcf/09/05/china.pentagon/.

22. It is still fairly easy for the suspected perpetrators to deny any involvement.

23. In both Gosler's article "The Digital Dimension" (published in *Transforming U.S. Intelligence,* ed. Sims and Gerber) and the Defense Science Board 2003 Summer Study on DoD Roles and Missions in Homeland Security, it was suggested that the intelligence community must aggressively collect, analyze, and report on the threats to our technology infrastructure. Moreover, this reporting must be actionable and supportive of our defensive strategy. In part because of our limited insight relative to a sophisticated threat, coupled with our reluctance to convey our current insights, the country has insufficient motivation to make the necessary investments to improve our defensive posture. Based upon the complexity and magnitude of the information assurance challenge facing the country, any future solution that allows us to appropriately balance the impact of compromise, defensive capability, and threat motivation and capability will likely infringe on the privacy of U.S. citizens. A necessary condition for the public to accept this potential for privacy reduction is a credible story with supporting evidence relative to the realness of this threat. The privacy implications are discussed in great detail in other chapters of this book.

24. Office of the National Counterintelligence Executive, *The National Counterintelligence Strategy of the United States of America 2007,* 1.

25. Michelle Van Cleave, "Counterintelligence and National Strategy" (Washington, DC: National Defense University, 2007), 9.

26. Ibid., 10.

27. Richard Proto, conversations with author relative to lessons from the Cold War, Fort Meade, Maryland, November 11, 2007. During most of the Cold War, the United States was the principal intelligence target of the Soviet Union. Because the United States was so heavily invested in top-end technology, the Soviets were forced to develop techniques that could exploit this advanced technology. At the same time, U.S. targets were using relatively simple technology and thus there was no need to develop technical approaches to compromise advanced systems. This is why the Soviets had a ten-to-twenty-year lead in exploiting high-end technology.

28. Basic Input/Output System (BIOS) refers to the firmware code run by a personal computer when first powered on. The primary function of the BIOS is to identify and initiate component hardware (such as hard drives, floppies, and CDs). This is to prepare the machine so other software programs stored on various media can load, execute, and assume control of the PC.

29. Bill Gertz, "China cyberwarfare," *Inside the Ring*, June 22, 2007. Available at www.gertzfile.com/gertzfile/ring062207.html.

30. Van Cleave, "Counterintelligence and National Strategy."

31. Robert Wallace and H. Keith Melton, *Spycraft: The Secret History of the CIA's Spytechs from Communism to al-Qaeda* (New York: Dutton, 2008).

32. Robert McMillan, "Hacker Finds Serious Flaw in Adobe PDF," *IDG News Service*, September 21, 2007. Available at www.pcworld.com/article/id,137456-c,hackers/article .html.

33. A buffer overflow is an anomalous condition where a process attempts to store data beyond the boundaries of a fixed-length buffer. The result is that the extra data overwrite adjacent memory locations. The overwritten data may include other buffers, variables, and program-flow data and may cause a process to crash or produce incorrect results. They can be triggered by inputs specifically designed to execute malicious code or to make the program operate in an unintended way. As such, buffer overflows cause many software vulnerabilities and form the basis of many exploits. Sufficient bounds checking by the programmer, the compiler, or the runtime can prevent buffer overflows.

34. The development of system access during the various stages of system life (design, fabrication, testing), in conjunction with the subversive modification of the system, is often referred to as the life-cycle approach.

35. Lin Ching-lin, "Chinese subcontractors blamed for trojan horses," *Taipei Times*, November 12, 2007. Available at www.taipeitimes.com/News/taiwan/archives/2007/ 11/12/2003387447.

36. Defense Science Board, *Report of the Defense Science Board Task Force on Mission Impact of Foreign Influence on DoD Software, September 2007.* Text used in this section of the chapter includes elements of this author's original submission to this DSB study.

37. In March 2005 Deputy Under Secretary of Defense for Technology Security Policy and Proliferation Lisa Bronson told the Counterintelligence for the 21st Century Conference at Texas A&M that "China has somewhere between 2,000 and 3,000 front companies in the US, their sole reason for existing is to steal, exploit US technology."

38. James R. Gosler, "The Digital Dimension," *Proceedings on Combating the Unrestricted Warfare Threat: Integrating Strategy, Analysis, and Technology* (Johns Hopkins University Applied Physics Lab, March 20–21, 2007), 264.

39. Ibid.

40. Defense Science Board, *Report of the 2006 Summer Study on Information Management for Net-Centric Operations, April 2007.*

41. Gosler, "The Digital Dimension," in *Transforming U.S. Intelligence*, ed. Sims and Gerber, 108.

42. Sergey Brin and Lawrence Page, "The Anatomy of a Large-Scale Hypertextual Web Search Engine." Available at www-db.stanford.edu/~backrub/google.html.

43. J. Doyle et al., "The 'robust yet fragile' nature of the Internet," *Proc. National Academy of Sciences 102* (2005). Also, P. Ormerod and R. Colbaugh, "Cascades of failure and extinction in evolving complex systems," *Journal of Artificial Societies and Social Simulation 9* (2006). R. Colbaugh, K. Glass, and G. Willard, "Scalable methods for vulnerability analysis of complex networks," patent application, National Security Agency, April 2007.

44. Within this context, a triangle is a communication pattern. Suppose that A, B, and C are people where B and C report to A. Normal communications patterns would reveal

that A talks to B, A talks with C, and B talks with C. In this case the communications "triangle" between A, B, and C is closed. In the case of terrorists, for operations security reasons, it is much more likely that B and C would not communicate. Thus, the triangle would not be closed, and this reduction in (closed) triangles compared with normal communication serves as an indication of covert behavior. R. Colbaugh, K. Glass, and J. Gosler, "Personnel security assessment via complex networks analysis," presentation to Office of National Counterintelligence Executive (ONCIX), September 2007.

45. Colbaugh, Glass, and Gosler, "Personnel security assessment."

46. P. Ball, "Bioweapons labs outed by own research," *Nature Science Update*, June 2004. Available at www.nature.com/news/2004/040531/full/040531–1.html.

47. Ibid.

48. K. Alibek, *Biohazard* (New York: Random House, 1999).

49. P. Ball, "Bioweapons labs outed by own research."

50. Colbaugh, Glass, and Gosler, "Personnel security assessment."

51. M. Salganik, P. Dodds, and D. Watts, "Experimental study of inequality and unpredictability in an artificial cultural market," *Science 311* (2006). R. Colbaugh and K. Glass, "Predictability and prediction of social processes," *Proc. Fourth Lake Arrowhead Conference of Human Complex Systems*, April 2007.

52. "To Catch a Spy," *Chicago Tribune*, December 9, 1999. Available at www.fas.org/irp/news/1999/12/991210-rus-spy.htm.

53. Gosler, "The Digital Dimension," *Proceedings on Combating the Unrestricted Warfare Threat*, 265.

54. Ibid., 259.

55. Glenn Gaffney, private communication, January 19, 2008.

56. While there are instances where attribution with sufficient confidence is achieved, these examples are typically associated with elementary exploitations by adversaries who does not seem to care whether they have been identified.

57. Seymour Goodman and Herbert Lin, *Toward a Safer and More Secure Cyberspace*, National Research Council, Committee on Improving Cybersecurity Research in the United States (Washington, DC: National Academy Press, 2007); "Hard Problem List," INFOSEC Research Council, November, 2005. Available at: www.infosec-research.org/docs_public/20051130-IRC-HPL-FINAL.pdf.

58. William O. Studeman (admiral, retired), former director of NSA and deputy director of central intelligence, discussion of Studeman's talking points for upcoming DSB Summer Study over dinner in Great Falls, Virginia, March 7, 2006; in attendance Bill Studeman, Joe Markowitz, and Jim Gosler.

59. M. Bazerman and M. Watkins, *Predictable Surprises: The disasters you should have seen coming and how to prevent them* (Boston: Harvard Business School Press, 2004).

60. Art Money, private communication, February 16, 2008.

61. John Kao, *Innovation Nation* (New York: Free Press, 2007), 24–25.

9

Harvey Rishikof

Economic and Industrial Espionage

Who Is Eating America's Lunch, and How Do We Stop It?

This case [*U.S. v. Meng*, 2007] highlights the vital importance of protecting the intellectual property and trade secrets not only in Silicon Valley but also for our country's businesses. The alleged economic espionage and theft and export of trade secrets such as these—visual simulation training software that has military application, no less—has real consequences that could jeopardize our country's military advantages in the world, in addition to creating substantial financial losses for our businesses which legitimately developed and owned this information. We are grateful to our law enforcement partners for taking swift and appropriate action here, and also want to acknowledge the pivotal role private industry's ready cooperation has in these investigations.

United States Attorney Kevin V. Ryan[1]

ECONOMIC OR industrial espionage is an old problem. As Joel Brenner, current National Counterintelligence Executive (NCIX) under the director of national intelligence (DNI), likes to muse, espionage itself is as old as Joshua reconnoitering the Promised Land, and it will be with us forever.[2] During the Cold War the archetype for technological counterintelligence, as well as industrial espionage, was the American-born Russian spy Dr. George Koval's penetration of the Manhattan Project for the atomic bomb.[3] But the paradigm is shifting in the economic era of globalization. The end of the Cold War, increased access to computers and the Internet, potential profits, poor prosecutorial tools, fear of reporting the theft, and inadequate federal and state laws have all contributed to the attractiveness of economic espionage.[4] In the words of Bernard Esambert, former chairman of the board of the Pasteur Institute, "Today's economic competition is global. The conquest of markets and technologies has replaced former territorial and colonial conquests. We are living in a state of world economic war and

199

this is not just a military metaphor . . . the companies are training the armies and the unemployed are the casualties."[5]

International commerce and advancing technology are increasing the likelihood of, and opportunity for, economic intelligence and industrial espionage, placing intellectual property and trade secrets at increased risk of appropriation. Consider the iPod. While it is developed by Apple, its 451 parts are made in several different countries, including Japan, the Philippines, Korea, China, and Taiwan.[6] Such outsourcing, although efficient and cost effective, leaves Apple open to foreign industrial espionage at critical stages of design. When viewed from the perspective of Brenner and the NCIX trying to protect economic secrets in a world of shifting boundaries, world supply lines, and spheres of influence, it is a monumental challenge:

> Boundaries of every kind are eroding—legally, behaviorally, electronically—in all aspects of our lives: Between the public and private behavior of ordinary people; for example, the sense of dress and decorum appropriate to the home, the street, the office, or houses of worship. Between the public and private—that is, secret— behavior of governments. Between the financing, legal norms, and research activities of public as opposed to private institutions; [and] universities, for instance. Between state and non-state actors and the relative size of the resources they control. Cyber boundaries are also eroding—and not always in ways we like—but simply because we are sometimes helpless to enforce them.[7]

But those in charge are still responsible for crafting a response to the new era of globalization, computerization, secrets, and spying. The mission, therefore, is increasingly difficult and will not go away because the stakes are so high. The "intellectual thieves" seem to have the upper hand at the moment, as Brenner elegantly explained at a recent public-private-sector conference:

> The fact is, intellectual thieves are eating our lunch—eating *your* lunch. The public and private sectors are both leaking badly. I'm not talking about just the pirating of DVDs and movies in Asia. I'm talking about significant technologies that are walking out of our laboratories on electronic disks, walking onto airplanes bound for foreign airports, and re-entering the country as finished products developed by foreign entrepreneurs. In effect, we're buying back our own technology. This is bad enough when we're talking about commercial innovation. But when we're talking about technology with substantial defense applications, we're talking about losses of intellectual capital that in wartime could cost many lives of our fellow citizens. These losses are occurring, and they are occurring in a targeted, systematic manner. Protecting innovative technology before it can be patented or classified is an urgent task, and it is difficult. If any of us knew how to do it, he'd be very rich, because it's a question of handicapping basic research.[8]

Protecting critical business information is not only a bottom-line issue but also increasingly a national security issue. Companies, however, are fearful of government classification schemes that will hinder innovation and openness. Given this reality and boundary erosion, perhaps it is not surprising that a former head of the French intelligence service in 1994 admitted that his agency spied on U.S. executives abroad and "bugged" first-class seats on Air France in order to monitor conversations.[9] Moreover, this arena is complicated not only by the fact that the key to our information networks is openness but that the information can be transmitted through standard business practices—mergers and acquisitions, joint ventures, strategic alliances, and licensing agreements. Therefore, both military friends and foes may be adversaries in the economic arena of espionage. Sometimes the attack is from government-sponsored espionage, other times it is the private illicit acquisition of proprietary information, and sometimes it may be a combination of the two.

A measure of the extent of the problem is the number of prosecutions for the illegal export of U.S. technology as reported by the 2003 Annual Report on Foreign Economic Collection and Industrial Espionage (FECIE). During fiscal year 2003, the U.S. Department of Immigration and Customs Enforcement (ICE) conducted more than two thousand investigations involving violations of the Arms Export Control Act, International Traffic in Arms Regulations, Export Administration Regulations, the International Emergency Economic Powers Act, and the Trading with the Enemy Act. Those investigations resulted in 120 arrests, 75 criminal indictments, and 55 convictions.[10]

According to a survey published in 2007 by the American Society for Industrial Security (ASIS), the financial impact of individual cases of espionage ranged from less than $10,000 to more than $5.5 million per incident, for a cumulative year-end total in the American economy of billions of dollars in losses—to reputation, image, goodwill, competitive advantage, core technology, and profitability.[11] But as we began to recognize in the late 1990s, corporations are of strategic interest to the United States on three levels since they (1) produce classified products for the government; (2) produce dual-use technology used in both the public and private sectors; and (3) are responsible for R&D and the creation of leading-edge technologies critical to maintaining U.S. economic security. Losses at any of these levels could affect U.S. international competitiveness and security.[12] Regardless of the source, the threat to American interests is real, and the United States is extremely vulnerable.

The 2005 Annual Report to Congress on FECIE reported that 108 countries—both friend *and* foe—were involved in information collection efforts against the United States.[13] China, Russia, and India top the list. The FECIE reports indicate that foreign collectors tend to target dual-use technology, which can be used for both peaceful and military objectives, and military technology. There is no dispute that foreign governments go after trade secrets for the sake of national security advantage. But what is the United States government's role in intercompany warfare? Should investigations be considered a counterintelligence or law enforcement matter? Do these old jurisdictional boundaries and responsibilities still work? What should be a secret, and what is the government's role in making that determination? What can be done to protect U.S. interests?

The critical issue in the new world of commerce is whether one can clarify the differences between economic and industrial counterespionage and explain why the latter is particularly problematic. To many, governments have long engaged in economic intelligence but have found the need to engage in economic espionage declining as more and more critical information is available through open sources. Industrial espionage, on the other hand, may be becoming the most prevalent form of economic espionage as governments seek industry-related information for the intelligence they need on battlefield capabilities, design of countermeasures, and preparation of the battlefield—including how to attack energy grids and industrial plants important for war making. Industrial espionage involving the theft of trade secrets perhaps at one time seemed restricted to an industrial sphere, but dual-use technologies erase what once was an easy distinction, as government involvement becomes more prevalent.

This essay will discuss these issues in three parts. The first part will discuss the period before the passage of the Economic Espionage Act of 1996 and the legal framework it created. In the second part I will examine the current state of prosecutions, highlighting the three most recent cases. The third part will explain where we are in 2008 as a matter of policy and the emerging trends.

How Did We Get to This Point?

Perhaps for the purposes of this discussion it is best to begin with the passage of the Economic Espionage Act (EEA) of 1996. Although the stakes were well known and recognized prior to 1996, the law was not structured for prosecution. Information and technology industries, followed by finance and trade sectors, had been the prime targets for decades, as noted by most espionage open-source reports.[14] Though the problem was recognized prior to 1996, there were, and still are, a dizzying array of entities involved in combating foreign industrial espionage. For example, the National Counterintelligence Center (NACIC), in drafting the 1995 annual report to Congress on foreign economic collection and industrial espionage, solicited input from several relevant executive branch government agencies.[15]

The NACIC was created in 1994 by Presidential Decision Directive/NSC 24, "U.S. Counterintelligence Effectiveness," to manage the perennial problem of fragmentation and coordination at all national levels of counterintelligence (CI) and domestic law enforcement activities (LE). A major problem was, and continues to be, how to create connectivity with the private sector and prioritize economic security within the two communities.

In 1995, as noted in the NACIC report, the FBI was the central U.S. government agency for collecting, analyzing, and investigating foreign threats to U.S. industry. Because of its mission as both the U.S. government's primary CI agency with regard to foreign intelligence activities within the United States and in its role as the lead criminal investigative agency, the FBI was able to use both statutory roles against economic and industrial espionage. The U.S. Customs Service, the primary border enforcement agency, however, enforced the Arms Export Control Act, the Export of War Materials Act, and the Export Administration Act.

To reach out to the domestic corporate community, the FBI had for over twenty years been running the Development of Espionage, Counterintelligence, and Counterterrorism Awareness Program (DECA) and the Awareness of National Security Issues and Response Program (ANSIR). Theoretically DECA and ANSIR coordinators in each of the FBI's fifty-six field offices had regular liaison with companies located in the field offices' territories and discussed the various methods employed by foreign governments to accomplish their intelligence collection goals. During fiscal years 1993 and 1994 the FBI briefed almost twenty thousand companies totaling nearly a quarter of a million personnel, in addition to briefings at academic institutions, laboratories, and state and local governments. In addition, the programs periodically published foreign intelligence threat information journals titled *DECA Notes* and *ANSIR-FAX*. Both classified and unclassified versions of *DECA Notes* and DECA briefings have been given to U.S. corporations throughout the United States. As part of the domestic framework, DoD, NRO, NSA, DOE, DOC, as well as other agencies, such as U.S. Customs, all fed the FBI information and analysis on economic espionage.

In theory, the State Department's Overseas Security Advisory Council (OSAC) and, on occasion, the CIA's National Resources Division were to provide more timely or relevant threat information to the private sector concerning overseas operations. In 1995 the State Department's OSAC was a joint venture by the department and U.S. businesses to work together on overseas security problems of mutual concern, including foreign economic threats. OSAC was administered under the State Department's Bureau of Diplomatic Security (DS). Over 1,400 private-sector organizations participated in its activities and received information and guidance. As part of the growing emphasis on the threat to U.S. business, OSAC established a Committee for Protection of Information and Technology that sought to improve the government-industry partnership. OSAC also oversaw "Country Councils" in selected foreign cities that consisted of U.S. embassy security officers and other post officials working with security managers of U.S. private-sector enterprises to exchange unclassified security information in a timely fashion. In 1994 the State Department had Country Councils in twenty-five foreign cities, with five more planned for 1995. Country Councils were set up so that OSAC could pass threat information to industry and gather information from U.S. corporations concerning threats to U.S. economic security.[16]

As noted over twelve years ago and often repeated, the problem of fragmentation and competition on the policy and operational roles between CI operations and law enforcement investigations was such that at times "these two communities have proceeded separately without effectively coordinating their efforts."[17] Then, as now, the policy option fixes were the standard remedies: increase resources for CI and law enforcement, institutionalize economic security as a priority in national security, and develop a coordinated CI and law enforcement approach to collection and analytical requirements.

By 1992 the CIA was sounding the alarms in open forums about the theft of U.S. proprietary information and technology by foreign countries and companies. The then-director of the CIA, Robert Gates, testified, "Some foreign intelligence services have turned from politics to economics, and the United States is the prime target. . . . Various governments in Asia, Europe, the Middle East, and to a lesser degree, Latin America, as well as some former Communist countries (some twenty countries or governments in all) are involved in intelligence activities that are detrimental to our economic interests at some level."[18] Without the proper criminal tools, the theft of trade secrets was subject to misdemeanor penalties. In hearings on economic espionage reform before the House Judiciary Subcommittee on Crime in 1996, FBI Director Louis J. Freeh laid out the growing government awareness of the post–Cold War shift to a new emphasis of economic and industrial espionage by foreign powers and private actors. Arguing for new legislation, he detailed the problems of trying to prosecute the nontangible nature of proprietary information under the Interstate Transportation of Stolen Property Act; the Mail Fraud, Wire Fraud, Computer Fraud and Abuse Act; the Conspiracy to Deprive the U.S. of Its Right to Honest and Competitive Bidding on Contract; and the Aiding and Abetting statutes.

Most significant, law enforcement efforts were constrained because federal law made it difficult to prosecute thefts of proprietary technology, proprietary information, or intellectual property since the laws did not specifically protect economic and technological information. Instead law enforcement officials cobbled together violations of espionage, fraud and stolen property, and export statutes to prosecute cases against foreign economic and industrial intelligence violators. In March 1996 the American Society for Industrial Security (ASIS) issued a special report entitled *Trends in Intellectual Property Loss*, detailing the loss of corporate information and stating that it had increased from 9.9 incidents per month in 1992 to an average of 32 incidents per month in 1995, or a 323 percent increase.[19]

At the same time "cybercrime" was beginning to loom larger on the government's radar screen. First, the FBI established the Computer Investigations and Infrastructure Threat Assessment Center (CITAC) and the National Infrastructure Protection Center (NIPC) at headquarters, and the field offices were opening local computer prosecution cells, while at the Department of Justice the Criminal Division Computer Crime and Intellectual Property Unit, established in 1991, was elevated to a Section (CCIPS) in 1996, though by 2000 the section had grown from five attorneys to only eighteen.[20] In short, cybercrime was still not a high priority with full resources.

Nevertheless, the stars were aligned, and with the support of Senators Arlen Specter and Herb Kohl on the Senate side and Congressmen Bill McCollum and Chuck Schumer on the House side, President Bill Clinton signed the Economic Espionage Act (EEA) of 1996 on October 1.[21] In his signing statement President

Clinton expressed the hope that the EEA "will protect the trade secrets of all businesses operating in the United States, foreign and domestic alike, from economic espionage and trade secrets theft and deter and punish those who would intrude into, damage or steal from computer networks."[22] History has not been kind to this aspiration.

For some the problem for the EEA began at its inception. It was passed during the period when the intelligence community was trying to find a new mission in the post–Cold War era and was searching for resources that emphasized the new and real threats to industry. From the perspective of Congress the national security side of the FBI was losing power to the criminal side, which was receiving prominence for its "helping hand" to law enforcement in the new emerging Russia. Fighting crime and securing borders were seen as the FBI's marquee missions, and resources were rapidly being moved to fulfill it. The national security division was in a desperate fight for resources, and a sense of urgency drove the new legislation.

The debate appeared to be weighted in favor of the security of huge corporations or defense contractors' chiefs (many former FBI agents) and not the leaders of emerging cutting-edge technology firms that were likely to be targeted by adversaries. Therefore, rather than a nuanced dialogue with industry CEOs that would allow consensus on how to protect trade secrets, debate was sidestepped in favor of a blunter approach in order to pass the legislation quickly. Although there was an underlying need for new laws, speed at the expense of analysis created an act that was both too broad and too narrow, but it did bolster the FBI's National Security Division budget.

The EEA protection of trade secrets has ten sections. The fundamental contribution of the act was in criminalizing the theft of trade secrets and providing a very broad definition of the term "trade secret" as follows:

> all forms and types of financial, business, scientific, technical, economic, or engineering information, including patterns, plans, compilations, program devices, formulas, designs, prototypes, methods, techniques, processes, procedures, programs, or codes, whether tangible or intangible, and whether or how stored, compiled, or memorialized physically, electronically, graphically, photographically, or in writing if—
>
> (A) the owner thereof has taken reasonable measures to keep such information secret; and
> (B) the information derives independent economic value, actual or potential, from not being generally known to, and not being readily ascertainable through proper means by, the public; and . . .
>> (4) the term 'owner,' with respect to a trade secret, means the person or entity in whom or in which rightful legal or equitable title to, or license in, the trade secret is reposed.[23]

The act covers any action concerning a trade secret when, without authorization, there is a copying, duplicating, sketching, drawing, photographing, downloading, uploading, altering, destroying, photocopying, replicating, transmitting, delivering, sending, mailing, communicating, or conveying. Using this broad definition the EEA contains two distinct provisions. Section 1831 addresses economic espionage directed by foreign governments or government-controlled entities and carries a prison penalty of fifteen years and a fine of up to $500,000 for individuals and $10 million for organizations. The other section, 1832, prohibits the commercial theft of trade secrets carried out for economic or commercial advantage, whether the perpetrator is a foreign or domestic entity and carries a prison penalty of ten years and fine of up to $5,000,000.[24]

Section 1831 was designed to apply only when there is evidence of foreign government-, instrumentality-, or agent-sponsored or coordinated intelligence activity. Under section 1831, the government must prove that: (1) the defendant stole, or without the owner's authorization obtained, destroyed, or conveyed information; (2) the defendant knew or believed that this information was a trade secret; (3) the information was a trade secret; and (4) the defendant intended or knew that the offense would benefit a foreign government, instrumentality, or agent. The term "foreign instrumentality" is defined as "any agency, bureau, component, institution, association, or any legal, commercial, or business organization, firm, or entity that is substantially owned, controlled, sponsored, commanded, managed, or dominated by a foreign government."[25]

Under section 1832, the government must prove beyond a reasonable doubt that (1) the defendant stole, or without the owner's authorization obtained, sent, destroyed, or conveyed information; (2) the defendant knew or believed that the information was a trade secret; (3) the information was in fact a trade secret; (4) the defendant intended to convert the trade secret to the economic benefit of somebody other than the owner; (5) the defendant knew or intended that the owner of the trade secret would be injured; and (6) the trade secret was related to, or was included in, a product that was produced or placed in interstate or foreign commerce. It is also illegal to attempt to steal a trade secret, or to receive, purchase, destroy, or possess a trade secret, which the defendant knew, was stolen.

The issues stemming from the act's narrowness immediately became apparent once enforcement began. According to the NCIX reports, one cannot be convicted under the EEA if it can be proven that the elements of a trade secret were discovered through parallel development or reverse-engineering. In addition, the EEA does not apply to individuals who seek to exploit their lawfully developed knowledge and abilities. The EEA also does not prohibit legitimate economic collection or reporting by personnel of foreign governments by lawful open-source means.[26] The EEA anticipates that victims of trade secret thefts are often faced with the dilemma that by reporting the matter to law enforcement authorities the trade secret might be publicly revealed during criminal prosecution. In an effort to preserve the confidentiality of a trade secret, the EEA under section 1835 provides for the continued status of information as a trade secret and will prevent the unnecessary and harmful disclosure of such information. Confidentiality agreements for counsel and experts to protect all proprietary information were part of the expected trial process.

What Is the Current State of Prosecutions?

The verdict on the first years of the EEA is somewhat mixed; to some critics the act has been more of a mousetrap than a bear trap.[27] In the first six years of the act the government prosecuted eighteen cases.[28] Between 2000 and 2003, seventeen more cases were brought, for a total of thirty-five.[29] The trade secrets involved in the first eighteen included a wide range of products: fiberglass, drugs for cancer, sensitive pressure devices, shaving systems, accounting software, hepatitis kits, laminates for countertops, veterinary products, Intel chips, mining diagrams, engineering drawings, industrial equipment, radiation therapy machines, IBM source code, 3Com Corporation source code, plans for oil field and pipeline machinery from Caterpillar, and well logs for oil drilling.

Interestingly, only three of the eighteen cases went to trial. All the cases were brought under the domestic section Sec. 1832, rather then the foreign section, and other federal statutes were also used, like the wire and mail fraud laws. Moreover, the defendants received relatively light sentences, ranging from two years probation to six months' home confinement to supervised release, and relatively small fines of up to $250,000, although the cases may have involved trade secrets valued at millions of dollars.[30]

AT THE TIME of the passage of the EEA, twenty-three to twenty-six countries were identified as practicing suspicious collection and acquisition activities, and twelve, in particular, were targeting trade secrets. The technology categories, many of which are dual-use technologies and are listed in the Military Critical Technology List published by the DoD, were of greatest interest.[31] The FBI had seen the number of cases of suspected economic espionage under investigation in its Economic Counterintelligence Program started in 1994 leap from four hundred to eight hundred cases by 1996. By 2005 the number of countries involved in collection efforts against sensitive and protected U.S. technologies had risen dramatically.

More specifically, the immediate issue is whether the government should be engaged in a backdoor industrial policy by determining which industrial products deserve protection with federal dollars. The criteria for prosecution might be based on direct relevance to national security, actually threatened industries, or a mixed strategy using a case-by-case approach. Recent cases brought under the EEA are illustrative of the range of potential problems for prosecution under the current charging schemes as the government tries to establish foreign involvement.

If the companies are selected according to their direct relevance to national security (i.e., they have defense contracts), then the contracting process becomes the tool the FBI and others use for building their database of which industries to help—regardless of whether the thief is a foreign government or a competing firm acting on its own. This is, of course, a very defensive posture but allows for a potential marshaling of resources. An example of such a national security case is *United States v. Meng*, which involved military technology, computer source code, and economic opportunity.[32]

In 2007 Xiaodong Sheldon Meng, formerly a resident of Beijing, China, and a resident of Cupertino, California, was charged with stealing military combat and commercial simulation software and other materials from his former employer Quantum3D, a company based in San Jose, California. Meng was charged under the EEA with stealing trade secrets from Quantum3D with the intent that they would be used to benefit the foreign governments of China, Thailand, and Malaysia.

Many of Quantum3D's products were designed primarily for military purposes, including military combat training in simulated real-time conditions during the day and night and the use of advanced infrared (IR), electro-optical (EO), and night vision goggle (NVG) devices. The indictment alleges that Meng stole numerous Quantum3D products, including "viXsen" and "nVSensor," which were used exclusively in military applications and designed for precision training of military fighter pilots in night vision scenarios among other applications. Both "viXsen" and "nVSensor" are classified as defense articles on the U.S. Munitions List and cannot be exported outside the United States without an export license.

In 2003, after a number of years of employment, Meng entered into a consulting agreement with Quantum3D in which he would serve as an independent consultant for Quantum3D in Asia. In this capacity he tried to sell sensitive source code to the Malaysian Air Force. In 2004 he severed his relationship with Quantum3D, joined a competitor, and attempted to sell Quantum3D products to the Chinese and Thailand.[33] In essence, Meng, given his knowledge of the products, became the carrier.

Another recent case highlights the overlap of economic and industrial espionage in the national security area and offers an example of the type of case that the EEA might be applied to. In the *Chi Mak* case, five members of a southern California family were charged with acting as agents of the People's Republic of China and with conspiring with one another to export United States defense articles to the People's Republic of China, a violation of the Arms Export Control Act. This technology theft ring focused on acquiring corporate proprietary information and embargoed defense technology related to the propulsion, weapons, and electrical systems of U.S. warships. The family, the father a naturalized citizen from China, had pursued a long-term plan of infiltration over years.

Though the object was clear, who sponsored the ring? Chi Mak was a support engineer at L-3 Communications working on Navy quiet-drive propulsion technology. The espionage effort appears to have been directed by a Chinese academic at a research institute for Southeast Asian affairs at Zhongshan University in Guangzhou, China. The Chi family encrypted the information it was passing back to China into a computer disk that appeared to contain television and sound broadcasts. It was literally embedded in the other data in encrypted form. This effort has all of the earmarks of professional espionage tradecraft and state-directed espionage, with sophisticated control and sophisticated clandestine communications means. The government university in Guangzhou could have been cover for a state-directed espionage effort. However, Chi Mak and his alleged coconspirators could just as well have been part of a sophisticated economic espionage operation run out of a university research institute. The future plea agreements will perhaps make clear the true nature of the conspiracy.[34]

This "direct relevance" approach would require prioritizing military programs and "tagging" all employees with access to high-value products. And as these cases illustrate, the targeting countries are not beyond "planting" potential operatives as "sleepers" whose goal is to join critical companies and plot long-term career paths.

Alternatively, the FBI and others could build a database of those industries actually threatened by foreign governments' intelligence activities, whether or not the United States uses the technology for national security purposes. The rationale here would be as follows: If a foreign government wants the technology, there is national security gain to be had, by definition, in keeping that technology from them. This approach is problematic because of its underlying assumption and because many nondefense firms do not necessarily want the federal government probing their businesses to discover what their R&D involves or interfering in their choices on how to develop, protect, or share such technologies.

Such a case was *United States v. Okamoto and Serizawa*, when Takashi Okamoto, a resident of Japan, and Hiroaki Serizawa, a resident of Kansas, were indicted for stealing trade secrets from the Cleveland Clinic Foundation (CCF).[35] Okamoto and Serizawa conspired to misappropriate from the CCF certain genetic materials called deoxyribonucleic acid (DNA) and cell-line reagents and constructs developed by researchers employed by the CCF, with funding provided by the CCF and the National Institutes of Health, to study the genetic cause of and possible treatment for Alzheimer's disease. Alzheimer's affects an estimated four million people in the United States alone and is the most common cause of dementia. The pharmaceutical market for this disease is a potentially rich profit center for any company in the field. The Alzheimer's disease market is forecast to continue to expand significantly over the next ten years. Aided by growing elderly populations, successive product launches have seen global revenues grow at over 35 percent.[36]

The goal of the conspiracy was to benefit the Institute of Physical and Chemical Research (RIKEN), a quasi-public corporation located in Saitama-Ken, Japan, which received over 94 percent of its operational funding from the Ministry of Science and Technology of the government of Japan. The Brain Science Institute (BSI) of RIKEN was formed in 1997 as a specific initiative of the Ministry of Science and Technology to conduct research in the area of neuroscience, including research into the genetic cause of, and possible treatment for, Alzheimer's disease.

Okamoto and Serizawa had committed economic espionage by stealing, altering, and destroying trade secrets that were property of the CCF, specifically, ten DNA and cell-line reagents developed through the efforts and research of researchers employed and funded by the CCF and by a grant from the National Institutes of Health.[37] Okamoto and Serizawa were also charged with transporting, transmitting, and transferring in interstate and foreign commerce DNA and cell-line reagents developed through the efforts of researchers employed and funded by the CCF.[38]

Should the FBI be focused on lucrative emerging world markets, as in the above case of *Okamoto and Serizawa*, and be using limited resources to protect private companies from losing market share? How can the federal government, given its limited resources, spread itself across such a large canvas? Will corporations want to cooperate with the government?

A third option is to develop a CI strategy that mixes the two previous approaches and determines, on a case-by-case basis, whether the efforts at acquisition by a foreign entity represent a national security threat. *United States v. Ye and Zhong* presents such a choice.[39] Fei Ye and Ming Zhong were arrested at the San Francisco International Airport with stolen trade secret information in their luggage while attempting to board an aircraft bound for China. Ye and Zhong admitted to possessing stolen trade secrets for an integrated circuit design from Sun Microsystems and Transmeta Corporation with the intent to benefit the People's Republic of China.

Ye and Zhong admitted that they intended to utilize the trade secrets in designing a computer microprocessor that was to be manufactured and marketed by a company that they had established, known as Supervision, Inc. They admitted that Supervision was to have provided a share of any profits made on sales of chips to the city of Hangzhou and the province of Zhejiang in China, from which Supervision was to receive funding. Mr. Ye and Mr. Zhong also admitted that their company had applied for funding from the National High Technology Research and Development Program of China, commonly known as the "863 Program."

Fei Ye is alleged to have possessed a corporate charter for Hangzhou Zhongtian Microsystems Company Ltd. at his house; the charter states that the joint venture will raise China's ability to develop superintegrated-circuit design and form a powerful capability to compete with worldwide leaders' core development technology and products in the field of integrated-circuit design.[40]

The problem here is that in addition to the issues raised by the first two previous enforcement approaches, the *Ye and Zhong* case introduces a third: acquiring the expertise within the CI community to analyze industrial R&D at its most cutting edge. And even if the community were successful in doing this, the FBI would have to employ a sliding authorization for use of counterintelligence tools (wiretaps, undercover surveillance, etc.) during the investigative process or risk alienating firms it might need to cooperate in an eventual prosecution. Any investigations that did not pan out as espionage would have to be prosecuted as crimes, unless companies decide to drop charges in the interest of pursuing profits instead. But could the corporations count on the federal government or IC to pull back once an interest had been pursued? For some of the proponents of the EEA in 1996, the act was an attempt to pursue this third option, but the infrastructure and groundwork has not materialized to pursue such a nuanced course.

These cases are of interest because they illustrate how difficult CI is when the focus is the private sector. What were the roles of the firms in each of the cases? Did they alert the FBI, or the other way around? How were decisions made regarding the use of CI versus countercrime techniques, and did internal FBI disagreements arise that complicated or slowed down investigations? These important questions demonstrate how difficult it is to pursue prosecutions in this area.

Where Are We in 2008? Questions, Issues, Trends, and Consequences

In the years since the passage of the Economic Espionage Act, more questions than answers remain. As the cases demonstrate, the fact patterns are complicated, and the relationships between government and the private sector remain obscure. The first problem as outlined by the 2001 Annual Report is that there is no consensus in the U.S. government as to the definition of "economic espionage." Moreover, it is difficult to prove espionage has been committed under foreign government sponsorship, and trade secrets or proprietary information is defined differently under state laws, different U.S. statutes, and international conventions. As stipulated by the NCIX report in the definitions section for economic espionage, industrial espionage, and proprietary information, we are at sea.

For example, in the section on "definitions," this is what the report contains:

Economic Espionage. There is no consensus within the US Government on the definition of economic espionage. For the purposes of this report, NCIX will use the US Attorney General's definition of economic espionage as "the unlawful or clandestine targeting or acquisition of sensitive financial, trade, or economic policy information; proprietary economic information; or critical technologies." This definition excludes the collection of public domain and legally available information that constitutes a significant majority of economic collection. Aggressive intelligence collection that is entirely in the public domain and is legal may harm US industry, but it is not espionage. It, however, may help foreign intelligence services identify and fill information gaps that could be a precursor to economic espionage. For a conviction under the Economic Espionage Act (EEA) of 1996 (title 18 U.S.C. Chapter 90), a person must convert a trade secret to an economic benefit in interstate commerce.

Industrial Espionage. According to the Justice Department, industrial espionage is defined "as activity conducted by a foreign . . . government or by a foreign company with the direct assistance of a foreign government against a private US company for the sole purpose of acquiring commercial secrets." This definition does not extend to the activity of private entities conducted without foreign government involvement, nor does it pertain to lawful efforts to obtain commercially useful information, such as information available on the Internet. Although some open-collection efforts may be a precursor to clandestine collection, they do not constitute industrial espionage. Some countries have a long history of ties between government and industry; however, it is often difficult to ascertain whether espionage has been committed under foreign government sponsorship, a necessary requirement under the Economic Espionage Act, Title 18 U.S.C., Section 1831.

Proprietary Information. Another term used in this report is *proprietary information*, the definition of which is information not within the public domain and that which the owner has taken some measures to protect. Generally, such information concerns US business and economic resources, activities, research and development, policies, and critical technologies. Although it may be unclassified, the loss of this information could impede the ability of the United States to compete in the world marketplace and could have an adverse effect on the US economy, eventually weakening national security. Commonly referred to as "trade secrets," this information typically is protected under both state and federal laws.[41]

The result of this definitional confusion is that prosecutions can be problematic. What is a lawful scientific investigation, and what is a violation of trade secrets? To some critics the problem is inherent in the act.

The EEA changes the common-law definition of trade secret, and although it follows the general contours of the Uniform Trade Secrets Act (UTSA), it provides a more detailed list of protected material, broadens the concept of secret from "relevant competitors" to the public, and redefines misappropriation far beyond the "improper means" under the UTSA.[42] Finally, its extraterritorial provision, Section 1837, expands and distinguishes the EEA from traditional patent and copyright laws and threatens the Trade Related Aspects of Intellectual Property Rights Agreement of 1995 (TRIPS) negotiated at the World Trade Organization at the Uruguay Round, which established uniform minimum standards of intellectual property protection for all member nations.[43]

This fear of potential reckless prosecution resulted in a letter to the Congress from Janet Reno, the attorney general at the time of the passage of the EEA, stipulating that any prosecution in the first five years of the EEA would require the express approval of the attorney general. The five-year harbor is over, and although Congress has not ratified TRIPS, in the event that the EEA's extraterritorial proviso would be enforced, the potential conflict with TRIP nations is apparent, particularly where cooperation would be required for extradition purposes.

This problem of enforcement, particularly in the international context, becomes most apparent in the major defense anticipated by the act—reverse engineering—since on its face the EEA prohibits practices that are otherwise lawful.[44] Reverse engineering, a practice "commonly accepted within the scientific community," is the process of studying an item in hopes of obtaining a detailed understanding of the way it works in order to create a duplicate or superior product using the original as a model.[45] For example, under copyright law, the Digital Millennium Copyright Act of 1998 (DMCA) allows for reverse engineering to achieve interoperability for source codes and algorithms.[46] Similarly, patent law anticipates reverse engineering for a variety of lawful purposes, as does the Semiconductor Chip Protection Act of 1984, and a number of state trade secret statutes.

For these critics reverse engineering is not misappropriation, and something that is more of a breach of contract of a "business relationship" based on a license or joint venture should not be criminalized. Criminal sanctions should be only for cases where it was "the intent of one party to enter a relationship to steal information from a partner." But given today's technology, and the complexity introduced by joint ventures, and cross-licensing, how nineteenth-century to be caught stealing in such an obvious way. Today a partner is a partner, whether or not the factory is in China or India. The technology to produce the product must be shared. Policing the information and know-how, once an employee leaves and decides to set up shop next door is a challenge.

Conclusion

"You might as well sell this to us. We are going to get it anyway."
> —FBI records quoting the U.S. representative of a firm brokering technology transfer to a major foreign power.[47]

The EEA thus far has not been the panacea envisioned by its authors. Vague legal categories, reverse-engineering defenses, the nature of sensitive information, obscure links between thefts and foreign entities, and the difficulty of international enforcement have proven to be formidable hurdles.[48] Estimates of the losses to economic espionage have been speculative to date. Perhaps a corporate-loss cause célèbre will bring the issue to the fore.

But if government regulations and enforcement continue to prove ineffective, the private sector may be the place where an attempted solution will be sought, in order to keep foreign interests from eating our lunch. The questions are these: (1) Are we willing to pay the price in terms of lost privacy, and will it work? and (2) What is a U.S. economic interest, and what is a multinational conglomerate interest, as they pursue their respective globalization strategies?

These issues of economic and industrial espionage bleed into other categories of security and competition. Recently Joel Brenner characterized the key three strategic challenges now confronting the CI community: (1) threats to our cyber networks and opportunities to understand and counter them; (2) acquisition vulnerabilities created by the international nature of our markets; and (3) the need for better collaboration in countering espionage.[49]

These are themes that the community has heard before. What is counterintelligence for economic interests? What is the intelligence community to do in this context? Can we keep on treating intelligence, the private sector, and law enforcement as separate communities? How can the private sector trust the law enforcement community, since to open its books and data to the government is to risk prosecution for transgressions not related to the vulnerabilities?

As pointed out by a fellow contributor to the volume, Rodney Faraon, the United States needs a comprehensive, integrated strategy and the creation of a counterintelligence or operational security culture within the private sector. Where are the crown jewels in the twenty-first century? Are they still in Manhattan-like projects or somewhere else? Are the key technologies only on the Military Critical Technology List (MCTL), and given the "dual-use" issues, since these technologies are also used for commercial applications, what is not critical?[50] Has the MCTL become our adversaries' wish list for Christmas?

These questions are fundamental to the themes explored throughout this book. Globalization and constant technological change are rapidly complicating CI policy. How can a CI strategy work within the context of our public institutions, our political culture, and the private sector? As some have pointed out, we just cannot do CI as well as our enemies, because we are not North Korea (a totalitarian regime) or even France (a highly centralized government with special relations with the private sector). There are certain approaches that we just do not want to do, even if we could do them. But if we want to increase our own CI abilities in the economic arena so that we can close the gap—can we do it without compromising our values?

What has become even more problematic is the fact that multinational companies are, in fact, multinational—foreign nationals are in the boardroom of Goldman Sachs.[51] Moreover, production that is divided among several countries will mean that all of these countries have access to security secrets and technology. Given the government's difficulties with prosecution and the stakes involved for the private sector, which desperately desires to keep the loss of trade secrets as nonpublic as possible, and given the potential adverse impact on corporate reputations and stock values, the growth of private security solutions should come as no surprise.

Recently it has come to light that Blackwater, the private security firm, has created a product for its corporate customers—Total Intelligence Solutions (TIS), with its own twenty-four-hour Global Fusion Center.[52] In the words of Cofer Black, chairman of Blackwater and former head of CIA counterterrorism, "We provide intelligence to our clients. It's not about taking pictures. It's business intelligence. We collect all information that is publicly available. This is a completely legal enterprise. We break no laws. We don't do anything near breaking laws. We don't have to."[53] TIS is an ambitious endeavor offering a terrorism research center, cyber security, economic information gathering, and risk management functions. In short, given the underperformance of government, corporate America is buying its own offensive capability to protect itself.

To many it is only a matter of time before corporate "intelligence functions" will expand to a more robust defensive corporate security and the monitoring of the private sector's own "critical secrets." Increasingly the private sector, as a condition of employment, will more closely monitor employee activities. The need, and the legal right, to request waivers to privacy, currently unavailable to government, may be part of the next round of economic and industrial counterespionage. Firms such as Globaltrackinggroup.com, Alltrackusa.com, smart-driver.com, davisnet.com, teensurance.com, and mobileteengps.com are marketing tracking devices to provide car locations, speeds, acceleration and braking records, and gas mileage from remote monitoring locations, including handheld devices.[54] Computer logging in, tracking, GPS for data, videosurveillance and more, are just around the corner.

As a condition of employment, employees may increasingly allow employers to monitor any activities that are corporate-related. In the most recent case of Chinese economic espionage of 2008, the Dongfan Chung case, involving the theft of trade secrets belonging to the Boeing Corporation, concerning fighter-jet aircraft design and Space Shuttle design manuals, Chung breached four private employee/employer conduct agreements.[55] As this case underscores, as the private sector becomes more aggressive in the area of trade secret protection, more extensive computer tracking and phone monitoring by the private sector are only a waiver way. What the government has failed to do in protecting economic secrets may become the business of business.

Once the information is gathered, however, it is only a subpoena away from a government investigation. In other words, what is private may become public. But the private sector will have to make the choice between involving the government or resolving the matter more quietly and delicately with its competitor. The balance between openness and protection are at the heart of the problem in economic and industrial espionage and may prove to be as elusive to the private sector as it has to the government, unless more extensive monitoring is envisioned.

New and expanded private security policies will dovetail with Homeland Security Presidential Directive 7 covering the seventeen critical sectors outlined by Rodney Faraon in this volume, since all private-sector companies will support the monitoring. More FBI expertise and resources for the protection of critical trade secrets will be called for as more cases are prosecuted and as the public better understands the nature of the threat.[56] In addition, more "sting" operations will probably be pursued.[57] As more countries begin to suffer from foreign industrial espionage, there may be support for more robust international conventions and regimes to respond to the economic losses suffered by U.S. business.[58] The incentives to steal trade secrets are high, since the penalties are not prohibitive, and if the stealing is government sponsored, the targeting sovereign will provide immunity.

A corporate security culture must entail a shift in the traditional notions of privacy. This shift will be a challenge to the previous zone of privacy many of us grew up with. Interestingly, the new generation of "MySpace," "FaceBook," and "YouTube" employees may approach the new transparent workplace with a different appreciation for the new corporate security culture of trade secrets. The government's responsibility historically has been to concentrate on the espionage side of the national security arena and not be so involved in the industrial, a more private-sector field. The private sector paid for its own slackness in lost revenue. Modern technology has helped to erode these two distinct arenas, and this has created new burdens for the government. As global economic warfare becomes more industrial based, the distinction between economic and industrial espionage becomes less relevant.

One reason for the erosion of this distinction is that our adversaries have taken just such a path, as in the Chinese 863 Program in the *Ye and Zhong* case. The 863 Program is a funding plan created and operated by the government of the People's Republic of China (PRC); it is also known as the National High Technology Research and Development Program of China. The program was designed by leading PRC scientists to develop and encourage the creation of technology in the PRC, and it focused on issues such as high-technology communications and laser technology, with an emphasis on military applications. The General Armaments Department (GAD) of the People's Liberation Army was responsible for the army, the navy, and the air force in the PRC, and oversaw the development of weapons systems used by the PRC. The GAD had a regular role in, and was a major user of, the 863 Program.[59]

This approach is perhaps more understandable in political/economic cultures that encourage state-owned enterprises. In countries where government interests often coincide with corporate interests intelligence agencies can be more easily instructed to assist the private sector. This perhaps explains why over ten years ago France established the *Ecole de Guerre Economique* (EGE), or School of Economic Warfare. The founder of the school contends that rather than teaching economic espionage, it is more the management of information to develop an economic strategy in the context of conflicts to gain market share.[60] For such state- and corporate-centric approaches the distinction between fair or unfair business practices can become blurred. Some have contended that the open competitive market–based system in the United States and our antitrust laws, combined with our Foreign Corrupt Practices Act, have made state-sponsored economic espionage a nonstarter.[61]

These three trends—government incapacity, a neo-privacy generation of leaders and workers, and the erosion of the distinction between industrial and economic espionage—may converge to create a twenty-first-century corporate security culture. Employee/employer hiring contracts may provide for more extensive monitoring as a price of doing business and maintaining trade secrets. These developments would greatly enhance our ability to stop and to prosecute industrial and economic espionage. In Andrew Niccol's 1997 science fiction film *Gattaca*, set in the near future, the Gattaca Aerospace Corporation has created a totally transparent workplace with technology that can manipulate genetic codes and monitor all employee interactions. Although the hero is able to fool the system, the world depicted is a conceivable future that would bring corporate monitoring to one logical conclusion. If we choose to travel down the path of a culture of corporate security, future generations will have to judge whether the price paid for corporate and national security, in order to keep competitors from eating our lunch, was in the end worth the meal.

Notes

The views expressed in this article are those of the author and do not reflect the official policy or position of the National Defense University, the National War College, the Department of Defense, or the U.S. government. Only public documents were used as sources for this article in order to have an open essay on this subject. In particular I would like to thank the editors, Jennifer Sims and Burton Gerber, for their assistance in framing the article and the many helpful suggestions from Anand Prakash and Megan Jackson. I want to acknowledge Patsy Bailin, whose research was extremely helpful in defining the issue, suggesting approaches, and uncovering material. Moreover, special thanks to my fellow authors for our working session on the book and to Trudi Rishikof for her comments.

1. See the Department of Justice website.Available at www.usdoj.gov/usao/can/press/2006/2006_12_14_meng.indictment.press.html.

2. See Remarks of Joel F. Brenner, ABA Standing Committee on Law and National Security, March 29, 2007. Available at www.ncix.gov/publications/speeches/ABAspeech.pdf.

3. See William J. Broad, "A Spy's Path: Iowa to A-Bomb to Kremlin Honor," *New York Times*, November 12, 2007.

4. See Chris Carr, Jack Morton, and Jerry Furniss, "The Economic Espionage Act: Bear Trap or Mousetrap?" *Texas Intellectual Property Law Journal* 8.2, no. 159 (2000): 163–70.

5. Wanja Eric Naef, "Economic and Industrial Espionage: A Threat to Corporate America?" *Infocon Magazine Issue One* (October 2003). Available at www.iwar.org.uk/infocon/print/espionage-cid.htm.

6. Hal R. Varian, "An iPod Has Global Value. Ask the (Many) Countries That Make It," *New York Times*, June 28, 2007. Available at www.nytimes.com/2007/06/28/business/worldbusiness/28scene.html.

7. See "Welcoming Comments by National Counterintelligence Executive Dr. Joel F. Brenner DNI—Private Sector Workshop on Emerging Technologies," *Carnegie Endowment for International Peace*, Washington, DC, December 7, 2006. Available at www.ncix.gov/publications/speeches/CarnegieSpeech20061207.pdf.

8. Ibid.

9. Carr, Morton, and Furniss, "The Economic Espionage Act," 161.

10. See NCIX, "Annual Report to Congress on Foreign Economic Collection and Industrial Espionage, 2003," 3 (hereafter cited as ARCFECIE). Available at www.ncix.gov/publications/reports/fecie_all/fecie_2003/fecie_2003.pdf.

11. ASIS International, "Trends In Proprietary Information Loss; Survey Report" (August 2007), 3. Available at www.asisonline.org/newsroom/surveys/spi2.pdf. The 2001 FECIE report stated that an estimated $100–250 billion was lost in sales at the end of calendar year 2000.

12. See statement by FBI Director Louis J. Freeh, "Hearing on Economic Espionage before the House Judiciary Subcommittee on Crime," May 9, 1996. Available at www.fas.org/irp/congress/1996_hr/h960509f.htm.

13. ARCFECIE, 2005, 1.

14. See ARCFECIE, 1995, Foreign Economic Threat; Sec. 2., The Industrial Sectors and Types of Information and Technology Targeted by Such Espionage, 16. Available at www.ncix.gov/publications/reports/fecie_all/FECIE_1995.pdf. Here is an excerpt from the report:

Targeted Information and Technology: The industries that have been the targets in most cases of economic espionage and other collection activities include biotechnology; aerospace; telecommunications, including the technology to build the "information superhighway"; computer software/hardware; advanced transportation and engine technology; advanced materials and coatings, including "stealth" technologies; energy research; defense and armaments technology; manufacturing processes; and semiconductors. Proprietary business information—that is, bid, contract, customer, and strategy—in these sectors is aggressively targeted. Foreign collectors have also shown great interest in government and corporate financial and trade data.

15. These agencies included the Federal Bureau of Investigation (FBI), National Security Division; the Central Intelligence Agency (CIA), Counterintelligence Center; the Department of State, Bureaus of Intelligence and Research and Diplomatic Security; the Director of Counterintelligence and Security Programs in the Office of the Assistant Secretary of Defense for Command, Control, Communication, and Intelligence; the Defense Intelligence Agency (DIA); the U.S. Army Intelligence and Security Command; the Naval Criminal Investigative Service (NCIS); the Air Force Office of Special Investigations (OSI); the Defense Investigative Service (DIS); the Personnel Security Research Institute; the National Security Agency (NSA); the Department of Energy (DOE), Counterintelligence Division; the Department of Commerce (DOC), Office of Export Enforcement; the Department of Treasury, Office of Intelligence Support; and the U.S. Customs Service, Office of Intelligence. Section 809(b) of the *Intelligence Authorization Act for Fiscal Year 1995* requires that the president annually submit to Congress updated information on the threat to U.S. industry from foreign economic collection and industrial espionage. There have been eleven published reports up to 2005; the report for 2006 is forthcoming. The act defined foreign industrial espionage as "industrial espionage conducted by a foreign government or by a foreign company with direct assistance of a foreign government against a private United States company and aimed at obtaining commercial secrets."

16. Moreover, as outlined in ARCFECIE, 1995, all the techniques of espionage or traditional methods were being applied to collect economic and proprietary information, and some more specifically tailored techniques were being tested. Traditional methods included Classic Agent Recruitment, US Volunteers, Surveillance and Surreptitious Entry, and Specialized Technical Operations and Economic Disinformation. Other Economic Collection Methods included: Tasking Foreign Students Studying in the United States, Tasking Foreign Employees of US Firms and Agencies, Debriefing of Foreign Visitors to the United States, Recruitment of Émigrés, Ethnic Targeting, Elicitation During International Conferences and Trade Fairs, Commercial Data Bases, Trade and Scientific Journals, Computer Bulletin Boards, Openly Available US Government Data, Corporate Publications, Clandestine Collection of Open-Source Materials, Foreign Government Use of Private-Sector Organizations, Front Companies, and Joint Ventures, Corporate Mergers and Acquisitions, Headhunting, Hiring Competitors' Employees, Corporate Technology Agreements, Sponsorship of Research Activities in the United States, Hiring Information Brokers, Consultants, Fulfillment of Classified US Government Contracts and Exploitation of DoD-Sponsored Technology Sharing Agreements, and Tasking Liaison Officers at Government-to-Government Projects

17. ARCFECIE, 1995, 3.

18. See Hearings before the Subcommittee on Economic and Commercial Law, Committee on the Judiciary, House of Representatives, "The Threat of Foreign Economic Espionage to Corporations," April 29 and May 7, 1992; quoted in Paul M. Joyal, "Industrial Espionage Today and Information Wars of Tomorrow," 19th National Information Systems Security Conference, October 22–25, 1996, note 20. Available at http://csrc.nist .gov/nissc/1996/papers/NISSC96/joyal/industry.pdf.

19. See ARCFECIE, 1996, Appendix A. Available at www.ncix.gov/publications/ reports/fecie_all/FECIE_1996.pdf.

20. See "Cybercrime" Statement of Janet Reno, attorney general of the United States, before the United States Senate Committee on Appropriations Subcommittee on Commerce, Justice, State, and the Judiciary and Related Agencies, February 16, 2000. Available at www.usdoj.gov/criminal/cybercrime/ag0216.htm.

21. Pub. L. No. 104–294, 110 Stat. 3488; Title 18 USC 1831 et. seq. Available at www .economicespionage.com/EEA.html.

22. President William J. Clinton, Presidential Statement on the Signing of the Economic Espionage Act of 1996 (October 11, 1996).

23. 18 USC Sec. 1839. Definitions.

24. See "The Economic Espionage Act of 1996: an Overview," George "Toby" Dilworth, Assistant United States Attorney, Computer and Telecommunications Coordinator District of Maine. Available at www.usdoj.gov/criminal/cybercrime/usamay2001_6.htm. Note: this paragraph and the following two on Sections 1831 and 1832 are drawn directly from the article with citations and references omitted and edited.

25. 18 U.S.C. § 1839(1).

26. See ARCFECIE, 1997. Available at www.ncix.gov/publications/reports/fecie_all/ FECIE_1997.pdf.

27. Carr, Morton, and Furniss, "The Economic Espionage Act," 159.

28. Ibid., 180.

29. See Robin J. Effron, "Secrets and Spies: Extraterritorial Application of the Economic Espionage Act and the TRIPS Agreement," *N.Y.U. Law Review* 78 (2003): 1491.

30. Ibid.

31. The categories for 1997 were as follows: Advanced material coatings, Advanced transportation and engine technology, Aeronautics systems, Armaments and energetic materials, Biotechnology, Chemical and biological systems, Directed and kinetic energy systems, Electronics, Ground systems, Guidance, navigation, and vehicle control, Information systems, Information warfare, Manufacturing and fabrication, Marine systems, Materials, Nuclear systems, Power systems, Semiconductors, Sensors and lasers, Signature control, Space systems, and Weapons effects and countermeasures.

32. The allegations, facts, and plea agreement for this section are drawn directly from the Department of Justice's websites. Available at www.usdoj.gov/usao/can/ press/2006/2006_12_14_meng.indictment.press.html.

33. The indictment charged Meng under a number of statutes with the following maximum penalties: Conspiracy, in violation of 18 U.S.C. § 371 (five years in prison, a fine of $250,000 or twice the value of the property involved in the transaction, whichever is greater, a three-year term of supervised release); Economic Espionage and Attempted Economic Espionage, in violation of 18 U.S.C. §§ 1831(a)(3), 1831(a)(4) (fifteen years in prison, a fine of $500,000 or twice the value of the property involved in the transaction, whichever is greater; a three-year term of supervised release; Arms Export Control Act,

in violation of 22 U.S.C. § 2778 (ten years in prison, a fine of $1,000,000 or twice the value of the property involved in the transaction, whichever is greater; a three-year term of supervised release); Misappropriation of Trade Secrets and Attempted Misappropriation of Trade Secret, in violation of 18 U.S.C. §§ 1832(a)(1), 1832(a)(4) (ten years in prison, a fine of $250,000 or twice the value of the property involved in the transaction, whichever is greater, a three-year term of supervised release); Interstate and Foreign Transportation of Stolen Property count, in violation of 18 U.S.C. §§ 2314 (ten years in prison, a fine of $250,000 or twice the value of the property involved in the transaction, whichever is greater, a three-year term of supervised release); False Statement to Government Agency, in violation of 18 U.S.C. § 1001 (five years in prison, a fine of $250,000 or twice the value of the property involved in the transaction, whichever is greater, a three-year term of supervised release). However, the court could impose any sentence following conviction after consideration of the U.S. Sentencing Guidelines and the federal statute governing the imposition of a sentence, 18 U.S.C. § 3553.

34. Case description quoted from the Testimony of Larry M. Wortzel, Before the Subcommittee on Crime, Terrorism, and Homeland Security of the House Committee on the Judiciary Hearing on "Enforcement of Federal Espionage Laws" January 29, 2008. Available at www.fas.org/irp/congress/2008_hr/012908wortzel.pdf.

35. The allegations, facts, and plea agreement for this section are drawn from the Department of Justice's websites. Available at www.usdoj.gov/criminal/cybercrime/Okamoto_SerizawaIndict.htm and http://www.usdoj.gov/criminal/cybercrime/serizawaPlea.htm.

36. See "Alzheimer's." Available at www.piribo.com/publications/diseases_conditions/alzheimers/pipeline_commercial_insight_alzheimers_disease.html.

37. The Indictment against Okamoto, which charges him with Conspiracy, Economic Espionage Act offenses, and the Transporting of Stolen Property in Interstate and Foreign Commerce, is still pending.

38. Thus far Hiroaki Serizawa has pleaded guilty to making false statements to the government. In the plea Serizawa admits that he falsely understated the number of vials of research material that Okamoto had taken from Serizawa's laboratory (hundreds of vials); initially denied any recent personal contact with Okamoto when in fact Serizawa had been in recent telephone, electronic mail, and personal contact with Okamoto; and initially denied any knowledge of Okamoto having accepted a research position with RIKEN when in fact Serizawa knew that Okamoto had accepted a research position at RIKEN. The false-statements offense carries a maximum penalty of five years incarceration and a $250,000 fine. Under the law, conspiracy carries a maximum penalty of five years incarceration and a $250,000 fine, while economic espionage carries a maximum penalty of fifteen years incarceration and a $500,000 fine, while interstate transportation of stolen property carries a maximum penalty of ten years incarceration and a $250,000 fine.

39. The allegations, facts, and plea agreement for this section are drawn directly from the Department of Justice's websites. Available at www.usdoj.gov/criminal/cybercrime/yeIndict.htm and www.usdoj.gov/usao/can/press/2006/2006_12_14_ye.zhong.plea.press.html.

40. Ye and Zhong were charged with a total of ten counts, including one count of conspiracy, in violation of 18 U.S.C. §§ 371, 1831(a)(5) and 1832(a)(5); two counts of economic espionage, in violation of 18 U.S.C. § 1831(a)(3); five counts of possession of stolen trade secrets, in violation of 18 U.S.C. § 1832(a)(3); and two counts of foreign transportation of stolen property, in violation of 18 U.S.C. § 2314.

41. These definitions are directly from ARCFECIE, 2001. Available at www.ncix.gov/publications/reports/fecie_all/fecie_2001.pdf.

42. Statutory framework for trade secrets, Uniform Trade Secrets Act (amend. 1985), 14 U.L.A. 437 (1990). See also Effron, "Secrets and Spies," 1491.

43. Effron, "Secrets and Spies."

44. See Craig L. Uhrich, "The Economic Espionage Act—Reverse Engineering and the Intellectual Property Public Policy," *Michigan Telecommunications and Technology Law Review* 7, no. 147 (2001).

45. Ibid.

46. DMCA, 17 U.S.C 120 (f); Ibid.

47. ARCFECIE, 2003, 1. Available at www.ncix.gov/publications/reports/fecie_all/fecie_2003/fecie_2003.pdf.

48. Under current law, companies must take positive steps to secure trade secrets such as: physically securing them; limiting documentation; limiting employee access; notifications of critical information on documents; and, partial information sharing with vendors to stop replication. See *U.S. v. Lange*, 312 F.3d 263 (7 th Cir. 2002).

49. Remarks by Joel F. Brenner, National Counterintelligence Executive, "Strategic Counterintelligence: Protecting America in the 21st Century," The NRO/National Military Intelligence Association Counterintelligence Symposium, Washington DC, October 24, 2007. Available at www.ncix.gov/publications/speeches/NRO-NMIA-CI-Symposium-24-Oct-07.pdf.

50. The Militarily Critical Technologies List (MCTL) is a detailed list of the technologies that the Department of Defense determines are critical to maintaining superior U.S. military capabilities. The acquisition of any of these technologies by a potential adversary would lead to the significant enhancement of the military-industrial capabilities of that adversary to the detriment of U.S. security interests. But as the 2003 Report also noted, the following areas of commerce were also of interest and targeted by foreigners: information systems, sensors and lasers, energetic materials and electronics. Pharmaceuticals, biometrics, nanotech/miniaturization, manufacturing processes, public safety systems, patent rights, computer technologies, biotechnology, and public security technologies (identity recognition, bomb detection, and emergency response), advanced computer chip technologies, such as proprietary and export-restricted processors, semiconductors, circuitry, energy, agriculture, automotive, machining, and environmental sectors, 7–8.

51. The United States does extremely well in encouraging foreign nationals to study, work, attend conferences, or guest teach in American universities: Almost 30 percent of the science and engineering faculty employed at U.S. universities and colleges are foreign born, according to National Science Foundation statistics. Annual foreign student attendance at U.S. institutes of higher education has averaged more than 570,000 since the beginning of the 2000 academic year, compared to an average of 460,000 students during the previous decade. More than 40 percent of PhDs awarded in science and engineering in the United States in 2004 went to foreign citizens; in physics and mathematics, the shares were around 55 percent. (See the 2005 FECIE Report, 10).

52. See Dana Hedgpeth, "Blackwater's Owner Has Spies for Hire," *Washington Post*, November 3, 2007.

53. Ibid.

54. See Elizabeth Olson, "Peace of Mind When They Ask to Borrow the Car," *New York Times*, November 3, 2007.

55. These included an Employee Action Notification Agreement (nondisclosure contract), a general Boeing Code of Conduct Agreement, a Non-Employee Code of Conduct Agreement (restrictions on post-employment) and Code of Conduct Acknowledgment Agreement. See *USA v. Dongfan "Greg" Chung*, Indictment, October 2007 Grand Jury.

56. In 2006 tips from executives led to the opening of twenty-seven trade-secrets and related cases over five months. See David J. Lynch, "FBI goes on offensive against China's tech spies," *USA Today*. Available at www.usatoday.com/money/world/2007–07–23-china-spy-2_N.htm.

57. Sting operations occur when the FBI uses undercover agents to act as illegal purchasers.

58. Germany's domestic security service Bundesamt fuer Verfassungsschutz (BfV) has accused China and Russia of massive economic and political espionage in Germany. See Germany's Domestic Secret Service Targeting Economic Espionage at Confab. Available at www.globalsecurity.org/intell/library/news/2007/intell-071203-irna01.htm. See also ARCFECIE, 2004, 15:

> **China**: In April 2004, a court in China sentenced a former engineer from a Wuhan Iron & Steel Company to 18 years in jail for taking bribes and industrial espionage, according to press reports. The individual was found guilty of selling sensitive corporate information to an unidentified foreign company bidding for the project to produce high-end steel products and cold-rolled steel sheet. The foreign company accused of receiving the information reportedly pulled out of the bidding process after the individual was arrested.
>
> **Russia**: In April 2004, Russia's Federal Security Service claimed to have uncovered an industrial espionage network that was preparing to pass information on Russia's satellite program to the Chinese. The theft would have enabled China to close the gap with Russia in satellite production and delivery, according to press reports.
>
> **South Korea**: In mid-2004, a South Korean employee of a Hong Kong–based cell phone distributor was arrested on charges of espionage for attempting to give 75,000 internal computer files from a South Korean handset maker to a Hong Kong firm. The computer files contained secret information about the South Korean company's technology for making mobile phones. Prosecutors estimated that if the information had leaked, it would have cost the company $3.8 billion in lost exports.

59. Ariana Eunjung Cha, "Even Spies Embrace China's Free Market: U.S. Says Some Tech Thieves Are Entrepreneurs, Not Government Agents," *Washingtonpost.com*, February 15, 2008. Available at www.washingtonpost.com/wp-dyn/content/article/2008/02/14/AR2008021403550.html.

60. See Kelly Uphoff, "Tilting the Playing Field: Economic Espionage Hasn't Gone Away; Since 9/11Costs to the U.S. Economy Could Be in the Hundreds of Billions of Dollars," Jewish Institue for National Security Affairs. Available at www.jinsa.org/articles/view.html?documentid=2835.

61. Nevertheless, in 2000 a small controversy erupted when James Woolsey, former DCI, maintained that the United States did not collect or even sort out secret intelligence for the benefit of specific American companies in response to European reports concerning alleged U.S./British spying on Europe under the *Echelon* program for industrial espionage purposes. See James R. Woolsey, "Why We Spy on Our Allies," *Wall Street Journal*, March 17, 2000.

STRATEGIES

10

Rodney Faraon

Private-Sector Counterintelligence Strategies

Principles for Consideration

IN OCTOBER 2007 some 7,500 public- and private-sector subscribers to the unclassified Department of Homeland Security (DHS) Daily Open Source Infrastructure Report suffered what amounted to a denial-of-service attack against their e-mail inboxes, with an estimated 2.2 million messages clogging servers for several hours.[1] The trigger was a request from a North Carolina businessman who inadvertently hit "Reply to All" when he asked DHS to send the report to another address. The result was a dizzying cascade of e-mails ranging from pleas for all to stop "replying to all," to e-mail jokes, business advertisements, weather reports, and even job inquiries.

The flood did not stop until one person, allegedly writing from Iran, asked, "Is this being a joke? Why are so many messages today? [sic]."[2] In response, another writer took the opportunity to lecture the group on the importance of counterintelligence, noting that many security professionals from the military, federal, state, and local governments, and the private sector had apparently just shared with a potential adversary details of their identities and contact information in their e-mail signature blocks. He wrote:

> Wow a reply from Iran . . . For those of you that have responded to this email from an official computer with your snazzy little signature at the bottom, especially those that have every piece of contact information listed, including those of you that have disclosed sensitive phone numbers and classified email addresses have knowingly provided this information to people all over the world some of which I am sure are deemed 'undesirables.' Folks wise up. . . . [T]hose of you that are in the military or provide services through any official office you should know better than

225

to advertise who you are and who you work for. The best tool that someone can use to gain access to information they should not have is to befriend you and what better way than through some harmless emails. . . . I know that I now have access to hundreds of IP addresses, email addresses, phone numbers, names of personnel in sensitive positions and locations, I am only a cover story and a fake letterhead away from trolling for intel. James Bond made it look cool but in its most simple form intelligence gathering can very easily start right here. Not good folks, and don't blame DHS for this, no one forced your hands to type.[3]

We may never know if the e-mail from Iran was genuine or a clever pretext contrived to scare people into stopping the deluge. Regardless, it illustrated that many public- and private-sector employees were far too oblivious to their information vulnerabilities. To be sure, the respondents from the public sector should have known better, given the training and education that most should have received as a matter of policy. But for the private sector, ignorance cannot excuse a failure of security, because what the private sector protects is no less of value than what the public sector protects. The private sector—the engine of the nation's economy—controls most of the nation's critical infrastructure and key resources and itself relies on this infrastructure and these resources; the private sector's interest, therefore, coincides with the government's interest. Fundamentally, both share responsibility for protecting the overall national interest. Thus, there is a consequent need for the private sector to develop strategies and practices to address information security vulnerabilities.

The Scope of the Challenge

Outside the classified world of the defense and intelligence industrial base, the American private sector has generally paid too little attention to the strategic threat of information compromise and, therefore, the discipline of counterintelligence. For example, according to a 2007 survey cosponsored by the leading security industry association ASIS International and the U.S. Government's National Counterintelligence Executive (NCIX), when asked about the total number of attempts to compromise or gain unauthorized access to proprietary information, 102 out of 144 companies responded that this information was "not available." The investigators interpreted this to mean that the respondents lacked access to these data, were reluctant to provide it, or had difficulty in quantifying the data.[4] At least two of the three rationales suggested a phenomenon of *not knowing*, which is a symptom of a weak counterintelligence and information protection infrastructure. And given that the survey covered a comprehensive cross-section of private-sector industries, this would appear to be a problem that dominates the U.S. commercial field.

The lack of attention to the issue flies in the face of well-documented risks to the private sector, prompted by threats from a broad and diverse spectrum of players. According to NCIX's *Annual Report to Congress on Foreign Economic Collection and Industrial Espionage 2005*, a record number of countries—108—

were involved in collection efforts against sensitive U.S. technologies from October 1, 2004, to September 30, 2005.[5] The specific foreign actors ranged from foreign intelligence services, defense establishments, and government-related and quasi-official organizations, to commercial entities and individuals with access to targets of opportunity. Companies that reported incidents of compromised information in the ASIS survey also identified the following as perpetrators: current employees with or without direct access to the compromised information, former employees, subcontractors, foreign and domestic competitors, foreign and domestic business partners, computer hackers, existing or potential customers, and information brokers.[6]

The globalization phenomenon—defined as the increasing interconnectedness of national economies coupled with lightning-speed advances in information technology (IT)—has compounded the problem by making the world smaller. The information assets of a company are more accessible to a wider variety of actors. Furthermore, globalization's imperative and incentive for U.S. firms to outsource company research, development, and manufacturing has introduced even more vulnerabilities.

In addition, accurately quantifying the full cost of information security breaches to companies at a national level is all but impossible, given the lack of good crime statistics, inadequate records kept by companies, and ignorance as to how much value to assign to individual information assets. The ASIS survey, for example, noted that "[a]lthough as much as 75 percent of the market value of a typical U.S. company resides in intellectual property (IP) assets, firms rarely perform formalized valuations of these assets." NCIX also illustrated the problem when it made this assessment:

> Calculating a precise dollar figure for [technology losses] would be difficult. Any such estimate must make fair market value estimates of the technologies lost by firms and the value of replacement technologies necessary to remain competitive.... One of the challenges that makes calculating the cost of industrial espionage particularly difficult is that the technology losses often are not readily apparent. The only indication a U.S. company may have that its research and development plans or its marketing strategies have been stolen is a shrinking or even a more slowly growing market share as foreign and domestic firms take advantage of price and product information to win customers.[7]

Even the few statistics available paint a disturbing picture. The NCIX 2005 *Annual Report to Congress* noted that from October 2004 through September 2005, the Federal Bureau of Investigation (FBI) opened 89 economic espionage cases with 122 pending at the end of the year.[8] Given the standard of evidence typically required to open criminal investigations, the volume of un-investigated, unreported, and undetected incidents undoubtedly is much higher. The ASIS survey noted that the number of attempts at information compromise was "comparable to or higher" in 2005 than in 2004, with respondents reporting "varying degrees of financial impact ranging from less than $10,000 to more than \$5.5 million."[9] Even then, how does one value damage to brand, reputation, or loss of competitive advantage?

Going beyond the economic losses and the damage to national security from the transfer of sensitive technology to potential adversaries, the lack, or underperformance, of counterintelligence efforts makes for strategic vulnerability in another arena: terrorism. Given the new norm of a post-9/11 heightened threat from terrorism, the fact that during preoperational preparation, terrorists have often employed surveillance and other collection techniques similar to those of intelligence operatives, and most important, the fact that the private sector owns, controls, and secures an estimated 85 percent of the nation's critical infrastructure, it stands to reason that corporate security personnel should be engaging in operations to detect and protect against the loss of sensitive information at the hands of determined adversaries.[10] In this case, the sensitive information is less an issue of intellectual property, but of critical physical vulnerabilities.

The private sector, however, has not been entirely absent from the counterintelligence field. With globalization an enduring phenomenon, both governments and companies have recognized the importance of protecting vital computer networks and personal and financial data from hackers and thieves. Laws and industry regulations and standards are in place to promote these measures.[11] Perhaps as a result, according to a 2007 survey of 7,200 IT, security, and business executives by PriceWaterhouseCoopers (PWC) and *CIO* and *CSO Magazines*, 57 percent of companies surveyed reported having some kind of "overall information strategy," up from 37 percent in 2006. But hinting at a heavy focus on information technology (IT) in these strategies, corporate security and IT departments in the same survey reported heavy investments in "technology safeguards such as network firewalls (88 percent), data backup (82 percent), user passwords (80 percent), and spyware (80 percent)."[12]

The Need for Comprehensive, Integrated Strategy

Although these IT solutions serve counterintelligence functions, because of their relatively limited scope, it is time for the private sector to place these efforts under the rubric of an explicitly stated counterintelligence strategy. Developing a corporate counterintelligence strategy that integrates responses to cyber-based threats with human-based threats could generate effective and efficient solutions for any company protecting its sensitive information, personnel, and facilities. It would also help protect against a more comprehensive set of threats and adversaries and, if done right, would help anticipate emerging or latent threats for which the company can prepare.

Companies without counterintelligence strategies may be building solutions, but these solutions are individual responses to protect against discrete threats. Without an integrated strategy, companies may continue to see information compromises as isolated incidents. Responsibility for information security and regulatory compliance in these cases could be scattered across different corporate functions, such as IT, legal, finance, and corporate security. Without an integrated strategy, such diffuse management will probably lead to inconsistency in the application of protective measures, missed opportunities, and blind spots. Perhaps even more important for the chief executive officer's bottom line, it would also probably lead to an inefficient and ineffective allocation of precious resources.

Solutions that address only information technology largely ignore other types of threats such as state- or corporate-sponsored human espionage or social engineering that may not exploit technology to obtain information. Such solutions by themselves do not consider the ramifications of publicly obtainable or openly published information that, when exploited by competitive intelligence analysts, could give a rival corporation an unintended edge. They would not give a commercial facility the means to detect and warn against potential terrorists conducting physical surveillance against its most vulnerable points. Indeed, according to Scott Berinato of *CIO Magazine*, who drafted the assessment based on the PWC survey mentioned earlier, security professionals "believe that the security discipline has so far been skewed toward technology—firewalls, ID management, intrusion detection—instead of risk analysis and proactive intelligence gathering."[13] The result has been an information security posture that is reactive, as opposed to preventive, and that is blind to several other threats.

For most companies, there is no integration of physical and information personnel and leadership. According to the PWC survey, a full 69 percent of respondents do not integrate both sides of the security house, and some 80 percent of these have no plans to do so.[14] Moreover, the trends are increasingly moving toward more dominance of the field by information technology. The four-year trend of increasing integration that began in 2003 appears to have reversed course, with 25 percent of respondents reporting separation of functions in 2006, compared to 46 percent in 2007.[15]

No Single Solution

When it comes to specifics, a big problem for the private sector is that there can be no such thing as a one-size-fits-all counterintelligence strategy because of the sheer diversity of commercial concerns and thus, the sheer diversity of the threats they face. The perpetrators themselves include foreign government spies and commercial competitors. Some threats have national security consequences, while others have only criminal consequences. Some adversaries seek to steal intellectual property, to enhance their negotiating positions, or to identify physical security vulnerabilities. Conversely, not all private-sector actors face all of the same threats.

To illustrate the diversity of private-sector responsibilities, Homeland Security Presidential Directive number 7 (HSPD-7), which governs what the federal government needs to protect the nation from terrorism, identifies seventeen separate critical infrastructure/key resources (CI/KR) sectors that are mainly composed of private entities.[16] One sector, commercial facilities, is essentially a catchall category to cover what the other sixteen sectors do not, including, for example, convention centers, theme parks, hotels, stadiums, film studios, retail facilities, and recreational vehicle parks. Although all may face counterintelligence and terrorism threats of one sort or another, the various "risks"—defined as the nexus of threat, vulnerability, impact, and likelihood—are not spread evenly in typology or quantity among the various private-sector entities.[17]

This chapter, therefore, does not seek to offer a single specific solution or strategy to meet the counterintelligence challenge. But it does make one recommendation: The essence of private-sector counterintelligence is the creation of a counterintelligence or operational security culture within the enterprise.

Five Principles of a Corporate Counterintelligence Culture

This essay suggests five general principles that corporate leadership should consider as it addresses the problem of how to build such a culture.[18] These principles are not meant to be a magazine of magic bullets to solve the counterintelligence problem, but a means to start dialogues within companies to assess what level of protection they may need, how to think about the issue, and how to act. They are as follows:

- Principle One: Understanding True Risk Factors, Developing a Tailored Mitigation Program, and Aligning It with the Business
- Principle Two: Establishing a Policy
- Principle Three: Accountability—Stewards and Constituents
- Principle Four: Education and Training
- Principle Five: Consistency in Ethical Standards and Brand Protection Goals

Understanding True Risk Factors, Developing a Tailored Mitigation Program, and Aligning It with the Business

The first step in building a counterintelligence culture in companies and corporations is to get all key leaders and stakeholders to agree that they need one and then to identify one that fits. The diversity of the private sector means that threats are similarly diverse. Obviously, the threat faced by a big, publicly traded contractor that is developing weapons technologies for the Department of Defense is different from that faced by a media entertainment corporation developing scripts for films. A major multinational may be engaged in sensitive negotiations with a state-run corporation with access to sophisticated national intelligence capabilities, but a restaurant probably will not. Even then, the assessment of threat may not be so simple, because the same media entertainment company could be working on advanced visualization technologies or special effects of interest to the intelligence community and, thus, to international adversaries.

As there can be no one-size-fits-all solution, each company must tailor its counterintelligence infrastructure to deal with the threats it realistically faces. A corollary to this is the fact that corporate security—as essential as it is—typically represents a cost center to a private-sector concern; security leaders need to be efficient in how they request, divide, and allocate what typically are hard-won financial and human resources. The key to devising a tailored response is to start with a thorough discovery of the threats a given company truly faces.

An excellent basis for such an assessment is to create a framework that enables security professionals to look at the problem systematically and methodically. One example of such a framework would be a matrix mapping specific threats against key axes: impact (a function of relevance) and likelihood (a function of a company's vulnerability and the prevalence of the threat), the result of which would be a visual representation of risk. "Risk" is defined as the nexus of impact and likelihood.

There are many ways to undertake such an analysis. Ideally, however, a team of security professionals (both IT and physical) and business unit personnel would jointly assess the risk of given threats to their company. This is useful because each side brings to bear unique expertise and perspectives on the subject; for example, business unit personnel may have a different perception of how much risk to tolerate, of how much information they can afford to lose, or whether certain kinds of information are sensitive or not. Joint assessments also have the advantage that the security professionals can get buy-in and essential support from the business units. The idea is to start a conversation by all stakeholders and thereby bring awareness of counterintelligence issues to the company.

Getting all sides to agree on the nature of the threat is important, because there appears to be dissonance between what business leaders and security leaders think. According to the 2007 Global State of Information Security survey, only 30 percent of respondents reported that their security policies were aligned with their business objectives, and only 22 percent reported that their security spending was aligned with business objectives.[19] Even more striking was the apparent disconnect between perceptions of a company's level of information security by chief executive officers (CEOs) and their security teams. The survey indicated that CEOs seemed to think their companies were more secure than their chief information officers (CIOs) and chief security officers (CSOs); moreover, the security teams—perhaps as a result—were more confident than the CEOs of a higher level of spending on security for the following year.[20]

A good way to incorporate the resource allocation aspects into the conversation is to start, not with an examination of the threats, but with a discussion of how much theoretical risk the company can tolerate. Ideally, the discussion would be highly abstract, focusing on generic categories such as "high impact–low likelihood" or "low impact–low likelihood." This discussion will result in participants shading those areas on the blank matrix that they in theory can or cannot tolerate (see figure 10.1). The shading will ultimately determine which threats should be the focus of the company's allocation and distribution of resources. The facilitators of the exercise should take care to emphasize that this is a nonbinding discussion, but one necessary to get the game started.

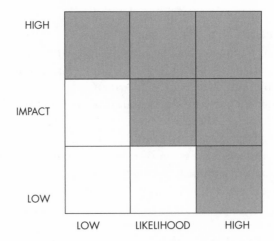

Figure 10.1 Predetermined Risk Areas for Resource Coverage

The next step would be to begin the dialogue on theoretical threats the company has or will face in the future. Again, although there are many ways to conduct this exercise, the key factor is to make it as systematic and methodical as possible. For example, the dialogue could begin with a brainstorming session on information security threats. Once the team has identified a universe of threats, and defined each one precisely, each participant should rate the likelihood and potential business impact of each threat specific to their company. The team may opt to use a numerical scoring system, which the facilitators would later tabulate and average into numeric scores that would permit them to visualize the threats on the risk matrix via a scattergram (see figure 10.2).

The third step in the process is to overlay the first diagram—showing the company's risk tolerance and resource allocation—on the scattergram, to identify the threats that the company believes it can tolerate and those it cannot (see figure 10.3). Inevitably, the results will lead to a debate, as some threats will unexpectedly fall into one or the other categories. This should in turn start another dialogue among team members to "check their work" and review the assumptions that each participant used in his or her assessment. In most cases, the exercise may highlight threats that team members individually would not have considered, or dispel preconceived notions about the most important or urgent threats. For example, a pandemic flulike event reveals itself to need more attention from security and business leaders than previously believed; alternatively, a given company may be less susceptible to a terrorism incident than it thought, and have to reallocate resources accordingly. The exercise may also show holes in preliminary assessments of a company's level of risk tolerance. In either case, a systematically derived assessment will go a long way toward educating corporate leadership on top priorities and demonstrating the need to address them.[21]

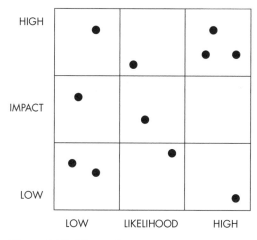

Dots represent actions by competiors/adversaries. One dot could represent "Surveillance against Headquarters Building by Terrorists," while another may be "Foreign Government X's Acquisition of Pharmaceutical Formula A."

Figure 10.2 Threat Scattergram

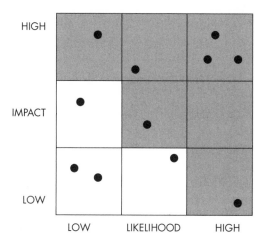

Figure 10.3 Risk/Resource Determination

Establishing a Policy

In today's interconnected society, and in a global economy dominated by knowledge, leadership must engender among their employees a respect for the power of information and the value of the information each employee controls. There is no better way of starting than to communicate directly with the workforce what the company's expectations are; therefore, an early step in building a corporate counterintelligence culture is to establish a formal, enterprise-wide policy mandating the protection of information and defining the sensitive information that each employee is responsible for protecting.

In the intelligence community new officers learn from Day One that the government places a special trust in them to protect the information that comes across their desks. In orientation classes—reinforced by on-the-job training and traditions passed by leadership, mentors, and peers—new officers learn the value of their security clearances, the differences between unclassified information and that marked Confidential, Secret, or Top Secret, and the damage caused by unauthorized disclosure. It is a matter of policy that the intelligence community communicates and fosters these values.

By contrast, practices vary widely in the private sector. Companies that are part of the defense and intelligence contracting business tend to adhere closely to the counterintelligence culture of the communities they serve, while companies in other industries may not be so systematic or bound by historical tradition or contractual requirements. In the studio entertainment industry, for example, scripts worth millions of dollars may be carelessly left on desktops as unattended or unescorted visitors wander the campus free to see or swipe them. In the unclassified world, busy employees may take work home or to wi-fi-enabled coffee shops on unencrypted laptops. At crowded malls, on Wall Street, at outdoor arenas, theme parks, or events, terrorists could be conducting covert surveillance to identify vulnerabilities to exploit for attacks, and without a workforce educated in how to identify suspicious behavior and told to report it, adversaries could be stealing critical infrastructure protection information. IT-based solutions or operations to achieve compliance with industry standards or federal law cover some of these issues, but not all of them. Lack of an overall policy to mandate protection of all sensitive information presents a vulnerability.

Accountability—Stewards and Constituents

Unless a company dedicates discrete resources, assigns a mission, and holds an organizational entity accountable for the success of information protection policies, a counterintelligence culture cannot germinate. By extension, unless a company holds its personnel individually responsible for knowing the policy, implementing it, and obeying the rules, the establishment of counterintelligence culture cannot succeed.

In many companies, counterintelligence and information protection are largely the responsibility of IT departments. According to the 2007 Global State of Information Security survey, some 65 percent of information security budgets is allocated to IT departments.[22] This is certainly appropriate, because much of the data that the private sector would like to protect resides in digital media and is potentially vulnerable to remote theft by hackers or insiders. It is only part of the battle, however, because not all of a company's sensitive information is digital. Physical theft (of laptops, for example) by other criminals, written documents contained in a briefcase or left on a desk in a hotel room, and sensitive business negotiation strategies discussed overseas on unsecure cellular telephones can expose vulnerabilities to competitors. IT departments cannot encrypt information contained in an employee's head, elicited by human collectors adept in "social engineering" techniques such as pretexting. Who should think about the sensitivity of information contained in promotional materials on websites, posters, or pamphlets that could be exploited for competitive intelligence? Who assesses the vulnerabilities of individual employees, both for their potential to be targeted as well as their potential susceptibility?

None of these is a natural fit for protection by the IT department. Left only to IT, a company that believes its information and operations are safe has put blinders on itself. According to Ron Woerner, a security consultant at TD Ameritrade, "We have to start addressing the human element of information security, not just the technological one."[23]

It is essential, therefore, that companies dedicate expert resources for the counterintelligence mission. Although larger companies may find it ideal to create a position of Chief Information Security Officer (CISO), it does not have to be a separate department; indeed, an alternative solution would be to assign the mission to both a company's IT (under a Chief Information Officer–CIO) and corporate security department (under a Chief Security Officer–CSO), forming an integrated task force to devise strategies, operations, and tactics to cover the comprehensive counterintelligence battlefield. This team should also be charged with building a business case for counterintelligence that they can "sell" to corporate leadership and business unit leaders.

Even then, the success of the mission rests largely in the hands of the company's workforce. Every employee also needs to be a steward. With a policy established, and organizational entities dedicated to promoting and enforcing the policy, employees need to bear the responsibility of complying with it. In the absence of a preestablished corporate counterintelligence culture, the only way to develop it and make it stick is to make protection of sensitive information a specific business objective used to evaluate departmental and employee performance, much like it is done in the government. Without a means to personalize the counterintelligence policy of a company to an individual employee, the culture cannot sustain itself.

Education and Training

For companies large enough to enjoy an in-house training and education apparatus, a quick perusal of their curricula would probably show courses in leadership and management, perhaps financial and logistical operations, racial/sexual harassment prevention, and perhaps even CPR, safety, and health and fitness. Some of these courses are mandatory, while others are designed to enhance an employee's career development prospects. It stands to reason that if a company has set a policy mandating protection of information, has dedicated a group to implementing and enforcing the policy, and expects its employees to comply with it as a part of their performance evaluations, the workforce requires training and education to know exactly what to do and when and how to do it.

Formal training courses—in virtual or physical classrooms—are a key part of getting the word out. Formal training has four objectives: to educate the students, to sell them on the importance of protecting information, to give them the tools to accomplish the mission, and to demonstrate the value that a company places on it. A sample syllabus ought to include at least some of the following elements: company policy, standards, definitions of sensitive information, how to classify information, procedures, tools, and behaviors to protect the information, awareness of counterintelligence threats, reporting mechanisms for security violations or pitches, and the business case for counterintelligence, to name a few.

At some private-sector companies, corporate leadership has set a policy mandating protection of information and communicated the policy and classification standards to all through mandatory online training sessions. Too often, however, that is the extent of the training, and an annual training opportunity becomes just that: something to think about once per year. For the culture to stick, counterintelligence stewards need to reinforce the message at regular intervals. Some examples of this would include posters promoting counterintelligence themes; articles in companywide newsletters; tips on company intranet websites; occasional reminders sent to all employees by e-mail; mention of the importance of corporate security by the CEO at his or her annual speech. Another effective mechanism is making the mission, and the consequences of failure, real to employees by periodically publicizing attempted information thefts by outsiders, breaches of company policy by employees, and the consequences to the company and to the offender.

The sine qua non for any of this, however, is a well-educated, expert counterintelligence/information security staff that understands the full scope of the problem and can pass that understanding to others. The question is, therefore, where does a company find such an expert, or how does a company develop such expertise? The private sector unfortunately, is largely left to its own devices to build expertise on the subject, again with the exception being in IT security. The easiest way to do so is to hire personnel who already have deep experience in counterintelligence and then charge them with the mission to share their knowledge and expertise. Barring that, however, companies may have to outsource the expertise to private security firms for training and education or even to accomplish the core mission.

One obvious source of help, the federal government, has made some (but not enough) resources available to the companies that comprise the private sector. The FBI's Counterintelligence Domain program offers seemingly extensive assistance to academia and defense/intelligence contractors to help them protect information and perhaps even to spot potential counterintelligence threats in the classroom. There appears, however, to be no ready way of getting the information unless you work for one of these entities and can prove one's value to the FBI's mission, with the InfraGard program—largely an IT security effort—being the exception.[24] The US-CERT program that the Department of Homeland Security operates offers a well-designed website to communicate IT vulnerabilities and mitigation strategies to the public, but similar to the FBI's InfraGard, this effort does not substantially address other counterintelligence problems, such as social engineering (except "phishing") and physical theft.[25] The trend may be changing, however: The National Counterintelligence Strategy of the United States of America in several places mentions the importance of partnership with the private sector and even defines the private sector beyond the traditional defense/intelligence contractor community.[26] On the heels of this strategy, NCIX hosted its second annual Counterintelligence Symposium for professionals in October 2007, focusing on executive-level (CEO/CSO) discussions of the convergence between cyber-threats and more traditional intelligence threats.[27]

Consistency in Ethical Standards and Brand Protection Goals

The success of a counterintelligence culture will depend on the success of the counterintelligence stewards to adapt it to the culture of the company for which they work. By definition, the establishment of a counterintelligence culture necessitates an investment in change by the company's leadership. At the same time, however, too much change too soon in the absence of a dramatic predicate—for example, a breach of IT or physical security resulting in tangible financial losses—can meet with resistance in any private-sector entity, no matter how imperative the change is.

Indeed, it is an absolute necessity to ensure that whatever programs a counterintelligence culture implements are consistent with the company's standards of ethical behavior and are sensitive to the need to protect its image and brand, not to mention federal, state, and local laws. For example, it would not be a surprise to the world if a defense contractor that provides substantial support for the intelligence community requires of its employees routine background reinvestigations, polygraphs, notification of all foreign travel and contacts, reviews and monitoring of e-mail and other correspondence, that in a typical, nonclassified private-sector concern might raise questions about privacy and propriety. Similarly, recent operations involving pretexting or technical intercepts, employed by security personnel at high-profile companies to identify illicit contacts with the press, not only caused controversy and hurt the reputation of these companies and their security functions, but also resulted in criminal charges against some of those responsible for the programs.[28]

In a similar hypothetical case, it would not be a stretch to say that even if these tactics were successful in achieving the counterintelligence mission, the controversy they caused would not make the end result worth the damage to a company's brand image and reputation. Moreover, even if certain counterintelligence measures were deemed to be legal, the question remains about whether such means were appropriate or consistent with the image that a company would like to portray to its constituents, both inside and outside the firm. This also underscores the importance of aligning security objectives with business objectives.

One way to identify ethical and image pitfalls and achieve success as a cultural change agent is for security personnel to build partnerships with key officers outside the security function. While a CEO's imprimatur is the first necessity, security personnel should build support among influential peers as well. These allies would by necessity include corporate counsel and might also include human resources, brand management, and management audit. Other allies would be leaders of important business units, particularly those with the largest number of employees; because the business of a private-sector company is business, it stands to reason that the leaders of revenue-generating organs have the most influence within a corporation. They also need to understand the benefits they can gain from an effective CI strategy.

Conclusion

The idea of information as power is not new, but in today's knowledge economy, information has never been more powerful. Consequently, the importance of protecting information and assets that are sensitive or critical for the survival of the country—or one's company—has also never been higher. With the vast majority of the U.S. critical infrastructure in the hands of the private sector, and with terrorists and other infrastructure threats employing increasingly sophisticated tools and methods—including some similar or even superior to those of the intelligence community—training security personnel in counterintelligence is essential. Communicating awareness of counterintelligence to the workforce as a whole is arguably even more important.

There can be no single counterintelligence model or infrastructure for every private-sector concern, given the diversity of companies and other entities that comprise the sector. What can be done, however, is the establishment of a culture within companies that values protection of information and assets as part of their competitive strategy and offers incentives to encourage the defense of that commodity from both internal and external threats. The question then is how to develop such a culture.

Although there are many ways to answer that question, this chapter has described five principles that security personnel and corporate leadership charged with that mission should consider. These principles recommend the development of a respect for information; assigning a mission manager and holding the stewards and users of information equally accountable; educating and training the workforce in counterintelligence techniques and principles; systematically and methodically determining realistic risks and opportunities, tailoring a counterintelligence program to address those risks, and ensuring the program is in line with business objectives; and making the culture stick by maintaining consistency with the law and a company's ethical norms.

The kinds of counterintelligence capabilities that the establishment of that culture produces within a company will vary, both in terms of appearance and most likely in terms of effectiveness. They should address both IT and human elements of the problem in order to be most effective. That said, given the low baseline that many private-sector entities have, even establishing a general awareness of counterintelligence principles—one that sticks—may be enough to help with many of the most common threats that they face. At the very least, it is a start, and that might be enough to turn the tide on the corporate counter-intelligence battlefield.

Notes

1. Eric Lipton, "Security Bulletin Problem Creates Message Flood," *New York Times*, October 4, 2007. Accessed on October 7, 2007, and available at www.nytimes.com/ 2007/10/04/us/04secure.html?ref=technology.

2. E-mail message to author, October 3, 2007.

3. E-mail message to author, October 3, 2007.

4. ASIS International, *Trends in Proprietary Information Loss, Survey Report August 2007* (Alexandria, VA: ASIS International), 23. Accessed on October 13, 2007, and available at www.asisonline.org/newsroom/surveys/spi2.pdf.

5. *Annual Report to Congress on Foreign Economic Collection and Industrial Espionage 2005*, U.S. Office of the Director of National Intelligence, Office of the National Counterintelligence Executive (Washington, D.C., August 2006), 1.

6. ASIS International, *Trends in Proprietary Information Loss, Survey Report August 2007*, 33.

7. *Annual Report to Congress on Foreign Economic Collection and Industrial Espionage 2005*, U.S. Office of the Director of National Intelligence, Office of the National Counterintelligence Executive, 1.

8. Ibid.

9. ASIS International, *Trends in Proprietary Information Loss*, 3.

10. *The National Strategy for the Physical Protection of Critical Infrastructures and Key Assets*, The White House (Washington, DC, February 2003), 8. Available at www.whitehouse.gov/pcipb/physical.html.

11. Examples include Sarbanes-Oxley (SOX), the Health Insurance Portability and Accountability Act (HIPAA), the Payment Card Industry Data Security Standard (PCI DSS), ISO/IEC 27002, and the European Union Data Protection Directive (EUDPD), to name a few.

12. Scott Berinato, *The Global State of Information Security 2007, A Joint Research Project of CIO and CSO in Partnership with PriceWaterhouseCoopers*, 4. Accessed on October 13, 2007, and available at www.pwc.com/extweb/pwcpublications.nsf/docid/ 114E0DE67DE6965385257341005AED7B.

13. Ibid., 4.

14. Ibid., 10.

15. Ibid.

16. Homeland Security Presidential Directive/HSPD-7, "Critical Infrastructure Identification, Prioritization, and Protection," December 17, 2003, section 18. Accessed on October 13, 2007, and available at www.whitehouse.gov/news/releases/2003/12/ 20031217–5.html.

17. As discussed earlier, threats to information security come from diverse sources and motivations. Threats from commercial enterprises are essentially criminal concerns; those from foreign governments are national security concerns. Ironically, although there is no one-size-fits-all strategy to address the problem, there is one solution: better counter-intelligence to protect sensitive information. This is true regardless of the consequence

of failure, whether it means the death of a company or a threat to critical infrastructure or sensitive U.S. government interests under the control of the private sector.

18. The scope of these principles encompasses the establishment of a defensive counter-intelligence program, the minimum beginning standard. Offensive CI, which values the development of an understanding of specific adversaries and would enable more proactive policies or decision advantage, is a key element of an advanced program that has already put in place the fundamentals of a security program. One must crawl, however, before one walks or runs.

19. CSOOnline.com, "New Security Survey Shows Organizations Are Strong on Infrastructure, Weak on Monitoring and Enforcement." Accessed on September 10, 2007, and available at www2.csoonline.com/info/release.html?CID=33166.

20. Berinato, *The Global State of Information Security* , 9.

21. Ultimately, what the scattergram shows is where it would make sense for the company to spend only a limited amount of time and money on security-related programs—say, on basic threat awareness. Above that level of risk, the company would explore a range of mitigation strategies depending on the likelihood and impact of a given threat, for example, by instituting mandatory training programs, incorporating technologies to better monitor outgoing company e-mails for transfers of sensitive information, and conducting technical security countermeasure sweeps of the CEO's office.

22. CSOOnline.com, "New Security Survey Shows Organizations Are Strong on Infrastructure, Weak on Monitoring and Enforcement." Accessed on September 10, 2007, and available at www2.csoonline.com/info/release.html?CID=33166.

23. Berinato, *The Global State of Information Security*, 8.

24. InfraGard is an intelligence-sharing partnership between the FBI and the private sector that began on a national level in 1998, with a primary focus on cyber infrastructure protection. InfraGard expanded its efforts to include physical threats to critical infrastructure after 9/11. In the personal observation of this author, however, IT security rather than general CI issues dominate much of InfraGard's attention. For more information about the FBI's counterintelligence domain program and InfraGard, see www2.fbi.gov/hq/ci/domain.htm.

25. Department of Homeland Security, United States Computer Emergency Awareness Team. Accessed on September 29, 2007, and available at www.us-cert.gov/.

26. U.S. Office of the Director of National Intelligence, Office of the National Counterintelligence Executive, *The National Counterintelligence Strategy of the United States of America, 2007*, 4–7. Accessed on October 1, 2007, and available at www.ncix.gov/publications/policy/CIStrategy.pdf.

27. U.S. Office of the Director of National Intelligence, Office of the National Counterintelligence Executive. Accessed on October 13, 2007, and available at www.fbcinc.com/cisymposium/.

28. In 2006 the state of California levied felony charges against Hewlett-Packard's board chairman and others for efforts by company-hired investigators to identify press leaks by board members. The investigators allegedly falsified their identities to obtain call records of suspected leakers from telephone companies. The state later dropped these charges after having reached a settlement. In a separate case, Wal-Mart fired a nineteen-year security employee for allegedly intercepting a reporter's telephone calls to help in investigating leaks. His supervisor was also fired and a vice president was demoted over the incident.

11

Timothy R. Sample

A Federal Approach to Domestic Intelligence

> The men and women of the World War II generation rose to the challenges of the 1940s and 1950s. They restructured the government so that it could protect the country. That is now the job of the generation that experienced 9/11. Those attacks showed, emphatically, that ways of doing business rooted in a different era are just not good enough. Americans should not settle for incremental, ad hoc, adjustments to a system designed generations ago for a world that no longer exists.[1]

DESPITE THESE words from the 9/11 Commission Report, our efforts over the last seven years to change how we collect, analyze, understand, and counter domestic threats have more resembled "incremental" and "ad hoc" adjustments than the bold restructuring that arose in the 1940s and 1950s. To be sure, there have been significant changes at the federal level related to our national security structure and processes.[2] But although these changes affected the roles, responsibilities, and, in some cases, capabilities of our national security structure, very few of them actually addressed the difficult issue of changing "the ways we do business" in this new environment of individualized threats operating both virtually and on our soil.

Instead, we have focused on individual problems that have been identified and highlighted by commissions and Congress in the aftermath of a national tragedy, rather than making the hard strategic, coordinated decisions to fundamentally change how we meet our national security needs. We have created a Director of National Intelligence (DNI) to better manage our existing intelligence capabilities and also signal an our understanding that the traditional barriers between foreign and domestic intelligence are quickly dissolving. We have created a new Department of Homeland Security (DHS), a move designed primarily to consolidate disparate federal security functions under one management structure to better coordinate existing efforts. The Federal Bureau of Investigation (FBI) has

241

created a new security division that is supposed to be intelligence and analysis based, and has declared counterterrorism to be its main national objective.[3]

We have placed our highest priority efforts on information sharing—something that has been recognized as a pre-9/11 fatal flaw in every subsequent commission report and national-security-related law—to ensure that information (especially threat-related intelligence collected at the federal level) is passed between our existing intelligence and security mechanisms within the federal government and with state and local governments and authorities. In all of these examples, finding better ways to accommodate existing bureaucracies and jurisdictional boundaries has been the key to our approach and to our strategies.

The heavy emphasis on information sharing has shortchanged the need to foster a comprehensive public debate, nor have we encouraged the development of new approaches to the way we conduct domestic intelligence. Information sharing is not domestic intelligence, and focusing on this as the major issue between federal, state, and local governments ultimately will not be effective in anticipating, detecting, and foiling plots, especially those that are homegrown and those that effectively utilize the protections contained within our laws until the very moment before execution.

What kind of domestic intelligence apparatus is most appropriate for our society? Who should conduct such activities? What kinds of activities to counter internal threats would we find permissible? Facing such questions and such threats will require a comprehensive domestic intelligence strategy that can establish a balance between our need for creating in-depth knowledge about our internal threat environment with the practical realities of Americans' expectations of freedom and privacy. Doing so will require an effective and dynamic oversight process that does not exist today. Finally, as the 9/11 Commissioners recognized, we need new ways of thinking about and implementing domestic intelligence capabilities that go beyond simply modifying existing operations to face a fundamentally new threat.

Defining Domestic Intelligence

Currently, the term "domestic intelligence" has no legal definition. A general definition can be considered, however, in the context of how we do foreign intelligence—that is, the process by which we gather information, identify gaps in knowledge, task collection assets to fill those gaps, analyze the information that we have, and present reasonable long-term and actionable short-term assessments to national security decision makers. Two stark differences exist, however, between foreign and domestic intelligence. First, in the case of foreign intelligence there is an expectation that laws (of the countries in which we are operating) will be broken, whereas we have an expectation that U.S. laws will not. As a result, we have traditionally left domestic intelligence operations as a matter for law enforcement officials in the context of building a case for prosecution. The second difference is that foreign intelligence operations rarely include interaction between state and local governments or take into account the jurisdictional responsibilities of those governments. Domestic intelligence operations depend on these interactions and remain highly sensitive to jurisdictional responsibilities.

Equally important is the concept of counterintelligence in a domestic context. Again, using the more familiar definition, domestic counterintelligence could be considered the actions taken to identify and understand activities on U.S. soil by actors who pose a threat to our security, with the goal of either neutralizing their activities or effectively controlling or manipulating them to our advantage. From a nation-state threat perspective, we understand the threat and have basically divided the responsibilities between the Central Intelligence Agency (CIA) and the FBI. Historically, the FBI has handled all counterintelligence operations on U.S. soil, while CIA has handled overseas operations. Obviously, such activities have been principally conducted against other nations' intelligence services, which are presumably operating illegally in our country. As mentioned elsewhere in this volume, there is significant concern over the priority given to counterintelligence, including the level of resources allotted, especially since the end of the Cold War. Clearly, although there are changes in the types of threats facing the nation, traditional counterintelligence capabilities and operations continue to have a place in our security.[4]

With the rise in threats from individual actors and small groups, however, the dynamic of our counterintelligence capabilities must also change. Although using traditional tradecraft to recruit and penetrate a terrorist cell within the United States is undoubtedly difficult, especially if the group is based on a very close-knit family or tribal connection, it might still be possible. However, whether our society can tolerate such activities regardless of whether any laws have been, or may be, broken by the individuals or groups in which we may have interest is an open question. Would Americans find it acceptable to penetrate—either directly or through recruited agents—a mosque or a church, a university's student body, or a prison population in order to gain knowledge about key actors, or about recruitment of individuals to act on radical teachings, regardless of whether any crimes have been committed or even suspected? And can we look at this activity as a federal intelligence responsibility, or is this best left, from a public policy standpoint, to elected state and local law enforcement officials who are more familiar with their own communities? If the latter, do they have the resources and skills to do such a job? Likewise, can these local resources be tasked to fill gaps in knowledge, and what are their responsibilities to take such action and report their results?

Given the rise in Islamic fundamentalists' use of the Internet as an effective tool for propaganda, recruitment, instruction on terrorist techniques and tactics, and command, control, and communications, our counterintelligence capabilities must evolve into the cyber domain. Running virtual agents and double agents, misleading a terrorist on our capabilities as well as our knowledge about their organization, plans, and intentions, and neutralizing their intelligence collection must be accomplished in ways that are just as effective online as they would be in person. One can argue that such capabilities are more important today than the more traditional ones, but both are necessary and vital within the realm of domestic intelligence. But, again, who should be responsible for conducting such counterintelligence operations? Should this be a key component of the FBI's work or should a state or local entity be responsible, especially when a website might be from a local group? What are the legal ramifications, and do our laws even contemplate such activities in the future?

In contemplating the strategy and architecture for domestic intelligence, we must address these questions in a comprehensive fashion, as opposed to the more piecemeal approach that has been used over the past decade. Moreover, given that these issues strike to the core of our beliefs about good governance, a public debate on domestic intelligence is also appropriate, rather than having a series of individual, and often political, criticisms by those representing only certain aspects of the issues. Such a debate has yet to begin.

One other key consideration is the priority placed on counterterrorism in our national security discussions. Clearly, terrorism has been a national security priority since 9/11. On September 20, 2001, President Bush declared a "global war on terrorism" that has become not only the focus of our national security activities, but the raison d'être of the changes to our national security structure.[5] But like information sharing, counterterrorism is not necessarily equivalent to domestic intelligence, although it will have a dominant role in the development of any federal strategy on domestic intelligence.

Finding the Balance

The concept of the federal government's conducting intelligence operations within our borders is anathema to the American psyche. Historically, such operations are specifically governed by law—and conducted by appropriate law enforcement entities—within the context of pursuing a crime and subsequent prosecution. Consequently, the concept of domestic intelligence tends to go against our very system of ideals and beliefs.

As other chapters in this volume discuss, certain factors shade any discussion of federal strategies or approaches to domestic intelligence and counterintelligence. These factors are rooted in our experiences and expectations as a nation. We generally accept that even in a democracy there is a place for national-level intelligence operations to protect our security, but that acceptance is premised on the belief that such activity should not impinge on our individual rights and freedoms; in fact, those are the very principles that we expect to be protected by our intelligence and national security efforts. As the House of Representatives' first Muslim congressman, Keith Ellison (D-MN), has stated, "The U.S. is founded on the idea that we're all connected to a set of ideas, not a set of histories. For all our criticisms, the idea of America is an amazing thing—a society organized around a set of principles instead of around racial or cultural identity."[6] Consequently, any strategy involving dedicated and robust domestic intelligence must address the preconceived principles it is trying to protect. Thus, before discussing specific strategies for domestic intelligence, it is important to understand the factors that generate the gravitational pull that often plagues the pursuit of a sound and consistent strategic course.

Factors Underlying Strategies

We are a nation of laws. We pride ourselves on our ability to establish laws for the common good, and we expect that everyone will respect and abide by those laws. We support a capability to punish transgressors of those laws. We use the Constitution—the foundation of our country's very existence—to set specific principles in place, including freedom, civil liberties, and an expectation of privacy. In the past 220 years, our founding principles have been amended only twenty-seven times. Thus, it is also fair to say that we are a nation that is reluctant to change its founding principles. Our level of pride in our own system of government and in the rights that it brings to individual Americans is such that we generally extend those rights to individuals who are not U.S. citizens, as long as they are legally within the boundaries of the United States. Our form of democracy has not been successfully replicated anywhere else in the world, and thus, the desire of others to experience the American dream of freedom and opportunity continues to be strong. We view terrorism foremost as a federal crime.

We are a nation that likes neatness, especially in our federal bureaucracies, although arguably such a pristine condition is rarely achieved. The Department of Treasury deals with financial matters, Commerce with trade, war is in the Department of Defense, foreign policy and diplomacy are entrusted to the Department of State, law enforcement and crime in the FBI, and so on. Intelligence was considered a matter external to our borders and handled by the intelligence community. Counterintelligence, defined as detecting and neutralizing others' intelligence operations, was also subjected to geographic delineation, with the intelligence community operating overseas and the FBI operating domestically as a law enforcement entity, even if the resulting punishment of a foreign agent is a diplomatic response in the case of state-sponsored intelligence operations.

We are a nation that is generally wary of the strength of its federal government; sometimes with good reason. Throughout history, individuals and leaders have warned about keeping the federal government in check. President Eisenhower warned of the potential strength and harm of the military-industrial complex. For the intelligence and law enforcement communities we have gone out of our way—given our experiences with other countries over time—to ensure that we do not have a secret police entity at the federal level, nor a formal federal-level domestic intelligence apparatus. When the concept of a centralized intelligence community was raised in 1947, our experiences with the German Gestapo, in part, resulted in a specific desire to separate CIA and FBI responsibilities. Watershed moments reinforced our wariness of domestic intelligence, including the Palmer Raids in 1919, the FBI's surveillance and documentation of citizens' political associations in the 1950s, and the revelations that unfolded during the Church and Pike Committees' reports in the mid-1970s, when civil liberties transgressions were discovered on a grand scale. These events shaped the American distrust of domestic intelligence operations, especially since such operations were often conducted against U.S. citizens seen as political threats to presidential administrations rather than as security threats to the nation.

We are a nation that is founded on a basis of federalism. Although the concept within the United States has been changed and molded over time, we were founded on the principle that there are specific responsibilities and actions that a centralized, national government should undertake (i.e., international trade and commerce) and there are responsibilities that are best left to the state governments (i.e., fire and police functions). This is why, in the aftermath of the 2001 terrorist attacks, President George W. Bush wrote in a letter that prefaced a new National Strategy for Homeland Security, "My Administration has talked to literally thousands of people—governors and mayors, state legislators and Members of Congress, concerned citizens and foreign leaders, professors and soldiers, firefighters and police officers, doctors and scientists, airline pilots and farmers, business leaders and civic activists, journalists and veterans, and the victims and their families. We have listened carefully. This is a national strategy, not a federal strategy."[7] Generally, intelligence has been considered a federal function performed by the intelligence community, although intelligence units within state and local police entities that focus on gathering leads and law-enforcement-related functions are common.

We generally are not, however, a nation that is good at strategy. More appropriately, we are a nation of reaction. Our formal entry into World War II was in reaction to the Japanese bombing of Pearl Harbor. Our technological awakening to a Soviet/Communist threat was in response to the Soviet Union's launch of Sputnik. In reaction to the terrorist attacks on September 11, 2001, we declared war on terrorists and put counterterrorism at the center of our national security activities. Our subsequent reactions included taking significant steps to upgrade security related to air travel (reacting to a previous threat), while initially ignoring any potential threat to our rail lines. Our initial reaction was to focus on individuals of Middle Eastern origin because they were the ones who conducted the September 11 attacks, despite the fact that large segments of terrorist organizations are working out of Indonesia and Europe. The creation of the Department of Homeland Security and the creation of the Director of National Intelligence were also in reaction to the terrorist attacks on September 11, 2001. In all of these cases, the reaction was motivated more by political necessity than by adherence to any national strategy.

It is no wonder, then, that there is a great deal of concern about what the federal government is doing about domestic intelligence, whether these actions will be effective, and whether these actions go too far in degrading civil liberties. An outsider to the workings of government might conclude that a federal strategy on domestic intelligence has been elusive, and they would not be far from the truth. Today's domestic intelligence strategy is at best made up of efforts by individual organizations and agencies that are tangential to a more global campaign against terrorism writ large, without an underlying approach to basic intelligence activities and operations within our borders or their ramifications. Countless hours have been spent debating which federal agency should have the "lead" in domestic intelligence; indeed some believe that the existing structures and agencies are inadequate to the task and have called for a separate domestic intelligence agency, similar to MI-5 in Great Britain. Moreover, given our history of federalism, state and local governments, in the absence of any truly identifiable federal strategy, have embarked on their own efforts. These range from an extensive, active intelligence capability in New York City to a rapidly growing number of fusion centers throughout the country, but there exists little understanding of how domestic intelligence should be conducted, nor of the importance of its integration into a larger national intelligence and threat equation.

But centering on the structural debate alone misses the key question that underpins any government strategy. Will we continue to perform intelligence functions domestically principally in the context of a law enforcement activity, with all of the judicial constraints and oversight that we expect in our concept of due process, or are we ready to consider intelligence domestically in a broader context and with prosecution of would-be lawbreakers being only one potential use of such information, and certainly not the primary one? Although not addressed in such scope, this is where the debate surrounding current collection programs by the National Security Agency—referred in the press as warrantless wiretapping—should ultimately lead, though it is doubtful that the current political environment will allow for such a significant expanded analysis. And although this chapter cannot answer this question, we can use the question to lay out options for strategies on domestic intelligence.

The Changing Threat Environment

American intelligence capabilities are deeply rooted in our experiences in World Wars I and II and are modeled on the threats of the Cold War. Therefore, our national-level collection and counterintelligence capabilities are designed to respond to threats from a nation-state whose intelligence activities and goals are generally understood (although specific Soviet activities were not always readily identified). The current desire to focus on establishing a more robust domestic intelligence capability stems from the changing threat environment that has developed after the Cold War. Although many of the traditional state-sponsored threats continue to be a priority, the emergence of nonstate organizations, such as al-Qaeda, have changed the dynamic of the threat, because these organizations are not wedded to geographic boundaries or government structure. Such organizations have successfully mastered the art of centralized strategy and planning with decentralized operations and execution. Of potentially greater significance is the emergence of empowered individual actors, who may take their lead from a centralized organization, but who operate independently—individually or in small groups or cells—in identifying, designating, and attacking targets.

The emergence of such threats does not conform neatly to our intelligence structure or our accustomed operations. In his book *The New Protective State*, Peter Hennessy identifies the differences between Cold War and counterterrorism intelligence as, first, a difference between battling a state (the Soviet Union) and battling a state of mind (Islamic fundamentalism), and second, a reverse in "secrets" and "mysteries." Hennessy notes that during the Cold War, "secrets" such as order of battle and the location of weaponry were obtainable through open and classified sources, while the "mysteries" were the specific intentions of the Soviet leadership. Today, with an organization like al-Qaeda, the intentions are "murderously plain," while the location of the operatives and the weapon is the "mystery."[8]

The availability of technology, especially in the areas of communications and information technology, including ready access to the Internet, has armed these organizations and individuals with a ready-made command, control, and communications capability that did not exist previously. Their knowledge of the impact of the visual message of an attack and their savvy use of it reveal an appreciation of modern information warfare. One stark example of this is the professionally produced, shot, and edited video statement of Osama bin Laden declaring war on the United States. This video statement was masterfully packaged and cued to go on the air as soon as the anticipated U.S. air strikes in Afghanistan commenced on October 7, 2001.[9] As Dr. Bruce Hoffman from the RAND Corporation noted during testimony before the House Permanent Select Committee on Intelligence:

> For bin Laden and his followers the weapons of terrorism are no longer simply the guns and bombs that they always have been, but now include the mini-cam and videotape, editing suite and attendant production facilities; professionally produced and mass-marketed CD-ROMs and DVDs; and, most critically, the lap-top and desk-top computers, CD burners and email accounts, and Internet and worldwide web access that have defined the information revolution today.[10]

For al-Qaeda, the Internet has long facilitated three critical functions: propaganda for recruitment and fund-raising and to shape public opinion in the Muslim world; terrorist training and instruction; and operational planning for attacks through both e-mail communication and the access it provides to an array of useful open-source information.[11]

Such access to communications and information has allowed terrorists to operate anywhere in the world. And terrorist activities within the United Kingdom have highlighted the changing complexion of the threat. Prior to her retirement as the director general of MI-5, Dame Eliza Manningham-Buller stated:

> Today, my officers and the police are working to contend with some 200 groupings or networks, totaling over 1,600 identified individuals—and there will be many we

don't know—who are actively engaged in plotting, or facilitating, terrorist acts here and overseas. . . . We are aware of numerous plots to kill people and to damage our economy. What do I mean by numerous? Five? Ten? No, nearer thirty that we currently know of. . . . These plots often have linked back to al-Qaeda in Pakistan and through those links al-Qaeda gives guidance and training to its largely British foot soldiers here on an extensive and growing scale."[12]

The bombings of the London transportation system on July 7, 2005, were perpetrated by British citizens. As noted in an FBI report, "The four suicide bombers were British citizens: three had been born in the United Kingdom, and the fourth had been born in Jamaica. The British citizenship of the bombers and the lack of strong ties between them and an international terrorist group illustrate the potential threat of "homegrown" terrorists as perpetrators of future attacks."[13] Such concerns must be considered within the United States as well. As mentioned in a *Newsweek* article on Islam in America (and noting the rise of religious conservatism of young Muslim Americans), a Pew study revealed that 26 percent of Muslims age eighteen to twenty-nine believe that suicide bombing can be justified. Thirty-eight percent of that group believe that Arabs did not carry out the 9/11 attacks.[14] Massoud Shadjareh, of the Islamic Human Rights Commission, noted of the British experience that "[o]ver 1000 arrests have been made under anti-terrorism since 9/11 and out of those, twenty-seven have been found guilty. Out of those twenty-seven, only nine have been Muslim."[15]

Another aspect of the changing threat involves the interactions of terrorists with other criminal enterprises to, for example, raise and launder money. The director of national intelligence (DNI), Mike McConnell, has noted that such activities underscore the need to share threat information with state and local law enforcement: "The unique contribution made by men and women on the ground is vital to U.S. national security. In 2000, for example, a county sheriff's investigation into a local cigarette smuggling case in Charlotte, North Carolina, uncovered a multistate terrorist cell supporting Hezbollah. In 2005 a local police detective investigating a gas station robbery in Torrance, California, uncovered a homegrown jihadist cell planning a series of attacks in Illinois."[16] Such instances underscore not only the need to share information with state and local law enforcement, but also the fact that terrorist activities within the United States are likely to be uncovered first by state and local law enforcement officials.

The Need for a Domestic Intelligence Strategy

The rise of terrorism—especially the potential for homegrown terrorists—has focused a spotlight on the question of whether the United States must now have a dedicated strategy and capability to conduct domestic intelligence. Our response, however, has been to focus on the infamous "connect the dots" concept post-9/11, rather than on the real issue of intelligence—or, more pointedly, having the ability to anticipate, assess, and evaluate activities aimed at damaging our interests when there are no dots or when the set is incomplete. Consequently, we have produced national strategies for national security, intelligence, homeland security, combating terrorism, and information sharing (among others), all of which stress the importance of intelligence and warning but fail to offer a true assessment of how such a capability is to be achieved. For the most part, the recommendations stemming from these strategies focus on information sharing within our government institutions rather than on creating a domestic intelligence function to obtain the information to be shared. Here are two examples:

> We must transform our intelligence capabilities and build new ones to keep pace with the nature of these threats. Intelligence must be appropriately integrated with our defense and law enforcement systems and coordinated with our allies and friends.[17]

> [Intelligence community efforts therefore must] Enable those outside the Intelligence Community with valuable counterterrorism information (such as police, corrections officers, and border patrol officers) to contribute to the national counterterrorism effort [and create] an information sharing environment in which access to terrorism information is matched to the roles, responsibilities, and missions of all organizations engaged in countering terrorism, and is timely, accessible, and relevant to their needs.[18]

Such references emphasize our long-standing focus on law enforcement as the primary intelligence apparatus within the United States. They also highlight the current cultural change within the intelligence community related to information sharing. DNI Mike McConnell refers to this change as a shift from "need to know" to "responsibility to provide."[19]

A consistent theme in all of these strategies and efforts is the recognition that a federal strategy must include state, local, and tribal capabilities and resources. Conversely, developments over the last six years have suggested that state, local, and tribal efforts without clear direction or leadership will naturally devolve to their own specific, and often tactical, interests rather than focusing on a larger national picture. Under a grants program from DHS, approximately fifty-eight fusion centers have so far been created, ostensibly to collect, analyze, and assess threat information, especially as it relates to terrorism. A recent study by the Congressional Research Service highlighted the challenges in this approach:

> CRS research indicates that one of the central challenges of designing a constructive and productive federal role in supporting these state and local fusion centers is working to ensure that the centers retain their state and local-level identity and support from those communities. According to many homeland security observers, one manifestation of this tension lies in the need to strike a balance between the national needs for a consistent provider of state and local threat information with the state's autonomy to pursue issues deemed of importance to local jurisdictions. This tension is often notable when reviewing the diverse, and at times incompatible, types of threat and warning products required by state leaders and contrasted to those requested by federal homeland security and law enforcement entities.[20]

As a result, a fusion center may well be as focused on natural disasters and recovery response and on consolidation of criminal information across jurisdictions as much as on intelligence or terrorism. These centers also generally do not understand the concept of fused intelligence. Again, the CRS research sheds light:

> It is unclear if a single fusion center of the forty plus that are currently in operation (or soon to be) has successfully adopted a truly proactive prevention approach to information analysis and sharing. No state, including its local jurisdictions, appears to have fully adopted the intelligence cycle to support fusion center operations. While some states have seen limited success in integrating federal intelligence community analysis into their fusion centers, research indicates most continue to struggle with developing a "true fusion process" which includes value added analysis of broad streams of intelligence, identification of gaps, and proactive collection of information to fulfill those gaps to prevent criminal and terrorist acts."[21]

To date, there is no formal plan or strategy that would promote such developments within these centers, although there is a growing belief within the federal government that such a development should occur if the centers are established or rely on federal funding. Indeed, one of the national strategies clearly sees an ability to govern fusion centers from a federal perspective:

> Individual departments and agencies of the federal government have been directed to work together to ensure that federal information and intelligence capabilities are brought together to form a national assured information sharing capability. These same individual departments and agencies have been directed to work together to ensure that state and major urban area fusion centers are interlinked with each other and federal information and intelligence capabilities to form a national information sharing capability."[22]

The advent of fusion centers does provide something that was not present prior to 9/11, namely a potentially integrated structure where federal, state, local, and tribal information can be exchanged. Such a development could serve to allow a federal-level domestic intelligence entity to effectively operate by consolidating the number of jurisdictions that the entity would have to engage.

Considering a Domestic Intelligence Strategy

As a nation, we are often resistant to change, especially in our laws and our bureaucratic structures. Consequently, when change is required, we often gravitate toward modifying existing structures and responsibilities rather than taking a new approach. This has been the case for domestic intelligence over the past seven years.[23] But precisely because domestic intelligence is not something that comes naturally to the United States, considering a strategy for such activities can be instructive and is a useful first step in understanding the complexity of the mission.

Ideally, a domestic intelligence strategy should do several things, all of which are equally important. First, it should have as its ultimate goal the ability to create assessments that provide decision advantage to those responsible for the safety of our citizenry prior to damaging events or crises. For those assigned the mission of domestic intelligence, providing indications and warning intelligence—sometimes speculative in nature—must take precedence over collection of evidence to build a case or providing information for disaster recovery, which are two different functions with different intelligence needs.

Second, the strategy should take into account both current and evolving threats, ensuring that required capabilities match anticipated challenges. As stated previously, counterterrorism does not include the entirety of our domestic intelligence concerns. Additional areas of concern include cyber threats to our national critical infrastructure, much of which is in commercial hands. Also, given the apparent growing links between terrorist activities and organized crime elements, having the ability to utilize so-called all-crimes information is important to the overall success of the strategy.

Third, the strategy should clearly define the relationships between federal, state, local, and tribal entities in terms of intelligence roles and responsibilities. Such a relationship is specifically important in terms of the domestic collection of information, including establishing clear mechanisms for tasking and guidelines for reporting. Here, it is just as important to specifically delineate responsibilities within the federal government relating to domestic intelligence as it is to clearly articulate the responsibilities between the levels of government and between the states themselves. Since 9/11, commission reports and legislation have generally been vague in their prescriptive approaches to domestic intelligence, leaving solutions open to interpretation. The Bush administration thus far has left execution of domestic intelligence to existing bureaucracies, leaving refinement of specific operating relationships subject to internal jurisdictional battles.

A fourth part of a strategy must develop, define, and implement specific guidelines for how collected information is protected and utilized. This is essential to protecting intelligence sources and methods, information related to gaps in our security, and specifically in protecting information on our citizenry. Such guidelines must address who can produce reports, who can receive the reports, and what level of detail—especially if the information is about a U.S. citizen—can be shared and with whom. This would include not only which decision makers could have access to the reporting, but how such information might be reported to law enforcement entities so that a case could be opened and pursued. Additionally, such guidelines should address the potential for modified and expanded reporting in the aftermath of a crisis.

A fifth component of the strategy should be the establishment of a domestic counterintelligence capability, along with the necessary authorities for this activity. Such an operational element is a necessity if our overall security strategy includes a desire to not only understand the intentions of hostile actors operating on U.S. soil, but also to neutralize, control, or manipulate their activities to our advantage. Our current domestic counterintelligence activities, which heretofore have been the responsibility of the FBI, need to be reconsidered and, as noted elsewhere within this volume, more thoroughly supported in terms of priority and resources. Moreover, the types of operational activities that may be required in order to successfully infiltrate the circles of the types of actors envisioned in the future may well benefit from a closer tie between analysis and operations than that currently existing between the CIA and FBI. Regardless of whether a new operational element for counterintelligence is ultimately desired or required, a fresh look at our existing capabilities and operating procedures must be accomplished to ensure that we can meet evolving domestic threats.

A sixth component of a domestic intelligence strategy must address a comprehensive legal framework that would underpin the strategy. Such a framework may require new laws as well as the modification of existing laws. In some cases, states and localities may need to modify their laws in order to appropriately and clearly define relationships, responsibilities, and authorities with one another and with the federal government within the overall framework. Although there have been changes to laws since 9/11—most notably the U.S. Patriot Act—recent debates within Congress illustrate the need for further examination. The debate that has been ongoing since 9/11 relating to the National Security Agency (NSA) surveillance program and to the Foreign Intelligence Surveillance Act (FISA) suggests the need to continually review and update laws to meet our current challenges as time and technology make laws obsolete. Likewise, the objections to the creation of a National Applications Office within DHS that would provide a mechanism by which state and local law enforcement could utilize national intelligence collection assets (especially satellite imagery) are largely based on the apparent lack of a legal framework that would ensure the protection of civil liberties.[24] These examples indicate the need for a comprehensive approach rather than continued reliance on actions by individual departments and agencies (and states) to support domestic intelligence needs. Without such a step, it is unlikely that we can achieve the necessary balance between our national security needs and the protection of our fundamental rights of privacy, probable cause, due process, and other civil liberties.

A final element would be the development and implementation of a comprehensive oversight mechanism that ensures the integrity of domestic intelligence operations within the legal framework, including the protection of civil liberties. Although traditional oversight resources (e.g., civil liberty officers and inspectors general) are necessary and can assist in internal consistency of oversight, external mechanisms that can provide some level of transparency for the public about our domestic intelligence operations could gain critical support and promote trust among the American people. Historically, oversight of federal operations and programs has been the role of Congress as the elected representatives of the American people. There are few debates more emotional than those engendered by intelligence needs and protection of civil liberties. Given our history with domestic intelligence, as described earlier in this chapter, debates on this topic are often highly politically charged, both between parties and between the White House and Congress. Creating and implementing a dedicated domestic intelligence strategy must take this reality into account.

Conclusion

There are no easy answers to the complicated questions surrounding domestic intelligence. Other countries that have dedicated national domestic intelligence entities have specific histories that have led them to establish such entities. Ironically, our history has led us to specifically avoid such an entity. Today, in American political debate, the British domestic intelligence entity, MI-5, is often touted as a model for our organizational approach. However, MI-5 operates under a different type of government with different, albeit similar, ideals regarding individual rights. Moreover, the sizes of the countries and their local constabularies are so vastly different, it is not clear whether such a model would be scalable to our needs.

Clearly, if we abandon our basic principles and civil liberties, the terrorists can rightfully claim victory in eroding and destroying our nation and its ideals. For this reason, the next administration must assess whether the actions taken on domestic intelligence thus far are sufficient for our future security. At the beginning of this chapter, I mentioned that we are a nation that is reactive in nature. The backgrounds of the creation of DHS, the DNI, the Patriot Act, and the Protect America Act are all similar in that these were congressional responses intended to assure the American people that their government was satisfying its basic and fundamental requirement to provide for the common defense. In every case, these actions were accomplished without an overarching, carefully considered strategy on domestic intelligence and the larger impact of the need to collect intelligence within our own borders.

Subsequent activities on domestic intelligence have been piecemeal in their approach, often working around bureaucracies rather than adapting them to new national security needs. Of potentially greater concern is the level of complacency that appears to have infected our national security actions. Although continuous debate on Iraq, Afghanistan, Iran, and other issues that are shaded by the rhetoric of the "Global War on Terrorism" are at the center of our nightly news, much of the debate hinges on internal political strategies more so than on a comprehensive understanding and approach to a new national security paradigm that takes the effects of terrorism, globalization, and technology into account as key factors. Thus, individual efforts by federal agencies and departments, and by state and local governments, have flourished in an attempt to react to threats in the absence of a strategy or structure that might effectively neutralize the security threats.

The next administration has an opportunity to consider a comprehensive strategy like that previously described. Such an undertaking is difficult even in terms of who should develop the strategy. Clearly, to be successful, the development must involve the legislative and judicial branches of the federal government as well as representation from governors and other state and local elected officials. In essence, it must be a national strategy, not a federal one, that is publicly endorsed by those key decision makers most affected by domestic threats.

In considering what type of structure our domestic intelligence might have, it is likely easiest for a new administration to start with how to organize the federal government. The federal government brings an array of capabilities for collection and analysis that can aid state and local governments and the private sector in identifying, understanding, and neutralizing internal threats. The intelligence community, specifically, can add a wealth of knowledge and understanding about external threats that can translate to internal ones. Of greatest potential benefit, however, may be the federal government's ability to provide a complete assessment of threats by being the focal point for all collected information—foreign and domestic—in order to provide a holistic, all-source analysis that would be difficult to achieve from a state or regional perspective. For example, the Terrorist Screening Center, with its goal of consolidating myriad watch lists, has been successful in linking information from local police officers with that contained within the databases of the intelligence community (including the FBI) in order to determine whether an individual stopped for a traffic violation has ties to terrorist organizations.

At the federal level, a domestic intelligence entity must be positioned to draw information not just from the intelligence community, but also from elements of the Departments of Homeland Security (e.g., the Coast Guard, TSA, and Border Patrol), Justice, Defense, Treasury, Commerce, Transportation, and others, especially in areas that contain elements of our national critical infrastructure. Ideally, this entity would report directly to the DNI, as the senior leader accountable for all intelligence activities, and who is best positioned to ensure that sufficient resources are available for both foreign and domestic activities. Moreover, given the extremely sensitive nature of domestic intelligence, a single point of responsibility/accountability is warranted, similar to the precedent of assigning responsibility of covert actions to the DCI. Such assignment of responsibility would also match the governing legislation that established the DNI as the leader of the intelligence community.

When the Department of Homeland Security was established, Congress believed that its focus would be homeland security and domestic intelligence. By bringing together the disparate components of our domestic security functions, a clearer, more concise understanding of our vulnerabilities and requirements would be realized. Proponents envisioned an intelligence-specific office of Information Analysis and Infrastructure Protection (IAIP), whereby the intelligence-related information from the other components within DHS could be gathered and consolidated with information from the intelligence community in order to create a more complete picture of the threats and vulnerabilities. Unfortunately, such a critical capability was not realized. The Bush administration's establishment of the Terrorist Threat Integration Center, and later the National Counterterrorism Center, effectively dampened the priority of the position, resulting in significant delays in hiring IAIP personnel (including management) and, ultimately, the lack of an IAIP allocation when the first DHS budget was submitted. Consequently, IAIP never became the focal point of domestic intelligence.

Regardless of this history, the intelligence position within DHS seems the most logical place to locate a domestic intelligence entity. Taking the example of the undersecretary of defense/intelligence (USD/I), who now also carries the title of director of defense intelligence under the DNI, the individual charged with domestic intelligence within DHS could be designated director of domestic intelligence, with a direct reporting line to the DNI, while maintaining the line of reporting to the secretary of the department. The advantages of recreating and recasting the intelligence position within DHS include

- its already-existing ties to the DHS infrastructure—representing a significant component of potential intelligence collection and reporting;
- some existing authorities that would help create a domestic intelligence entity;
- existing links to state, local, and tribal governments;
- and a position outside of both an intelligence agency and the Department of Justice that sets it apart as an unbiased, outside arbiter without the baggage of existing intelligence and law enforcement bureaucratic cultures.

Such a move also has the advantage of avoiding the additional bureaucracy of a new department that would be inherent in an MI-5-like organization.

Placing the domestic intelligence component within DHS also complements work being done in the development of state fusion centers. As mentioned earlier, this work is in its infancy, but the potential is there to fully develop fusion centers as the regional hubs for domestic intelligence, still bringing together each state's assets on terrorism and all-crime related activities and thus answering the demands of state governments. Such a structure also allows the federal government to set at least basic standards for the formation and operation of fusion centers, placing intelligence as a key priority.

There is no doubt that recasting the existing component of the DHS intelligence effort is a major undertaking that would require significant reprioritizing and resources, but any effort to create a domestic intelligence entity will require a major effort regardless of where it falls within the government. By placing domestic intelligence operations in DHS—but reporting to the DNI—a balance is also created between the major intelligence consumers: Homeland Security and the Department of Defense. Thus, future intelligence systems planning and acquisition strategies—often dominated by DoD today—would significantly take into account the needs of domestic intelligence.

Settling on a federal component for domestic intelligence is only a portion of the issue. The other components of the strategy are equally important. Specifically articulating which decision makers at various levels of government have what types of information is fundamental to the success of our overall domestic intelligence efforts. If warning information cannot be tailored and provided to a local decision maker in time to prevent a crisis, our efforts have failed. Some work on this issue has been done in the efforts related to information-sharing initiatives, but more work is needed.

The issue of domestic intelligence collection is also critical, and procedures in that arena have not yet matured. As noted in the examples given earlier in this chapter, state and local first responders play a lead role in confronting potential threat activities and suspicions. However, ensuring that these individuals can report such activities and suspicions must be addressed in both a legal and practical manner. Likewise, the issue of tasking collection from state and local entities must be addressed, as their day-to-day roles focus on protection and law enforcement of their areas, not intelligence collection.

Whether this federal domestic intelligence entity should have its own domestic human collection resources is another question to be considered, as is whether this entity should have its own domestic counterintelligence resources. Finally, taking all of these elements and constructing a legal framework will be a massive undertaking that is steeped in complexity. Not only will adjusting federal guidance and jurisdiction prove difficult, but the inevitable concerns about states' rights will make the legal effort a politically charged proposition.

The issue of oversight must be addressed, regardless of whether the development and execution of a comprehensive domestic intelligence strategy is attempted. Post-9/11 interactions between Congress and the Bush administration have made the subject of domestic intelligence highly politicized and polarized. The debate over the FISA was tinged with political overtones as the Democratically controlled Congress has tried to "check" the Republican administration. As reported, "The debate in Congress about whether to allow Americans to sue companies that participated in the National Security Agency's warrantless surveillance activities has little to do with punishing Big Telecom for its role in domestic spying. Rather, keeping alive the 38 pending civil suits against AT&T, Verizon, and other companies have become congressional Democrats' best chance to hold the White House accountable for the controversial NSA program. The lawsuits also offer the hope of an official ruling on whether the program was ever legal, something that Congress has been unable to determine on its own."[25]

Congressional oversight of homeland security (including domestic intelligence) has become fractured and dispersed among many committees claiming jurisdiction. This is especially true when considering oversight of DHS. Due to the various components that made up DHS from its implementation, multiple committees and subcommittees claim some portion of jurisdiction, including authority over the intelligence activities of the department. A recommendation from the Homeland Security Advisory Council in January 2008 specifically highlighted the issue by stating in its recommendations, "Implement 9/11 Commission recommendations to reduce the number of Congressional oversight committees and subcommittees from its current unwieldy eighty-six."[26]

One of the driving principles for the creation of the intelligence oversight committees in the 1970s was the lack of focused, formal oversight on intelligence activities and budgets. From their creation until 9/11, these committees have generally provided the kind of oversight that was required. Since 9/11, however, oversight of homeland-security-related activities, including intelligence, has been diluted. And although the intelligence oversight committees continue to have some marginal effect on oversight of the intelligence community, a focused effort on oversight of a domestic intelligence entity would likely not be possible in today's environment without major changes to existing jurisdictional authorities of the committees of Congress. Thus far, Congress has been specifically resistant to such changes.

Given the current circumstances in Congress, combined with the importance and necessity of having focused oversight of the implementation of a strategy like the one envisioned in this chapter, a separate, independent oversight mechanism should at least be considered. Such a mechanism, which could take a form similar to those found within the financial sector (e.g., the Federal Reserve or the Securities and Exchange Commission), might provide the type of constant, unbiased, apolitical oversight on domestic intelligence operations, activities, and needs. This oversight body would report equally to the White House and to Congress, with some reporting to governors and state legislators. It might also periodically produce an unclassified report for the public in order to boost public confidence in the process. Realizing that establishment of such a body is currently as unlikely as Congress's willingness to reform itself, it is doubtful that such a step would be immediately embraced as viable by a new administration. That does not mean, however, that it should not be considered.[27]

It has been seven years since 9/11, and we have not suffered another terrorist attack. Whether this is because of our actions and activities through our intelligence, defense, and homeland security mechanisms or whether this is a result of calculated waiting by terrorists is unclear. Both are probably true. The piecemeal and often tactical approaches to our existing domestic intelligence efforts do not suggest that we are on a path to achieve true and sustained decision advantage for homeland security. As the 9/11 Commissioners challenged the generation experiencing these attacks to change the way we do business related to domestic intelligence, so too must the next administration be charged with taking the opportunity to assess whether a comprehensive domestic intelligence strategy and its implementation would better serve our interests.

Notes

1. National Commission on Terrorist Attacks on the United States, *The 9/11 Commission Report* (New York: W. W. Norton, 2004), 399.

2. In October 2001 Congress passed the Uniting and Strengthening America by Providing Appropriate Tools Required to Intercept and Obstruct Terrorism Act (USA PATRIOT Act), changing the way the federal government operated and interacted on issues such as intelligence and information sharing, in response to the terrorist attacks on September 11, 2001. In November 2002 Congress passed the Homeland Security Act, establishing the

Department of Homeland Security (DHS). And in December 2004 Congress passed the Intelligence Reform and Terrorist Prevention Act, establishing the Office of the Director of National Intelligence.

3. Robert S. Mueller III, "Statement Before the Senate Select Committee on Intelligence" January 11, 2007. Available at www.fbi.gov/congress/congress07/mueller011107 .htm.

4. Joel Brenner, the national counterintelligence executive, has stated that "the United States remains the number one target of "virtually every significant espionage service on the face of the Earth." Noting that China, Cuba, Russia, and Iran are most aggressive at spying on the United States, he opines, "These services are eating our lunch." Bill Gertz, "China's Spies 'Very Aggressive' Threat to U.S.," *Washington Times*, March 6, 2007.

5. Address to a Joint Session of Congress, September 20, 2001. Available at www.whitehouse.gov/news/releases/2001/09/20010920-9.html.

6. Lisa Miller et al., "American Dreamers; Muslim Americans are one of this country's greatest strengths. But they're vulnerable as never before," *Newsweek*, July 30, 2007, 26.

7. *National Strategy for Homeland Security*, Office of Homeland Security, July 2002, iii. Available at www.whitehouse.gov/homeland/book/nat_strat_his.pdf.

8. Peter Hennessy, *The New Protective State: Government, Intelligence, and Terrorism* (London: Continuum, 2007), 15–16.

9. Mohammed El-Nawawy and Adel Iskandar, *Al-Jazeera: The Story of the Network That Is Rattling Governments and Redefining Modern Journalism* (Cambridge, MA: Westview, 2003), 143, 146–47.

10. Bruce Hoffman, "The Use of the Internet by Islamic Extremists," Testimony before the House Permanent Select Committee on Intelligence, May 4, 2006.

11. Ibid.

12. "MI5 tracking '30 UK terror plots,'" *BBC News*, November 10, 2006. Available at http://news.bbc.co.uk/2/hi/uk_news/6134516.stm.

13. Report published by the U.S. Department of Justice, FBI, *Terrorism 2002–2005*, 23.

14. Miller et al., "American Dreamers," 29.

15. "MI5 tracking '30 UK terror plots.'"

16. Mike McConnell, "Overhauling Intelligence," *Foreign Affairs* 86, no. 4 (July/ August 2007): 55–56.

17. *The National Security Strategy of the United States of America*, Office of the President of the United States, September 2002. Available at www.whitehouse.gov/nsc/ nss.pdf.

18. *The National Intelligence Strategy of the United States of America: Transformation through Integration and Innovation*, Office of the Director of National Intelligence, October 2005. Available at www.dni.gov/publications/NISOcboer2005.pdf.

19. McConnell, "Overhauling Intelligence," 55.

20. Todd Masse and John Rollins, *A Summary of Fusion Centers: Core Issues and Options for Congress*, CRS Report, September 19, 2007, 12.

21. Ibid.

22. *National Strategy for Information Sharing: Successes and Challenges In Improving Terrorism-Related Information Sharing*, October 2007, 29. Available at www.whitehouse .gov/nsc/infosharing/NSIS_book.pdf.

23. An excellent synopsis of both Congress's and the Bush administration's initiatives after 9/11 can be found in Bruce Berkowitz, "Homeland Security Intelligence: Rationale, Requirements, and Current Status," in *Analyzing Intelligence*, ed. Roger Z. George and James B. Bruce (Washington, DC: Georgetown University Press, 2008), 289.

24. "Administration Set to Use New Spy Program in U.S.," *Washington Post*, April 12, 2008. Available at www.washingtonpost.com/wp-dyn/content/article/2008/04/11/AR2008041103655_pf.html.

25. Shane Harris, "Telecoms as Trojan Horses," *National Journal*, December 7, 2007.

26. *Report of the Administration Transition Task Force*, Homeland Security Advisory Council, January 2008. Available at www.dhs.gov/xlibrary/assets/hsac_ATTF_Report.pdf.

27. After reading my own conclusions, I found a similar idea regarding the creation of an independent oversight body for intelligence in Randall J. Larson, *Our Own Worst Enemy* (New York: Grand Central Publishing, 2007), 176–82.

12

Richard A. Posner

Counterintelligence, Counterterrorism, Civil Liberties, and the Domestic Intelligence Controversy

I HAVE WRITTEN at some length about intelligence (with particular though not exclusive emphasis on domestic intelligence), and the issues of civil liberties that intelligence methods present.[1] I have barely touched on counterintelligence, however, and I hope to repair that neglect in this chapter. My focus is mainly on the civil libertarian concerns that counterintelligence and counterterrorist intelligence (which are not always clearly separated either in practice or in analysis) present. I do not attempt to assess the threat of espionage, which is the particular concern of counterintelligence, or the performance, which has been criticized, of our principal counterintelligence agency—the Federal Bureau of Investigation (FBI).[2] But I do give some attention at the outset to the question of where counterintelligence belongs in a rationally organized intelligence system.

I.

Familiar though it is, the word "counterintelligence" does not have a single, agreed-upon meaning; and the definitional difficulty turns out to have practical and not merely semantic significance. At its broadest, "counterintelligence" refers to efforts to prevent any covert activities inimical to our national security, not only espionage by foreign powers but also penetration of the nation by sleeper cells that might someday be awakened to engage in sabotage or terrorist attacks. At that level of generality "counterintelligence" includes counterterrorism intelligence; and indeed until recently (approximately the 1990s) counterterrorism intelligence was a more or less undifferentiated part of counterintelligence. More commonly, "counterintelligence" refers to efforts to prevent and detect espionage ("protecting secrets, frustrating attempts by foreign intelligence services to acquire those secrets, and catching Americans who spy for those foreign intelligence services"), while at its narrowest the term refers to efforts to detect employees who are actually enemy agents ("moles").[3] As serviceable a definition as any, and carrying an official imprimatur to boot, is that given by Joel Brenner, the national counterintelligence executive: "Counterintelligence is the business of identifying and dealing with foreign intelligence threats to the United States. Its core concern is the foreign intelligence services of foreign states and the similar organizations of nonstate actors—transnational terrorist groups such as al-Qaeda and Lebanese Hezbollah, for instance. Counterintelligence has both a defensive mission—protecting the nation's secrets and assets against foreign intelligence penetration—and an offensive mission—finding out what foreign intelligence organizations are up to in order to better defeat their aims."[4]

An initial organizational question is the relation between counterintelligence and security, in the sense of the use of background investigations of applicants for employment, along with encryption and other security protocols (including limiting access to classified material on the basis of "need to know"), to prevent penetrations. Both are preventive, but security intervenes earlier. Yet the relation is so close that they ought to be under common direction. A further reason for such a merger is the excessive risk aversion of officers whose only task is to prevent security breaches. Counterintelligence officers have a broader perspective because of their close relation to the intelligence function.

Counterintelligence in any of the senses that the word bears is often conducted abroad; our armed forces stationed abroad have counterintelligence units tasked with preventing espionage, and the CIA engages in counterintelligence abroad. But most counterintelligence is domestic, and might therefore seem indistinguishable, from the standpoint of civil liberties, from domestic intelligence in general and thus from domestic surveillance. But this I shall argue is not true. Traditional counterintelligence concentrates on the efforts of foreign intelligence services to conduct espionage in the United States. Those services tend to operate largely out of the foreign countries' embassies in the United States, and so counterintelligence has a well-defined target consisting of embassy and other nominally "diplomatic" personnel (though there is increasing concern about foreign agents who do not operate under diplomatic cover and therefore are more difficult to identify), and of the American citizens whom those personnel attempt to suborn. Surveillance focused on the activities of representatives of foreign governments tends therefore to be circumscribed, unless there is a concern not just with foreign espionage but also with a domestic minority or political opposition that is believed to be inspired by or supportive of foreign enemies (perhaps to the extent of spying for them—American communists provided a rich source of recruits for Soviet espionage in the 1930s and 1940s—but Japanese Americans were mistakenly suspected after Pearl Harbor of being a fifth column), or to be incubating revolution or inciting violent protest. That is not a major concern today, unless one thinks that Iran might try to stir up the Iranian minority in the United States against the U.S. government, and that seems unlikely to succeed, since most Iranians in the United States oppose the current Iranian regime.

A more serious concern from a civil libertarian standpoint is that the line between threats to national security, on the one hand, and civil unrest incident to political conflict, on the other hand—think of the aggressive, even when not (seriously) violent, protests against the Vietnam War in the late 1960s and early 1970s—is not a sharp, unwavering one. We do not want an agency concerned mainly with foreign-originating threats to national security to interest itself in peaceful, political protest, even when the protest involves a degree of interference with traffic or with property rights (as in the civil rights sit-ins of the 1960s). To make such protest the business of a counterintelligence agency is to imply that even peaceful political protests can endanger national security—an implication that could have a chilling effect on legitimate political advocacy. The charter of a counterintelligence agency should therefore be precisely and narrowly defined.

There is a further definitional problem. The targets of counterintelligence work, when limited to dealing with foreign-state threats, tend to be fairly well defined and identified, as I have said; but this is not true of counterterrorism intelligence. There the threat tends to be diffuse rather than focused. The potential targets of terrorists are essentially unlimited, because terrorists striking almost anywhere can do immense damage. And the magnitude of the potential harm from a terrorist attack is growing with the increasing availability of weapons of mass destruction, especially biological weapons. Terrorists, moreover, can also be homegrown, with few or even no links to foreign terrorist groups. Presenting a broader and more immediate threat than that of penetration by agents of foreign states, modern terrorism, if is to be countered effectively, requires that counterterrorist intelligence cast a wider net, and have a finer mesh, than counterintelligence narrowly defined.

Yet there is a counterterrorist dimension to counterintelligence, even when the existence of a boundary between counterterrorism intelligence and conventional counterintelligence is acknowledged. Terrorists can and do engage in espionage. Rare is the terrorist attack that is not preceded by surveillance, or "casing," of the target. Terrorists have often been apprehended at the target-surveillance stage. But the counterintelligence challenge posed by terrorist espionage is less ominous than that posed by foreign-state espionage. No terrorist group has nearly so sophisticated an espionage service, especially for spying inside the United States, as many nations have. Although exceptional cases occur, successful espionage in this country requires a considerable support infrastructure consisting of training facilities, communications, recruitment, technical know-how, logistics, finance, and management. It is unlikely that any terrorist group has such an infrastructure. And most of what terrorists need to know in order to plan and execute attacks in the United States is public knowledge, so that not only would the costs of establishing a sophisticated espionage apparatus be very high for a terrorist group but the incremental benefits would be meager. A greater danger is that terrorists' moles or sympathizers, or freelance traitors, in national security agencies might obtain vital information on intelligence sources and methods and seek to give it or sell it to terrorist groups, or use the information to compromise or disrupt national security computer systems, or to conduct other sabotage. These dangers exist even if the terrorist group does not have a substantial organization for conducting espionage.

The *methods* of counterintelligence and counterterrorism overlap even when their targets do not. Both emphasize surveillance and prevention rather than punishment, and so both reject the proposition, dear to the FBI and to Justice Department lawyers, that criminal prosecutions are always the best way to neutralize terrorists. Yet the principal federal counterintelligence agency, like the principal domestic intelligence agency for counterterrorism, is a component of the FBI, still predominantly a criminal investigation agency and lodged in the Department of Justice. The Bureau's Counterintelligence Division is, along with the Counterterrorism Division, the major component of the FBI's recently created National Security Branch. True, there are many other counterintelligence agencies in the federal government, some lodged in intelligence agencies (like the counterintelligence division of the CIA, and military counterintelligence), and some in agencies or departments only peripherally involved in intelligence. The national counterintelligence executive is tasked with coordinating, promoting, and improving the scattered counterintelligence units, but does not control or manage them. For my purposes in this chapter I do not have to delve deeply into the structure of U.S. counterintelligence. I can treat the FBI's Counterintelligence Division as the core of the nation's overall domestic counterintelligence system.

I have been distinguishing between counterterrorism intelligence and counterintelligence, and of course between counterintelligence and intelligence, but now I want to blur these distinctions. The difference between diffuse and focused targets for counterintelligence work is important, but it does not map as neatly as I have suggested onto the distinction between counterterrorism and counterintelligence. A terrorist group can operate much like a foreign state, with a defined geographical locus, a definite target set, and a formal management structure; Hamas and Hezbollah approximate this model. Terrorism can also be state-sponsored. And, on the other side of what I am suggesting is an artificial divide, foreign-state threats can be diffuse. A foreign state might, at the same time that it was conducting espionage out of its embassy in the United States, be sending officers and agents to study at U.S. universities or work for U.S. firms, or recruiting agents from among the U.S. population of the same ethnicity as the people in the foreign state. Such NOCs (that is, intelligence officers lacking the official cover, and therefore diplomatic immunity, provided by working out of an embassy) present a diffuse rather than a focused target for counterintelligence efforts.

One can imagine an organization of the intelligence system that made no hard-and-fast *organizational* distinction between counterintelligence and counterterrorism intelligence, between security and counterintelligence, or even between intelligence and counterintelligence, since the methods are so similar and intelligence officers often shuttle between the two activities. Even so, there is an inherent tension between intelligence and counterintelligence—intelligence operations officers recruit agents to do spying; counterintelligence officers suspect all agents of actually working for the enemy; sometime they suspect intelligence officers as well, especially given the precedent of Aldrich Ames. But outweighing these points is that intelligence officers are likely to have the best leads to who among the officers or the agents they recruit might be a mole, and that, because the techniques used in intelligence are similar to those used in counterintelligence, counterintelligence officers can profit from the "corporate" knowledge of the intelligence officers, and indeed officers can and are, as I noted, rotated between the two functions.

There is also a serious tension between counterintelligence and counterterrorism that results from the difference between focused and diffuse threats to national security. Dealing with a diffuse threat requires the pooling of information gleaned from a great variety of sources, which in turn requires fast information sharing through connected databases and easier access to them. But this is a nightmare from the standpoint of counterintelligence, because the easier the access to more information, the more damage a mole who gains access can do. Although terrorist groups have much more limited capabilities for conducting espionage than nations do, hacking into a computer database does not require an elaborate espionage infrastructure.

A further point is that at the response, as distinct from the detection, stage, counterterrorism favors a wide diffusion of detailed threat information, and again the counterintelligence officer worries: The wider the diffusion of the information, and the more detailed (and hence useful to the responders) it is, the greater the danger that a mole will obtain the information and be able to draw inferences about its sources and about the methods by which those sources were tapped. Counterintelligence officers favor compartmented data with access even by persons having the requisite security clearances limited by the "need to know" principle.

Once again, however, the tension arises not from the difference between counterterrorism and counterintelligence as such but from the difference between diffuse and focused threats, and so might arise within a counterintelligence agency that was trying to counter a diffuse threat. In short, conventional boundaries between intelligence organizations—counterterrorism/counterintelligence, intelligence/counterintelligence, counterintelligence/security—may be arbitrary. Of course, different threats require different responses, different teams, but not necessarily different organizational divisions or different, nonintersecting career paths.

One organizational distinction, however, should remain solid—that between domestic and foreign intelligence (including in "intelligence" counterintelligence, counterterrorism intelligence, and security, as well as intelligence more narrowly defined). For there are three ineradicable differences between domestic and foreign intelligence, which have particular importance in U.S. culture and require separate though closely coordinated domestic and foreign intelligence agencies. They are, first, the difference between the tactics that intelligence agencies can use abroad and those used within the United States; second, the need to integrate a national domestic intelligence capability with the "eyes and ears" capability of the thousands of state, local, and private police and security forces, along with federal security personnel in customs, visa control, and (other) border control; and third, the need to recruit officers, and not merely agents, from the local population. We cannot, as a practical matter, recruit CIA officers from foreign populations. Instead, our mainly all-American CIA operations officers recruit agents from the populations of the foreign target country. But in the United States it is important for the FBI and other agencies to recruit intelligence officers from subpopulations that are of interest to counterintelligence (such as the Iranian or Pakistani minority), for that increases the pool of informants and moles (as distinct from intelligence officers) and also heightens understanding of the subpopulation in question.

So placing a counterintelligence group in the same agency as a counterterrorism group (as in the FBI and the CIA, both of which do both counterintelligence and counterterrorism) makes good sense, but not their lodgment in a criminal investigation bureau, for reasons that I have addressed in detail in my writings on domestic intelligence. Just as domestic and foreign intelligence belong in separate agencies, so intelligence and criminal investigation belong in separate agencies. I have argued elsewhere that both counterintelligence and counterterrorist intelligence belong in an MI-5– or CSIS (Canadian Security Intelligence Service)–type domestic intelligence agency, which we do not have. We are unlikely to get it in the foreseeable future, in part because of the bitter opposition of the FBI to the creation of a domestic intelligence service not controlled by the Bureau, and in part because of a misunderstanding of the effect of such an agency on civil liberties. In fact, the threat posed to civil liberties is enhanced when domestic intelligence (including domestic counterintelligence) is placed inside a criminal investigation agency because the latter has the power of arrest, which a domestic intelligence agency does not. So in the rest of this chapter I shall be discussing not only the nature and gravity of the danger that counterintelligence poses to civil liberties, but also how that danger would be affected by the creation of a domestic intelligence agency.

II.

The activities of domestic intelligence that trouble civil libertarians, whatever the precise goal of the intelligence activity—whether it is aimed at moles or other spies or at terrorists—fall into four groups: surveillance (both electronic and what is called "physical surveillance," consisting not only of "eavesdropping" in the traditional nonelectronic sense but also of open-source collection, questioning of neighbors, and the like); detention and custodial interrogation; neutralizing threats, as by disrupting plots through bribery, threats, and disinformation; and aid in prosecution. Prosecution is not an intelligence function, but it is often aided by information obtained by intelligence activities, and it can of course terminate a threat by locking up its source. I shall describe these activities briefly and then describe and assess the specific civil liberties concerns that each of them engenders.

Surveillance is the most important function of a domestic intelligence agency. It includes open-source intelligence (trolling the Web, for example); technical intelligence (mainly electronic surveillance, including wiretapping and the interception of e-mails); and traditional human intelligence, including the immensely labor-intensive work of tailing suspected foreign agents (or purely homegrown terrorist suspects), collecting information about them from banks, universities, libraries, and other institutions patronized by them (including prisons) and from their acquaintances and employers, recruiting and running undercover agents, and listening and observing in public places frequented by suspects, such as mosques that cater to Islamic extremists.

Surveillance so defined does not involve overt personal contact between a domestic intelligence officer and a suspect. At times, though, effective investigation of a threat may require interrogating a suspect, and custodial interrogation, inherently intimidating even when no coercive methods of interrogation are used, will often be more effective than interrogation in a setting in which the person being interrogated can terminate the interrogation at will. Arrest and detention are police rather than intelligence functions, but interrogation can of course be an intelligence function.

One tends to think of intelligence as the collection and analysis of information. But intelligence officers, having detected a threat, are often also well placed to thwart it. Just revealing the plot may do the trick, or threatening the plotters with arrest if they do not abandon it, or using threats or bribes to turn them into double agents, or blackmailing them, or feeding them with plausible disinformation that causes their plot to miscarry, or even merely revealing to their accomplices that they have been turned, are suspected, or just have been questioned. Once the plot has been detected, and especially if the intelligence service has managed to place an undercover agent among the plotters, enabling it to manipulate the group, send it off on wild goose chases, or otherwise induce it to expend resources on futile endeavors, the threat posed by the plots may be neutralized without any need for prosecution. Intelligence services hesitate to advise prosecution because the publicity attendant on it, and the possible revelation in the course of a public trial of sensitive information concerning the plans and capabilities of the intelligence service itself, may cause a defendant's accomplices to scatter and later to regroup with a better understanding of how to outwit and outrun their pursuers.

But in many cases, indefinite detention, usually requiring that formal legal proceedings be instituted, is an unavoidable last resort. The spy or terrorist may be too dangerous to leave at large; too elusive (even if he could in principle be tailed, it may be too costly to keep track of him given the number of officers—at least twenty, and often more—needed to maintain around-the-clock physical surveillance); or there may be no more information to be obtained from him or his accomplices and hence no benefit from continuing to play him along. Punishment may also have a deterrent effect—even on spies or terrorists who place little value on their survival, for they may be highly averse to a long spell in prison if their quest for martyrdom fails. When a prosecution is instituted, the information that has been obtained by the intelligence service and that prompted the prosecution may be vital to obtaining a conviction, yet the service may be unwilling that it should become public in a public trial.

At each of these junctures, there is a potential for conflict with the values that inform what we call "civil liberties," such values as privacy; freedom from fear, from harassment, and from groundless accusations and punishments; and freedom of movement, thought, and expression. So consider the potential conflict that is created by surveillance (distinguished, as before, from custodial interrogation). When it is pinpointed on persons who, there is probable cause to believe, are agents of foreign powers or terrorist groups—the situation in which a conventional search warrant or wiretapping warrant can be obtained from a judicial officer—the impact on civil liberties is minimal. This is especially true when physical surveillance is contemplated; the high labor costs of that surveillance require as a practical matter that it be limited to the most suspicious characters.

Valid concerns about inroads on civil liberties arise when the surveillance is more encompassing and therefore more indiscriminate. Suppose, for example, that the National Security Agency vacuums a very broadly defined class of telephone conversations and e-mails and uses computer search methods (analogous to Google or to the traffic-analysis software programs used by credit card companies to detect fraud) to identify communications that are sufficiently suspicious to justify their being read by intelligence officers. The computer searches are bound to produce many false positives, that is, interceptions that turn out to be of innocent communications. At this point, when an innocent communication is read or heard by a government employee, there is an infringement of privacy, which is one of the values that cluster under the term *civil liberties*.

Is it a serious infringement? Are there offsetting benefits? And can the infringement be minimized without unduly impairing the benefits? The answers are no, yes, and yes. Much as people claim to value their privacy, the actual behavior of Americans suggests that most of us are willing to surrender it for very small rewards. An example is one-click shopping for books and movies, which enables vendors such as Amazon.com to create profiles of customers' tastes, including their political preferences. People do not worry much about their privacy being compromised in this manner because they realize that the vendors do not have malign motives in creating such profiles; the vendors just want to be able to make more effective sales pitches, which benefit consumers as well as the vendors. People are more suspicious about infringements of privacy by the government. Americans have a tradition of distrust of government, a tradition reinforced by a well-publicized history of abuses by the FBI, the CIA, local police, and other government agencies engaged in security, although a neglected aspect of that history is that with notable exceptions, the abuses have rarely done serious harm to the persons whose privacy was invaded. But in any event the rise of hyperaggressive media, of whistleblower protections, of a culture of leaks and of disregard for security classifications, and of accountability checks such as departmental inspectors general, have greatly reduced the incidence and likelihood of such abuses even in the present era of political polarization, fear of terrorism, and continued concern with commercial and military espionage by powerful foreign countries that are actual or potential rivals of the United States, such as China and Russia. A further point is that labor costs (again) greatly limit the number of intercepted communications that intelligence officers can actually listen to or read. The intelligence services therefore have a strong interest in acquiring computer search programs that select only the most suspicious communications to be read by an intelligence officer.

So the danger that electronic surveillance poses to privacy, as well as to freedom of thought and expression, as illustrated by the practices of the communist countries in their heyday and as classically depicted in George Orwell's *Nineteen Eighty-Four*, seems to me modest.[5] On the other side the threat to national security posed by terrorism and foreign-state espionage is serious, especially as we move inexorably, it seems, into an era of widespread availability of weapons of mass destruction. This balance provides a strong argument for permitting surveillance, including domestic surveillance, even more extensive than is (so far as one can judge from public sources) being undertaken at present. The danger of homegrown terrorism, though it does not *at present* seem to be a serious danger in the United States, casts doubt on the wisdom of distinguishing as sharply as the Foreign Intelligence Surveillance Act does between surveillance of foreigners on the one hand and "U.S. persons" (U.S. citizens plus noncitizen residents who are eligible to receive a green card). Britain has been plagued by Islamic terrorists who are British citizens, as has Canada. But of course FISA is the *Foreign* Intelligence Surveillance Act. The American public does not seem ready for that word to be deleted.

There are measures by which any danger to privacy from even more extensive surveillance could be minimized without undermining the efficacy of such surveillance. I have sketched such measures elsewhere and will not repeat the discussion here, partly because Congress is currently considering extensive revisions of the Foreign Intelligence Surveillance Act, which governs electronic surveillance conducted for national security purposes.[6] Such a discussion is also somewhat peripheral because, as I shall be stressing, while indiscriminate surveillance is an important tool of counterterrorism intelligence, it is not a common tool of counterintelligence. (It would be one if, as in the 1940s and 1950s, a domestic group was believed to be subject to recruitment by foreign intelligence services.) As noted above, foreign-state espionage can present the kind of diffuse threat that terrorism does, and it has done so at various junctures in our past history, but I do not expect the counterintelligence services to be pushing for expanded electronic surveillance. Such an expansion, furthermore, is not likely to be embraced even as a counterterrorism tool in the present political climate.

Old-fashioned, preelectronic surveillance—eavesdropping in its original sense, but also such other forms of snooping like combing through public and corporate records, following people surreptitiously, questioning friends and neighbors, opening private mail, and other investigative methods—continues to be a source of concern to civil libertarians. Suppose the FBI recruits a Muslim to take notes on sermons delivered by a radical imam, to listen in on the conversations of the members of the congregation, to pose as a radical in an effort to elicit radical comments from members, and to report all this to the Bureau. As word of such activities spread, free, open, and candid political and religious expression by Muslims, especially those sympathetic to Salafism and other radical versions of Islam, would, to some unknown extent, be inhibited. There would be no violation of the laws that limit electronic surveillance and physical searches and seizures, but there would be incompatibility with the spirit of the free-speech clause of the First Amendment, which has long been interpreted as immunizing even radical political advocacy from government suppression.

But one must resist exaggerating the absolutist strain in the concept of free speech in the American legal and popular culture. There is a rhetoric of absolute rights that has undoubted appeal, but it creates a misleading impression of the actual legal situation. Much of the speech (in the broad sense in which the word has come to be understood), including fulminations by the Ku Klux Klan and neo-Nazis, the burning of the American flag, and, yes, the advocacy of jihad by radical imams, has negative social value in the current political and social culture of the United States. Moreover, freedom of speech is not, as a *legal* matter, absolute. Speech can lawfully be regulated, and even punished, when it defames an individual or corporation, infringes copyright, reveals military secrets, violates contract, invades privacy, misrepresents the quality of products or services, is obscene, disrupts traffic, makes threats—or incites to crime. But merely creating an atmosphere conducive to criminal activity is not punishable as incitement. Preaching the Salafist version of Islam may prime the preacher's audience for a subsequent pitch by a recruiter for a terrorist gang, but according to the standard interpretation of the First Amendment, such preaching could not be punished unless it contained unmistakable calls to commit illegal acts imminently. Even the United Kingdom—which does not have nearly so expansive a conception of free expression as the United States and appears to face a graver threat from Islamic terrorism than the United States does—and so has criminalized "glorifying" terrorism, nevertheless requires that the glorification has reached the level of an incitement.

And that is too late. An important recent study by the New York Police Department (which has an extensive domestic intelligence program and staff) finds that the process of becoming an Islamic terrorist unfolds over years of gradual inculcation of jihadist thinking, but that the final phase of this evolution—the phase in which the recently radicalized Muslim becomes a participant in actual terrorist plotting—can take place in a matter of weeks.[7] Such a rapid transition will often escape detection, so it is essential that the government be able to keep tabs on radicalized Muslims before the transition to the final phase begins. There is an extra dividend from such surveillance if it causes the radical imams to temper their rhetoric. But this tab keeping will often require the kind of old-fashioned, preelectronic surveillance that I described earlier. The benefits to public safety from such surveillance have to be traded off against the costs in deterring what would ordinarily be considered constitutionally protected speech. Such trade-offs are not at all alien to our constitutional tradition. The exceptions that I listed to the constitutional protection of freedom of speech are based on such trade-offs. So if the government can make a compelling case that the kind of mosque surveillance that I have described is important to public safety, the First Amendment will not, or at least should not, be interpreted to block it if the surveillance is unobtrusive. If it is obtrusive—especially if it is intended to intimidate extremist Muslim preachers and their followers—this will tilt the balance toward protection of freedom of speech. It will do this both by increasing the likely effect of the surveillance in deterring speech and by engendering additional costs, which it will do by alienating the Muslim community, a process that has reached alarming proportions in the United Kingdom.

There is a further concern about surveillance, however, that takes me back to the civil libertarians' worries over loss of privacy. To understand it requires consideration of the various methods of surveillance (broadly defined) in tandem rather than in isolation from one another. We are to imagine the government using the resources of electronic surveillance, the Web, public records about persons, private records that can readily be obtained by government (such as library checkouts, book purchases, and travel information maintained by electronic highway-toll systems such as E-Z Pass), the surveillance cameras sprouting in streets, parks, and other public places in our cities, and reports of human surveillance in mosques and other public venues, to create a comprehensive, continuously updated dossier of every person in the United States. That is not feasible at present, but it will be, and it will probably not be vulnerable to a successful legal challenge based on the Constitution. Contrary to widespread impression, the Constitution does not provide robust protection for privacy in the sense of concealment, as distinct from, say, "privacy" as the name of the right to have an abortion. But the objection to such dossier compilation, like the objection to requiring Americans to carry identification papers (the "internal passport" required in many other countries), is so strong that the government is unlikely even to try to overcome it.

And perhaps that is right, as well as realistic. I have suggested that Americans' primary concern about privacy is instrumental: It is not so much that other people, firms, and government agencies know a lot of private facts about us, but that they might have motives for using those facts against us. This fear is a stubborn fact, whether fully rational or not, of American culture, and it suggests an important distinction between lack of privacy and lack of a sense of autonomy. We can live with the former, to a considerable extent, but not with the latter—not with the sense that our ability to self-fashion, self-express, self-define, and generally control the terms on which we deal with the world has been destroyed because the government knows everything about us and follows our every move.

So realism—technological, political, and ultimately psychological—counsels limiting the compilation of detailed, continuously updated dossiers on persons reasonably suspected of being actual or potential participants in terrorist or other hostile activities. But setting realism to one side, should we be troubled if domestic security agencies undertook to compile comprehensive dossiers on all Americans? At least from the standpoint of counterintelligence (an important qualification), probably not. The objection to the government's compiling a comprehensive dossier on a person evaporates when the person is a known foreign agent or reasonably suspected to be one. What is more, a principal activity of a counterintelligence agency is hunting for moles in agencies involved in matters germane to national security; persons employed in such jobs are required to sign away most of their rights as a condition of employment, so subjecting them to the most searching and intrusive surveillance is unlikely to present constitutional or other legal issues.

But from the standpoint of counterterrorism (hence the importance of distinguishing counterterrorist intelligence from counterintelligence analytically but not organizationally), the answer may well be yes, especially given growing concern with homegrown terrorism as distinct from terrorism directed from abroad. There are two to three million American Muslims, and we are soon likely to see an influx of Iraqis who have been working with U.S. forces in Iraq. Thus far, there are no signs of widespread disaffection in our Muslim community, as there are in the Muslim communities of Great Britain, France, the Netherlands, and other European countries, but of course this may change—and change quite suddenly. We are not prepared for that change. Should it occur, it will require an urgent rethinking of the value of privacy—and not just the privacy of Muslim Americans. To avoid exacerbating Muslim disaffection by use of ethnic and religious profiling, a program of widespread dossier compilation or internal passports would have to embrace the entire adult American population.

Surveillance is much less intimidating—and therefore less effective in eliciting information possessed by persons of interest to security agencies—than custodial interrogation, to which I now turn. Such interrogation is not a normal method of counterintelligence, or even of counterterrorism when it is conducted by an intelligence agency. Classic domestic intelligence services do not have the power to arrest or prosecute, though they often assist in prosecution. But sometimes it will be impossible to foil or even detect a plot without forceful interrogation of a suspect; and the question then is just how forceful such interrogation can legally be. Custody itself is intimidating, and prolonged custody, especially without access to a lawyer or a family member or anyone else from the world outside the detention facility, is much more so. The grounds and length of permissible detention and isolation present one set of issues that agitate civil libertarians, and the permissible techniques of interrogation another.

Regarding the first set of issues, there is a general impression that due process of law mandates that no one be detained by the government without being brought before a judicial officer within forty-eight hours of his arrest for a hearing to determine whether there is probable cause to prosecute him. Probable cause, in this case, means more than a bare suspicion but (much) less than proof beyond a reasonable doubt. This impression of the state of the law is imprecise. The Supreme Court has made clear that longer detention (though it has not said how much longer) is permissible if there is an emergency or other extraordinary circumstance.[8] The exception would permit Congress, without violating due process, to authorize detention in national security investigations for a longer period before the probable-cause hearing—perhaps for the twenty-eight days permissible for this purpose under British law with judicial supervision. This seems a sensible approach. A longer period would be objectionable because it would entail a greater deprivation of freedom but would likely yield little incremental benefit in information obtained from interrogation. This is partly because the longer it takes to extract information from a suspect, the likelier it is that the information, once extracted, will be stale.

It would be imprudent to entrust the screening of applications for such detention entirely to the courts. Warrant applications are ex parte and, in the case of FISA warrants, secret rather than adversary and public, and a judge hearing in secret from only one side of a dispute will have difficulty finding the holes in the argument. An important supplement to judicial review is executive accountability—requiring that national security and other high-level executive officials approve detentions beyond the standard forty-eight-hour prearraignment period, so that if a detention proves to be unjustified, the public knows whom to blame besides the rather hapless judges.

What methods of interrogation should be permitted during the detention of a suspected spy or terrorist? The United Nations Convention Against Torture, to which the United States is a signatory, forbids not only torture but any other form of cruel, inhumane, or degrading treatment of a person.[9] But just what methods fall under this ban is unclear. The question is largely academic with respect to counterintelligence. Interrogating a suspected spy is rarely as urgent as interrogating someone who has knowledge of an imminent attack, and a spy usually will not have that knowledge; he is a snooper, not an attacker or an attack planner. It is circumstances of urgency—which are more likely to arise in a counterterrorism investigation—that create pressure to increase the coerciveness of interrogation toward, and perhaps reaching, outright torture.

Even the efficacy of torture as a method of interrogation is disputed. What is indisputable is that torture produces many false positives—lies designed to stop the torture, including confessions to nonexistent crimes. But that is not the killer riposte to apologists for torture that its opponents think. The frequency of false positives in interrogation by means of torture just places another cost on the cost side of a cost-benefit analysis of torture, and it is possible to imagine offsetting benefits. The notion put forth by many civil libertarians that torture never succeeds in extracting true information is implausible. If it is ineffectual, why has it been used for thousands of years to extract information? Why would debate over its efficacy not have long since ceased, as debate has ceased over the efficacy of animal sacrifice for bringing rain? Of course some torture is sadistic, and some is designed to extract confessions to nonexistent crimes, such as sorcery, and political crimes in totalitarian nations. But much torture is designed to extract information, and the fact that it continues to be used for that purpose suggests that at least in some circumstances, there are no efficacious substitutes.

But of particular importance to my concerns in this chapter, the question of permitting torture in *any* circumstances seems moot with regard to counterintelligence, where it would rarely, if ever, be required to counter espionage. Even with regard to counterterrorism, the question is answered emphatically in the negative by existing law.

I turn now to the use of intelligence, including both counterintelligence and counterterrorism intelligence, as sword rather than just shield. Detection, or information gathering, is the principal task of an intelligence agency. (Analysis is important but secondary, in part because it can be performed outside an intelligence agency, as is largely done in the British intelligence system.) But neutralizing threats by the methods that agencies use to collect intelligence is also, as I mentioned earlier, a task of intelligence.

Recognition of this point is impeded by the tendency to identify this task with the "covert action" conducted by the CIA, which tends to be thought of in quasi-military terms and has sometimes taken that form. The "Special Activities Division" of the CIA is a paramilitary organization, and the best-known successes and failures of the CIA, largely during the Cold War, have involved covert warfare (though more often propagandistic, financial, and psychological than paramilitary) against hostile nations that were not, however, planning attacks on or even conducting espionage against the United States. Most covert action, both abroad and domestically (where it is cabined by U.S. laws that generally do not apply to the conduct of military or civilian American officers abroad), is not paramilitary, but involves tactics similar to those by which intelligence agencies gather information. Blackmail, bribery, deceit, threats, impersonation, and burglaries (clandestine searches, but authorized by search warrants) can be used by an intelligence agency not only to extract information but also to break up a plot by inducing the plotters to abandon it or, by turning a plotter into a double agent, by manipulating the plot to the benefit of the agency. Thus in World War II, MI-5 succeeded in taking over the German espionage rings in Great Britain and using them to feed disinformation to Germany concerning the Normandy invasion.[10]

Such operations are unlikely to raise serious concerns about civil liberties. Since at the stage of seeking to thwart an enemy plot (whether the plot involves espionage, sabotage, or a terrorist attack) at least some of the plotters are known, warrants based on probable cause to believe that a search will yield evidence of crime can be obtained, physical searches and electronic interception authorized, and agents planted (or double agents recruited) without concern that lawful activity will be deterred or disrupted. It is the *indiscriminate* character of effective counterterrorism surveillance that arouses justified concerns about infringements of civil liberties. To sound a recurring theme in this chapter, it is because counterintelligence in the information-collection stage, but especially in the active response stage, is usually targeted rather than indiscriminate that it engenders fewer civil liberties concerns than counterterrorist intelligence.

But this is in general rather than in every case. Probably the most notorious example in American history of serious, widespread infringement of civil liberties in the name of national security was the internment of more than a hundred thousand American citizens of Japanese origin during World War II. This was not a counterintelligence operation, but one motivation was the fear that Japanese people (including Japanese Americans) on the West Coast would conduct espionage or sabotage on behalf of our Japanese enemy. Surveillance of American communists during the Cold War was a counterintelligence operation, and like the internment of the Japanese, it infringed civil liberties. It did so in part because the threat was diffuse, and diffuse threats, as we know, rationally invite indiscriminate responses. The responses to both threats were also contaminated by politics and, less discreditably, by a desire to show unflinching resolve in the face of a serious foreign threat. But a repetition of such indiscriminate domestic-security programs seems unlikely in the foreseeable future. For one thing, they are extremely costly and therefore, likely to be undertaken only in times of acute national emergency. Moreover, since both the cost of implementing domestic security measures and the cost of those measures to their targets rise with the scale of the measures, there is an automatic check on the kinds of massive draconian policies, like mass internments, that civil libertarians are rightly most indignant about.

The remaining task of domestic intelligence that engenders civil liberties concerns is assistance in prosecution. Much of the traditional concern of civil libertarians is with the rights of criminal defendants; most of the provisions of the Bill of Rights regulate the criminal process. A domestic intelligence agency that does not have powers of arrest and prosecution has greater latitude in obtaining information than police detectives, or the FBI's criminal investigators, have, because it is less invested in gathering information that would be admissible in a trial, and so, less concerned with whether its methods would taint any leads to otherwise admissible evidence that the information had produced. But at some point it will often be desirable to prosecute a foreign spy, saboteur, or terrorist rather than continue monitoring his activities or neutralizing him by the means ("offensive intelligence") described earlier. Civil libertarians are concerned that intelligence agencies will feed criminal investigators information, gathered by means that are improper in criminal investigations, and that the investigators will in effect "launder" the information, not presenting it directly at trial but instead using it as a source of leads to admissible evidence.

Often, however, laundering will not work, and the prosecution will want to present the original evidence obtained by the intelligence agency, and the question is whether it should be admissible if it was obtained in the course of a legitimate intelligence investigation and whether the sources and methods used in the investigation must be revealed at trial even if disclosure would impair the intelligence agency's effectiveness, as well it might. I cannot see why, if it was a lawful intelligence investigation, its fruits cannot be used to prosecute a spy or terrorist.

There is the further question of whether information concerning a crime unrelated to national security, but obtained accidentally in the course of a legitimate intelligence investigation, can be used to prosecute the perpetrator of the crime. Two types of cases must be distinguished. In one, although the crime is unrelated to national security, the criminal is a spy, saboteur, or terrorist, and prosecuting him for the unrelated crime may be the simplest way of taking him out of circulation. That is unproblematic. But in the other type of case, the criminal is not someone of interest to an intelligence agency. The agency just stumbled on him in the course of an investigation, and the question is whether it should report him to law enforcement authorities.

There are two legal principles that might appear to furnish, between them, the answers to these questions. The first is the "plain view" doctrine. Suppose the police obtain a valid warrant to search a house for narcotics, and in the course of their search they discover in plain view a stolen artwork. Suppose further that they could not have obtained a warrant to search for the artwork because they did not have probable cause to believe it was in that house. Nevertheless they can lawfully seize it and use it as evidence to try the occupant of the house for theft.

At its broadest this principle would allow any evidence obtained in the course of a lawful intelligence investigation to be used in a criminal prosecution, even if it could not have been obtained otherwise. The principle is built into the Foreign Intelligence Surveillance Act, which permits evidence obtained pursuant to a FISA warrant to be used in a criminal prosecution, provided that "a significant purpose" (it need not be the only or even the primary purpose) of seeking the warrant was to investigate a threat to national security even though such FISA warrants do not satisfy the requirements that the Fourth Amendment imposes for getting a warrant to search for contraband or other evidence of crime.[11]

The second principle is that trials are public proceedings and that criminal defendants are entitled to confront the witnesses against them and to test the reliability of their testimony. These principles should not pose a serious obstacle to the use of intelligence information in criminal trials, however, unless the principles are pushed to an unreasonable extreme. Even outside the national security context it is permissible to keep some types of evidence, such as trade secrets, or the identity of a child victim of sexual assault, out of the trial's public record. And the problem of sensitive intelligence evidence can usually be solved by allowing the prosecution to present the evidence in edited form, provided the judge, having reviewed the full evidence in camera, agrees that the deletions will not impair the defendant's ability to defend himself against the criminal charge.

It might seem that if this pair of defendant-protective principles can be finessed, the way is open for the "plain view" doctrine to allow all lawfully obtained intelligence information to be used in prosecutions. As a matter of law, this may well be so. But as a matter of proper regard for the concerns of civil libertarians, it is not so, when a legitimate intelligence inquiry turns up evidence that someone who is *not* a threat to national security is engaging or has engaged in criminal activity; and the question is whether this discovery should be shared with law enforcement authorities. I think not, except in extreme cases like murder. There is a very large amount of minor criminal activity, in this as probably in all societies, that rarely results in prosecution. Examples are small-scale income-tax evasion, nonpayment of Social Security taxes for household help, household employment of illegal immigrants, petty thefts from employers (such as inflated claims for reimbursement of travel expenses, or appropriating office supplies for personal use), illegal gambling, consumption of illegal drugs, underage drinking, teenage sex, shoplifting, reckless driving, fraudulent insurance claims, perjury—the list is endless. The more indiscriminate that electronic surveillance aimed at protecting the national security is, the more evidence of minor criminality wholly unrelated to national security the intelligence agencies will obtain without seeking it. The search engines used to identify communications that might be of interest to an intelligence agency are crude and, as a result, produce many false positives—communications that turn out to have nothing to do with threats to national security. But some fraction of those false positives will contain evidence of minor crimes committed by someone of no interest to the intelligence agency that discovered the evidence. If the agency is required or even just permitted to turn such evidence over to law enforcement authorities, the exposure of the American population to criminal prosecution will be greatly broadened. This could be considered a good thing or a bad thing. I am inclined to consider it bad, not because I think it would be bad for the nation if our population were more law abiding but because the public's acceptance of the kind of comprehensive surveillance that may be necessary to protect the nation is likely to dwindle if people discover that a random sample of their phone conversations and e-mails are being read by the police.

Most Americans, as I have argued, regard privacy as an instrumental value. It is the concealment of sensitive, personal information from people who we think might use it against us. We surrender it willingly to those we think will not use it against us when there is compensation, for example, by buying books online. But if intelligence agencies used information obtained for national security purposes to expose people's minor crimes, many people would feel that they were giving up privacy to institutions that meant them no good and that they were getting nothing in return. Some people might applaud the reduced incidence of crime due to the greater risk of other people being caught, but I suspect they would be in a distinct minority. And so resistance to comprehensive national security surveillance would be reduced if people could be assured that the information obtained through such surveillance would be used only to protect national security—assured, in other words, that intelligence agencies are not adjuncts to the police except insofar as crimes that threaten the nation's security are concerned.

Once again, the problem I have identified is not likely to be serious in the case of counterintelligence. It is true that even when it is narrowly defined, counterintelligence and counterterrorism intelligence have a great deal in common. But it is precisely with respect to civil liberties that a gulf between them emerges. The threat to civil liberties posed by counterintelligence activities is in most regards far less serious than that posed by counterterrorist intelligence activities, because in general the former are much more focused on identified enemies and the latter are necessarily far more indiscriminate. This gulf must be kept in mind in considering the design of legal regimes for the two classes of intelligence activity. But also to be kept in mind is the permeability of the boundary between counterterrorist intelligence and counterintelligence and the overriding distinction between diffuse and focused threats to national security. And since counterintelligence, even when concerned strictly with foreign-state threats, can find itself opposing a diffuse threat, it cannot avoid all potential collisions with the values that cluster under the rubrics of civil liberties and privacy. And so, this chapter can fairly be interpreted as advocating an (incremental) shifting of the security/liberty balance in favor of security.

In closing I wish to consider briefly the familiar argument that any curtailment of liberty operates as a ratchet, or more dramatically as placing us on a sharp downward slope, at the bottom of which is tyranny. Historically that is quite false. Curtailment of civil liberties, beginning with the Alien and Sedition Acts, continuing with Abraham Lincoln's curtailment of habeas corpus at the outset of the Civil War, and culminating (rather tepidly, however) in the Patriot Act and other post-9/11 security measures, has been episodic. The crisis past, more precisely the crisis better understood, the curtailment has been eased (we are seeing that today, with the post-9/11 measures); and when civil liberties are fully restored, the restored liberties become a platform for further expansions in, not curtailments of, those liberties. Moreover, no mechanism has been proposed by which a curtailment of civil liberties in response to a perceived emergency becomes the platform for further curtailments. The degree of curtailment is vital. All the curtailments have been marginal to the basic political institutions and cultural traditions of the United States (the same pattern can be observed in Britain). Democracy and liberty are more robust than civil libertarians believe. We need not sacrifice security to liberty. We can have both, while shifting the boundary slightly toward the former.

Notes

I thank Tara Kadioglu for her valuable research assistance, and I thank John Lenkart, Joel Brenner, Jennifer Sims, and other participants in an Intelligence Salon organized by Sims, for exceedingly helpful comments on a previous draft.

1. Richard A. Posner, *Preventing Surprise Attacks: Intelligence Reform in the Wake of 9/11* (Lanham, MD: Rowman & Littlefield, 2005); Posner, *Uncertain Shield: The U.S. Intelligence System in the Throes of Reform* (Lanham, MD: Rowman & Littlefield, 2006); Posner, *Countering Terrorism: Blurred Focus, Halting Steps* (Lanham, MD: Rowman & Littlefield, 2007). See, in particular, chapters 4 and 5 of *Uncertain Shield*, and chapters 5 and 6 of *Countering Terrorism*; see also Luis Garicano and Richard A. Posner, "Intelligence Failures: An Organizational Economics Perspective," *Journal of Economic Perspectives* (Fall 2005): 151. See Richard A. Posner, *Not a Suicide Pact: The Constitution in a Time of National Emergency* (Oxford, UK: Oxford University Press, 2006).

2. On the criticism see William E. Odom, *Fixing Intelligence: For a Secure America* (New Haven: Yale University Press, 2004), 167–72, and other works cited in Posner, *Countering Terrorism*, 162n44.

3. Frederick L. Wettering, "Counterintelligence: The Broken Triad," *International Journal of Intelligence and CounterIntelligence* 13 (2000): 263. Wettering's article contains an excellent description of the variety of techniques used in counterintelligence (see pages 267–84). Yet—illustrating the ambiguity of the word "counterintelligence"—he includes background investigations of applicants for security clearances and "need to know" limitations on access to classified materials (see pages 272–75), tasks usually not classified as part of counterintelligence or assigned to counterintelligence officers, though I argue here that such tasks should be regarded as forms of counterintelligence.

4. Joel F. Brenner, "Strategic Counterintelligence," March 29, 2007, http://dni.gov/speeches/20070329_speech.pdf. See also the compendious definition in Vince Bridgeman, "Defense Counterintelligence, Reconceptualized," in this volume: "the broad subset of intelligence focused on the intelligence efforts of a competitor."

5. The most unrealistic feature of that great novel is precisely the infeasibility of real-time surveillance of an entire national population without the use of digitized search methods that did not exist in 1948, when the novel was published, and were not foreseen by Orwell.

6. See, in particular, Posner, *Countering Terrorism*, chapter 7. Also, Foreign Intelligence Surveillance Act, 50 U.S.C. §§ 1801 et seq.

7. Mitchell D. Silver and Arvin Bhatt, *Radicalization in the West: The Homegrown Threat* (New York Police Department, Aug 2007). See NYPDShield.org. See also Marc Sageman, *Understanding Terror Networks* (Philadelphia: University of Pennsylvania Press, 2004).

8. *County of Riverside v. McLaughlin*, 500 U.S. 44, 57 (1991).

9. Convention Against Torture and Other Cruel, Inhuman or Degrading Treatment or Punishment, 1465 U.N.T.S. 85 (1984).

10. J. C. Masterman, *The Double-Cross System in the War of 1939 to 1945* (New Haven: Yale University Press, 1972). On "offensive" counterintelligence generally, see *Counterintelligence and Counterterrorism—Defending the Nation against Hostile Forces*, ed. Loch K. Johnson (Westport, CT, Praeger Security International, 2007).

11. 50 U.S.C. § 1804(a)(7)(B). Compare §§ 1802 and 1804(a), with the text of the Fourth Amendment.

13

Jennifer E. Sims and
Burton Gerber

The Way Ahead

ONE PREMISE of this volume has been that designing new or fixing old organizations will not address the larger problem of poor strategic vision in the counterintelligence domain. The authors' chapters suggest that weaknesses in strategic vision and purpose are probably the most significant problems for U.S. counterintelligence. These weaknesses have had at least three root causes: technological change, confused purposes, and political culture, mind-sets, and bureaucratic rigidity. Address these challenges and the need for new organizations may fall away. Fail to do so, and any new organizations are likely to founder in the same ways the old ones have.

Technological Change

New detection or communications technologies are always disruptive for counterintelligence because they present practitioners with both opportunities and threats. The chapters by Wallace and Gosler underscore this point. These challenges are best understood and addressed when collectors and defenders within an intelligence service work together and, ideally, in collaboration with industry and other organized groups in the private sector. Such collaboration need not be sophisticated. It can even be left to private initiative so long as training, open communications, or even prearranged protocols help local decision makers understand how collaboration can work to everyone's benefit. But it remains uncertain how much of this collaboration can and or should be scripted beforehand. For example, in January of 2006, an employee at a Circuit City store in New Jersey contacted the Mount Laurel police after customers asked to have copies made of an incendiary video. When the police contacted the FBI with the Circuit City information, they provided the critical tip foiling a plot to attack hundreds of soldiers at Fort Dix.[1] How can we ensure that such linkages happen in every case? Should we? Or do we need to learn to live with some risk and accept that these linkages may sometimes fail to occur?

Such collaboration works best when it is institutionalized so that even simple cases such as the Fort Dix one, do not turn on ad hoc decision making. As Kathleen Kiernan has observed in her chapter, cities such as Chicago, New York, and Los Angeles have already recognized the importance of partnering and have developed programs to educate, train, and support merchants on the front line.[2] But the problem should be seen as geographically larger than these programs and these cities. Shopkeepers in Afghanistan have admitted to both repairing the hard drives of al-Qaeda operatives and selling them for the right price to reporters from the U.S. media.[3] Applying lessons from city defense to overseas operations is haphazard and sticky if it happens at all. The problem also ought not to be seen as involving only counterterrorism and traditional brick and mortar businesses. In June 2007 the *Atlantic Monthly* reported how private scam baiters have learned to troll the Internet, entrapping con artists in sophisticated cyberstings using deception strategies worthy of the best offensive counterintelligence operatives.[4] When nongovernmental networks get good at counterintelligence operations and come across a threat in the making, whom do they call and how are they protected?

In fact, the United States could do more to further cooperation among private-sector, law enforcement, and counterintelligence communities. Firms may understand the need for security against theft and even employ business counterintelligence themselves, but most likely believe that partnering with intelligence agencies or federal law enforcement to counter foreign intelligence services poses more risks than gains. Customers, including foreigners, represent markets and contracting opportunities as well as competition. Although some firms make serious efforts to protect their proprietary information, Rodney Faraon has shown that businesspeople often seem to believe that a culture of wariness is incompatible with good business practices. In contrast, the U.S. national security community is accustomed to such a culture and often addresses technological threats with rules, regulations, and licensing. All of these measures, necessary as they may seem to counterintelligence professionals, represent costs to producers. For example, when private firms developed sophisticated encryption software in the 1990s, a boon for protecting businesses responding to the forces of globalization, the U.S. government moved swiftly to try to stop its use and then to control its export as a counterintelligence *threat*, which, of course, it was—but only in part. It was also a boon for the protection of proprietary information—a mission with which, as Harvey Rishikof has shown, the FBI was struggling and against which it had contemplated using intrusive surveillance methods. When unbalanced and uncoordinated, the government's approach can make domestic intelligence seem harder than it is and make collaboration between counterintelligence and business communities more difficult as well.

Now the private sector is on the cutting edge of an information revolution that is moving from rapid data processing and communications to the development of new sensors, such as biometrics, and new platforms, such as robots and micromachines. The world of remote, digital spying, captured in the Gosler and Wallace chapters, is upon us. Rapid advances in private-sector surveillance, developed for such purposes as preventing crime, marketing products, or making buildings more comfortable for their occupants, are creating treasure troves of private-sector information both threatening to, and potentially useful for, national security. On the one hand, the government's use of commercial technologies may make government agencies vulnerable to digital spies for which, as Gosler has noted, no effective defense may yet be available.[5] On the other hand, government interest in gaining access to private databases that may contain indications or warnings of attack presents serious legal issues. In any case, as government institutions spend months and even years planning costly and time-consuming overhauls of their computer systems, foreign operatives, organized into wireless networks, may be sifting through the latest catalogues to buy or steal the access they need.

Confused Purposes

Without a good grip on what the purposes of counterintelligence are, performance is bound to slip. It is reasonably well understood among most national security professionals that counterintelligence is not simply security and that its purpose is to empower decision making in the national interest. As several chapters in this volume have pointed out, the business is supposed to involve "playing" the adversary to learn all that he knows. Beyond catching spies, counterintelligence involves penetrating, analyzing, degrading, disrupting, and manipulating an adversary's intelligence activities in order to gain a competitive advantage. Done well, counterintelligence involves offensive as well as defensive measures and provides its masters with a unique kind of decision-making advantage—an advantage gained not solely by blocking an adversary's intelligence but by learning from it and using it creatively in the service of overarching strategy.[6]

Yet, the legacy of the Cold War, in which intelligence services knew pretty much what each other was after, together with the prominent role that federal law enforcement plays in the U.S. counterintelligence community, has meant that the mission, particularly in its domestic dimension, has had a distinctly defensive and legalistic aura. It became mostly about operational security for CIA and catching spies for the FBI. U.S. counterintelligence has long emphasized defense over offense, making the countering of new threats seem harder than it has needed to be. Though CI's overarching purpose is to protect national security, its means are often and wrongly considered to be exclusively defensive, even by experts. Catching a single spy is often far less effective than recruiting an agent ("mole") in a foreign intelligence service, thereby learning about the activities of many of them. Thus, the FBI's job and, by extension, Americans' constitutional protections, are strengthened by a more effective CIA.

The prior statement is no analytic sleight of hand. Historical records demonstrate that a sophisticated counterintelligence strategy that balances offense with defense or even combines them can diminish the adversary's intelligence threat and thus lighten the burden for one's own defenses.[7] In any case, measuring each side's success at eliminating or prosecuting the other's agents (as distinct from recruiting "moles") may be an inadequate way to determine which side in a conflict is gaining competitive advantage over the other. Recruiting moles and perhaps even keeping the adversary's spies active, but deluded, may prove just as effective. In any case, the division of counterintelligence tasks among competing agencies during the Cold War may have rigidified the U.S. approach against more agile and operationally unified transnational networks.

To make matters worse, in the post-9/11 world, counterterrorism (catching terrorists) and counterintelligence (controlling or defeating hostile intelligence efforts) have been conflated in the minds of many government officials and the general public. Because the counterterrorism effort crosses so many bureaucratic lines, the debate over which organization should have responsibility for intelligence-related domestic operations has eclipsed proper focus on the similarities and differences in these missions. As Posner has pointed out, these missions—linked but distinguishable—may demand a more sophisticated approach than any bureaucratic fix alone might provide. Posner has argued that while the logistical techniques that have made al-Qaeda's attacks so virulent are available to the intelligence services of hostile states as well, techniques for countering terrorists may be necessarily more aggressive at the local level than those aimed at traditional intelligence services. In any case, strategies to address counterintelligence threats from hostile states and criminal organizations operating within U.S. borders should not necessarily be designed by agencies responsible for domestic *counterterrorism* programs where capacity for interdiction is often the paramount objective. Similarly, as Sample suggests in his chapter, the tradecraft and lessons derived from counterterrorism efforts should not remain the preserve of counterterrorism centers, but rather shared more widely with those confronting other threats in the homeland.

Political Culture, Bureaucratic Rigidity, and Mind-sets

To some extent confusion over our counterintelligence purposes is a matter of political culture. Here, three issues seem paramount. First, as Yamada and Fox and Warner remind us, Americans' historical diffidence about counterintelligence reflects unease about the costs for American civil society—particularly when transnational adversaries are involved. The government's effort to hunt terrorists on phone lines or through Internet services raises more than privacy concerns; it also suggests an interest in controlling, or at least fighting in, cyberspace as well, which raises the stakes even more. Governments are inclined to limit public access to certain information and possibly engage in interdiction, disinformation, and disruption—all of which could entail collateral damage, including erosion of the very political liberties that the U.S. government was created to protect. This sense of jeopardy has led some to frame the question starkly and ominously: How much physical security is society interested in buying at what cost in civil liberty? The authors in this volume have suggested that sound counterintelligence strategies need not involve such Faustian bargains: purchasing security at the expense of social values and liberties. Indeed, sound strategies will incorporate ways to distinguish true threats from less important ones and protect constitutional rights as carefully as they do buildings, infrastructure, and lives. The defense of U.S. interests requires protecting the American way of life as vitally and energetically as protecting property or persons.

Second, and somewhat ironically, counterintelligence policy may have suffered from its good press. Because the popular view is that counterintelligence is mostly about catching spies or terrorists, it would seem that the United States is pretty good at it. The Venona transcripts, released in the 1990s, revealed how U.S. counterintelligence efforts exposed Soviet penetration of U.S. and British intelligence throughout the 1930s and 1940s. More recently, Americans watched *Breach*, a film about FBI agent Robert Hanssen, who had been moonlighting as a spy for Moscow. According to the film, federal agents pursued Hanssen, meticulously documented his treachery, and then arrested him red-handed on February 18, 2001. Between Venona and Hanssen, federal agents made a number of high-profile arrests, including John Walker, a chief petty officer and communications specialist for the U.S. Navy and several members of his family, Aldrich Ames, the CIA spy caught in 1994, and Jonathan Pollard, the Israeli spy. And since 2001 the United States has apparently done well in countering terrorism; since 9/11, according to government sources, a number of plots have been foiled. New York City has erected new defenses and is rebuilding the World Trade Center site, creating what some believe to be the "gold standard" in security for other threatened regions. Kiernan has discussed in her chapter the important means by which such local successes have been achieved: joint terrorism task forces, terrorism early warning centers, and similar operations designed to fuse intelligence, law enforcement, and counterintelligence operations.

Yet, recalling that counterintelligence is an interactive and dynamic game, such popular perceptions are not the best metrics to use. Generalizations based on selective counterintelligence successes are, unfortunately, incomplete and misleading; they map where hostile services have been, not necessarily where they are going. And even in New York City, several officials have acknowledged that their relatively successful counterterrorism program depends in critical ways on the forceful leadership of Police Commissioner Raymond Kelly and a network of individuals with informal connections.[8] Well-funded federal partnerships with localities, designed to address the counterintelligence aspects of major infrastructure projects, remain lacking. The New York model is, in any case, difficult to replicate in places such as Los Angeles, where multiple jurisdictions prevent the kind of centralized control available to New York's Commissioner Kelly, or in Columbus, Ohio, where resources are scarcer and police cannot afford to dedicate as much energy to counterterrorism as they do in cities that have had more direct and recent experience with attacks. Robert Wallace reminds us that while the U.S. historical record of catching spies has been impressive, a balance sheet would show that their damage has been great. The Venona intercepts were a counterintelligence coup, but it was only much later that the full scope of Soviet espionage was realized and partially uncovered. Hanssen was caught, but he also fooled the Washington establishment for fifteen years, giving away highly sensitive technical programs as well as jeopardizing the lives of U.S. agents. Aldrich Ames contributed to the deaths of at least ten U.S. agents. John Walker helped the Soviets decipher over one million encrypted naval messages and gave up Army, Air Force, and NATO secrets as well.[9]

Third, vulnerability to deception has also been, as Robert Jervis explains, an enduring problem for the United States. In a separately published piece, former International Atomic Energy Agency (IAEA) inspector David Kay has shown that during the 1980s, Saddam Hussein had such sophisticated knowledge of U.S. intelligence strategies that he was able to deceive Washington about his most destabilizing weapons programs.[10] In fact, it wasn't until after Desert Storm that U.S. intelligence learned that Saddam had been close to producing a nuclear device—a counterintelligence (and positive intelligence) failure that may have led to a compensatory bias in weapons assessments prior to the Iraq war of 2003.[11] Before the second Iraq war, Washington was deceived again—this time by agents of influence, such as Chalabi, and bad sources, such as Curveball, who fed erroneous information about Iraqi weapons of mass destruction through intelligence liaison services. That such weaknesses do not adhere to American political culture as well as memories of FBI and CIA overreach do, perhaps reveals less a complacency with national security than a misunderstanding of what is required for its strong defense.

Even inside the profession, some experts have argued that the U.S. counterespionage portfolio remains distasteful because of the memory of James Jesus Angleton, the famous former head of counterintelligence in the CIA, whose relentless pursuit of suspects made creative use of double agents and walk-ins difficult and tainted his specialization within the ranks of the CIA. Others argue that Angleton was less the cause than the result of a system that lacked adequate strategies and methodologies for developing counterintelligence skills, incorporating them into intelligence practices from the ground up, and integrating these practices into decision making at the highest levels of the government. A few continue to believe that Angleton saw what turned out, in the Ames and Hanssen years, to be the intelligence community's central weakness: its own gullibility unmatched by an independent capability to sense and deal with deceit.[12]

What Next?

Post–Cold War adjustments to U.S. counterintelligence have been too slow in coming. If effective intelligence must be a fabric, cooperatively woven by those responsible for both offense and defense and for tactics and strategy, then the U.S. weavers were not communicating with one another prior to 9/11 and failed

to see holes that in retrospect seem obvious. Both policy and intelligence practitioners did ask how the coming years would be different from what came before, but in doing so they implicitly anchored themselves to the past, adapting
their own past practices rather than looking for new ones or exploiting existing
capabilities owned by others outside of Washington.[13] Congress, working on the
basis of too little information and too little time, made a rather arbitrary series of
line item cuts to the budgets of legacy intelligence institutions and programs.[14]
The folly in this approach was not exposed until 2001. From a counterintelligence standpoint, we came to the battle late, divided amongst ourselves and
underequipped.

What then, are the practical steps the United States can take right away to
improve counterintelligence capabilities? Although many might be listed here,
we will mention six that seem most pressing:

1. First, do no harm. Washington is rightly focused on counterterrorism and,
in its name, is moving smartly to increase federal powers. But the United States
has considerable nonfederal counterintelligence powers that, because they are
unrecognized, remain at risk. Perhaps the first among them is the willingness
and capability of most Americans to stop terrorists themselves. This point, recently made by Stephen E. Flynn of the Council on Foreign Relations, is not a
minor one.[15] The Capitol probably stands today because a few Americans on
United Airlines flight 93 decided to use their cell phones, and once informed of
the threat, they took control of their destiny to crash the plane. This is the stuff
of America; it is precious and powerful. The lesson is that democracies are willing to fight—beginning at the grassroots level.

How they will do so is another question. American may be willing to report
suspicious activities to decision makers whom they trust—generally local officials and community leaders—but to the extent that intelligence-led policing
means Washington-led, it is unlikely to be accepted for long. Citizens, inherently
concerned about the security of their neighborhoods, are critical to national defense; but, as Yamada discusses in his chapter, they are also inherently skeptical
of federal power, especially if sustained by mysterious color-coded threat levels.
Community-led policing, enabled by good intelligence practices, continues to
be the foundation of sound domestic counterintelligence practice, whether the
battles are against counterfeiters, mobsters, white collar criminals, smugglers
or terrorists. Where Washington can help, it should; but it should probably seek
less to expand its own powers than to build local and regional capabilities that
permit smooth working relationships during crises. Businesses with surveillance cameras, companies with marketing data, cops on the street, hospitals
monitoring emergency rooms, and dock workers emptying ships can identify
anomalies that might be indicators or warnings of attack. But the fusion of such
information should stay local until a demonstrable federal interest arises. The
question local decision makers rightly have is whether they will be left free to
do their work saving lives, selling goods, arresting crooks, and shipping goods

while also enabled by Washington to do more when the time comes—again with the least amount of federal interference possible. The answer they need from Washington is yes.

So, how do we get to yes? The Department of Homeland Security (DHS) might consider studying the strongest and most successful local initiatives and provide the results to others whose situations are similar. When good choices are made that can be replicated, Washington should help do so. DHS could provide funds to hospitals tracking traffic in emergency rooms or the use of their high-priced diagnostic equipment so that national security protocols are added to these data-bases: when metadata show the possible indicators of biological attack, data would be automatically transferred to a national site for analysis, such as the Centers for Disease Control, and counterterrorism officials in Washington. In this way local investments can have ripple effects, allowing other local governments to benefit in a timely way. This is true value-added service that builds on local initiative. Companies wiring their buildings with sensors for environmental or health related reasons, could be offered federal funds to have operations centers equipped with extra ones—trip wires that permit those same buildings to sense chemical, biological or other terrorist related attacks and provide status reports to first responders. The question is not what the private sector can do for Washington, but what Washington can do for the private sector before the terrorists make their next move. In this regard, the intelligence community might amplify its Razor program, which helps intelligence analysts understand the law enforcement context for information collected domestically. This could, in fact, become an analytic specialization within the intelligence community that feeds into a new capacity for net assessment at the national level.

It should be remembered, however, that even though the federal government can and should help with the domestic counterintelligence mission, the homeland is, inherently, a hostile place for terrorists to operate. This last point deserves special emphasis—especially because the opposite point is so often made. Counterterrorism, like counterinsurgency, is a special kind of competition to which intelligence must adjust. To succeed, terrorists need either to win the population over or break the trust they have in their governors by creating panic and confusion. Citizens are therefore more than targets; they are critical decision makers who ultimately decide the contest. Their elected leaders in Washington, including intelligence agencies, can win if they treat them accordingly—not just as potential victims who need to be herded or otherwise controlled.[16] Terrorists instinctively know their weaknesses here, since their intent is to make the population their target. So they seek to "decontrol" the territory in which they hide or strike in order to enlarge their operating space.[17] On the way to this safe zone, they exploit or provoke maximum distrust and confusion between the population and their governors. Total lack of trust is the ultimate aim of strategic terrorism because as long as trust is preserved, the governors will get stronger with every attack against the citizens they serve. Washington's best counterintelligence strategy in such a contest, is to build trust with Americans by limiting the federal footprint at the local level, while at the same time, bolstering the capacities for resilient, multilayered decision making among first responders. We ought not build new organizations but should network instead. America is already getting wired up and connected through the Internet, Bluetooth technologies, fiber optics, and massive data processing. Turning that latent power into a weapon for community defense and a source of community resilience just makes good sense.

2. **At the federal level, reconnect counterintelligence with national security strategy and decision making**. The best way to do this is to lessen the influence law enforcement directives have over the role and agenda of the NCIX and to bind this office's work more clearly and effectively to all those agencies with operational CI roles and to the policymakers they support. The idea would be to make the strategic whole greater than the sum of its parts through coordination, selective secrecy, and deft delivery of decision advantages to the president. DNI McConnell has already recognized the critical importance of decision advantage in his "Vision 2015" for the intelligence community. The next step is to assert the DNI's indispensable role in delivering it to the president through CI means. Such an initiative should not increase executive oversight, which is best left to the operator's home agencies, nor should it involve a heavy managerial hand. It is often forgotten that one of the most effective counterintelligence systems of the twentieth century, the Double-Cross System of the British during World War II, was highly compartmented, multiagency and blessed with carefully nuanced and light managerial direction at the top. John C. Masterman, a university don and cricket master, headed the committee, which had no executive power itself. Operations were coordinated, but left tied to the purposes of the decision makers they served until the moment arose for a combined coup de grâce. In this regard, it would not be unreasonable to consider the latent American capacity for deception, as outlined in the chapter on mission-based counterintelligence.

3. **Reconsider personnel policies that create any kind of homogeneity in the workforce**. Effective counterintelligence involves an artistic, choreographic and musical sensibility in that it requires understanding how meaning is derived from events or circumstance. On occasion, quirky, nonlogical thinking may be necessary—thinking of the kind that finds meaning in seemingly disconnected ideas or actions. Although intelligence agencies may have employees with such qualities, they rarely encourage their development or reward their use. One of the most important programs the intelligence community has developed in recent years is the DNI's Galileo Award, which encourages employees to submit innovative ideas and rewards the best of them. This program should have more consistent follow-through so good ideas are actually tested and rewarded for their feasibility. It should also be expanded to include innovative ideas from state, local and tribal intelligence units as well as members of the broader national security community. Intelligence and counterintelligence involve partnership with policymakers; ideas should come from all who contribute to the function.

In addition, winners should be permitted to work on the implementation of their ideas, with additional rewards for doing so successfully.

4. **Managers should eschew both inflexible denial and blanket "need to share" policies in an effort to build up the capacity for selective security**. The United States no longer has a good process for determining when and how to release classified information for the purpose of achieving strategic gains or timely advantage. Instead, declassification is usually a negotiated enterprise: proposed by policymakers seeking influence and gains overseas but resisted by the intelligence community, which is duty-bound to protect sources and methods. Releases have been episodic, as when the Kennedy administration released classified imagery to allies during the Cuban Missile Crisis or Secretary of State Powell brought imagery to bolster his arguments for war to the UN Security Council in 2003. During the era of strategic arms control, an ongoing process was in place to consider what intelligence might be released as part of institutionalized arms control negotiations. Then it was important to keep some information from the Soviets while at the same time ensuring that they knew enough not to miscalculate their advantages and over-reach. Such manipulation of an adversary's perceptions through selective secrecy, traditionally part of the art of managing intelligence liaison, is no longer a well-honed or routinely practiced art—in part because it requires policymakers willing to engage their opponents either in direct or tacit negotiations. But regardless of policymaker preferences, the intelligence community needs the capability to offer up the options, which it cannot do if it does not practice generating them. Such an approach requires, in the first place, a sophisticated attitude towards the design of collection systems and the protection of their sources and methods. As Sims has discussed in her chapter, collection managers can purposefully design systems that are expendable and can purposefully "take the hit" for more classified programs; but funding for them cannot be sustained unless this kind of constructive redundancy is valued by congressional authorizers and appropriators and defended not just by collection managers, who may be seen as self-serving, but by a credible national counterintelligence staff.

The capability to generate these kinds of options thus requires a re-invigoration of counterintelligence management as an intelligence discipline across the intelligence enterprise. These managers should be intelligence brokers skilled at designing, building, merging, and opening compartments in the service of both long-term collection and policymaking, recognizing that gaining and using advantages is the purpose of having sources and methods. Put another way: counterintelligence is not just about keeping secrets; it is for gaining advantages as long as the competition is in play.

5. **The U.S. intelligence community, including the NCIX, should submit to Congress a comprehensive rationale and architecture for what is evolving to be the national domestic intelligence capability**. Congress will obviously not be legislating its establishment, but lawmakers should understand its composition

and how and why it is growing as it is beyond Washington's customary purview. We agree with Posner's premise that countering terrorism and its cohorts in the criminal world poses a structurally different kind of threat from those posed by more traditional intelligence services. These adversaries fuse intelligence to operations in a highly tactical and decentralized fashion. To operate against such an adversary requires rapid and integrated intelligence and decision making; it requires manipulating the time available for the terrorist to observe and to act so interdiction and disruption have some chance for success.[18] Local "counter-intelligence" officers—often but not always law enforcement officers—may occasionally have to act against these adversaries in their capacities as intelligence collectors and national security decision makers, noting and reporting suspicious incidents in the communities they serve much as the Circuit City employee did in the example cited earlier. This meshing together of policy, intelligence, and counterintelligence operations is nerve-wracking for professionals trained to keep such functions apart. Yet, in certain critical circumstances, fuse they must. After all, against these particular adversaries, U.S. intelligence is not so much countering another intelligence service, as it did when working against the KGB or GRU during the Cold War, as countering networks of decision makers doing intelligence on the fly. We have these too: police officers, fire fighters, and community leaders. We need to support them, paradoxically, by helping them to keep their intelligence capabilities both highly tuned and reliably curtailed—a most difficult balancing act.

Such support might begin by considering the evolution of local defense on a national stage—the floors of the House and Senate. There, a broad-based political consensus on risk management at the federal level may ultimately be achieved, based less on a federal solution to perceived gaps in Washington's domestic intelligence apparatus than on the positive changes underway at the state and local level. A national debate of this kind would also help citizens understand what their cities, municipal officials, and state governors are doing so they can take appropriate steps to make their views known. While the authors in this volume may differ over the precise form this architecture should take, they all recognize that it is developing anyway as a natural outgrowth of city and state measures for local defense. Local decision making is empowered by a new national security mandate. It would be wise, therefore, for federal officials to propose any needed changes, such as partnerships with the private sector, that build on these developments while at the same time ensuring that they do not jeopardize constitutional protections for civil liberty. In any case, neighborhoods and communities are more likely to build trusted counterintelligence networks around policemen, doormen, and private-sector security cameras than they are around a federal agency newly designed to spy. And given the technological changes underway, this kind of arrangement may actually be best for early warning of attacks and threats of all kinds.

Of course, the federal government need not and should not control this evolution, but should support localities by subsidizing training for police, the use of new technologies for collection, and the use of sensor and wireless communications networks in hospitals, transport hubs and skyscrapers so that standardized data could flow seamlessly and appropriately to federal emergency management officials should serious suspicions arise concerning a potential terrorist attack or should one happen again in the homeland. The critical point for federal oversight is the moment when local information is handed off as national intelligence for potential federal action.[19] To preserve civil liberties, such hand-off should be rare, crisis-related, and strictly temporary so that such national intelligence is as reliably deleted as it is created in time of need. This task is important and difficult to execute in the United States; it is, nonetheless, absolutely essential. Again, the NCIX could help with this mission while helping to ensure that national intelligence systems are positioned to meet the needs of decision makers dealing with the integrity of shipping lanes, rail, and air transport systems.

6. Fix intelligence and counterintelligence oversight in Congress and at the state and city levels. U.S. law enforcement can work comfortably with intelligence institutions only if those responsible for oversight are well informed and willing to accept responsibility for their decisions. After the Cold War, when members of the intelligence oversight committees allowed their roles to become politicized, two-way communication started to break down between intelligence agencies and congressional overseers and between the those agencies and the White House.[20] As the media published revelations that clearly caught the oversight committees by surprise, confidence that Congress was doing its job declined and the willingness of intelligence to take risks, including independent and edgy collection operations for critical decisions, apparently also declined.[21] While the accelerated growth of this gap after 9/11 was hardly surprising, the failure to fix it and, indeed, the headlong rush to make it worse through imbalanced action (on the one hand, assuming additional intelligence authorities without simultaneously enhancing the scope and depth of oversight; on the other hand, using oversight to punish instead of rebuild trust) seems astonishing.

Both congressional and executive oversight could be improved by making the core staff members on the intelligence committees (the Senate Select Committee on Intelligence and the House Permanent Select Committee on Intelligence) bipartisan professionals hired by Congress but trained by the executive branch as public servants. Policymakers, lawmakers, and legal counsels need to understand the relationship of intelligence advantage to state power and the purposes and consequences of effective oversight. Members of oversight committees should also understand that there is a natural constituency beyond Washington for their intelligence-related work: state and local police, private-sector businesses, and first responders who collect and use intelligence—albeit not for institutions with "intelligence" in their names. More effective domestic intelligence must begin with a reinvention of American oversight and, thus, the compact between the country's safekeepers and its citizens.

$$\bullet \quad \bullet \quad \bullet$$

SUGGESTIONS THAT the United States is bad at counterintelligence because spies have been discovered, terrorists have struck, or history has examples of over-reach or of poor CIA-FBI coordination, are no more valid than arguments drawing the opposite conclusion. In fact, the roots of sound counterintelligence practice lie deep in American practice.[22] The point here is that reform of the U.S. counterintelligence effort is urgent; it should not be delayed because of past successes, nor should it overlook these successes and, in so doing, fail to build upon them.

Notes

1. "As terrorism plots evolve, FBI relies on Agent John Q. Public," *Los Angeles Times*, May 12, 2007.

2. The Chicago Police Department developed Chicago Alternative Policing Strategy (CAPS) in the late 1990s to increase community involvement in police operations; the New York Police Department supports SHIELD, a program designed to train local businesses on best practices, lessons learned, counterterrorism training opportunities, and information sharing; the Los Angeles Police Department's Commercial Crimes Division partners with the private sector to better combat property and financial crimes.

3. Bruce Berkowitz, *The New Face of War: How War Will Be Fought in the 21st Century* (New York: Free Press, 2003), 9–10.

4. Ron Rosenbaum, "How to Trick an Online Scammer into Carving a Computer Out of Wood and Other Ingenious Acts of Cyber-vengeance," *Atlantic Monthly*, June 2007, 78–84.

5. See, in addition to James R. Gosler's chapter in this volume, his chapter in our previous book: James R. Gosler, "The Digital Dimension," in *Transforming U.S. Intelligence*, ed. Jennifer E. Sims and Burton Gerber (Washington, DC: Georgetown University Press, 2005), 96–114.

6. For example, if Country "A" is engaged in a conflict with adversary "B," who is using photographic imaging to locate A's troops from space, it might choose to eliminate B's satellite in order to block the activity. This would be a classic counterintelligence move and would also in most circles be considered an act of war. Country A might instead choose to conceal from B the fact that it knows it is being watched during the day. This latter choice would offer A's decision makers the option to deceive Country B—perhaps by setting up fake activity during the day while redeploying at night for the purpose of an assault on B's flank.

7. See various essays in Loch K. Johnson, ed., *Strategic Intelligence Volume 4: Counterintelligence and Counterterrorism—Defending the Nation Against Hostile Forces* (Westport, CT: Praeger Security International, 2007).

8. Conclusions based on interviews with senior officials of the NYPD and the Port Authority, including Deputy Commissioner of Intelligence Dave Cohen (NYPD) and Commissioner Anthony Coscia (Port Authority), July 16, 2007.

9. Carol Clark, "Alleged spy crimes 'the most traitorous actions imaginable,'" CNN.com. Available at www.cnn.com/SPECIALS/2001/hanssen/overview.html.

10. David Kay, "Denial and Deception: The Lessons of Iraq," *U.S. Intelligence at the Crossroads: Agendas for Reform*, ed. Roy Godson, Ernest R. May, and Gary Schmitt (Washington, DC: Brassey's, 1995), 109–27.

11. Failure to uncover deception programs run by adversaries is a counterintelligence failure even if those deceptions are not necessarily run by the hostile intelligence service. Intelligence and counterintelligence are functions that can be performed by agents and agencies outside the formal "intelligence establishment" of a state.

12. See, for example, William Hood, "Angleton's World: Lessons for US Counterintelligence," in *Intelligence at the Crossroads: Agendas for Reform*, ed. Roy Godson, Ernest R. May, and Gary Schmitt (Washington, DC: Brassey's 1995), 128–45. This article includes commentary by James Nolan and Samuel Halpern.

13. The problem of perceptual "anchoring" has been described most usefully by Richards J. Heuer in his book *Psychology of Intelligence Analysis* (Washington, DC: Center for the Study of Intelligence, 2000).

14. Former DCI George Tenet has written about the downsizing of intelligence after the Cold War in his memoir *At the Center of the Storm: My Years at the CIA* (New York: Harper Collins, 2007).

15. Interview with Stephen E. Flynn, Council on Foreign Relations, January 28, 2008.

16. Ibid.

17. Ibid.

18. For more on the problems of countering terrorist organizations before they act, see the NYPD's study of the process of radicalization: "Radicalization in the West: The Homegrown Threat," New York Police Department Intelligence Division, 2006. Available at NYPD Shield.org. "Observe, Orient, Decide, Act" has been called the "OODA loop" and was made famous by military strategist John Boyd. For a detailed examination of Boyd's ideas, see Frans P. B. Osinga, *Science, Strategy and War: The Strategic Theory of John Boyd* (London: Routledge, 2006).

19. We *are not* here recommending that mail carriers routinely report to the secretary for homeland security. We *are* suggesting that the federal government help train mail carriers, fire fighters, and police to recognize the precursors to terrorist events, report them locally, and allow their employers to work with federal officials ahead of time to determine if, when, and how to hand such information over to federal officials.

20. Numerous works have been written on the political turbulence of this period and the later breakdown of intelligence oversight. For a focused and highly personal account of the law enforcement paradigm applied to CI, see Louis Freeh, *My FBI: Bringing Down the Mafia, Investigating Bill Clinton, and Fighting the War on Terror* (New York: St. Martin's Griffin, 2005). For more on the breakdown of intelligence oversight, see L. Britt Snider, "Congressional Oversight of Intelligence after September 11," in *Transforming U.S. Intelligence*, ed. Jennifer E. Sims and Burton Gerber (Washington, DC: Georgetown University Press, 2005), 239–58.

21. Revelations concerning secret detention and domestic surveillance after 9/11 have shown that even when edgy operations were pursued, Congress, by then a suspect overseer, was poorly informed. Apparently fear of retribution also led CIA officers to destroy tapes of harsh interrogations, despite apparent support for the techniques the interrogators employed. Wholly apart from the tapes destruction, by all accounts a serious matter, the fact that the oversight committees have spent so much time on this issue has meant that other pressing matters have been left unattended.

22. It is worth remembering that when fears of a terrorist attack during the millennium celebrations were at a high point, FBI, Department of Justice, CIA, and customs officials collaborated in apprehending would-be bombers. In preparing for the Olympics

in Atlanta and Athens, similarly high levels of cooperation were achieved but failed to make headline news. And such successes have occurred not just in recent years. In 1957, for example, the CIA and the FBI cooperated in one of the first of many captures of spymasters and terrorists. An aide to the KGB illegal William Henry Fisher [aka "Colonel Rudolf Abel"] turned himself in to the CIA overseas and provided details of Abel's operations. The CIA then passed this information to the FBI, which subsequently arrested Abel. See Allen W. Dulles, *The Craft of Intelligence: America's Legendary Spy Master on the Fundamentals of Intelligence Gathering for a Free World* (Guilford, CT: Lyons Press, [1963], 2006), 118. Other and more telling examples can be cited, such as U.S. Army work with FBI and CIA to run double agents in the 1980s.

CONTRIBUTORS

Vincent H. Bridgeman is a Marine officer and a graduate of the Security Studies Program at the Edmund A. Walsh School of Foreign Service at Georgetown University. His most recent posting was at Marine Corps Forces, Special Operations Command (MARSOC).

Rodney Faraon is a partner with the Crumpton Group, LLC, a strategic business advisory practice in Washington, D.C. Before joining the Crumpton Group, he was The Walt Disney Company's founding director of global intelligence and threat analysis, and had earlier served fourteen years with the Central Intelligence Agency as a manager, senior analyst, and a briefer for the President's Daily Brief. He is a graduate of the Edmund A. Walsh School of Foreign Service at Georgetown University.

John Fox Jr. has been the FBI historian since 2003. He has recently had articles published in the *Law Enforcement Executive Forum*, *Studies in Intelligence*, and the *Journal of Government Information*, as well as numerous pieces on the FBI's website. He contributed a chapter to *The Gouzenko Affair: Canada and the Beginnings of the Cold War*, edited by J. L. Black and Martin Rudner for Penumbra Press. Fox has also been heavily involved in the FBI's tour renovation and a number of cooperative museum projects, especially a temporary exhibit on the FBI and the media put together by the Newseum. He was awarded a Ph.D. in modern American history from the University of New Hampshire in 2001 and an M.A. in political science from Boston College in 1993.

Burton Gerber is retired from the Central Intelligence Agency after thirty-nine years as an operations officer. Subsequently he has lectured and written on intelligence subjects, particularly intelligence ethics. He now teaches at Georgetown University. With Jennifer Sims he is the coeditor of and contributor to an earlier volume, *Transforming U.S. Intelligence*, published by Georgetown University Press in 2005.

James R. Gosler is a fellow at Sandia National Laboratories. His areas of interest include information operations, information assurance, nuclear weapon security, cryptography, critical infrastructure protection, terrorism, and space superiority. He is a member of the Defense Science Board and the National Security Agency Advisory Board. In conjunction with these boards, he regularly assists the Department of Defense and the intelligence community through his participation on numerous studies and panels. Previously, he was a visiting scientist at the National Security Agency, the director of the Clandestine Information Technology Office at the CIA, and commanding officer of three units in the U.S. Navy Reserve. He is the recipient of several awards, including Lockheed Martin's NOVA Award, the CIA's Director's Award, the CIA's Directorate of Operations Donovan Award, the Intelligence Medal of Merit, and the U.S. Navy's Legion of Merit. He received his M.S. in mathematics from Clemson University.

Robert Jervis is Adlai E. Stevenson Professor of International Politics at Columbia University. His *System Effects: Complexity in Political Life* (Princeton University Press, 1997) was a cowinner of the APSA's Psychology Section Best Book Award. *The Meaning of the Nuclear Revolution* (Cornell University Press, 1989) won the Grawemeyer Award for Ideas Improving World Order. He is also the author of *Perception and Misperception in International Politics* (Princeton University Press, 1976); *The Logic of Images in International Relations* (Princeton University Press, 1970; 2nd ed., Columbia University Press, 1989); and *The Illogic of American Nuclear Strategy* (Cornell University Press, 1984). His most recent book is *American Foreign Policy in a New Era* (Routledge, 2005). He was president of the American Political Science Association in 2000–2001 and has received career achievement awards from the International Society of Political Psychology and ISA's Security Studies Section. He is a Fellow of the American Association for the Advancement of Science and the American Academy of Arts and Sciences.

Kathleen L. Kiernan is a twenty-nine-year veteran of federal law enforcement and is the CEO of Kiernan Group, an international consulting firm that supports federal and civil clients in the areas of both strategy and policy. She previously served as the Assistant Director for the Office of Strategic Intelligence and Information for the Bureau of Alcohol, Tobacco, Firearms, and Explosives (ATFE), where she designed and implemented an intelligence-led organizational strategy to mine and disseminate data related to explosives, firearms, and illegal tobacco diversion. She is a Senior Fellow of the George Washington University Homeland Security Policy Institute, and the Director of Intelligence Analysis Programs at Johns Hopkins University. Dr. Kiernan is currently a special advisor to the director of the Combating Terrorism Task Force in the Department of Defense and to the Office of the Director of National Intelligence, exploring the parallels between criminality and terrorism. Dr. Kiernan holds a doctorate in education from Northern Illinois University and masters' degrees from the Joint Military Intelligence College and George Mason University.

Richard A. Posner, a judge of the U.S. Court of Appeals for the Seventh Circuit since 1981 and a senior lecturer at the University of Chicago Law School, is the author of many books and articles. His most recent books are the seventh edition of *Economic Analysis of Law* (2007); *Countering Terrorism: Blurred Focus, Halt-*

ing Steps (2007); and *How Judges Think* (2008). His current academic research includes national security and intelligence reform, the law and economics of catastrophic risk, and judicial behavior. He and economist Gary Becker write weekly commentaries on issues of public policy. See "The Becker-Posner Blog" at http://becker-posner-blog.com/.

Harvey Rishikof, former chair, Department of National Security Strategy at the National War College in Washington, D.C., is currently a professor of law and national security studies. He specializes in the areas of national security, civil and military courts, terrorism, international law, civil liberties, and constitutional law. Mr. Rishikof's career includes experiences with the college where he has taught and served as a law school dean; in the private sector with Hale and Dorr; and in public service with the federal judiciary and the Federal Bureau of Investigation.

Timothy R. Sample has over twenty-five years of intelligence and policy experience as both a supplier and user of intelligence. His assessments on the future direction of U.S. intelligence led to his integral service to the House Permanent Select Committee on Intelligence (HPSCI) as both a contributing author and managing editor of *IC21: The Intelligence Community of the 21st Century*. His government positions have included staff director of HPSCI, executive director of the DCI Counterproliferation Center, and deputy U.S. negotiator for the START I talks. His private sector experience includes being vice president for Strategic Intelligence Strategies and Programs at General Dynamics Advanced Information Systems. He served as president of the Intelligence and National Security Alliance, a nonprofit, nonpartisan public policy forum focusing on intelligence and national security issues, from November 2005 to July 2008. He is currently working as an independent consultant.

Jennifer E. Sims is professor in residence, director of intelligence studies, and member of the core faculty of the Security Studies Program, Edmund A. Walsh School of Foreign Service, Georgetown University. She has served as deputy assistant secretary of state for intelligence coordination and as the Department of State's first coordinator for intelligence resources and planning. She has also served as Senator John Danforth's designee on the staff to the Senate Select Committee on Intelligence. She is the recipient of the national intelligence community's Distinguished Service Medal and is a member of the International Institute of Strategic Studies. Dr. Sims received her B.A. from Oberlin College and her M.A. and Ph.D. from Johns Hopkins School of Advanced International Studies, where she has also taught. Her publications include *Icarus Restrained: An Intellectual History of Nuclear Arms Control, 1945–1960*, as well as numerous articles on arms control and intelligence. She co-edited with Burton Gerber, *Transforming U.S. Intelligence*, and contributed two chapters on American intelligence culture and reform efforts (Georgetown University Press, 2005).

Robert W. Wallace retired from a thirty-two-year career at the Central Intelligence Agency in 2003 and founded Artemus Consulting Group to provide strategic planning, program assessment, and representational services to government and corporate clients. He is the author of *Spycraft: The Secret History of the CIA's Spytechs from Communism to Al-Qaeda* (2008) and *Nine from the Ninth* (2002), a memoir of service with the 75th Infantry Rangers during the Vietnam War. Wallace's CIA assignments included three tours as chief of station and director of the Office of Technical Service. He is a member of the oral history staff of the CIA's Center for the Study of Intelligence and a contributor to its *Studies in Intelligence* journal. Mr. Wallace holds a B.A. from Ottawa University and a master's degree from the University of Kansas.

Michael Warner serves as chief historian for the Office of the Director of National Intelligence. He received his Ph.D. in history from the University of Chicago. He has written and lectured extensively on intelligence history, theory, and reform, serving first as an analyst and then as a historian at the Central Intelligence Agency. His recent publications include "Intelligence as Risk Shifting" in Peter Gill et al., editors, *Intelligence Theory: Key Questions and Debates* (Routledge, 2008); "Building a Theory of Intelligence Systems," in Greg Treverton, ed. *Mapping the State of Research on Intelligence* (Cambridge University Press, 2008); and "The Divine Skein: Sun Tzu on Intelligence" in the journal *Intelligence and National Security*, 2006. Dr. Warner is also adjunct professor at American University's School of International Service in Washington, D.C.

Austin K. Yamada served for twenty-five years as a career civil servant in the Department of Defense, where he served most recently as the deputy assistant secretary of defense for Special Operations and Combating Terrorism. Prior to his retirement in 2003, Yamada held various positions in the Office of the Secretary of Defense, where he was conferred the rank of Meritorious Executive in the Senior Executive Service, and at the Defense Mapping Agency (now the National Geospatial-Intelligence Agency). His father, Hatsumi Yamada, was one of over 125,000 Japanese Americans interned during World War II, and later served in the Office of Strategic Services and at the Central Intelligence Agency. Mr. Yamada is currently vice president for national security solutions at ManTech International Corporation in Fairfax, Va. He received his B.S. degree from Montana State University and his master's degree in engineering from Virginia Tech University.

INDEX